Planning the Low-Budget Film

Planning The Low-Budget Film

Robert Latham Brown

Los Angeles

PLANNING THE LOW-BUDGET FILM.

The author is grateful for the permission to use the following previously copyrighted material: "Producers Code of Credits," Producers Guild of America; script supervisor's notes, the budget, and portions of the script of *The Anarchist Cookbook*, Freedonia Productions LLC.

FIRST EDITION.

Library of Congress Cataloging-in-Publication Data is available.
LIBRARY OF CONGRESS CONTROL NUMBER: 2005930350

ISBN-13: 978-0-9768178-0-2
ISBN-10: 0-9768178-0-2

0 9 8 7 6 5 4 3 2 1

To the crew members who have supported and helped me in so many ways, through so many years.

Contents

Acknowledgements

Since 1996, I have been privileged to teach Production Planning to undergraduate students in the School of Cinema/Television at the University of Southern California. During that time, I have been challenged by my students on every aspect of what I teach, and I am deeply grateful to all of them. It is said that the best way to learn a subject is to teach it, and I have found this to be true. The class has forced me to think about the procedures and methods I have used since entering the film business in 1974. Doing so has caused me to refine and distill these ideas, and to be able to anticipate many of the questions that newcomers arriving in this field may have. The information in this book is a result of that process and my over thirty years in the business of making feature films. It is intended as a source of practical information, presented in a way that I hope is both entertaining and instructive.

No book is created in a vacuum and this one is no exception. I want to thank Jordan Susman, writer, director, and fellow producer of *The Anarchist Cookbook,* for allowing me to use his film as an example; Alan Bell, editor extraordinaire, for proofing the chapter on post production; Bruce Block, producer, professor, author, and friend, for his advice and guidance on navigating, which for me were the uncharted waters of authorship; and finally Howard Kazanjian, producer and author, who has been my mentor since I started in this business as a trainee.

This book could not have been completed without the extraordinary help and encouragement of my editor, my partner, and my wife. Fortunately for me, they are all one person, Karen Kalton. While it is generally true that to be edited is to be humbled, to be edited by Karen is to be given unfair advantage over one's shortcomings.

Introduction

Making a film is a complex undertaking. It is equivalent to building a skyscraper or carrying out a small invasion. It involves synchronizing the efforts of vast numbers of people over months or years, and sometimes such a project can cost a hundred million dollars or more.

I have often marveled at the complexity of a modern skyscraper (while scouting its deepest dungeons for a film location), tracing the various utility lines running like nerves and blood vessels to unknown places. How do we build such complex structures? Through planning. No one is capable of fully imagining such a structure in its entirety all at once. In order to conceive the complexity of such a construction, it is necessary to break the project down into manageable parts.

So it is with film. To plan a film production intelligently and efficiently, it must also be broken down into manageable parts or we become overwhelmed with the details. In *Jurassic Park* when the water in the mud puddle vibrated from the footsteps of the *Tyrannosaurus rex*, the crew did not just show up with all of its equipment hoping to find a mud puddle that they could film. Someone had to choose where the puddle would be, someone else had to dig the puddle, someone else had to fill it with water, and finally, someone had to work out a way to make it vibrate on cue. Of course, this is in addition to all the people and equipment it took to put the image of the vibrating water on film.

Before any of the above could happen, someone had to plan it. That person is the unit production manager and/or the line producer. The Directors Guild of America (DGA) defines a unit production manager (also simply referred to as the *production manager or UPM*) as that person who:

> *...under the supervision of the Employer, is required to coordinate, facilitate and oversee the preparation of the production unit or units (to the extent herein provided) assigned to him or her, all off-set logistics, day-to-day production decisions, locations, budget schedules and personnel.**

It goes on to enumerate further the duties of the unit production manager to include, but not be limited to, the following:

1. *Prepare breakdown and preliminary shooting schedule.*
2. *Prepare or coordinate the budget.*
3. *Oversee preliminary search and survey of all locations and the completion of business arrangements for the same.*
4. *Assist in the preparation of the production to insure continuing efficiency.*
5. *Supervise completion of the Production Report for each day's work, showing work covered and the status of the production, and arrange for the distribution of that report in line with the company's requirement.*
6. *Coordinate arrangements for the transportation and housing of cast, crew and staff.*
7. *Oversee the securing of releases and negotiate for locations and personnel.*
8. *Maintain a liaison with local authorities regarding locations and the operation of the company.* †

The Producers Guild of America (PGA) officially calls the line producer the *co-producer*. They define a co-producer as:

1. *...the individual who reports directly to the individual(s) receiving "Produced By" credit on the theatrical motion picture.*
2. *The Co-Producer is the single individual who has the primary responsibility for the logistics of the production, from pre-production through completion of production; all Department Heads report directly to the Co-Producer.* ‡

---

* Directors Guild of America, *2002 Basic Agreement*, 11.

† Ibid. 11-12

‡ Producers Guild of America, "Producers Code of Credits," *Membership Roster 2004-2005*, 20.

A production may operate with just a unit production manager or both a UPM and a line producer. A film must include a production manager if it is made under the Directors Guild of America contract. Often a line producer is an experienced UPM, and can take on the functions of both jobs.

The busiest and most intensive time on a picture for a production manager or line producer is during the pre-production or planning phase. Once the picture starts shooting, the line producer tracks the progress of the picture, maintains its efficiency, and runs as fast as he or she can to keep up. A line producer can be compared to the Greek mythological character Sisyphus rolling a huge boulder up a hill only to have it roll back down again and again. Unlike the myth though, eventually the boulder does get to the top of the hill and starts to roll down the other side of its own accord. At that point, Sisyphus, our line producer, has to run for all he or she is worth just to keep up. Without the proper planning, it can only end in disaster.

'Ready when you are, CB'

This famous story exists in many forms and it may or may not be true. It is valuable, however, since it illustrates how the unexpected can happen. Here is how it was told to me.

One morning, Cecil B. DeMille, the great epic director, started rehearsing one of the most difficult scenes in *The Ten Commandments*. The scene involved thousands of extras, hundreds of horses, chariots, Egyptian legions, hoards of Israelites, and hundreds of crew members. They started at 6 AM, working out all of the various cues for each of the groups of people. An army of wranglers prepped the horses and made sure each had an experienced rider on board. The special effects crew rigged all of the exciting effects, and by late afternoon the camera crews had all three cameras in place. The assistant director told DeMille that he thought they were ready. DeMille gave the order to shoot immediately since they had only enough daylight for one take.

The assistant director raised his megaphone and called for quiet. "Roll cameras!" he shouted.

"Action!" commanded DeMille. The Egyptian army surged forward. The Israelites went into mock panic. The horses charged. The special effects went off flawlessly. A charioteer flew through the air as planned when his chariot lost a wheel. Finally, his face flushed with excitement, DeMille shouted, "Cut! Cut! That was beautiful! Perfect! Did we get it?"

The A camera operator came running up from his camera position. "I'm terribly sorry, Mr. DeMille," he said, "The bloody camera jammed right at the beginning."

You could see the disappointment in DeMille's face but he said, "No matter. You weren't the only camera. B camera, how did you do?"

The B camera operator was pulling himself out from under the wreckage of an overturned chariot while the camera assistant gathered up what was left of his camera. "Not well, I'm afraid," he moaned.

DeMille turned to the C camera operator perched high up on a hill. He had the wide shot and would have caught all the action. DeMille grabbed the assistant director's megaphone and waved to the operator.

"C camera, how did you do?" he shouted.

The C camera operator cheerily waved back and replied, "Ready when you are, CB."

Apocryphal or not, the story is funny because it contains truth. Anyone who has ever worked on a film will attest to this. In fact, many of the procedures that will be outlined in this book got their start because of someone's misfortune or disaster. For instance, if this scene were being filmed today, there would have been five or more cameras, not just three. In addition, the director would never have called "Action" until every camera operator confirmed he was rolling with a shout of "Speed!"

Murphy Is In Complete Control

Along with change, Murphy's Law is a constant in film production. *Whatever can go wrong will go wrong* are wise words to remember. Throughout this book, I will use actual disasters on actual films as a way of illustrating what can go wrong and how to prepare for it. Avoiding disaster is a large part of production planning and it is important to anticipate what could go wrong.

A Little History

It is helpful in understanding the concepts I will be writing about if one understands their origin. Film complexity has evolved, and with it so have the methods of dealing with that complexity.

In the early days of film production, the shooting schedule was the same length as the running time of the film. There were no cuts or coverage. You just set up the camera and staged everything in front of it as though the camera were the audience. Most of the early Edison films were done this way. They never amounted to more than a sketch and their running time was never more than a few minutes. The scripts were patterned after short play scripts and there were no numbered scenes. Watching these early films was much like watching a vaudeville performance.

When films became longer and they began to involve more than one location or set, the scheduling became more difficult. It was no longer practical to shoot the separate scenes in story order. If the story returned to a specific location at three separate times in the script, it made better sense to shoot those three scenes all at once, eliminating the need for the shooting company to return to the same place again.

In order to better organize the shoots, filmmakers began to number the scenes in the script. They would put the scene number and a short description of the scene on index cards which they would then pin to a cork board. In this way, they could organize the cards according to which scenes they would shoot on specific days.

In the mid-1920s, German director Fritz Lang improved upon this method by replacing the index cards with strips of adding machine tape. This afforded more space for the filmmakers to include elements necessary to each scene such as cast, extras, props, animals, vehicles, and special equipment. An example of why this was beneficial is if a cast member was only available on certain days, the scenes with that cast member could be identified at glance and moved to the days that the actor was available.

To accommodate the importance of scene numbers, the film script evolved into its current format with numbered scenes and descriptive sluglines (see Chapter 3). The collections of adding machine tape pinned to a wall evolved into the modern production board. We will go into detail on both script format and production boards in later chapters.

Stages of Preparation

Even before you can secure financing, you need to determine what your film will cost. Whether your project is a student film or a hundred million dollar epic, the preparation of a film for shooting (and in the process learning what it will cost) can be broken down into a few major stages. Outside of securing financing, the stages of pre-production are briefly:

- Breakdown of the script
- Creation of a schedule
- Making a Budget

- Securing Sets and Locations
- Casting the Roles
- Hiring a Crew

We will go into further detail in each of these stages, and along the way, you will learn to look at film production in an entirely new way.

Part I
THE BASICS

1

Why Low-Budget?

For most people, the answer to this is a lack of funds. If they had access to more money, they would gladly use it. However, a high budget does not guarantee high returns. Many low-budget directors have found themselves suddenly in great demand when their low-budget, original and creative film hits it big. They then go on to make huge, big budget, studio-financed pictures, which sometimes fail.

When I was a graduate film student at UCLA, I heard Roger Corman speak. After his presentation, he took questions from the audience. Corman was considered king of the B pictures at the time, and I asked him if he ever considered making a large-budget studio film. He answered me with an emphatic, "No." He explained that if he were to raise his budgets he would have to involve the studios to help him finance his pictures, and if he did that, he would lose control. He was not just being an egomaniac. Being in control of your project is crucial to it coming out as you envisioned it.

Picture yourself in a meeting with the studio creative execs. They tell you that you will get a *green light* (approval to start) on your film if it can be cast satisfactorily, and they hand you a list of suggestions for the role of Mother Teresa. You glance down the list, anxious for the expert advice from these people who know film and the film business inside and out, and your eyes lock on the top name on the list.

"Paris Hilton?" you gasp.

"Hey, she was great in that TV thing she did," the exec tells you. "It made a bundle...and we'd want to modify the habit she's wearing of course. Oh, and she's willing to leave the dog at home. She's really hot."

You hesitate, "But..."

"Look," the exec says, "do you want to make the picture or not?"

Okay, I'm exaggerating, but not by much. I actually have had a studio executive say those very words to me, *Do you want to make the picture or not?* Do you do what they ask with a possibility of going on to fame and fortune, or do you go back to waiting tables for the rest of your life? It's not an easy question to answer, even with the prospect of Paris Hilton playing Mother Teresa. I certainly don't mean to cast aspersions on the talents of Ms Hilton, but as Mother Teresa? But then, she *is* really hot...

And look at it from the studio's point of view. With the $60,000,000 they are going to give you to make your film, they need some assurance that it will make some money. Paris Hilton might guarantee a certain level of box office return. And with that huge investment, shouldn't they have some say?

Control is also crucial to your production being satisfying and fun. On big budget movies, the dollar dictates everything and you must answer to the studio for the decisions you make. You must justify your every move to the people in charge. On a low-budget production, *you* are the person in charge. You make the decisions and live or die on the consequences. You don't have to check with six people before you can make a deal. The decision is yours. You are answerable only to your investors. There is great responsibility in freedom, but there is great freedom in that responsibility.

What is a Low-Budget Film?

Low-budget is a relative term. These days a studio would consider a film costing $5,000,000 low-budget. In fact, it is very low-budget when compared to their usual fare of projects costing $40,000,000 to over $100,000,000. Studios make these extravaganzas in hopes of generating box office returns in the hundreds of millions of dollars. Nevertheless, a big budget does not guarantee box-office success..

The Union Definitions

The Screen Actors Guild of America (SAG) has several levels of budgets that they recognize under various conditions. (See 809-00 Talent in Chapter 18.) Their standard definition defines a low-budget film as any theatrical film under $2 million. There are exceptions which can increase this amount. The Directors Guild of America used to define a low-budget film as any theatrical film costing $500,000 or less. They defined a medium-budget film as any theatrical film costing over $500,000 up to and including $1,500,000. Anything over $1,500,000 was termed a high-budget film. Most recently, the DGA has revised their definitions to list four separate levels of low-budget films ranging from $1,030,000 and under up to $7,000,000. They are even exploring special consideration for projects under $500,000. These budget totals are known as the negative costs of a picture, meaning the cost of producing the final cut negative which does not include release prints, marketing expense, and distribution expense.

These definitions by the guilds are important to you only in how they affect the rates that you will be paying for people employed under the respective guild contracts. We will go into more detail on this when we discuss budgeting.

What Is It Really?

If you are truly rolling in money, your budget will probably be in the $5,000,000 range. However, it is more likely to be in the $2,000,000 and under range. Some very successful films have been made for less than $500,000. *The Blair Witch Project* cost somewhere between $19.95 and who knows how much—the producers aren't talking.

Let's say you raise $2,000,000. Until recently, the DGA would have said you are making a high-budget movie. Is it a high-budget movie? Maybe for D. W. Griffith. That is why they have revised their definition. If you plan to pay everyone, and your uncle does not own Panavision, you will be using all the tricks I can teach you to stay on budget.

2

How Do I Get Into This Business?

This is the single question asked most often by my students at USC. There are no set routes. Ask ten people in the business how they got there and you will get ten different stories. Formal apprenticeship programs are few and far between. The Editors' union, Local 700 and the Script Supervisors' union, Local 871 in Los Angeles have on occasion conducted apprenticeship programs. The DGA and the Association of Motion Picture and Television Producers (AMPTA) jointly sponsor the Assistant Directors Training Program.

My experience in my own career and in observing the careers of others is that the single most important quality you can have in pursuing a motion picture career is persistence. Rumor has it that you may even get an Oscar, if you live long enough.

Pursue Your Dream

A very holy and devoted saint died after a long and selfless life. When he arrived in heaven, God wanted to reward the saint's virtue and asked if he could build the saint a heavenly mansion in which to spend eternity. The saint smiled a shy smile and said that although God's offer was most generous and greatly appreciated, the saint was used to living in his simple room with a hard pallet as a bed. God then said that he would bestow upon the saint a handsome limousine with angelic retainers at his disposal so that he might wander through heaven in comfort and style. The saint bowed his head and said that he hoped God would not be offended but that the saint preferred his quiet walks in heaven's gardens where he could meditate alone on the beauty of God's work.

God was filled with respect and admiration for this humble servant. "Is there nothing I can grant you in reward for your life of service to others?" God asked.

The saint thought for a moment, and that same shy smile flashed fleetingly across his face. "Well," he said, "I *would* like to direct."

Most students in film school today want to direct, write, produce, or become a director of photography. Those without these specific ambitions enter film school thinking that they want to become a "filmmaker." Very few enter film school with the idea that they want to become a production manager, assistant director, special effects technician, costume supervisor, makeup artist, propmaster, set dresser, or fill any of the other numerous positions essential to the production of a film today.

If you are a student, or someone just starting out on a career path, this is the most flexible time of your life. You most likely do not yet have a mortgage or a family to support. You can afford to work cheap, delay rewards, and try different things. If you *are* encumbered with those responsibilities, you can still go after your dreams in your spare time and on weekends.

Internships and production assistant (PA) positions are useful as places that you can use to learn about the different areas of film production and to see what each has to offer. However, there is a lot of competition to land one of these spots. Networking and meeting as many people in the business as possible will help tremendously in finding opportunities. Also, check the trades for films starting up or ads looking for people.

However, if you want to direct, go direct. Direct anything you can get your hands on. Direct commercials. Direct student films. Direct theater. Direct video productions of your own scripts. Direct music videos for local bands. Direct 30-second public service videos and give them away to local stations.

If you want to write, go write—every single day. Don't stop writing. Study films, read scripts, immerse yourself.

If you want to produce, go produce. Produce your friends' short or feature length film scripts. Produce your own ideas. Produce ads for local businesses. Produce videos for local actors to show off their skills.

If you want to be rich, go into investment banking.

What is important here is to follow your heart's desire. Follow your dream. Joseph Campbell said, "Follow your bliss." Fame and riches can and often do follow. But if they don't, you are still rich because you are doing what you love to do.

DV—The Great Equalizer

That's all very well, you may say, but film production costs thousands and thousands of dollars. But who said it has to be *film* production.

In the old west, Samuel Colt gave to the world the "great equalizer," a six-shooter that allowed any 98-pound weakling to take on the toughest hombre in town, as long as his hand did not shake too badly. There is a new equalizer on the frontier and it is called Digital Video or DV, and if *The Blair Witch Project* is any indication, it does not matter if your hand does shake. *Blair Witch* was shot on DV and was purposely made to look amateurish to reinforce the conceit that it was a tape found in the woods. DV can look a lot better.

Not long ago, an article titled "In This Day and Age, Everyone's a Director" appeared emphasizing DV's accessibility (*Los Angeles Times* April 8, 2000).

> *DURHAM, N.C.—Matt Brutacao was a sophomore in high school when he wrote, shot, directed and edited "Stealing Can Be Murder," a two-hour action-adventure movie with an original score and more than 80 cast members. He filmed it over nine months in about 30 locations, including his school bus and the local jail—where a friend's father worked—and premiered it in his school's gym. His total cost was $130.*

Although DV does not have the resolution one would normally expect in a feature film release, it is more than adequate for broadcast, DVD, or online. It can even be tolerated on the large screen if you have a gripping story with fully developed characters to distract everyone from a less than perfect image. A 3-CCD DV camera costs in the $2,000 to $3,000 range to buy and about $100 per day or weekend to rent. A separate microphone is essential for recording on-camera dialog. With broadband Internet connections becoming more common, a DV camera, a microphone, a few friends, and a computer loaded with Adobe Premier® or Apple's Final Cut Pro® can put you and your films in front of millions of people. A number of World Wide Web sites are springing up solely to provide a venue for independent filmmakers. One of the more reputable sites is AtomFilms (**http://www.atomfilms.com**). Also, check out the quantity seller program on Amazon (**http://www.amazon.com**). If you go this route, be sure you know what you are giving away in exchange for distribution, and be sure you have full rights to the film and all of its content.

3

The Script

The Blueprint

It all starts with the script. Whether you wrote it or you have acquired it from someone else, the script is the blueprint for the final film, and as such, it is central to planning your film. It is important that the script be in a standard format so that you can accurately judge the amount of material to be filmed.

Screenplays come in two basic formats: the master scene format (fig. 3.1) and the shooting script format (fig. 3.2). They are very similar except for a few important differences. Both examples show a page from *The Anarchist Cookbook* written by Jordan Susman. The master scene format of the screenplay is written for only one purpose, to sell itself. For that reason, it is written in a manner that is easy and quick to read. The writer wants the prospective buyer of his script to see the movie he is describing and not be too distracted by the process of reading.

Each page of the script is numbered. Each scene begins with a slug line which is printed in all caps. The slug line tells the reader whether the scene is an interior or an exterior scene. This is done by the abbreviations "INT." or "EXT." at the beginning of the slug line. The slug line also tells where the scene takes place and the time of day. The first scene of the page shown in figure 3.1 takes place outside on the campus of Southwestern Baptist College in the early morning. If some part of the information of the slug line is redundant from the previous slug line, or is assumed to be understood, it is often left out as was done in the case of the third slug line

1.

EXT SOUTHWESTERN BAPTIST COLLEGE - EARLY MORNING

A mist hovers over the grassy knolls of the serene campus.

Joggers take their early morning runs past the magnolia trees, live oaks and colonnaded buildings.

In the dead center of campus is a fountain and beside it, a towering FLAGPOLE. Atop the pole, three flags snap in the morning breeze: The Stars and Stripes, the Texan flag, and at the very top, a large BLACK and RED FLAG.

EXT. SOUTHWESTERN BAPTIST COLLEGE - LATER

A group of 20 bright-eyed FRESHMAN tour the campus. The TOUR GUIDE is a sophomore who was on this tour a year earlier. He carries a university pennant so the groupdoesn't get lost.

PUCK (V.O.)
Be all that you can be.

INT. LIBRARY

The group ogles the endless rows of books that await them.

PUCK (V.O.)
Be the best and the brightest. A mind is a terrible thing to waste.

INT. CAFETERIA

The group is duly impressed by the lunch line.

TOUR LEADER
And this is where those of you on the meal plan will eat...

PUCK (V.O.)
Feed your head. Feed the beast. Feed the children. Feed me Seymour.
(beat)
It's food for thought.

INT. DORM - DAY

It's the Holy Grail of going to college -- the dorms. The group heads down the hallway, excitement building...

TOUR LEADER
This Floor is girls' only. Affectionately known as "chastity castle."
(nervous laughter)
Just kidding. No one really calls it that. It's just that boys are allowed
(MORE)

Fig. 3.1. The first page from ***The Anarchist Cookbook*** showing the master scene format.

WHITE Revision - 5-1-01 1.

1 EXT SOUTHWESTERN BAPTIST COLLEGE - EARLY MORNING 1

A mist hovers over the grassy knolls of the serene campus.

Joggers take their early morning runs past the magnolia trees, live oaks and colonnaded buildings.

In the dead center of campus is a fountain and beside it, a towering FLAGPOLE. Atop the pole, three flags snap in the morning breeze: The Stars and Stripes, the Texan flag, and at the very top, a large BLACK and RED FLAG.

2 EXT. SOUTHWESTERN BAPTIST COLLEGE - LATER 2

A group of 20 bright-eyed FRESHMAN tour the campus. The TOUR GUIDE is a sophomore who was on this tour a year earlier. He carries a university pennant so the groupdoesn't get lost.

PUCK (V.O.)
Be all that you can be.

3 INT. LIBRARY 3

The group ogles the endless rows of books that await them.

PUCK (V.O.)
Be the best and the brightest. A
mind is a terrible thing to waste.

4 INT. CAFETERIA 4

The group is duly impressed by the lunch line.

TOUR LEADER
And this is where those of you on
the meal plan will eat...

PUCK (V.O.)
Feed your head. Feed the beast. Feed
the children. Feed me Seymour.
(beat)
It's food for thought.

5 INT. DORM - DAY 5

It's the Holy Grail of going to college -- the dorms. The group heads down the hallway, excitement building...

TOUR LEADER
This Floor is girls' only. Affectionately
known as "chastity castle."
(nervous laughter)
Just kidding. No one really calls it
that. It's just that boys are allowed
(MORE)

Fig. 3.2. The first page from ***The Anarchist Cookbook*** shooting script showing numbered scenes and revision label at the top of the page.

which reads "INT. LIBRARY." In this case, the time of day had not changed so the writer felt it was not necessary to repeat it.

The large blocks of text describing the visuals and the action of the scene are called "Action." Dialog is indented under the character's name which is indented even further. The abbreviation "V.O." stands for "voice-over" indicating that the speaking character is not seen, but only his or her voice is heard.

The script is written in a 12-point Courier font with one-inch margins all around. This standardization of format and font help filmmakers judge how long the finished film will be and how long it will take to shoot. We will go into this in further detail later. For now, just remember that on average, one page of script equals one minute of screen time.

Figure 3.2 shows the same page from the script after it had been modified into a shooting script format. To be useful, a shooting script needs to have its scenes numbered as in this example. This makes it easy to refer to any scene in the script and have everyone know which scene you are talking about. Also notice that a revision name is typed at the top of the page. When the script is changed for any reason, a new version of the revised page is issued on a different color of paper. Each revision is named for the color of paper that it is issued on. To help further identify what was changed on a revised page, an asterisk is printed in the right hand margin on each line that was changed. Figure 3.3 shows a revised page.

Scene numbers are conserved in shooting scripts. This means that if a scene is omitted, a notation is written in the script that the scene has been omitted as shown in figure 3.3, and that scene number is never used in that script again. If a new scene is put in place of the one omitted, then a new number is created by appending a letter to the previous scene's number as can be seen again in figure 3.3. This policy helps prevent confusion and costly mistakes.

It should be noted here that a numbered scene in a shooting script is not the equivalent of a scene in a play. In a play, if the scene starts in the drawing room, that scene continues until the action is concluded and we leave the drawing room. In a film script, a new scene number and a new slug line can occur with a change of camera angle, point of view, or new visual emphasis while the action continues.

Working from a Master Scene Format

Several years ago, I was hired by a television producer to do a shooting schedule and a budget for a television production of Tennessee Williams's

PINK Revision - 5-8-01 20.

44 CONTINUED: 44

PUCK (VO) (CONT'D)
Ground Zero for American anarchy.
Lee Harvey Oswald was from Dallas.
David Hinkley was from Dallas. Ross
Perot is from Dallas. Need I say
more?

44A EXT. CITY STREET - DAY 44A

Puck and D stop by a rug salesman on the side of the road and pickup a BEARSKIN RUG.

45 EXT. SAM - DAY 45

Puck and Double D pick up the rest of the crew in the SUV.

46 EXT. NEIMAN MARCUS - DAY 46

Above the entrance to the store is a banner:

"May is Mink Month"

And outside on the sidewalk are PROTESTERS with signs in the vein of "Love animals. Don't wear them."

47 EXT. NEIMAN MARCUS, SERVICE ENTRANCE - DAY 47

The SUV pulls up. The team dashes out.

48 EXT. SIDEWALK - DAY 48

Gin, Sweeney, Puck, Johnny Black and numerous trolls crawl around the sidewalk like minks with large fake furs on their backs. Karla and Johnny Red attack them with oversized cardboard cleavers. The crowd stops and stares.

Johnny Black BITES Johnny Red's hand to the crowd's amusement, then RUNS off.

Puck chases after him around the building. *

49 OMITTED 49*

50 OMITTED 50*

50A EXT. NEIMAN MARCUS, SERVICE ENTRANCE - DAY 50A*

Johnny Black arrives at the loading dock, where mannequins *
with fur coats and cages with minks are waiting to be taken *
inside. *

Above them is a large banner: "PICK YOUR OWN MINK" *

PUCK *
What are you doing?

Fig. 3.3. A revised script page from ***The Anarchist Cookbook***. Each changed line is marked with an asterisk. Omitted scenes are marked as such and retained in the script. This page would have been issued on pink paper.

A Street Car Named Desire. After discussing what the approach to the film would be and at what cost level he wanted the budget, I asked if he had a copy of the shooting script that I could use to start working on. He said, "Of course," reached into his desk and handed me a copy of the Penguin edition of *A Street Car Named Desire*.

To understand why I was taken aback, you need to realize that a play and a film are two very different entities. A play takes place on a stage in front of a live audience. You can only change story location by changing the set, although this is done in very inventive ways in many play productions. A film is much more realistic in that when the story location changes, you actually change locations. You can be in the drawing room in one scene and at the South Pole in the next. This obviously has huge implications in budgeting and scheduling. For example, in *Streetcar*, the characters talk of being in a bowling alley. In a film version you might want to actually show them at the bowling alley—or you may not. The moment Stanley is outside the apartment yelling up to Stella is handled very cleverly in the play by a split set which shows the audience both Stanley on ground outside and Stella upstairs in the apartment. In a film, you would need to be EXT. THE APARTMENT HOUSE AND STREET for Stanley's shots, and INT. STANLEY'S APARTMENT for Stella's shots. In order to do the schedule and budget, I needed to make decisions that normally would be up to the screenwriter and ultimately the director. I decided to provide for going to the bowling alley and was pleased to see that they did exactly that in the finished film.

Occasionally, you may find yourself needing to work from a master scene formatted script. Hopefully it will be a screenplay and not a play script. On these occasions, usually all that is required is to number the scenes. This means numbering each of the slug lines and shots. A "shot" looks like a slug line in that it is written in caps and flush left but without the INT./EXT. designation or the time of day. It usually indicates a new camera angle or focus. Some examples would be

```
CLOSE ON
a hand as it reaches for the knife.
```

or

```
A BLINDING FLASH
all but obliterates the group of protestors.
```

or

```
INSERT
the timer stops at "0:07!"
```

Begin numbering the slug lines and shots starting at the number 1 and continue consecutively through the end of the script. Each of these numbers stands for a "scene" even though it may only be part of a larger continuing action. In a typical dramatic film, there might be 90 to 150 scenes. An action or special effects film may have well over 200 scenes.

Chain of Title

Whether you are working with your own script or one you have acquired, it is important to be able to demonstrate the Chain of Title. "Chain of Title" simply means being able to prove that you lawfully own the script. You do this through copyright registration. Although by law a work is copyrighted the minute it is written, it can be difficult to prove ownership without copyright registration with the U.S. Copyright Office. Before a distributor will take your film on, the distributor will want to see proof of copyright registration. Even the Screen Actors Guild will insist on a copy of the copyright form before they will let you sign their contract.

Fortunately, it is very easy to register a script. To obtain the proper form, go to the Library of Congress web site at **http://www.loc.gov** and click on "U.S. Copyright Office." Under "Publications," click on "Forms." Once you have the list of forms, choose "Form PA" or "Form PA w/instructions" to down load a PDF file of the form. As of this writing (2005), the fee to register a script is $30 in the form of a check or money order.

Do not confuse this with registering the script with the Writers Guild of America. The WGA provides a service in which they will hold a copy of your script in their files for five years, at which time you may choose to renew the registration. This service was first established for their members to serve as proof in disputes among the members of when a given script was written and by whom. They offer this service to nonmembers for a fee of $20. This registration is also a very simple process and can be accomplished in person at the WGAw headquarters building in Los Angeles or by mail at:

WGAw, Intellectual Property Registry
7000 West Third St.
Los Angeles, CA 90048

Alternatively, the WGA now allows you to register your script online at **http://www.wga.org**. The WGA registration has no legal standing. It is not proof of ownership and does not establish Chain of Title. It merely documents the date at which time the completed script was in your possession. A copyright registration proves ownership. Be sure to retain a copy of the Form PA that you file with the U.S. Copyright Office, as it will be weeks or even months before you get the completed registration back by return mail.

PART II
THE SCHEDULE

4

The Shooting Sequence

What is a Shooting Sequence?

In order to break down your film into those easily managed parts I mentioned, you need to understand the concept of the shooting sequence. When I first began teaching at USC, I found that none of the names in use for this construct were adequate. People often referred to it as a "scene" as in "We're filming the 'shoot-out' scene tomorrow," or "I've rewritten the heroine's death scene." As we have seen earlier, "scene" is a very vague term and can describe a continuous action that actually covers several numbered scenes in the script. If you have a phone call "scene," you may actually be talking about a part of the script that cannot be shot in one location, especially if you are going to film both sides of the conversation. I realized I needed to come up with a new term. This term needed to describe a piece of the script that one would shoot in a specific place over a specific period. Sequence is also an overused and vague term so I settled on the term *shooting sequence*.

A shooting sequence can consist of part of a scene, or a whole scene, or several scenes. It consists of continuous action that is to be filmed at one location, at one time, with specific characters. Think of the Greek unities of time, space, and action. To those three parameters, we will add cast. If any of the four parameters of time, space, action, or cast changes in a fundamental way, a new shooting sequence has begun.

The Four Unities

The four unities of a shooting sequence (action, cast, time, and space) govern how each part of the script will be shot. This is why they define a shooting sequence.

Unity of Action. It makes sense to stop filming a sequence once the main action of the sequence ends and a new action begins. It is a natural stopping point. At that point in the film, even if all the other unities stayed the same, the audience would expect a change in camera angle and the filmmaker would want a change in angle to signal the new direction. In a long complex scene taking place in one set over a continuous period of time with the same cast, a change in the action will give the filmmaker a convenient place to break the sequence.

Unity of Cast. If you have a scene in which the cast substantially changes, you probably also have a change in the action. More to the point, it does not make sense to have called in a large number of cast members for the sequence, only to have half of them wait around, unused, and racking up overtime while the other half works. Such a sequence would be better scheduled as two separate shooting sequences, one for each group of cast. This does not mean that every time one character enters or leaves a scene a new shooting sequence starts. Unity of cast is broken when a substantial number of the cast members in a scene change.

Unity of Time. If there is a time lapse at some point in a sequence, that is also a natural place to break the shooting sequence. A time lapse indicates that some aspects of the sequence have changed. Time is defined by change. Imagine a scene in a movie showing a nervous group of people hiding in a ruined building from a marauding band of terrorist bandits. The filmmaker does not want to make the audience sit through three days of boredom watching the cast grow evermore haggard. Instead, the filmmaker will cut the camera, and using makeup and costume changes, make the group appear in the next shot as though they have been there for a long time. This is not a sequence to be filmed all at once. It would naturally break. The new sequence would begin with the cast looking haggard.

Unity of Space. It is important to understand that the unity of space applies to both story location and shooting location. A change in story location invariably requires a change in shooting location, even if it is only a move to the set next door. Nevertheless, a change in shooting location can occur even if there has been no change in story location. Any change in shooting location must break the shooting sequence since the filming would have to stop and not continue until the company arrived at the new location. A change in story location is a way of determining a change in shooting location. Other indicators may be moving from exterior to interior (or vice versa); cutting between two nearby story locations that may or may not actually be near one another; and the incorporation of shots coming from different sources such as miniature units, visual effects shots, and second units.

Analyzing a Script Passage

Read the following short sequence with the above discussion in mind. Using your imagination, visualize the film as you read.

11 INT. SHERIFF'S OFFICE - DAY 11

Sheriff Curry reclines in his chair, dozing with his feet on the desk. Howie barges into the office.

HOWIE
Sheriff! Sheriff! You got to come to the saloon real quick like!

The Sheriff jerks awake and almost falls over backwards in his chair.

SHERIFF CURRY
Damn! Howie. Don't you know how to knock?

HOWIE
Mean Jim's in the saloon and he's acting real ugly.

SHERIFF CURRY
Mean Jim's back?

He stands and buckles on his gun belt.

SHERIFF CURRY
Thanks, Howie.

12 EXT. MAIN STREET - DAY 12

Sheriff Curry strides down the street toward the saloon. Various townspeople watch him, concern etched into their eyes.

The sheriff suddenly glances toward the sky.

13 SHERIFF'S POV 13

A buzzard glides noiselessly in a lazy circle.

14 BACK TO SCENE 14

Sheriff Curry turns his attention to Newman's Drygoods and finds the one pair of eyes he wishes weren't watching him.

15 HELEN, 15

overcome with emotion, rushes inside her father's store.

16 SHERIFF CURRY 16

clenches his jaw and continues on to the saloon.

He strides up to the front of the saloon and shoves his way through the doors.

17 INT. SALOON - CONTINUOUS 17

The normal hubbub ceases as soon as he enters. The only sound comes from the two saloon doors flapping to a standstill.

The sheriff scans the room and finds his man leaning on the bar.

18 MEAN JIM 18

swallows a shot of whiskey, slams the glass down on the bar, and turns to face the sheriff.

MEAN JIM
You really know how to put a damper on a party, Sheriff.

Sheriff Curry glides across the room toward Mean Jim, his eyes locked onto his quarry.

SHERIFF CURRY
I told you not to come back.

MEAN JIM
Yeah? I guess I got homesick.

19 CLOSE ON MEAN JIM'S HAND 19

which inches stealthily toward his gun.

SHERIFF CURRY
I'll be taking your gun.

MEAN JIM
I don't think so.

Suddenly, Mean Jim's gun is in his hand pointed right at the sheriff's chest. The sheriff has grabbed the gun from the top around the cylinder. Mean Jim smiles.

MEAN JIM
This here's a double action colt, Sheriff. Your're a dead man.

Mean Jim tries to pull the trigger but it won't budge as long as Sheriff Curry keeps the cylinder from turning.

The sheriff jerks down on the gun, wresting it from Mean Jim's hand. He then smacks Mean Jim across the face with the gun. Mean Jim staggers back against the bar.

The sheriff grabs him by the neck and hustles him out

```
through the doors into the street. Mean Jim collapses in
the mud.

                    MEAN JIM
          This ain't over!
```

How many shooting sequences? If you are not sure, go back and read it again. Remember the continuity of time, space, action, and cast. Now let's go through these scenes together. It's a good idea to try to think how and where a particular scene will be shot. We start with Scene 11, Int. Sheriff's Office, with the sheriff suddenly awakened by Howie coming in the door. How and where would this be shot? Are we outside with Howie before he enters the Sheriff's Office? The way that the scene is written indicates that we are with the sheriff and that we are surprised, along with him, when Howie interrupts his snooze. Therefore, you would assume that we are not outside the office with Howie.

Why is this important? It is important because we need to know where we are going to shoot the scene. Let's look at the possibilities:

1. We are shooting inside a real sheriff's office in some remote 19th century western town.
2. We are shooting inside a "practical" set in a western town backlot or on location.
3. We are on a sound stage inside a Sheriff's Office set.

Of these three possibilities, which is most likely? I would put my money on number 3. Maintaining a film crew on location is expensive, and most backlot western streets do not have practical interiors that can be used without extensive work. Also, location filming offers much less control than filming on a stage set does. If you need to see the outside as the door opens and Howie enters, that can be accomplished by a scenic backing outside the door on the stage. This would make Scene 11 a complete shooting sequence within itself. It takes place in one place, it is continuous action over a continuous time, and it uses a specific group of cast: unity of time, place, action, and cast.

Now imagine if Howie had been unable to wake the sheriff and left while muttering about sheriffs who sleep all day. Let's say that the next scene was later in the day, but again, inside the Sheriff's Office and Howie returned with 10 townspeople to help him wake the sheriff. Is this still part of the first shooting sequence where Howie tries to wake the sheriff? Look at the unities of time, place, action, and cast. Is it the same continuous time? No, it's later in the day. Is it the same place? Yes, it's in the Sheriff's Office. Is it the same action? Yes, Howie is still trying to wake the sheriff.

Is it the same cast? No, it involves another 10 people. Is it a new shooting sequence? Yes, it lacks unity of time and cast. Individuals can enter or leave a scene without affecting the unity of cast, but if you involve a completely new set of characters, that usually will break the unity of cast.

In Scene 12, we are out on Main Street. The time is immediately after Scene 11; the place is EXT. MAIN STREET; the action is the sheriff walking to the saloon; and the cast involves the sheriff, Helen, and several unnamed townspeople who will probably be played by *extras*. (We will discuss extras in more detail later.) Since we have broken the unity of place from Scene 11 (we have gone from interior to exterior), Scene 12 begins a new shooting sequence. Where does this shooting sequence end? We are EXT. MAIN STREET through Scene 16, when the sheriff enters the saloon. Does this shooting sequence include all the scenes from Scene 12 through Scene 16? Consider each scene in turn.

In Scene 12 we learn that several townspeople watch the sheriff with concern expressed in their faces. This will necessitate shots of those people watching him go by and looking appropriately concerned. Are those shots new shooting sequences? No. They are simply coverage of the ensuing action. The scene encompasses the whole street and everyone in it. The townspeople's reaction to the sheriff can be conveniently combined with the shots on the sheriff himself. In addition, the townspeople will necessarily be in the background when we focus on the sheriff, so they will have to be present. And what do we make of the close-up of Helen? This again is coverage on the scene as a whole. Helen should be present even when we are focusing on the sheriff. It would make a great deal of sense to shoot her close-up along with the rest of the action. So, Scenes 12, 14, 15, and 16 would all appear to be part of the shooting sequence.

Now look at Scene 13, the buzzard circling in the sky above Main Street. Isn't this more coverage of the scene? To answer this question, we must think about how the shot will be accomplished. Will we show up at our western street location and hope a buzzard flies by? Only if we are extremely foolish. This shot will be accomplished in one of three ways:

1. Stock Shot – we will buy a shot of a buzzard in flight from a stock shot library;
2. Second Unit – we will dispatch a small 2nd unit (consisting of a camera operator and assistant) out into the dessert and tell them to find a buzzard and get the shot;
3. Second Unit – we will use a slightly larger 2nd unit crew, rent a buzzard, hire a buzzard wrangler (animal handler), and have them go out and film the trained buzzard against the sky.

Notice that none of these choices includes the sheriff or any of the rest of our cast, or Main Street, or even the main shooting crew on the production. Each of these choices is from a source other than our main shooting unit thereby breaking the unity of space. In addition to lacking unity of cast and place with the surrounding scenes, Scene 13 lacks unity of time (it could be anytime) and action (the buzzard is circling overhead, not walking down Main Street). Scene 13 is definitely a shooting sequence unto itself. Note that the buzzard shooting sequence interrupts, and is in the middle of, the Main Street shooting sequence.

Scene 17 takes us Int. Saloon. Even if the interior of the saloon exists on our Main Street location, it is always wise to separate interiors from exteriors. This allows us to schedule the interior separately from the exterior. Whether we shoot this set on location or on a stage, it is a separate shooting sequence. The action has changed. We are no longer walking to the saloon, we are in the saloon and confronting Mean Jim. The cast is very different. The only cast member in the saloon who also appears on Main Street is Sheriff Curry.

Scene 18 focuses our attention and the camera on Mean Jim. However, note that there is action in Scene 18 that cannot be seen while we are focused on Mean Jim, namely Sheriff Curry's movement toward Mean Jim at the bar. Technically, the writer should have created another shot that said

```
18A  SHERIFF CURRY                                          18A

     glides across the room...
```

The writer did not do this because he was not writing the script for our convenience. He was writing his script so that it would read easily and he probably felt the added shot was intrusive. Instead, he implied the shot by the way he focused the reader's attention on the sheriff. Whether the shot is explicitly described or implicitly hinted at, it is still the same action (confronting Mean Jim), the same place (Int. Saloon), the same time (continuous from the action before), and the same cast (everyone inside the saloon). This shot is part of the ongoing shooting sequence.

Scene 19 explicitly focuses our attention and the camera on Mean Jim's hand as it inches closer to his six-shooter. This again is coverage and belongs with the greater shooting sequence we have been discussing. Again, the writer added much more to the action than just Mean Jim's hand moving toward his pistol. There is a physical confrontation where the sheriff grabs the pistol, dialog where Mean Jim tells the sheriff he's a dead man, the sheriff pistol whipping Mean Jim and throwing him out onto the street, and finally, Mean Jim's line of dialog from the street. Obviously we are not just staring at Mean Jim's hand during all of this. The writer has not broken this scene up, but we must. Everything up to the sheriff throwing Mean Jim through the saloon doors is still part of the Int. Saloon shooting sequence. However, once we move outside, we have broken the unity of space and need to start a new shooting sequence, even though the unity of time, action, and cast have not been broken.

Typically, this transition from Int. Saloon to Ext. Main Street or Ext. Saloon would be handled with a cut. We would see the sheriff rushing Mean Jim toward the saloon doors and just as Mean Jim hit them, we would cut outside to see him bursting through the doors and landing in the street. These two shooting sequences would then be edited together to give the impression of continuous action. The exception to this would be if the director decided to have the camera follow Mean Jim through the doors and into the street. This could only be accomplished if the Int. Saloon set actually existed within the Ext. Saloon set on the Main Street location. In this instance, it could be argued that we have not broken the unity of space since one could actually walk from Int. Saloon to Ext. Main Street, and we have not started a new shooting sequence by going outside. In fact, under those circumstances, it could be argued that the material from when the sheriff first walks down Main Street through Mean Jim landing in the mud (except the shot on the buzzard) could all be one long shooting sequence. However, if we were to do that, we would be getting away from the reason to divide a script into shooting sequences, namely to create manageable parts.

If you know with certainty, that the director wants to follow Mean Jim through the doors and that you have a location or set that physically allows that action, then by all means, add Mean Jim landing in the street to the Int. Saloon shooting sequence. Even under those circumstances, I still would not recommend adding the Main Street shots prior to the Int. Saloon since that would be a rather unwieldy shooting sequence which does break the unity of cast. Normally, at the early stages of planning, you would not know if the director wants to shoot the scene in that way, nor would you know if you had a location that would permit it. It is therefore usually safer to split the scene into interior and exterior shooting sequences. If you later find that you will be following Mean Jim through the doors, then you can schedule the two shooting sequences side by side.

So how many shooting sequences are in this short piece of script? Five: (1) Int. Sheriff's Office, (2) Ext. Main Street, (3) Ext. Sky (buzzard), (4) Int. Saloon, and (5) Ext. Main Street & Saloon. I have described these shooting sequences by the set in which they take place. There are probably other Ext. Main Street shooting sequences elsewhere in this script. To fully describe a shooting sequence you would need to include other information such as the action, cast, and time of day, or in other words, include the other three of the four shooting sequence unities. We will be doing exactly that in our discussion of breakdown pages.

Problem Situations

There are a number of problematic situations in which it is easy to become confused as to where a shooting sequence begins or ends, or what it includes. It is usually best, as we did above, to think how the sequence will be filmed and where. Ask yourself, where will the camera be, and what will it see? Let's look at a few examples.

Int. / Ext.

As stated earlier, it is always best to separate interiors from exteriors, making them separate shooting sequences. They usually indicate a change in shooting location. Interiors require different lighting, different film stocks, and different conditions under which they can be shot. For example, if you see some characters enter a building, they then have a scene inside the building, and then they exit the building and drive away in a car, it would be best to split the exterior scenes from the interior scene. It might even make a great deal of sense to split the two exterior scenes apart and make them separate shooting sequences since there would be a period of time between when the characters entered the building, when they exit, and when they drive away (unity of time). In doing this, one would be able to shoot the two exterior sequences early in the day while there was plenty of sunlight, and then move inside to shoot the interior sequence where the lack of sunlight would not be a hindrance.

A more complicated situation is the balcony scene in *Romeo and Juliet*. In Shakespeare's play, Juliet is on her balcony, Romeo in the garden below, and Juliet's nurse is inside Juliet's bedroom. Let's say that we are filming this scene, we have built a set on a soundstage of Juliet's bedroom, and we are using an actual location for the exterior of the house and garden. The location has a balcony at the end of a hallway that we will use for Juliet's balcony. What shooting sequences will we have? Imagine where the camera will be, and what it will see. Romeo is standing in the garden, so all of his shots must be on location. Romeo's POV (*point of view*) of Juliet must also be on location since the camera will be in the garden and will be seeing the exterior of the Capulet house. The Nurse's shots must be on our stage set since that is the only place the bedroom exists. What if the Nurse spies Romeo through the bedroom window? Where would her POV of Romeo from inside the bedroom be shot? It would have to be on location since Romeo is in the garden, not in the bedroom. The shot would most likely be made from a platform at the height of the bedroom, shooting through a window unit which matched the window units in the set. So in this situation, there would be two shooting sequences: (1) Int. Juliet's Bedroom, and (2) Ext. Capulet House – Balcony & Garden.

Vehicles

Vehicles provide a special case in that even if you are inside a vehicle, you see what is outside the vehicle. Shooting inside and outside of a stationary vehicle is equivalent to being outside. You might as well make such scenes all one shooting sequence and not differentiate between interior and exterior. If the camera is inside the vehicle, we will see outside, and if the camera is outside the vehicle, we can certainly see inside. For this reason, vehicle interiors shot on location should be considered exterior shots.

A moving vehicle presents a slightly more complicated situation. Often in the past, the interior of a moving vehicle was shot on a soundstage against a projected moving background while the exterior shots of the vehicle zooming by were done on location. These exterior shots are known as *run-bys*. In a situation such as this, it makes sense to separate the interior moving vehicle shots from the exterior moving vehicle shots. Even if the interior moving vehicle shots are done on location, the exterior run-bys may be done by a separate unit such as a second unit or stunt unit. If they are not done by a separate unit, they will probably be done at a separate time by the main unit. Rigging a vehicle with mounted cameras and lights takes a great deal of time, and the main unit would want to shoot all of the interior vehicle shots together once they were rigged for it. Because of this, you should separate exterior moving vehicle shots from the interior shots, yet still treat the interiors as exteriors.

Day/Night

Imagine a foreign legionnaire trekking endlessly through the trackless desert. He treks and treks and treks. Day becomes night, night becomes day. Is all of this one Desert Trekking shooting sequence? How do the unities apply? We cannot tell where he is since in this trackless desert every place looks like every other place. The unity of space is maintained. He is monotonously trekking. The unity of action is maintained. The unity of cast is maintained since we only see our hapless legionnaire. But, at the very least, you will need to shoot some of it in daylight and some of it at night. The unity of time is broken. Therefore, you will have, at minimum, two shooting sequences: the Day Trekking sequence and the Night Trekking sequence. These two sequences can then be cut up to appear like two weeks or more of endless trekking if the editor and director desire since nothing else is changing.

Lapse of Time

The passage of time can be subtle. How much time must pass before we have broken the unity of time? In the 1960s and the 1970s, a number of avant-garde filmmakers, such as Andy Warhol, were making films in which they set up a camera and kept it running continuously for extended periods, pausing only to change film magazines. Twenty-four hours of the Empire State Building is one long, incredibly boring shooting sequence. But what about the unities? Let's examine them. The unity of space is preserved in the extreme. The camera never moves. The unity of action is preserved since there is none. There are only people coming and going. The unity of cast is preserved since there are no particular people coming and going, just a faceless mass. But what about the unity of time? First it is day and then it is night, just like the Desert Trekking sequence. In the Desert Trekking sequence, we were not actually going to have our actor playing the legionnaire walk through the desert for thirty-six hours and follow along, pausing only to change magazines. We needed to create a schedule that normal human beings would be willing to work. No one wants to work thirty-six or even twenty-four hours straight, and if they did, it would be prohibitively expensive. In *Twenty-four Hours of the Empire State Building*, they did shoot for twenty-four hours. Therefore, the unity of time was not broken. So how much time must pass? The answer often depends on the unity of action.

High Noon, starring Gary Cooper, preserves the unity of time. Throughout its 85 minute length, screen time equals real time. What separates this story into shooting sequences is the breaking of the unities of action and space. Gary Cooper's character moves through the town, unsuccessfully trying to convince first this person and then that person to help him fight the evil killers who will be coming to exact their revenge.

Sometimes the shooting sequences can be defined by parameters which have nothing to do with the story. Alfred Hitchcock's film, *Rope,* is another film where screen time equals real time. The film was designed to appear as if the camera never cut. Actually, the camera did cut at the end of each thousand-foot reel (approximately every ten to eleven minutes), and the cuts were disguised by various means such as having someone's dark jacket fill the screen. This film was made up of eight ten-minute shooting sequences defined by the amount of film a camera magazine could hold at one time.

In *Twelve Angry Men*, *Sleuth*, and *'Night Mother*, the unity of cast and space are preserved. The shooting sequences are defined by the action. All of these films take place in a small defined space: a jury room in the first, an apartment in the second, and a house in the third. Also, each has a small defined cast which is essentially present throughout the film, although *Twelve Angry Men* at times has a subset of the cast on the screen by themselves. In all of these films, the time that passes can be separated into shooting sequences by the action that is taking place. Each film is made up of discreet movements that propel the story forward.

By analyzing how a film is to be shot and understanding how the story is structured, even extreme examples can be broken into shooting sequences.

Visual Effects Elements

Consider the following snippet of script.

```
74  INT. COCKPIT OF THE SPACESCOUT RANGER - DAY                    74

      Cmdr. Egan fights to bring the craft under control after
      the devastating explosion. Lt. Harley raises her arm and
      points.

                            LT. HARLEY
                  Commander!

      Cmdr. Egan follows her pointing finger out the forward
      viewport.

      A lifeless JACK SIMMONS smashes into the thick screen and
      bounces off into space spinning madly.
```

How many shooting sequences? As always, it really depends on how it will be shot. If you can really go out into space and have some actor float by and collide with the viewport, it would be just one. The camera would be inside the ship and would film the action as described. However, it seems it will be a few years before we can do this sort of thing, so next we need to consider visual effects.

Visual effects influence shooting sequences by how the various elements are supplied. The action inside the cockpit of the ship is straightforward. It would be shot in a set on a soundstage. Out the window, or viewport, would be a *blue screen*. A blue screen can be easily removed from the frame either optically or on a computer and replaced by another shot. The filmmakers could put whatever they wanted outside that window, from a swirling black hole to an undersea coral reef, or even the courtyard at Windsor Castle. How we come up with that element outside the window is going to determine the shooting sequences.

In the current example, we would hang the actor playing Jack Simmons in a harness that would allow him to spin and tumble in front of another blue screen, and we would then swing him toward a camera shooting behind a transparent barrier. We would bounce him off the barrier and swing him away from camera as though he were tumbling out into space. Next we would have a matte artist come up with a background that we could put behind him showing the cold limitless reaches of space. These three elements, the live action in the cockpit, the shot of Jack hanging in space, and the space background would then be composited together to create the shot described in the script. How many sequences? At least three: (1) Int. Cockpit, (2) Ext. Space (Jack floating around), and (3) the background produced by the matte artist. Each of these sequences will have to be accounted for in the schedule.

At one point in *Indiana Jones and the Temple of Doom*, Indy is high up on a cliff. We are looking down on him from above. Far below him we see crocodiles swimming in the river. I'm not sure why the crocodiles were necessary; to paraphrase the line from *Butch Cassidy and the Sundance Kid*, "Hell, the fall would kill him." How many shooting sequences? Did the filmmakers actually dangle Harrison Ford over a crocodile infested river? I think not. So there would be probably three shooting sequences: (1) Harrison Ford on a nice safe soundstage dangling over a blue screen, (2) Ext. Cliff looking down on a river for the background, and maybe (3) Crocodiles created by a *visual effects* company to be inserted into the background shot.

Low-budget films rarely have the luxury of dealing with $100,000 visual effect shots, but even low-tech films can have shooting sequences required by visual effects. In *Robin Hood: Men in Tights*, there is a scene toward the end of the film where Robin is dueling with the Sheriff of Nottingham while Maid Marian lies restrained and helpless nearby. At one point in the duel, the Sheriff's blade snags a cord around Robin's neck, cutting the cord, and sending a locket it supported flying up into the air. The locket hits a stone archway, explodes into a million shimmering golden pieces and releases a key. The key tumbles through the air in slow motion and ultimately lands in the lock of Maid Marian's chastity belt.

The budget for this film did not allow any high-tech computer visual effects. A 2nd unit was organized to shoot a sequence which started with the locket flying through the air, and ended with the key landing in the padlock on the chastity belt. That was a shooting sequence within the dueling shooting sequence, and it needed to be scheduled separately from the rest of the scene. (See the appendix to read how the shot was done.) How did the unities apply? Time: the unity of time was preserved in that the sequence was contiguous with what went before. Space: the unity of space was broken in that a specially modified set was required to make the effect work. Action: the unity of action was preserved since the locket was flying into the air as a direct result of the duel. Cast: the unity of cast was broken since we used a photo double for Maid Marian (those are not Amy Yasbek's hips, she was needed elsewhere during the filming of this shot), and Robin and the Sheriff were not required at all.

Overlapping Shooting Sequences

There are instances where a shooting sequence can be laid right on top of another shooting sequence. Do not confuse this with sequences such as the buzzard sequence mentioned previously. The buzzard sequence is inserted into the Main Street sequence, not laid on top of it. Scene 13 will not be filmed when the shooting company is at the Main Street location. To be more explicit, you could physically cut Scene 13 out of the scripts of the cast and crew, and they would not need it while they were shooting the Main Street sequence.

Overlapping shooting sequences happen mainly in two dramatic constructs: phone calls and when there is a film within the film. In these situations, the same part of the script page is filmed in two separate locations. This will become clearer as we examine specific cases.

Phone Calls

Phones are ubiquitous in movies. Often a scene goes something like this: a phone rings, a character answers it and mumbles something back, hangs up, and says something like, "They're at the old warehouse. Let's go." That's a very simple shooting sequence. We are seeing only one side of the conversation. When both sides of the conversation must be filmed, it gets trickier.

We have all witnessed something like the following scene in a movie:

```
32  INT. VANDERLING'S LIVING ROOM - NIGHT                    32

    Mr. and Mrs. Vanderling sit together on the couch,
    obviously distraught. A dozen uniformed policemen and
    several detectives swarm through the house.

    The phone RINGS.

    The Vanderlings look at each other and then at Detective
    Winston. He nods to them to pick up the phone.

    As Mr. Vanderling picks the phone up, Detective Winston
    picks up an extension at the same time.

                          MR. VANDERLING
               Hello?

33 INTERCUT                                                  33

    Joey, in a phone booth in a seedy part of town.

                          JOEY
               Listen carefully, dude. Bring the
               money ALONE to the east end of
               the 6th street bridge. Come alone,
               dude, or the kid's history. You
               understand?

                          MR. VANDERLING
               I...I want to talk to my daughter.

                          JOEY
               You'll talk to her when I get the
               money.

                          MR. VANDERLING
               I won't come unless I can talk to
               my daughter.

    Detective Winston nods his approval to Mr. Vanderling.

                          JOEY
               Don't push me, dude.

    Joey lowers the receiver down to Jessica, held firmly at
    his side.

                          JOEY
               Say something, kid.

                          JESSICA
               Daddy?

                          MR. VANDERLING
               Jessica?

    Joey takes the receiver back.
```

```
                    JOEY
          You got two hours, dude.

     He hangs up.

34   INT. VANDERLING'S LIVING ROOM - CONTINUOUS              34

     Mr. Vanderling slowly lowers the phone.

                         DETECTIVE WINSTON
          We'll have the bridge surrounded.
          He won't get away.
```

Scenes 32 and 34 are easy. That's a shooting sequence shot in the Int. Vanderling Living Room, which preserves all four unities. However, Scene 33 is somewhat different. First, where is it? Is it in the Living Room or the Phone Booth? And what does the writer mean by *Intercut*?

Scene 33 is in both the Living Room and the Phone Booth. *Intercut* means that the editor will be cutting between the two sets as he or she sees fit. We will not know in which set any specific part of the phone conversation will be seen. What does this mean to us as the filmmakers? It means that we will need to shoot all of Scene 33 in *both locations*. Why would we not just film each person saying his lines? Because it might be more interesting seeing the other person listen. When Jessica screams out "Daddy?" the editor may think it's better to see the effect his little girl's voice has on Mr. Vanderling. Each side of the phone conversation must be filmed completely. We have two shooting sequences: (1) Int. Vanderling's Living Room consisting of Scenes 32, 33pt., and 34; and (2) Int. Phone Booth consisting of Scene 33pt. (The abbreviation for *part* of a scene is *pt.* and it means that Scene 33 will appear in more than one shooting sequence.) Both of these shooting sequences occupy some of the same real estate on the script page but the unity of space is broken because they take place in two different locations.

A similar situation occurs when a movie has a film within the film:

```
43 INT. VANDERLING STUDY - NIGHT                            43

     Mr. Vanderling pours himself a scotch and sits down at
     his desk. He picks up the remote and clicks on the TV
     and the tape player.

     Jessica's happy smiling face beams out from the screen.

                         MRS. VANDERLING (O.S.)
          How old are you today, Jessica?

     Jessica holds up three fingers.

     Mr. Vanderling swoops into the video frame, and picks
     his daughter up and spins around with her.
```

```
                    MR. VANDERLING (ON TAPE)
          That's my girl!

     At his desk, Mr. Vanderling drinks his scotch while the
     tears roll down his face.

                    MR. VANDERLING (ON TAPE)
          That's my girl!

     Mr. Vanderling turns off the video and buries his face
     in his arms on his desk sobbing uncontrollably.
```

This should be simple. Mr. Vanderling is sitting in his study watching a video of himself and his daughter. However, you need to film the video also. Therefore we have two shooting sequences occupying the space of one scene on the page: (1) Int. Study, Scene 43pt; and (2) Ext. Backyard Party, Scene 43pt. These two shooting sequences break all four unities. The unity of time is broken because the two sequences obviously take place at different times. The unity of space is broken because one sequence is in the Study and the other one is in the Backyard. The unity of action is broken because in one sequence Mr. Vanderling is pining over his missing daughter, and in the other sequence, he is playing with that same daughter. Finally, the unity of cast is broken because Mr. Vanderling is in the Study alone, but in the Backyard, he is with his daughter.

Creative Geography

Sometimes a scene can be split into two shooting sequences merely because the geography of the scene does not exist. It must be created. In essence, this breaks the unity of space in a scene in which that unity appears to be preserved. Let's consider the following scenario. Two men sit at a sidewalk café, observing the front of a hotel directly across the street. They are watching two detectives standing in front of the hotel. There is dialog between the two detectives, and there is dialog between the two men watching the detectives. In addition, the director wants to shoot a shot of the front of the hotel with the two men sitting at the sidewalk café in the foreground (fig. 4.2). You find you have only one problem. Nowhere within a hundred miles can you find this location. You can find hotels and you can find sidewalk cafés, but nowhere can you find a sidewalk café directly across the street from a hotel. Shot *C* in figure 4.1 can be achieved only by creating a geography that does not exist.

First, you would film the two men at the sidewalk café, angling your shots so that the café is in the background (fig. 4.1 shots *A* and *B*). Once

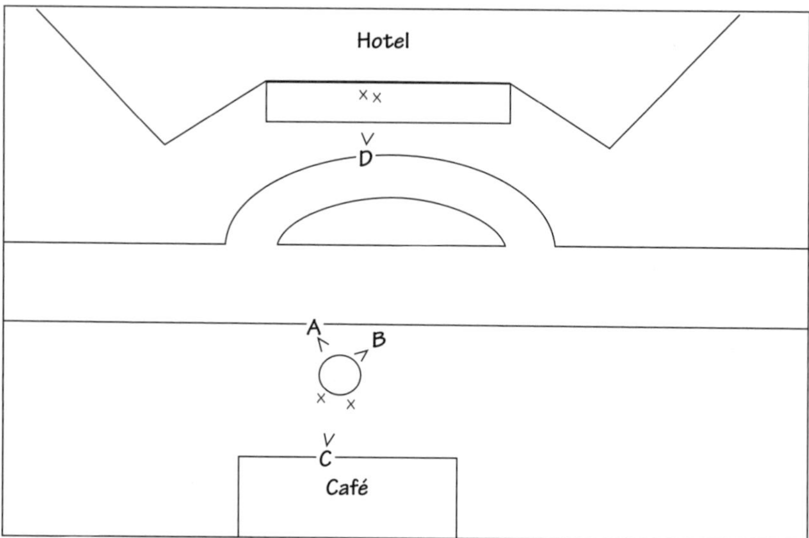

Fig. 4.1. A plan of the shots needed of two men at a sidewalk café watching two other men across the street standing in front of a hotel. The hotel and café do not exist in this relationship to each other and the location must be created filmically. The actors are marked by Xs and the camera angles are marked by Vs. The open end of the Vs point toward what the camera sees.

those shots are completed, you wrap that location and move to a hotel across town that has been selected. You stage the dialog between the two detectives in front of the hotel (fig. 4.1 shot *D*), keeping the hotel's facade in the background. In order to tie the two locations together, you then put tables on the sidewalk across the street from the hotel, seat your two men there, and shoot over them toward the detectives in front of the hotel (fig. 4.1, shot *C*, and fig. 4.2). By doing this, you have overcome a disunity of space to make it appear as though there is none, but you nevertheless have had to shoot two shooting sequences to make that one scene.

A similar situation occurred in the making of *Hollow Man*, directed by Paul Verhoeven. There is a scene early on in that film where a group of scientists led by Sebastian (Kevin Bacon), are celebrating in one of the finer restaurants of Washington, D.C. Thereafter, Linda (Elizabeth Shue), realizes that Sebastian has left the table and gets up to find him. She ambles out onto the restaurant's balcony and sees him at the railing with the U.S. Capitol building glowing in the background. This geography does not exist. The interior of the restaurant was filmed in a very fine restaurant located on the ground floor of a Washington hotel. The balcony was filmed on the roof of the U.S. Department of Labor building which is in close proximity to the U.S. Capitol building. Elements of the restaurant, including the doorway, were duplicated on the roof location in order to

Fig. 4.2. Shot C from fig. 4.1. This relationship of the café to the hotel exists only in the filmmaker's mind.

smooth the transition from one location to the other and to enhance the illusion of the space being continuous. It was not known at the time of the first breakdown of the *Hollow Man* script that the restaurant described did not exist. However, the restaurant scenes were broken into two shooting sequences anyway since, in moving onto the balcony, the unity of space and the unity of cast were broken.

Although some of the above examples are extreme, they are not unusual. When confronted with complex situations, always go back to the basic rule. Whenever any of the four unities are broken, it's a good indication that the last shooting sequence has ended and a new one has begun. Being able to break a script into its shooting sequences is the key to managing its complexity.

5

The Production Board

1 Shooting Sequence = 1 Strip

The goal of breaking a script down into manageable parts is to assemble those parts onto a production board (fig. 5.1). The information regarding each shooting sequence in the script is written on a cardboard strip, and then the strip is placed on the board. A production board is an organizing and sorting tool. It allows you to display each shooting sequence independently of all the others, and to sort all of the shooting sequences into a coherent and efficient shooting schedule.

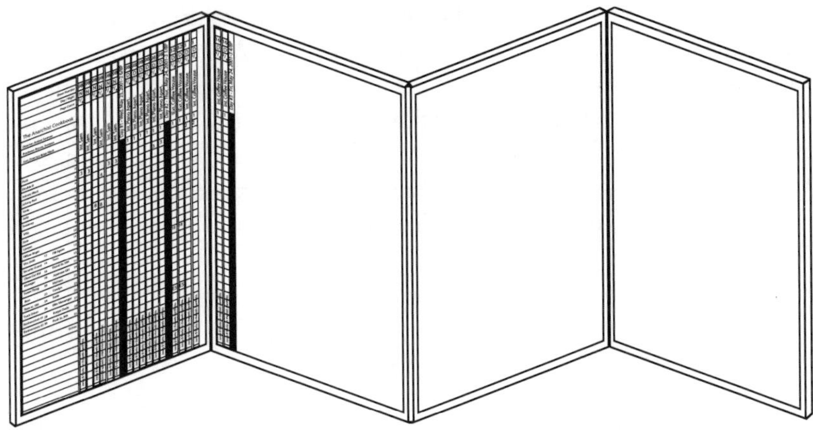

Fig. 5.1. A production board in the process of being assembled.

The components of the production board consists of the board itself, a header, and various cardboard strips (fig. 5.2). The board serves to hold the header and strips securely in any given order. Boards come in various sizes that are designated by the length in inches of the strips that they are designed to carry. Standard sizes of production boards used over the past several decades from oldest to newest are 18 inches, 15 inches, 14 inches, and 11 inches. These strip lengths were based on the size of the paper that was used to manufacture the strips. In more recent developments, the 14 and 11-inch boards were based on using legal and letter size paper respectively, since these boards are printed out by computerized scheduling programs.

The Header

The header board (fig. 5.2A) acts as a key to the production board and determines the order of the information presented on the strips. The order and information that is called for at the top of the header board can vary, but typically, it will list the strip number, whether the shooting sequence is day or night, and the length in pages of the shooting sequence.

Below the upper segment is an information block in which the title of the picture and often the director, producer, assistant director, and script date are listed. Below this general information is a list of the cast. Notice that the cast list has had to be doubled up to conserve space. In doing so, the numbers printed on the board have had to be revised.

Other needed elements such as extras, stunt players, vehicles, and anything else a filmmaker may want to track, including various makeup states or hair length, may be tracked on the board. Usually, it is desirable to track anything that might impact scheduling. In the first incarnation of the *Santa Clause 2* script, the character played by Tim Allen (Scott) was seen in various stages while transforming from Santa to a normal human being. His makeup changed progressively throughout the picture. Switching him from one makeup change to another would take hours, so the filmmakers tried to schedule scenes with the same look on the same day. For that reason, it made sense to track the makeup changes on the production board (fig. 5.3).

The Strips

The first thing you may notice when examining the strips on a production board is that the strips are in many different colors. (See the foldout

				B
			Sheet Number:	174
			Day / Night:	D
			Page Count:	5/8
Title: The Anarchist Cookbook				Int. Son of Sam - Liv. Rm. Sc. 219
Director: Jordan Susman				
Producer: Brown, Susman, Greenspun				
Asst. Director: Brian Mack				
Script Dated: April 5, 2001				
Character			No.	
Puck			1	1
Double D			2	
Johnny Black			3	3
Johnny Red			4	
Karla			5	
Jody			6	
Sweeney			7	
Gin			8	
Milo			9	9
Rich			10	10
Dale			11	11
Mr. Gold			12	
Lawyer			13	
Tour Leader	14	Sweet Thing	15	
Officer Roger	16	Boss sc. 155	17	
FBI Agent	18	Teen sc. 186	19	
Mrs. Gold	20	Truck Driver	21	
Teen	22	Business man	23	
Security Guard	24	Business woman	25	
Guard sc. 50A	26	Newsman	27	
Clean-cut Kid	28	Black Man	29	
Japanese Girl	30	Latina sc. 67	31	
Manger sc. 76	32	Ticket Guy	33	
		Extras:	24	E/18
			25	Johnny Black comes in and wants to know what's going on
			26	
			27	
			28	
			29	
			30	

C: End of Day 17 - Tue, Jun 12, 2001 - 5 2/8 pgs.

D: End of Week #3 - Sat & Sun, June 16 & 17, 2001

E: Company Moves to Elm Street

F: End of Principal Photography

G: Stock Footage

A B C D E F G

Fig. 5.2. The components of a production board: (A) the header board; (B) a shooting sequence strip; (C) a day strip; (D) an end-of-week banner; (E) a company-move banner; (F) an end-of-principal-photography banner; and (G) a stock-footage banner.

of *The Anarchist Cookbook* production board located at the back of this book.) The colors usually signify the time of day and whether the shooting sequence is to be shot interior or exterior, and whether it is on a stage

BP Helicopter Pilot	30		30	
Karl	31	Sidewalk Santa	51	
Situation Room Elf	32	Woman sc. 163	52	
Scott's hair dyed black			B	
Scott heavy no beard			HNB	
Missing tooth			MT	
Scott in normal makeup	N	Scott in Santa makeup	S	
Scott normal face, fat body	NF	Half normal, half fat butt	1/2	NF
			Extras:	E:6
			Stunts:	
				edical

Fig. 5.3. A portion of the header board and a strip for ***Santa Clause 2*** showing how Tim Allen's makeup changes were tracked.

or at a location. A typical color scheme might be: white for interior stage day, light blue for interior stage night, yellow for exterior day, darker blue for exterior night, tan for interior location day, green for interior location night. Other colors can be used to designate special shooting sequences such as visual effects elements or second units.

Starting at the top of the strip shown in figure 5.2B, we see that this strip was created from breakdown sheet #174. (The strip number and the breakdown sheet number are the same.) The shooting sequence represented by this strip takes place in the daytime and it occupies 5/8 of a script page. If you cock your head to the left, you can read the set and scene numbers. The set is Int. Son of Sam - Living Room, and the scene number making up the shooting sequence is Scene 219.

In the lined area below the set, the numbers of the appropriate cast are entered aligned with each cast member's line on the header board. If it is necessary to enter two cast members who occupy the same line, such as Mrs. Gold and Truck Driver, then the second number is put in the next space below the first number. In this sequence, we will need the parts of Puck, Johnny Black, Milo, Rich, and Dale.

Below the cast are entered the other items that are being tracked on the board; in this instance, the extras. There will be 18 extras or background players working in this sequence. At the very bottom of the strip, written vertically from bottom to top, is a brief but unique description of the action of the shooting sequence. We will discuss this in more detail when we cover the breakdown pages in Chapter 7.

The Day Markers

The day marker strips (fig. 5.2c) are black with a white space on which the day number, date, and total page count for the day can be written. Think of the day markers as *end-of-day* markers. They are placed to the right of the work for that day.

Banners

Banners are informational strips (fig. 5.2d, e, f, & g). Four different types of banners are shown in the illustration. Figure 5.2d is an *end-of-week* banner. End-of-week-banners are especially useful in longer shooting schedules. If you see that a piece of equipment must be used from week two through week five, you know that it will be needed for four weeks without having to count the weeks on the board.

Figure 5.2e shows a *company-move* banner. It is important that the crewmembers know if a midday move is planned so that they are able to have the trucks packed and ready.

Figure 5.2f is an *end-of-principal-photography* banner. The end of the main shooting period is an important time in the making of a film since many contracts will reference the end of principal photography in outlining terms of an agreement or contract.

Figure 5.2g shows a banner that would preceed a section of the board devoted to *stock footage* (footage that will be bought from a library and not shot by the production company). Other board divisions that might be announced by a banner would be *second unit shots, visual effects shots*, and *omitted scenes*. Banners are usually made by writing the information on the plain white backside of a strip.

The Next Step

I have given this brief introduction to the production board to help clarify the reasons for what follows next. As we go through the lining of the script and the making of the breakdown sheets, keep in mind where we are headed. It's all necessary in order to make an accurate and complete production board. Now that you know our destination, let's look at how we get there.

6

Lining the Script

Where to start?

The first thing you must do when you are given a new script to breakdown is to fnd a comfortable chair, sit down, and read it from beginning to end. As you allow yourself to be transported into the story, it is important to visualize the movie that is being described. In the process, you will also start to learn the writer's style and perhaps get a sense of the style of the picture as well. During this initial read, try not to worry about shooting sequences and mechanics. Just enjoy the story. If there are parts of the script that are confusing or that are unclear, make a quick note and try to get clarification from the director or writer later. Above all, it is important that you understand what happens in the story.

Next, determine if you have a shooting script or not. Are the scenes numbered? If not, start at the first slug line and number all the scene headings and shots from the beginning to the end. As mentioned in chapter 3, the slug line is the line written in all caps that introduces each scene. If you are numbering the script, be sure that your numbers are communicated to whoever is distributing the scripts so that all the scripts can be number the same as yours. When you refer to Scene 27, you want to know that everyone else's Scene 27 is the same as yours. The best and quickest way to number the scenes is to do it in the scriptwriting program in which the script was composed. The two leading scriptwriting programs, Final Draft® and Movie Magic Screenwriter®, each have a function to number the scenes. Once the scenes are numbered in the scriptwriting program, the script is locked, meaning that any further changes to the script will be highlighted and the page that they occur on will be marked as a revised page. If this is not done and the script is revised without the changes being marked, most of what you are about to do will have to be redone.

Once you have a numbered script, get yourself a pencil, a ruler, and a set of highlighter markers. Remove the brads holding the script together and either place it unbound on your desk or put it into a three-ring binder that will open flat. My preference is to use a three-ring binder so that I will not misplace any pages. You want it free of the brads so that you are not fighting to keep the script open and you are able to place the ruler flat across the open page.

The Point of Lining the Script

Your goal at this stage is two-fold. You want to divide the script into shooting sequences, and you want to highlight all important elements in each sequence. What are the important elements? They would be cast, extras, vehicles, animals, props, special effects, visual effects, special makeup, notes about the set, lighting changes, costumes, and anything necessary to the filming of the sequence and which might affect the budget and/or the schedule.

It is not necessary to make exhaustive lists of set dressing and props at this point. Your set decorator and your propmaster will do that. The elements that you want to highlight are the ones which are necessary to shooting the sequence and/or which are mentioned or inferred by the script. For example, in a shooting sequence set in a bar, it is understood that there will be tables, chairs, liquor bottles, barstools, and glasses, so it is not necessary to note these items. However, you should note the breakaway barstool that one character uses to smash the head of another since that is an unusual item and is necessary to film that particular scene. In highlighting these elements, it is useful to color code them.

Highlighter Colors – Keep It Simple

After leaving graduate film school, I lined my first script and made my first production board under the tutelage of Howard Kazanjian, an assistant director at the time, who later went on to produce *Return of the Jedi* and *Raiders of the Lost Ark,* among other films. I could not have had a finer teacher. Howard was known for his careful and accurate breakdowns, and his fine, artistic production boards. His production boards were such works of art with their skillful use of color and their neat, legible, handwritten strips, that the studio executives would leave them hanging on the wall long after the pictures were complete. They were a pleasure to look at *and* to use. Howard had a scheme of colors that he used when lining a script that gave each element a specific color depending on which category it belonged. For example, he might highlight each actor in red, extras in pink, special effects in blue, props in green, etc. You could look at any shooting sequence in a script that he had lined and see immediately what elements were required.

When I began to breakdown large and complex scripts, I found I was spending most of my time removing and replacing the caps on the fist full of markers in my hand. I needed to come up with a more streamlined system, so I settled on a scheme that used only two colors: a warm color such as pink, red, or orange for all people (cast and extras), and a cool color such as blue or green for everything else. This made my marker maintenance more manageable without diminishing the value of the system. Normally, a highlighted item is self-evident as to which category it belongs. If there is any ambiguity, a quick note penciled in the margin will make it clear.

Lining Off Shooting Sequences

In lining the shooting sequences, you need to draw a line across the page at the beginning and end of each shooting sequence (see figs. 6.1 and 6.2). Use solid lines to separate shooting sequences. Solid lines are always used except for a very specific instance that we will address below, under the section on overlapping shooting sequences. I use a ruler and a pencil. The ruler is a hold over from my training under Howard Kazanjian. It is important to keep the script neat and legible. Use pencil so that if you change your mind about a line you have drawn, you can erase it completely. If a sequence ends at the bottom of a page, draw a line at the bottom of the page *and at the top of the next page.* That way, you don't have to waste time paging back and forth to see whether or not a sequence continues from a previous page. If there is a line at the top of the page, then that is where the sequence begins. Remember that shooting sequences begin and end with the breaking of at least one of the four shooting sequence unities: time, space, action, and cast. If you encounter omitted scenes, ignore them. Do not line them off; do not cross them out. Just pretend that they don't exist.

```
WHITE Revision  -  5-1-01                                        1.

1  EXT SOUTHWESTERN BAPTIST COLLEGE - EARLY MORNING                 1

   A mist hovers over the grassy knolls of the serene campus.

   Joggers take their early morning runs past the magnolia trees,
   live oaks and colonnaded buildings.

   In the dead center of campus is a fountain and beside it, a     3/
   towering FLAGPOLE.  Atop the pole, three flags snap in the
   morning breeze:  The Stars and Stripes, the Texan flag, and at
   the very top, a large BLACK and RED FLAG.

2  EXT. SOUTHWESTERN BAPTIST COLLEGE - LATER                        2

   A group of 20 bright-eyed FRESHMAN tour the campus.  The TOUR
   GUIDE is a sophomore who was on this tour a year earlier. He
   carries a university pennant so the groupdoesn't get lost.

                        PUCK (V.O.)
             Be all that you can be.
___________________________________________________________________
3  INT. LIBRARY                                                     3

   The group ogles the endless rows of books that await them.     1/

                        PUCK (V.O.)
             Be the best and the brightest. A
             mind is a terrible thing to waste.
___________________________________________________________________
4  INT. CAFETERIA                                                   4

   The group is duly impressed by the lunch line.

                        TOUR LEADER
             And this is where those of you on                    2/
             the meal plan will eat...

                        PUCK (V.O.)
             Feed your head. Feed the beast. Feed
             the children. Feed me Seymour.
                 (beat)
             It's food for thought.
___________________________________________________________________
5  INT. DORM - DAY                                                  5

   It's the Holy Grail of going to college -- the dorms.  The
   group heads down the hallway, excitement building...

                        TOUR LEADER
             This Floor is girls' only. Affectionately           2/
             known as "chastity castle."
                 (nervous laughter)
             Just kidding. No one really calls it
             that. It's just that boys are allowed
                        (MORE)
```

Fig. 6.1. Page one of ***The Anarchist Cookbook*** with shooting sequences lined off and page count annotated.

WHITE Revision - 5-1-01 2.

5 CONTINUED 5

TOUR LEADER (CONT'D)
up here only after signing in with
the R.A.

The Tour Leader displays a KEY.

TOUR LEADER (CONT'D)
So without further ado. Jenna Connors
and Melissa Flanagan, welcome to
your room.

Jenna and Melissa can barely control themselves.

The key is turned. The door opens. The group pours into:

6 INT. DORM ROOM - CONTINUOUS 6

A cramped space, made all the more cramped by the presence of 6 ragged PEOPLE crashed on the beds and on the floor.

The kids on tour are confused: College wasn't supposed to be like this.

The Tour Leader whips out a WALKIE-TALKIE. 8/

TOUR LEADER
I have crashers in chastity castle.
Room 306. Again.

The freshmen ar agog at the sight.

PUCK (V.O.)
Bigger is better. Too much is not
enought. My eyes are bigger than
my stomach. You can have it all.
Happiness is only a purchase away.
He who dies with the most toys wins.

Two SECURITY GUARDS push past the freshmen.

SECURITY GUARD
Good morning sleepy heaads.

The crashers open their eyes to this rude awakening. Among them is PUCK, 24, good-looking in the extreme (but wholly unaware of it) with pierced ears and piercing eyes.

PUCK
Housing is a right, not a privilege.

PUCK (V.O.)
So I told them. But they were in no
mood to argue social theory.

BILLY CLUBS drawn, the guards charge towards the crashers.

Fig. 6.2. Page two of ***The Anarchist Cookbook*** with shooting sequences lined off and page count annotated.

Page Count

You may recall that the production board header had a line for the length of the shooting sequence. This is called the *page count*. Page count is always measured in pages and eighths of pages. Figure 6.1 shows a script page divided into eighths. If you have an even number of eighths, you do not reduce the fraction; 4/8 is shown as 4/8, not 1/2. The page count is an estimate, but any two production managers or assistant directors will independently come to approximately the same page count total for any given script. If a sequence takes up a complete page, it is 8/8 of a page long. If a sequence starts at the top of the page and ends at about the middle of the page or even with the middle hole, it is 4/8 of a page long. Halfway between the top margin and the middle of the page is 2/8 and half of that is 1/8. On a standard script page, an eighth of a page is approximately one inch, but don't waste your time measuring it. This is not an exact science and you should be able to visually judge the length.

The page count for each shooting sequence is written in the right hand margin in pencil. It is not necessary to write the "8" over and over. Save yourself a few seconds on each sequence by writing the page count as a number with a slash after it. In other words, don't write "7/8", instead just write "7/." The slash tells you that the number is a page count and not something else. Write only the page count on any given page that occurs on that page. In other words, if a shooting sequence begins on page 15 and continues on to the following page, on page 15 only write that part of the page count that occurs on page 15. Do not add up the page counts on pages that are before or after the current page. Deal only with each page in its turn. Figures 6.1 and 6.2 show two consecutive script pages that have been lined and that have had their page count noted in the margin.

An Example

Let's line the script pages we have seen previously involving Sheriff Curry and Mean Jim. Assume for the moment that the pages of this book are standard script pages. Standard script page size is of course 8 1/2 x 11 inches. Further, assume that a light gray shading is actually a pink highlighter mark and that white letters on a black background represent a **blue highlighter.** I will begin by drawing a line across the page at the beginning of the sequence. Refer to the script on the next two pages as you read the analysis.

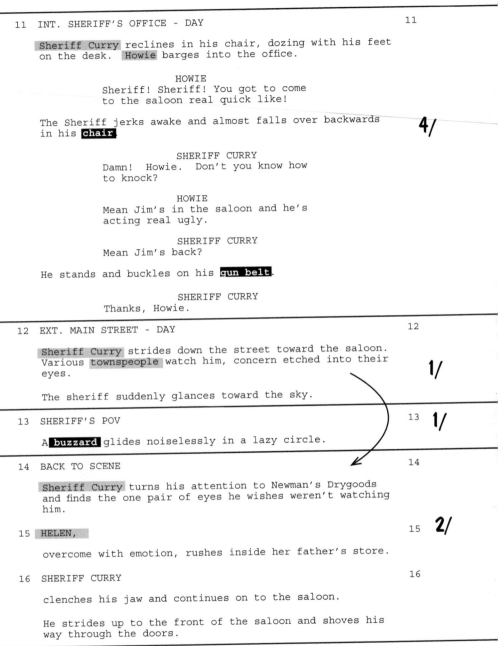

11 INT. SHERIFF'S OFFICE - DAY 11

Sheriff Curry reclines in his chair, dozing with his feet on the desk. Howie barges into the office.

HOWIE
Sheriff! Sheriff! You got to come to the saloon real quick like!

The Sheriff jerks awake and almost falls over backwards in his **chair**. 4/

SHERIFF CURRY
Damn! Howie. Don't you know how to knock?

HOWIE
Mean Jim's in the saloon and he's acting real ugly.

SHERIFF CURRY
Mean Jim's back?

He stands and buckles on his **gun belt**.

SHERIFF CURRY
Thanks, Howie.

---

12 EXT. MAIN STREET - DAY 12

Sheriff Curry strides down the street toward the saloon. Various townspeople watch him, concern etched into their eyes. 1/

The sheriff suddenly glances toward the sky.

---

13 SHERIFF'S POV 13 1/

A **buzzard** glides noiselessly in a lazy circle.

---

14 BACK TO SCENE 14

Sheriff Curry turns his attention to Newman's Drygoods and finds the one pair of eyes he wishes weren't watching him.

15 HELEN, 15 2/

overcome with emotion, rushes inside her father's store.

16 SHERIFF CURRY 16

clenches his jaw and continues on to the saloon.

He strides up to the front of the saloon and shoves his way through the doors.

17 INT. SALOON - CONTINUOUS 17

The normal hubbub ceases as soon as he enters. The only sound comes from the two saloon doors flapping to a standstill. FX

The sheriff scans the room and finds his man leaning on the bar.

18 MEAN JIM 18

swallows a shot of whiskey, slams the glass down on the bar, and turns to face the sheriff.

MEAN JIM
You really know how to put a damper on a party, Sheriff.

Sheriff Curry glides across the room toward Mean Jim, his eyes locked onto his quarry.

SHERIFF CURRY
I told you not to come back.

7/

MEAN JIM
Yeah? I guess I got homesick.

19 CLOSE ON MEAN JIM'S HAND 19

which inches stealthily toward his gun.

SHERIFF CURRY
I'll be taking your gun.

MEAN JIM
I don't think so.

Suddenly, Mean Jim's gun is in his hand pointed right at the sheriff's chest. The sheriff has grabbed the gun from the top around the cylinder. Mean Jim smiles.

Stunt dbl.

MEAN JIM
This here's a double action colt, Sheriff. Your're a dead man.

Mean Jim tries to pull the trigger but it won't budge as long as Sheriff Curry keeps the cylinder from turning.

The sheriff jerks down on the gun, wresting it from Mean Jim's hand. He then smacks Mean Jim across the face with the gun. Mean Jim staggers back against the bar.

The sheriff grabs him by the neck and hustles him out through the doors into the street. Mean Jim collapses in the mud. FX

1/

Sheriff Curry

MEAN JIM
This ain't over!

The Analysis

The first thing that you can always do to get started on a script is draw a line across the page at the beginning of the first sequence. It helps to get things going. In Scene 11, after drawing the first line, I highlighted "Sheriff Curry" and "Howie" with a pink highlighter. Note that it is only necessary to highlight elements once in each shooting sequence. I then took my blue highlighter and marked the chair and the gunbelt. The sequence ends at the end of the scene so another line was drawn after the line, "Thanks, Howie." I've written "4/" to indicate that the sequence is 4/8 of a page long.

Scene 12 begins the EXT. MAIN STREET sequence. Because we have drawn a new line, Sheriff Curry's name and "townspeople" are again highlighted in pink. We have to almost immediately draw another line because the buzzard sequence starts. I have drawn an arrow from Scene 12 to below Scene 13 to remind myself that the Main Street sequence continues after the buzzard sequence. This part of the Main Street sequence (Scene 12) is 1/8 of a page long.

In Scene 13, the buzzard sequence, I have highlighted the buzzard in blue. The sequence is 1/8 of a page. Notice that Scene 12 is actually a bit longer than Scene 13 even though they are both counted as 1/8 of a page.

Because I drew new lines indicating the buzzard sequence, I have highlighted Sheriff Curry again in Scene 14 even though he has been highlighted already in this sequence (Scene 12). Always start highlighting anew when you have crossed a line. If I was being really consistent, I would have written in "townspeople" and highlighted that in pink too, since they are still present. In addition to Sheriff Curry, I have highlighted "Helen" in pink. The sequence ends when Sheriff Curry enters the saloon so I drew a line at the bottom of the page. The page count for this portion of the Main Street sequence is 2/8.

Because I drew a line at the bottom of the previous page, the first thing I do on this new page is draw a line at the top. This tells me that the INT. SALOON sequence begins on this page and not on a previous page. Scene 17 begins the INT. SALOON sequence. This sequence runs until Sheriff Curry and Mean Jim exit the saloon. The first item I highlighted in this sequence is "hubbub." What is a hubbub? Well, I highlighted it in pink so it must be a person. This is my lazy way of not having to write out "saloon patrons." By highlighting "hubbub," I know that it will mean extras to me since there has to be some people present to create a "hubbub." I have also highlighted Sheriff Curry and Mean Jim. The props I found were whiskey, the glass, and a gun, which I have highlighted in blue. Note that, at this point, Sheriff Curry also has his gunbelt on and has had it since the Int. Sheriff's Office sequence. If he usually has his gun, it's only necessary to highlight it when it is mentioned. If he does not always have his gun with him, then it would be best to mark it down whenever you think it *should* be present, even if it is not mentioned.

Near the top of the page, I have highlighted "saloon doors flapping" in blue and written "FX" in the margin. This means that the special effects crew should be prepared to make those saloon doors flap if they don't do it on their own. Further down on the page, I have written "Stunt dbl" with an arrow pointing to the action in which the sheriff pistol whips Mean Jim. (He deserved it.) This means that I should possibly provide a stunt double for Mean Jim.

Notice that this shooting sequence ends in the middle of a sentence describing the action. This is not unusual. If the Int. Saloon set were on stage, then the camera would cut once Mean Jim and the Sheriff hit the doors. The next shot in the cut movie would be shot on the western street location and would show the two men flying out of the saloon doors. The entire sequence is 7/8 of a page long.

The last shooting sequence begins with the two men flying out the door, and ends with Mean Jim's line. Notice I have written in "Sheriff Curry" since he is not mentioned in the shooting sequence, but he must be there. I have highlighted "mud" in blue and put a note in the margin ("FX") indicating that a special effects crew is needed to create the mud. At this point, you should go back to the Ext. Main Street sequence and write in "mud" and "FX" in scene 12 in order to be consistent. It would be strange if the only spot in the whole street that's muddy is exactly where Mean Jim lands. That correction would look like this:

```
12  EXT. MAIN STREET - DAY                                    12
                                               Mud - FX
    Sheriff Curry strides down the street toward the saloon.
```

Overlapping Shooting Sequences

Previously, I discussed overlapping shooting sequences that occurred when there was a phone call in which both sides of the conversation were depicted, or when there was a film within the film. You may recall that these sequences were overlapping because we were going to have to shoot the same parts of the script in two separate locations at two separate times. We need a way to show that the sequences are overlapping, and we need to discuss how to handle the page count.

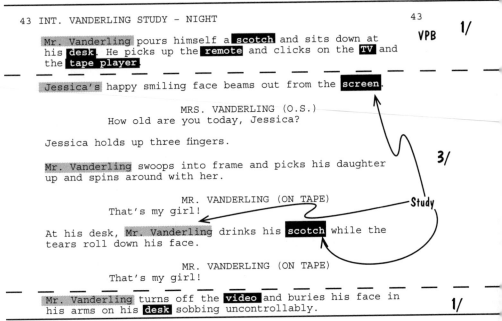

```
43 INT. VANDERLING STUDY - NIGHT                          43

    Mr. Vanderling pours himself a scotch and sits down at      VPB    1/
    his desk. He picks up the remote and clicks on the TV and
    the tape player.
- - - - - - - - - - - - - - - - - - - - - - - - - - - - - - - - - -
    Jessica's happy smiling face beams out from the screen.

                    MRS. VANDERLING (O.S.)
            How old are you today, Jessica?

    Jessica holds up three fingers.                                  3/

    Mr. Vanderling swoops into frame and picks his daughter
    up and spins around with her.

                    MR. VANDERLING (ON TAPE)
            That's my girl!                                   Study

    At his desk, Mr. Vanderling drinks his scotch while the
    tears roll down his face.

                    MR. VANDERLING (ON TAPE)
            That's my girl!
- - - - - - - - - - - - - - - - - - - - - - - - - - - - - - - - - -
    Mr. Vanderling turns off the video and buries his face in
    his arms on his desk sobbing uncontrollably.                     1/
```

We will use our previous scene example of the distraught Mr. Vanderling watching the video of his daughter's birthday party in his study (reproduced above.) It's easy to see where the study sequence begins and ends; it begins at the beginning of the scene, and it ends at the end of the scene and is about ⅝ of a page long. But what about the video sequence that is laid on top of the study sequence? First we should mark where it begins, just after the line where it says that Mr. Vanderling turns on the video ("VPB" or *video playback*). In order to show that the Int. Study sequence does not end here but rather continues through this point, we will use a broken or dashed line. Think of it as if the spaces in the broken line allow the study sequence to continue through. The video sequence ends when Mr. Vanderling turns the video off. Since the study sequence continues past this point, we will use another broken line. If both sequences had ended when the video was turned off, we would have used a solid line.

Notice that I have highlighted everything anew after *each* sequence line. You will need to remember or to make a note that the "screen" and "scotch" are in the study, not at the backyard birthday party. Mrs. Vanderling is not highlighted because she is not seen and it will not be necessary for her to be there. (*This should be confirmed with the director.*) Her voice will be added to the soundtrack in the post production process.

Note that the overall length of the Int. Study sequence is the sum of the separated parts (⅛ + ⅜ + ⅛ = ⅝), while the length of the backyard sequence is only ⅜. This total is not added up or written down at this point in the process. It is only necessary to mark the length of each of the separate lined off sections.

How Many Eighths Equal One Page?

This is not a foolish question. There may be short pages due to added material or omitted scenes in which there are less than 8/8. Or you may have a page that is so complex that there are more than 8/8 on the page. Figure 6.3 shows a page from an early draft of the script of *Hollow Man* that has been lined. (Notice the hand written scene numbers.) These sequences are from the portion of the film where the characters of Linda and Matt are climbing up the elevator shaft from the underground laboratory. If you count the lined off sequences, you will see that there are 12/8. Let's count the sequences and analyze why there are so many. The shooting sequence unities that are broken in each instance from the previous sequence are shown in parentheses.

1. At the top of the page is the end of Scene 218, which involves a large explosion on the laboratory set. This will be shot as a live-action sequence. (Space, action.)
2. Scene 219 takes place in one of the tunnels of the laboratory complex. The highlighted phrase beginning with the words, "... phase shifted animals," was highlighted in yellow to indicate a visual effect which will be created by the visual effects house after the filmed sequence is delivered to them. To film this sequence, a second unit will go to the set and film an explosion staged by the special effects crew. (Space, action.)
3. Scene 220 will be shot in the 75 foot high elevator shaft set that will be erected outside on the backlot. We will see Linda and Matt climbing the ladder attached to the side of the shaft. The special effects crew will cause the ladder to vibrate and shake. (Space, cast, action.)
4. Scene 221 will be filmed by a 2nd unit inside a ventilation shaft which is part of the laboratory complex set. The special effects crew will create the fireball. (Space, cast, action.)
5. Scene 222 will be filmed by the 2nd unit in the laboratory tunnels and at the elevators in the laboratory complex set on stage. Again, the special effects crew will create the explosions and cause the elevator to fly up. (Space, action.)
6. Scene 223 consists of numerous shooting sequences. It first

120.

A FLASH OF LIGHT. A HUGE EXPLOSION rips through the laboratory.

219 INT. TUNNEL.

(2U) The EXPLOSION rips through the lab doors. A MASSIVE FIREBALL rolls down the tunnel swallowing everything in its path.

One of the phase shifted animals gets caught in the flames. We see its shape briefly before it disappears in a wall of fire.

220 INT. ELEVATOR SHAFT.

The ladder begins to shake.
The entire shaft begins to rumble.
Linda pushes Matt up as they scramble toward safety.

221 INT. EXHAUST VENT.

(2U) The FIREBALL blows into the vent. Starts rolling down it also.

222 INT. TUNNELS.

(2U) More explosions... CHAIN REACTIONS. BOOM! BOOM! BOOM!

(MIN) THE EXPLOSION rolls toward the OPEN ELEVATOR. Slamming into it... The elevator flies upward.

223 INT. ELEVATOR SHAFT.

The rumbling worsens.
The two desperately cling to the ladder.
They look down to see...

MIN THE ELEVATOR SURROUNDED BY FLAMES flying up toward them, lifted by the explosion's SHOCK WAVES.

LINDA
Oh shit.

MIN The carriage accelerates toward them, faster and faster. Its loose cables whip around the shaft, slapping the walls around the pair.

It's gonna hit them!

Linda pulls herself close to the ladder and closes her eyes. She's pressed against Matt.

MIN The elevator... 50 feet... 40... 30... WOOOOOOOSH!

It flames RIGHT BY THEM.

When Linda opens her eyes, the elevator is HUNDREDS OF FEET ABOVE THEM and a wall of fire is below them, closing in.

Fig. 6.3. A reproduction of a page from an early draft of the ***Hollow Man*** script. The page count for this one page is 12/8.

takes us back to the elevator shaft set with Linda and Matt as they cling to the ladder. We see them look down…(Space, cast, action.)

7. …at a miniature of the elevator car flying up at them with flames around it…(Space, cast.)
8. Back to Linda realizing that they are in trouble…(Space, cast.)

9. Back to the miniature elevator car accelerating toward them. (Space, cast.)
10. We see the elevator cables in the elevator shaft set whipping back and forth (they are being whipped around by the special effects crew) as Linda and Matt hug the ladder and the wall. (Space, cast.)
11. Another miniature of the elevator car coming closer…(Space, cast.)
12. …and finally the special effects crew pulls a full size, lightweight, mockup of the elevator car right by Linda and Matt clinging to the ladder in the elevator shaft set. (Space, cast.)

An *eighth* is just a convenient unit because there are usually eight of them on each page. As can be seen above, however, the way the page is lined off and the number of eighths present is dictated by the content of the page and how it relates to the four unities of space, time, action, and cast.

7

The Breakdown Pages

1 Shooting Sequence = 1 Breakdown Page

A *breakdown page* (also called a breakdown sheet) is simply a form designed to collect the essential elements of each shooting sequence. This is why you highlighted all those items during the lining of the script. Each shooting sequence is recorded on its respective breakdown page. The first shooting sequence will go on breakdown page one. The next shooting sequence will go on breakdown page two, and so on. Let's examine a standard breakdown page and discuss the information that it records (fig. 7.1).

At the top of the page is a space for the *Title* of the project. This only needs to entered on the first page. Next to the title is the *BD Page No.* (Breakdown Page Number). As stated before, the first page is numbered "1" and the following pages are numbered consecutively thereafter. If you find at a later time that you need to insert a page into the sequence, do not renumber all your pages; just append a letter to the page number prior to the one you are inserting. In other words, if you wish to put a new page in between pages 18 and 19, number the new page 18A. The space for the *Production No.* (Production Number) is, like the title, only necessary on the first page. The production number is an accounting device used by the major studios to assign charges to the proper project. An independent production company really has no need for a production number so in that case this space can be ignored. The *Location or Stage* blank allows you to write in where the shooting sequence will be shot, on location or on a stage set. In the early stages of planning a film, you will only be able to circle "location" or "stage." Even if you are not certain, you should give it your best guess with the information you have at hand. In later stages, when some of the locations have been selected, you can write in the actual address or description of the location.

Day or Night is self-explanatory. Write in either "D" or "N," or circle the appropriate word. However, occasionally a script will use time of day designations such as *late afternoon*, *twilight*, *evening*, *sunset*, *sunrise*, *morning*, or *dawn* and these can be written in the blank. If your script has a number of these designations, be sure you know what the writer means by them. You will be shooting the sequence in daylight, at night, or at some point in between. It is the in-between state that is the most variable. When the writer says *late afternoon* or *evening*, what is the state of the natural light? Is the sun up or very low in the sky? Does the writer distinguish between evening and twilight? Again, what does that mean? Has the sun set? How light is the sky? Does the writer mean *magic hour*? "Magic hour" is a term used to refer to that time of day after the sun has set and the sky still retains a deep indigo color. It may last for twenty minutes or less depending on the time of year. It is magical in the sense that the light is unusual and very flattering toward a photographic subject.

An entire shooting sequence set at magic hour, twilight, or evening can not be shot in one day. Under these circumstances, the filmmaker has two choices: (1) shoot the sequence at magic hour over several consecutive days, or (2) shoot the wide master shot of the sequence at magic hour, and then shoot the remaining tighter coverage shots at night with appropriate lighting. An example of a film shot in the first manner is *Tess*, based on the novel *Tess of the D'Urbervilles,* directed by Roman Polanski, and photographed by Geoffrey Unsworth and Ghislain Cloquet. Messrs. Unsworth and Ghislain won an Academy Award for Best Cinematography, due in part, by waiting for the appropriate time of day to shoot each shot. Although it provides for spectacularly beautiful footage, it is an inefficient and expensive way to shoot a picture. For most films, the latter choice is an excellent compromise.

The *Set* is typically taken from the slug line. It usually takes a form such as Int. Bedroom or Ext. Forest. However, often the slug line does not give the set, as in Scene 13 on page 53 in our example of the Main Street sequence. The slug line in Scene 13 reads "Sheriff's POV." This is obviously not a set. The set must be inferred from the context and entered as Ext. Sky. The following scene's slug line is "Back to Scene." Again, context tells us that this is a part of the Main Street sequence and that the set is Ext. Main Street.

The space labeled *Script Pages* (sometimes called *page count*) is where the

Breakdown Sheet

Title			BD Page No.
Production No.	Location or Stage		Day or Night
Set			Script Pages
Scene Nos.			No. of Scenes
Synopsis			
Cast	Atmosphere	Props	
	Picture Vehicles/Livestock	Special Effects	
Costume	Art Department	Special Equipment	
Notes			

Fig. 7.1. A standard breakdown page or breakdown sheet.

total length of the sequence is recorded. If a shooting sequence is spread over several pages, add up all the eighths of the sequence from each page and convert it to an integer and eighths. For instance, if a shooting sequence was spread over four pages and the page length written on each of the pages was 1⁄, 8⁄, 8⁄ and 3⁄ respectively, then the total length would be 20⁄8 and should be written as "2 4⁄8."

Scene Nos. (Scene Numbers) is merely the list of scenes making up the shooting sequence. It is important to explicitly list each scene number in the sequence and not use shortcuts, such as *52–57*. The reason for this is that the range 52–57 may have scenes not contained in the shooting sequence, it may include one or more omitted scenes, or the sequence may have added lettered scenes that are not apparent by simply stating a range. The range 52–57 written explicitly might actually be 52, 53, 54A, 55pt., 56, 56A, 56B, 56C, 57, where Scene 54 is omitted and Scene 55 is a part of another shooting sequence. When a scene number appears on more that one breakdown page either because of overlapping shooting sequences (see the discussion beginning on page 56) or because of a shooting sequence ending in the middle of a scene (see the examples on pages 54 and 56), it is always written with *pt.* appended to it as in *32pt.* This would be read as *Scene thirty-two part.*

I have never found *No. of Scenes* useful. It relates neither to the length of time to film a sequence, nor to the screen time of a shooting sequence. Therefore I ignore it. Since scene numbers are merely convenient mileposts to identify specific areas of the script, it seems irrelevant how many there are in any one shooting sequence.

The *Synopsis* should be a brief, but unique description of the shooting sequence that allows instant identification of it. In a film heavy with phone calls, "Phone call." is brief but *not* unique and therefore useless as a synopsis. The phone booth sequence shown on pages 35 and 36 (Scene 33pt.) could be described as "Joey tells Vanderling he has two hours." The Int. Living Room sequence shown on the same pages (Scenes 32, 33pt., and 34) could be described as "Vanderling takes call from Joey, police listen in." If you find yourself writing a long complicated synopsis, it may be an indication that the sequence is not broken down completely, and that the unity of action may not have been preserved.

Cast

The box labeled *Cast* is where all those people covered by the Screen Actors Guild (SAG) agreement are listed. That would include actors (characters with lines), stunt players, and aircraft pilots (whether on-camera or off). If a character has a line at any point in the script, then that character is an actor and should be listed here, even in shooting sequences where the actor does not speak. Very often, you may have a character in a script that has no lines at all, yet the level of acting demanded by the role would require that an actor play the part and the character be listed under cast. In the film *Gigot*, Jackie Gleason played the title role. The main character, Gigot, was a deaf mute and therefore had no lines, yet the role required an actor with a high degree of skill. The part of Gigot would have been listed under *Cast.*

Stunt players are used any time an action requires a high degree of physical skill or strength, or involves some measure of risk. This is not because actors are less skillful, or less strong, or are adverse to risk. Many actors have a high degree of physical skill; some even began their careers as stunt players. The reasons for using stunt players in place of actors are for very practical and pragmatic purposes. If a mishap should occur and an actor becomes injured, the entire production may have to be shut down thus jeopardizing the completion of the film. If a stunt player is injured, as cold as it may sound, a replacement can be found, usually without any delay. In addition, stunt players practice constant physical training just as professional athletes do, and are knowledgeable in the ways of making dangerous looking stunts safe. The goal is not to sacrifice the stunt player in place of the actor. The goal is to hire the person most appropriate for the job and to insure that *no one* is injured.

When listing stunt players, be specific. If a stunt person is needed to double for a specific role, list the stunt player specifically as in "Dbl. Mean Jim" where *dbl* is an abbreviation for *double*. If you were filming a car chase with a number of near misses with unknown drivers in other cars, those unknown drivers would be *utility stunt players*. They would be listed with a number quantifying how many are needed, i.e. "5 utility stunts," or "3 stunt drivers." The stunt players doubling your cast members who are involved in the chase would be listed the same way as Mean Jim's double is above. (Cars driven normally, with the flow of traffic while observing all traffic laws, can be driven by extras.)

Pilots are listed under cast because the SAG agreement requires that any pilot who appears on-camera in a film covered by the SAG agreement work under an SAG contract. Pilots who do not appear on-camera, such as those flying helicopters used as camera platforms, will usually insist on being hired under the SAG contract also.

Atmosphere (Extras) - Listing What Is Not Mentioned

Atmosphere is the place to list all non-speaking characters in the film. These are known as *extras*. It is important to indicate a number when listing a group of extras as in "25 bar patrons," or "50 pedestrians," or even "150 crowd." This will be a great time saver in the budgeting stage. Often the script does not help much in informing what extras are required and how many are necessary. It is usually the person breaking down the script who initially decides this. Later, consultation with the director confirms or revises these numbers. Take our Ext. Main Street sequence for instance. It mentions "townspeople" but does not say how many or who they are. Only Helen is mentioned by name and she is a cast member since she has lines in other sequences in the script. So, how many townspeople? Ten? Twenty? Fifty? When you read the sequence, how many did you see in your mind? I saw about twenty-five. This is a subjective judgment and is subject to change by the director, by the selection of a location, or by a reassessment of your estimate. Be careful in deciding this number. It is startling how quickly a crowd is swallowed up by a large space. On the other hand, why pay for 300 extras when 250 would suffice?

This number is also important because it can have many repercussions throughout the budget. I was involved in the planning of a film that was to be shot in Spain and Morocco. One sequence involved a large group of horsemen riding down from a hill into a column of medieval soldiers. I must admit I was influenced in my thinking by having seen *Geronimo*, directed by Walter Hill. In that film, Mr. Hill skillfully used 50 horsemen to appear like a huge number by placing his cameras inside the action. My first breakdown of the scene in question showed fifty horsemen. The director thought he would need 150 horsemen so I amended my breakdown page. After thinking about it some more overnight, the director told me that he would need 400 horsemen. I began trying to figure out where I could corral 400 horses, how much feed they would eat, how many wranglers* it would take to handle them, and how much time they would take to get to the set each morning. Then the director amended the figure again to 800 horsemen. In addition, I had to consider how long it would take to get all those horses and horsemen back to their start marks for take two. That was a lot of horses, and a lot of wrangling, and the effect on the budget was part of the reason that the film was never made.

The listing of extras is an opportunity to add some creativity to the production. Rather than listing "50 pedestrians" for a city sidewalk sequence, break them down into specifics. The 50 pedestrians might become 30 business men, 15 career women, 2 sidewalk vendors, 2 winos, and a postman.

Photo-doubles are another class of extras that are sometimes needed. Photo-doubles are extras that are hired because they can be made to look like the actor playing a specific role in the film and can therefore be used in place of the actor in some shots. The intent in the use of a photo-double is not to spare the actor inconvenience. In fact, most actors dislike the use

---

*A *wrangler* is a person trained to handle large domestic animals such as horses or cattle.

of photo-doubles if they can do the shot themselves. They would rather do the scene themselves, even if they are only driving by in the background of a scene. If an actor is of the sort that only wants to be on set when he or she has a line to say, then maybe that is not the best actor to hire. There are real and valid reasons to use photo-doubles. In *The Parent Trap*, directed by Nancy Meyer, Lindsay Lohan played both roles of a set of twin sisters. A photo-double was used in certain shots when both of the twins were in the frame and one of them had her back to the camera. This saved the production company the time and visual effects expense of having Miss Lohan play both roles in those particular shots.

Props

The space labeled *Props* is where you write down all the props highlighted in the sequence. A prop is any object handled by an actor. As stated earlier, the property master (propmaster) will make a complete prop breakdown listing many props that are not in your initial breakdown. You should note here any props that are mentioned in the script or that you know must be present in order for the sequence to be filmed. Props which are known to be an intrinsic part of a set or location, such as silverware in a restaurant, are assumed to be present and need not be put into an initial breakdown unless, of course, one character is stabbing another with a fork from the table. At that moment, the fork becomes an essential prop and it should be noted.

There can be some confusion as to whether the props or set dressing department should handle an individual item. Typically, the matter is decided in favor of props if the item is manipulated in any way by an actor, as noted in the example of the fork above. In our saloon set, all of the chairs are manipulated by the people sitting in them, whether extras or cast. However, this is normal use and since the chairs are part of the normal furnishings of the room, set dressing would supply them. If Mean Jim had picked up a chair to hit the sheriff, then that chair would be a prop and would be handled by the propmaster. The reason for this distinction is that the chair may need to be made of special materials, or be prepared to break up easily (known as a "breakaway" chair). Another reason for the distinction between items which are handled by the actors and those that are not, is that the prop crew is present on the set during shooting while the set dressing crew is often away preparing the next day's set.

Picture Vehicles and Livestock

Picture Vehicles / Livestock cover all real vehicles put before the camera, from covered wagons to jet aircraft, and all animals from cockroaches to herds of cattle. These two seemingly disparate categories are lumped together because on a union film, the teamsters handle both of them. Back in the horse and buggy days before the widespread use of motorized trucks, teamsters were the people who hauled freight in horse or ox-drawn wagons. In the early days of filmmaking, it was only natural that the teamsters, because of their extensive experience, be used to handle horses and other large animals in the westerns which were so popular at the time. From horses and cattle, their expertise spread to cover all animals needed in a scene.

When listing animals, note how many are needed, i.e. "25 sheep," or "6 sled dogs." When listing an animal that has been given a name in the script, list the animal by name as in "Lassie." A quantity of one is assumed in a listing of this sort, so if you know that the animal will be played by more than one animal actor, list them by their uses such as "Jumping Lassie," "Fetching Lassie," or "Falling Trigger," "Rearing Trigger." I think it has become common knowledge that Lassie was actually played by several male collies, a situation that is not unusual.

Picture vehicles should also be listed with a quantifying number as in "30 n.d. cars" ("n.d." meaning non-descript or average looking). Vehicles that are specifically described in the script should be listed with their full description, as in "red 1958 Ford Thunderbird." If the script calls for a 747 jet or any other aircraft, it would be listed here as long as it is the exterior of the plane that is needed. Interiors are usually shot on mockup sets which would be treated like any other stage set. Nevertheless, if it is anticipated that the sequence would take place in an actual plane, then it should be listed under Picture Vehicles. Motorized boats of any size, from an outboard skiff to an aircraft carrier, would be listed here. Smaller boats such as canoes or kayaks could be listed under props. Helicopters used as camera platforms would not be listed here but rather under *Special Equipment*. If you list a vehicle that you intend to be moving in a shot, be sure that you have listed an appropriate driver, whether it is a cast member, a stunt player, or an extra, under the appropriate category. All aircraft that have their engines running must be assigned an actual pilot with a current FAA pilot's license. The pilot must be on board the aircraft at all times when the engine is running.

Special Effects

Special Effects, sometimes called *floor effects* or *mechanical effects*, should not be confused with visual effects. Special effects are created at the time the scene is shot and include smoke, wind, rain, wet downs, steam, fire, explosions, and bullet hits. If a doorknob spookily turns by itself, it is turned by a special effects technician. If a trail of gunpowder burns up to a powder keg and explodes, the special effects crew handles the burning powder and the resulting explosion. In the locket sequence from *Robin Hood: Men in Tights* mentioned earlier and described in the appendix, the special effects crew made the locket, exploded it, and blew the key out of the padlock with an air hose. In listing special effects, it is enough to just list the effect such as "smoke," "rain," "sparks," "mud," etc. There are many times when the effect may not be mentioned in the script but must be deduced. If a film has a sequence which takes place in a movie theater, the audience will expect to see the light beam coming from the projector. The light beam will not be visible unless there is dust in the air. This is accomplished by having the effects crew create a light smoke haze in the room. In John Carpenter's *The Thing*, it was decided that the audience would expect to see the breath of the actors when they were exploring the wrecked Norwegian South Polar Station. This sequence was being filmed in July in Los Angeles on a sound stage. The special effects crew cooled the stage down to about 48°F with portable air conditioners and installed water misters in the trusses of the stage to raise the relative humidity to about 98%. Under these circumstances, the actors' breath was quite visible, although it was a miserable environment to work in.

Costume

Any notes pertaining to the actors' *costumes* go here. If a character's clothes are commented on by the writer, it should be copied here. In addition, notes pertaining to any successive stages of a costume which may occur throughout the film would go here. A good example of this is the steady deterioration of Tom Hanks's clothing once he was stranded on the desert island in *Cast Away*, directed by Robert Zemeckis.

Art Department

Art Department notes regarding the set or set dressing would go here. If it were important that the saloon have a mirror that ran the length of the bar, it would be noted here. Other examples would be if it were a story point that a room be painted a specific color or perhaps a yard be overgrown or strewn with junk.

Special Equipment

Special Equipment includes items that would not normally be carried by the shooting company such as an insert car, crane, helicopter used as a camera platform, steadicam, special lenses, special lights, etc. By noting sequences that need these items, it will be possible to track these items on the production board or create a separate schedule for them, thereby making it possible to the rent them only for the period needed.

Notes

Put *Notes* here for any items not covered in any of the other categories such as notes to the set lighting department about a light change within a sequence (eg., "Elec – light chg.") All of the items written on the breakdown pages will eventually be seen on the full shooting schedule released to the crew prior to the beginning of principal photography.

Dealing with Revised Pages

As mentioned in Chapter 3, revised pages may be issued at any time throughout the production. On some pictures, the script becomes a multicolored rainbow of revised pages. The changes will be marked on each revised page with an asterisk in the right hand margin. These pages should be lined, inserted into their proper places in your script, and the affected breakdown pages should be brought up to date. Always mark the changes on the breakdown pages first before changing the board or editing an updated edition of the schedule.

8

Creating the Production Board

The Cast List

In order to make the production board, it is necessary to list the entire cast in approximate order of their importance. The best way to accomplish this is to make a list of the cast members from the breakdown pages and then count how many breakdown pages each cast member appears on. By sorting the roles in descending order based on the number of shooting sequences each cast member is a part of, one can generate a list organized in order of approximate importance each character has to the film. *Importance* is not intended here as a value judgment. It is merely a way to rank the roles by their anticipated cost to the film. The principal players will be at the top of the list because they will, by definition, be involved in the most shooting sequences. The supporting cast hired on a weekly basis will appear next on the list, followed by the day players (roles which may appear in only a few sequences and which will probably work less than a week).

The Header Board

The next step is to fill out the header board. As can been seen in the pull-out at the end of this book, the title of the film, the director, producer, and assistant director should be written in the appropriate blanks. The cast list should be transferred to the header board by listing the roles in the order of "importance" as discussed above. Often there are more characters than there are lines to put them in. Header boards generally come divided into two columns labeled *Character* and *Artist*. These are intended to provide a place to write the names of each role and the actor who will play it. At the early stages of planning, it is usually not known what actor will play each role, and therefore the "Artist" column that appears on some header boards is useless for its intended purpose. In addition, it is never really necessary to put the actors' names on the board since the character names are more relevant. For these reasons, it is usually best to double up a long cast list and use both columns to list all of the roles as shown in figure 5.2A. When both columns are used for character names, be sure to change the numbers preprinted on the board so that each character has a unique number. If there are still not enough lines, then another header board should be added to accommodate the overflow of names.

Below the cast list are listed the stunt players, extras, and anything else that is needed to be tracked on the board. The stunt players can be listed as individual doubles such as "Dbl. Sheriff," "Dbl. Mean Jim" (in which case they need their own unique ID number), or they can be listed as a sum showing how many stunt players are needed in any particular sequence. In the latter case, the header board would show on one line "Stunts S/," where the S/ would take a number after the slash on the strip to show how many stunt players are needed. In other words, on a strip for a shooting sequence in which five stunt players were needed, the strip would show "S/5" on the stunt line. Extras are handled in a similar way as a sum, using "E/" on the header board. Other items that might be tracked are makeup changes, vehicles, special equipment, etc. It is best to devise symbols for these items rather than ID numbers so that they are not confused with the cast. Makeup changes might be designated MU1," "MU2," etc. Vehicles might be labeled "BT" for blue truck, or "TT" for a tractor-trailer rig. Make the label that you use something that will be easily understood.

Leave a space of about two inches at the bottom of the header board. This will be equivalent to the area on the strip where you will write the synopsis. Once the header board is complete, you can begin making the strips.

The Strips

The first task in making the strips is to decide on a color scheme. This will be dependent on how many different colors of strips are available to you, and how many different categories of strips you want to code. At the very least, you should differentiate between interiors, day exteriors, and night exteriors. In addition, you can use different colors for stage interiors as opposed to location interiors. The use of these colors helps to see at a glance how the film is laying out. It is most useful to be able to see how the nights are scheduled, and to be able to differentiate quickly between interiors in which daylight or weather is not a factor, and other sequences which are daylight or weather dependent. A typical color scheme might be stage interiors – white; location interiors – tan; day exteriors – yellow; night exteriors – blue. In addition, depending on the project, you may want to set colors aside for stock footage, visual effects shots, or other items that you want to be able to easily separate. If you have need of a specific color strip that you are unable to find, you can simply run the appropriate colored highlighter over a white strip.

The next step is to start transferring the information from your breakdown pages to the strips. Start with breakdown page 1, select the appropriately colored strip, turn it sideways on the desk in front of you and write the set and scene numbers in the blank space near the top (fig. 8.1). Next, write the brief but unique synopsis in the bottom two inches of the strip. It is at this point you will learn the importance of the term *brief.* When the strip is held vertically, the set, scene numbers, and synopsis should read from bottom to top. After the set, scene numbers, and synopsis are entered, turn the strip vertically and align it with the header board. Write in the breakdown page number in the top space; this also becomes the strip number (see the pullout at the end of this book). Below that, on the appropriate lines, write in whether the sequence is day or night, and the page count. Write the page count in pencil since any script revisions may make it necessary to change it. Next, write in the ID numbers and codes for the cast, stunts, extras, and other items you may be tracking. When the strip is complete, put it in the production board, leaving room to insert the header board before it (to the left of the first strip). Proceed in this manner until you have made a strip for each breakdown page.

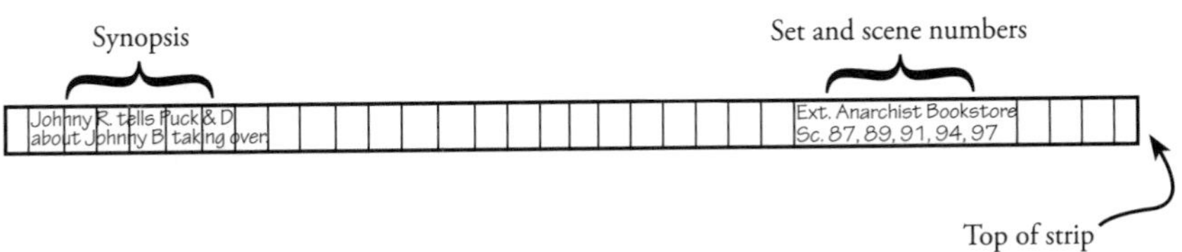

Fig. 8.1. A strip positioned to allow the writing of the set, scene numbers, and synopsis.

9

Scheduling the Board

Exteriors First

Once the strips are completed, you are ready to sort the board into a schedule. You begin by sorting the strips by set, and moving the stage work to the end of the schedule (far right of the board), and the locations toward the beginning of the schedule (far left of the board). The reasoning behind this is to get the exteriors done first so that you do not become weather dependent at the end of the schedule. If you have exterior work scheduled for your last day and a huge storm system moves in, you would probably be shut down and prevented from shooting. This can be costly and can threaten your delivery date. It is better to have stage work scheduled at the end of the period so that if it does rain on a day that you are scheduled to be outside, instead you can move to the stage and continue shooting. This is known as "going to cover." A cover set is any stage set you hold in reserve for this purpose. Of course, if you do not need to use the cover sets during the schedule, then you would shoot them during their scheduled days at the end. When selecting sets to use as cover sets, it is important that the actors who work in the sequences on those sets always be available. For that reason, cover sets normally involve sequences with your main cast, or cast that are so inexpensive that you can hold them on payroll throughout the length of the schedule.

How much work makes a day?

With the board sorted by set, with the locations first and the stage work at the end, you can divide the work into days. Determining how much work to put into each day is a function of how many days you can afford to shoot, and how many pages are in the script. The latter question is answered by adding up the page count from all your strips. This may be more or less than the actual number of pages in the script due to the various effects of short or long pages, complex pages, and overlapping sequences.

Large studio pictures, with schedules of 60 days or more, try to shoot 2 to 2½ pages per day. A low-budget independent may have to shoot 4 pages or more per day. Let's say that you have a script whose page count adds up to 110 pages. If you shoot 4½ pages per day, you will need a schedule that is about 25 days long (110 pages divided by 4½ pages per day equals 24.44 days). Typically, a film with a budget of about $2,000,000 will need to confine its schedule to 25 days or less. Sometimes the number of days is a given quantity. This can happen if the producer needs to deliver the film by a specific date. In that case, you can divide the number of pages by the number of days available to get how many pages per day you must average in order to finish on time. However, keep in mind that not all eighths are equal. Consider the following two sequences:

```
17 INT. KITCHEN - DAY                                    1/      17

     Janet breaks an egg into the frying pan.
```

and...

```
86 EXT. LITTLE BIG HORN CREEK                             1/     86

     The band of Sioux Indians rides down on Custer's men,
     slaughtering them.
```

Both of these sequences are one eighth of a page in length. The first sequence may take less then an hour to light and shoot. The second sequence could take a week or more. So, although you may need to average 4½ pages per day, there may be days that you will be doing much less, and that in turn will cause you to do more pages on other days. Generally, when a sequence consists mainly of dialog with just a few actors, you can shoot more than your average page count. On days with complex scenes that have large casts, complicated camera moves, heavy action, stunts, special effects, or visual effects, you may need to lighten the load considerably.

Other factors which can slow down the schedule are sequences with children or animals, or sequences which take place on water. Children have very special rules under which they must work, and these rules give you considerably less time with them on set than you have with adult actors. (See "Working With Minors" later in this chapter.) Animals are another case. Animals will perform until they are bored or tired. Once the animal decides to stop, there is very little that you can do. Even if the animal is well rested, it will still only do what it wants to do. On one occasion, I worked on a film which had a sequence involving an alligator. In the sequence, the alligator had to move from point "A" to point "B." On that particular day, the stage was rather cool, and the animal trainer had fed the alligator that morning in an effort to keep it from attacking the crew. When the alligator was given "action" it stayed where it was as if it were made of fiberglass. It did not move one muscle. If you look at the situation from the alligator's point of view, it makes sense: it had eaten and was content to sit and digest its meal. In addition, the stage was cool and as the alligator was a cold blooded animal, it didn't really have the energy to move, so it did the next best thing—nothing.

Keeping all of the above in mind, start putting in the black and white day strips to divide the board up into individual days of work. If you find that the work doesn't divide well into single days, but you know that you will accomplish it over a multiple day period, you can put several day strips together to show that the given shooting sequences will be shot over those days. When you come to the end of a week, put in an *end-of-week* banner using the back of a white strip. This is helpful on longer schedules to know where you are, or to figure out how many weeks an actor or piece of equipment is needed without resorting to counting.

Banners can be used for a number of different informative purposes. It is helpful to put in a *company-move* banner when mid-day moves are contemplated. A company move occurs when you move your base camp of equipment trucks and trailers to a new location. Banners can also announce holidays, specific shooting units, or other instructions.

Finish Each Location Before You Leave It.

As you move through the board, grouping the strips into days of work, try to finish each set or location before going on to another set. It is wasteful of both time and money to have to return to a set. In addition, if the set is not finished, you must often leave equipment such as lights or set dressing on the set, extending the rental and increasing your expense. Occasionally, it will not be possible to finish the set in the first visit. When that happens, try to return as soon as possible.

Cast Carry

The SAG Basic Agreement requires that an actor be paid from the actor's first day on the set until the actor is finished with the picture, whether or not the actor is needed on the intervening days. If an actor is not needed on a particular day, the actor is said to be "on hold." Actors on hold are paid a minimum day for each day they are on hold. Under the feature agreement, an actor can be dropped on a one-time only basis if there are ten or more intervening days (including weekends) between work days, as long as the actor has been given a definite *pickup* or return date. Once that return date arrives, the actor goes back onto your payroll until you release the actor from the picture. If you find that because of schedule changes, you no longer need the actor as early as anticipated, contact the actor's agent. You may get the agent to agree to move the pickup date. The reason that the agent might do this is that it gives the agent an opportunity to provide more work for the actor on another project. Under the low-budget contract ($2,000,000 or less), you are not required to pay for intervening hold-days.

Whether you are operating under the low-budget contract or not, you should try to keep an actor's hold-days to a minimum. Often an actor's work falls into a limited number of sets and his or her work days can be consolidated to a great extent by choosing carefully which sequences to film in succession. Occasionally however, there will be the odd role that works 8 days and is on hold for 18. In that situation, it is better to have the actor on hold and not have to return to sets.

Second Units

Stunt scenes, vehicle "run-bys", aerial shots, establishing shots of locations that the first unit (main shooting unit) will never shoot at, and other shots that do not involve the actors are best done by a *second unit*. A second unit can be smaller and quicker than the first unit, and therefore can be more economical to use for shots requiring elaborate and lengthy setups, or to go to far flung locations for a few exterior establishing shots. The second unit's sequences can be grouped at the end of the board after a banner which reads "Second Unit," or, if the second unit will be operating concurrently with the first unit, it is sometimes handier to schedule the second unit shots on each day, grouping them after the first unit shots. Again, there should be a banner on each day the second unit operates, designating which sequences belong to them.

Stock Footage

Strips should be made for all stock footage shots, and they should be grouped at the end of the board after the last day strip following a banner which reads "Stock Footage." This accounts for those scenes which otherwise would be missing from the board, and alerts the crew that those particular sequences will not have to be prepared.

Working with Minors

As stated earlier, having minors as actors or extras can have a large effect on the amount of work that can be accomplished each day. This is due to several reasons. Children are limited by law as to the amount of time they can spend on the set each day and as to the times they can be made available. If a minor's school is in session on the day of filming, then the minor must be schooled on the set. Also, a child does not have the capacity of an adult for sustained work. Recognizing these facts, and with the understanding that many parents and most children are naive about the entertainment industry, the State of California has encoded within its laws the conditions under which minors may work on films. The complete text of these rules can be found in the *California Labor Code – Title 8*. The primary purpose of these laws is to protect the child, and in doing so, they will protect the filmmaker, too. A comprehensive summary of the rules can be found in the Entertainment Partners Paymaster. It is to the filmmaker's benefit to follow these rules to the letter whether the filming takes place in California or not. California's long experience with children working in the film industry has made its child labor laws among the strictest in the nation. If you are following the California rules, you will meet the requirement of most other jurisdictions. However, it is always advisable to check the rules of the state or country in which you are filming. What follows is a brief summary of the California rules.

Definition of a Minor

A minor, in accordance with the *California Labor Code* [Section 11750] is any person under the age of 18 years who is subject to California's compulsory education law. Minors who have a high school education or its equivalent are exempt from the regulations. However, emancipated minors are not necessarily exempt from the regulations, since emancipation does not automatically exempt a minor from the compulsory education laws. An emancipated minor is not required to obtain parental consent to work. A work permit must still be obtained from appropriate school authorities. The only minors exempt from work permit requirements are those with a high school education or its equivalent.

Parents

A minor under the age of 16 years must have a parent or guardian present on the set at all times.

Work Permits

To be eligible for work in a film, a minor must have a valid work permit issued by the California Division of Labor Standards Enforcement (DLSE).

Permit to Employ Minors

A production that wishes to employ minors must obtain a permit to do so from the DLSE.

Meals

Minors follow the same rules as for adults. Minors must break for meals for no less than ½ hour and no later than 6 hours from their call time or their last meal.

Travel Time

As with adults, travel time counts as work time, but since you have so much less time to work with a child, this becomes crucial. Travel from a studio to location and vice versa is part of the minor's work day. With regard to "report to" locations (in which the child is driven to the location by the parents), the Labor Commissioner's position is that the travel time from the studio to the report to location is to be calculated and only that time is credited against the minor's work day.

Turnaround

Turnaround is the rest period an actor is given from the time he or she is dismissed on one day until the time the actor is required to report the next day. As with adult actors, a minor must be given no less than 12 hours from dismissal to report time. If the minor is dismissed from the set less than 12 hours from the beginning of his regular school day, he must be schooled the following day at the set and is on payroll for that additional day.

Studio Teachers

Studio teachers are responsible for the education of minors under 18 years, and for the health, safety, and welfare of minors under 16 years. Although they are paid by the employer of the minors, a studio teacher can refuse to allow a child to work on a set or location which jeopardizes the child's health, safety, and/or morals. Such a decision may be immediately appealed to the Labor Commissioner, who may confirm or countermand this action. A production company cannot discriminate against any studio teacher for carrying out responsibilities concerning health, safety, and morals standards, or for filing an oral or written complaint with the DLSE.

When school is in session, there must be one studio teacher for every ten minors. When school is not in session, there must be one studio teacher for every twenty minors. In determining the number of teachers to hire, remember that not all of the minors may be on set a the same time. For example, you may have ten minors on a particular day, only need five of them on set while the other five remain in the on-set classroom. In that situation, you would need two teachers, one to cover the set, and one to supervise the classroom.

California minors working outside of California must have a California studio teacher. Out-of-state minors working in California must also have a studio teacher and adhere to *Title 8*. If you film out-of-state with out-of-state minors, none of the California rules apply — the rules of the state in which you're filming do apply, and it is incumbent upon you to know what those rules are. However, any minor hired in California and then taken out of state by the employer is covered by the California rules. All minors working under a SAG contract, regardless of place of employment, are covered by the California rules. As stated earlier, if you follow the California rules, you will most likely meet the standards for the rest of the nation.

Ages	Time on Set	Work Time	School	Rest and Recreation	Total Time Including Meal
15 Days – 6 Mos.	2 Hours	20 Minutes		1 Hour 40 Minutes	2½ Hours
6 Mos. – 2 Years	4 Hours	2 Hours		2 Hours	4½ Hours
2 Years – 5 Years	6 Hours	3 Hours		3 Hours	6½ Hours
6 Years – 8 Years	8 Hours	4 Hours	3 Hours	1 Hour	8½ Hours
School not in session		6 Hours		2 Hours	
9 Years – 15 Years	9 Hours	5 Hours	3 Hours	1 Hour	9½ Hours
School not in session		7 Hours		2 Hours	
16 Years & 17 Years	10 Hours	6 Hours	3 Hours	1 Hour	10½ Hours
School not in session		8 Hours		2 Hours	

Table 9.1. Permitted work times and required rest times for minors working under the California *State Labor Code*.

Work Hours and Rest Time

Minors cannot start work before 5:00 AM and minors under the age of 8 years must be dismissed no later than 10:00 PM. Minors who are 8 years of age and older must be dismissed by 10:00 PM on days preceding schools days, although they can be retained as late as 12:30 AM on days preceding non-school days.

Minors are limited to the number of hours they can work on any one day based on their age. One should always follow the laws of the state governing the minor's employment, but California law says that in no case can a minor exceed the following limits on total work hours per day:

- 6 hours for minors 2 years through 5 years of age,
- 8 hours for minors 6 years through 8 years,
- 9 hours for minors 9 years through 15 years, and
- 10 hours for minors 16 years and older.

In computing the start and stop times for minors, remember that work time does not include meal time, but does include a mandatory 5 minute break required each hour. Do not ask the studio teacher to waive these limits or grant extensions. It is not within the teacher's powers to do so. Any waivers must be sought from the Labor Commissioner. Table 9.1 summarizes the work hours for each age group.

Babies

The use of babies or infants in a film requires special considerations and proper preparations. There should be a quiet area set aside, equipped with a crib, sterile garments, blankets, and kept at a comfortable temperature. If other children are being schooled on a day that an infant under six months old works, a separate studio teacher should be hired in addition to the teacher or teachers required for the school-aged children. For very young babies (fifteen days to six weeks old), there should be a teacher and a nurse for every three babies. With older infants (six weeks to six months old), the ratio can be increased to provide a teacher and a nurse for every ten babies.

We have all witnessed the scene in films or television in which an infant is shown on-camera for a few seconds and thereafter the only evidence of the infant is a bundle of blankets being cradled in a character's arms. The reason for this is the extremely limited amount of time an infant or baby is allowed to work and be present on the set. All babies from fifteen days to six months may be at the place of employment for a maximum of 2½ hours including meal time. (See table 9.1.) Babies can be called to work between 9:30 AM to 11:30 AM and 2:30 PM to 4:30 PM. An exception to this is that babies under six months of age may work during any two hours between 5:00 AM and 12:30 AM if the parent or guardian and the studio teacher approve, and if proper facilities are available for the baby to eat and rest. It is always wise to try to structure the shooting day to take advantage of a baby's active times. The best times for the baby can be learned by interviewing the mother. A tired and fussy baby will only make the work go slower.

Finally, a baby cannot be exposed to a light of greater than 100 foot-candles* intensity for more than thirty seconds at a time. For this reason, it is best to have the lights flagged off and to remove the flags once the camera is rolling. Be sure to shield the baby's eyes when removing the flags so that the baby's eyes are not suddenly exposed to the increase in intensity of light.

Because of the heavy restrictions on the time babies and children in general are able to be on set, many companies elect to use twins or triplets to play the roles. This can be very helpful and can extend the work day. However, proper facilities must be provided for the child who is not working at the moment. Usually when using twins or triplets, one parent or guardian will be bringing them to the set. This means that all the siblings will actually be present for the total time that they all work. This should be dicussed in advance with the studio teacher so that the teacher's recommendations can be followed in removing the idle child from the work environment in order to stay within compliance of the laws.

In *The Parent Trap*, the reverse was true. The talented Lindsay Lohan played twin girls and did it with great expertise, giving each twin her own personality. However, this multiplied our problems by giving Miss Lohan twice the work in that she was playing both roles. One way we addressed the situation was by scheduling shots with her only for part of the day, and then by filling out the day with shots that involved only adults, or other children that had not been used earlier in the day.

* A foot-candle is a standard measure of luminance equivalent to the light produced by a standard candle at a distance of one foot. One foot-candle is equal to one lumen incident per square foot.

Working with Animals

Do you have an animal in your film? If so, it will affect your scheduling. Now you're probably thinking, *but these animals are trained.* In the previously cited alligator incident when it stood motionless on a cold stage for an hour and a half, no one remembered, including the trainer, that alligators are cold blooded and are unable to function below a certain temperature. Whether or not they are trained, animals do just what they want to do—no more, no less. I can illustrate this with an incident that happened on *Starship Troopers.*

In the original script, Carl Jenkins (Neil Patrick Harris of *Doogie Howser* fame) practiced his telepathic abilities on his pet African bullfrog by mentally beaming an image into the frog's brain of a fly on his mother's leg. The frog hops up the basement stairs to the kitchen and we hear Carl's mother scream. Carl and Johnny Rico (Casper Van Dien) have a good laugh over this.

No big deal, we thought. We get a trained frog. I started calling animal trainers and found one that had a grotesque, huge, yellow, African bullfrog. So far, so good, I thought.

"Will he hop on cue?" I asked.

"Of course."

"Will he hop up a set of stairs?" I asked.

"Of course, as long as they aren't too high."

"What's too high?" I asked.

"Keep the risers under eight inches."

A little alarm went off in my head.

"Can we test it?"

"Of course. Give me a week to train it."

When the test day arrived, the director, the producer, the assistant director, the director of photography (DP), and the art director were gathered on a stage to film the test on a small set of 3 stairs with the risers that were just under eight inches high. The stage was a comfortable temperature (frogs are cold blooded, too), and all seemed to be ready.

When the trainer arrived with the frog, I asked the trainer how he planned to get the frog to jump on cue.

"We just hit his little bottom with a puff of air whenever we want him to jump."

How clever, I thought. That is what happens when you hire a professional.

It took a moment for the trainer to rig his air hose to deliver the little puff of air, but soon he was ready. The trainer placed the frog on the lowest step and turned the frog so that it was facing the riser. You could feel the anticipation building.

The assistant director called, "Rolling!"

The camera operator turned on the camera and called, "Speed!"

The director said, "Action!"

The trainer delivered his little puff of air.

The frog jumped—off to the right side.

The trainer replaced the frog on its mark, delivered the puff and the frog jumped off to the left side. The trainer replaced the frog on its mark, delivered the puff, the frog jumped backwards off the stair. The trainer replaced the frog on the mark, puff, the frog jumped off to the right side again. The trainer replaced the frog, puff of air, puff of air, puff of air…and the frog just sat there.

Look at it from the frog's point of view. You find yourself placed on this platform with a wall in front of you that is twice your height and someone blasts your behind with cold air. Do you bound over the towering wall in front of you? No, of course not. It's much easier just to hop off to the side. Then suddenly you are back in front of the wall again and another blast up the butt, so you go the other way. However, no matter what you do, you always end up back at this wall. So what do you do now? You quit. You just sit there—butt puffs and all.

That is why Carl has a weasel in the movie.

The point of this example is that animals do what they want to do, and when they are done, they are done. Period. Trainers are very clever and are able to take advantage of behavior that the animal does naturally. When the animal does something the trainer likes, the trainer encourages the behavior with a treat and lots of praise. The animal thinks, not a bad gig, and continues the behavior. The animal is now trained. The animal thinks that the *trainer* is now trained. When the animal has had enough, or becomes bored, or is no longer hungry, it stops. That is why you don't get some animal superstar that does all the tricks that are called for. That is why you have the play-dead Lassie, the roll-over Lassie, and the stand-on-the-edge-of-the-well-whimpering Lassie. That is why Lassie is actually six different dogs.

Sometimes you can reason with a child. With an animal, you are out of luck. The animal is calling the shots, literally. If you are scheduling a scene with an animal, you must allow for extra time. After all, you need them, they don't need you.

10

Locations

Location or Stage?

This fundamental question should be answered early in the scheduling process. To answer it, we need to understand the advantages and disadvantages of each choice. These fall under a few main categories: control, access, availability, production value, and cost.

Control. There is obviously much more control on a sound stage than there is on a public street. You can control who goes onto a sound stage and you control the environment. There is little interference with unwanted noise. You can make it rain; you can make it sunny; you can make it night or day. The temperature is usually comfortable, and the hours are normal. The walls of a stage set are removable to allow camera movement and expansion of the work area. You have a great deal of control on a sound stage.

On a location, you have very little control. You are at the mercy of the weather, time of day, surrounding noise, city traffic patterns, governmental regulations, cooperation of the public (or lack thereof), and the whims of property owners. I have been threatened, shot at, and I have had full cans of beer tossed out of 4th story windows above me. In the area of control, the stage wins without question.

Access. By definition, a stage should have great access. There should be adequate parking for the equipment trucks, and there should be large doors known as "elephant doors" which provide easy access to bring in equipment, sets, or props.

Access on locations can be a problem. After a long search on *Starship Troopers*, an existing house was chosen for Johnny Rico's house. This house was located in the Santa Monica Mountains overlooking Malibu, California. It had a unique, futuristic look since it was clad in stainless steel panels, and it sat on top of a hill with a wide view of the surrounding area. The director loved it. Unfortunately, it had very limited access. The only way you could get to the house was by way of a narrow, curvy driveway that was about a quarter of a mile long. To make matters worse, the Rico family's transporter booth (a large boxy set piece) sat at the end of the driveway taking up the only available space to turn a normal vehicle around. The driveway emptied onto a two-lane blacktop road with limited shoulder space. The equipment trucks all had to be parked along one side of the two-lane road, and all the equipment and crew had to be shuttled up to the house by gasoline powered vehicles similar to golf carts. This was not great access. Usually, the stage wins the access competition.

AVAILABILITY. Once you have booked a stage, it is available until you are done with it. If you run over your end dates, you will be given some leeway by the stage owners as long as you keep them informed. They know that shooting schedules are not written in stone and that things change. Even if the stage owners have given you a date by which you must be out, you can choose when to shoot on stage and when not to within your booked dates.

Locations are usually only available at the property owner's convenience. If there are tenants on the property, their schedules will complicate the matter. Weather can affect availability, too. If you are trying to shoot a scene in the middle of a pasture, the field will not be available if there has been a heavy rain recently. Your equipment and your crew would turn that lovely pasture into a muddy wasteland. The stage wins here, too.

Why would any sane person shoot on location? Because of production value and cost. These two categories are especially relevant for low-budget films where you must make every dollar work overtime.

PRODUCTION VALUE. Shooting on location gives your film a reality and a look that would be hard to achieve on a stage. There is no better way to get the look of a city street than by shooting on a real city street. Location wins in the production value category.

COST. This is the primary reason that low-budget films shoot on location. For a few thousand dollars per day, you can have a set that might cost millions to build. If the location is chosen wisely, you can make your two million dollar movie look like twenty million. Dollar for dollar, location almost always wins in the cost category.

How Do You Find What You Need?

In America, you go scouting. In Europe, you go on a "recce" (pronounced "wrecky", short for "reconnoiter" or "reconnaisance.") Scouting should initially be done by an art director or production designer and a location manager. There is no sense wasting the director's time dragging him or her around to places that may not be right for the story. It is better to start the search with as few people as possible. This can mean something as basic as getting in a car and driving around. Sometimes it's necessary to scout an area by helicopter or airplane first, although this can become expensive. However, there are other ways of finding sites. In large cities, there are often location reps or agencies which will show you folders upon folders of photographs of various locations that they represent. Film commissions can be very useful. When we needed to locate areas that could pass for distant planets in *Starship Troopers*, we sent requests out to the various state film commissions throughout the western half of the U.S. We were deluged with photos of very strange looking places. In areas where there are no location agencies or film commissions, you can simply start asking around. Talk to people and tell them what you are looking for. Someone will know where you can find the perfect site.

It's sometimes possible to narrow your search to people who will have the information that you need. If you need a swimming pool that has a specific look, ask pool maintenance companies. If you need a barn, ask around at feed stores or large-animal veterinarian clinics. If you want a high tech interior of an office building, check with commercial real estate agents. Be creative and don't forget the internet. A Google image search can sometimes find you exactly what you are looking for.

Coverage

Once you have found a location possibility, it must be photographed in a way that will convey the look and circumstances of that locale. This is called *coverage* and it should be done in a very specific way. You want the director to be able to eliminate the obviously inappropriate sites by looking at the photos so that time is not wasted traveling to locations that will be rejected out of hand. In the past, this has been done using a standard 35mm camera with a 50mm lens. A 50mm lens is chosen since it approximates the field of view and sense of perspective that your eye has. Recently, digital cameras and even video tape have been used.

To photographically cover locations, stand in an area that affords a broad overview of the location and begin snapping shots as you pivot in place. Each shot should overlap the previous one so that later these photos can be pasted together to provide an extremely wide view (often 180° to 360°). It is important to not only provide angles of the primary view which may have caused the location to be picked, but the opposite direction should be photographed as well. It is necessary for the director to know that while the view of the old mill may be perfect, when the camera shoots the reverse angle, the sewage treatment plant will be seen. Once a site that is visually appropriate is found, there are several other items that need to be checked.

Is It Right For The Story?

Is the location appropriate to the period of the film? If you are shooting a western and there are high-tension power lines visible on the horizon, then the location will not be appropriate without expensive visual effects to remove the wires. *The Patriot* used the old waterfront area of Charleston, South Carolina, for some of its scenes. The buildings have changed very little in the last two hundred years and the filmmakers only had to spread dirt on the streets in order to cover the modern looking asphalt.

Can the action be physically staged at the location? Is there room for the actors to move around or are there any impediments to the action? For instance, if you are looking at an interior of a house, do the rooms connect in a way that will work for the action described in the script? If the script says that the front door can be seen from the dining room table, make sure that it can be seen.

Who Owns It?

This is a vital question and the answer is not always apparent. You may be dealing with a tenant who is claiming to be the owner. Property ownership can always be checked through the Public Assessor's office. You must have the permission of the tenant *and* the owner.

Another piece of information that must be discovered is the governing body for each location. Is the property in the jurisdiction of the federal, state, county, city, or municipal government? Is it designated as a park? If so, it could be under the National Park Service, the National Forest Service, a state park system, or a local park system. The local or state film commission can be of great help in determining this. If the property is under military jurisdiction, you will need approval of your script from the Department of Defense. This process can take weeks or months and should be started as early as possible. Typically, the military will cooperate only when the film depicts the services in an accurate and positive manner. However, don't despair because your film is not a recruiting vehicle for the services. The film *Hollow Man* received Department of Defense approval even though it was not particularly pro-military. That speaks to the sincerity and objectivity of our government.

Is It Available?

Is the location available for the dates that you will need it? What happens if you have to reschedule? Can the property owners be flexible with the dates? How much notice do they need in the event of changes to the schedule? It's best to answer these questions before you show the property to the director. Once the director falls in love with a location, nothing else is going to look as good.

What Will Be Required Of The Production Company?

In our search for otherworldly planets for *Starship Troopers*, one of the locations we checked out was the Valley of Fire just north of Las Vegas, Nevada. The Valley of Fire is under the National Park Service jurisdiction. The National Park Service admirably takes its stewardship of the nation's parks very seriously and guards them against any who might damage them. I realized that we wanted to do some things that might cause the Park Service to reject our request, but I also knew that one of the *Star Trek* features had filmed there and felt reasonably comfortable that we would be able to do the same.

The Valley of Fire is a spectacular, arid, red landscape cut by deep gorges and high cliffs. When we arrived at the site, we were met by the ranger in charge. He was enthusiastic and very proud to show off "his" park. Paul Verhoeven, the director, wanted to walk into the park and get a closer look, so I followed him. We went up cliffs and down cliffs, into gorges and back out again. Finally, we returned to the road and I began to talk to the ranger about where the director wanted to film. The more I spoke, the more concerned he seemed to become. I told him about the giant bugs, the troopers' fort, the huge explosions, the 800 troopers charging over the desert and he finally shook his head.

"I don't think it's possible," he said.

"Why not," I asked. "Didn't *Star Trek* shoot here?"

He nodded, "Oh, yes, they set their spaceship up here in the parking lot and aimed their camera out over the valley so that it looked like they were surrounded by the red rock."

Star Trek had cheated and they had been very smart. They had gotten the look of the Valley of Fire without having to actually go into the park.

"What would happen if we tried to film back in the canyon?" I asked.

He pointed to the ground around us.

"This is all native vegetation. If you were to damage any of it, you would have to replant it with similar native vegetation and pay to have it watered for a year until it became re-established."

We were standing on dry, gravel-strewn ground. Here and there were small clumps of what I assumed were weeds. The native vegetation stretched out as far as I could see.

"How could we possibly not damage this stuff?" I asked.

"Well, I suppose you could build an elevated walkway," he answered.

I had visions of 200 crewmembers dragging enormous amounts of equipment into the valley and 800 troopers chasing giant bugs while dodging explosions and fire balls. I quickly concluded that we did not want to film at the Valley of Fire. Be sure you know what will be required of the production company before you get too excited or committed to the location.

Access

As stated earlier, access is of paramount importance, and this includes more than just being able to park the trucks near the set. Will your set dressing and construction crews have the access they need to prepare the location? This might occur over several days or even weeks prior to the filming date. Will there be someone on hand to admit the crews? Will that person stay during the day? Will there be access for the strike crews after filming at that location?

During shooting, where will the cast, crew, and extras park? Where can you set up a feeding area? How close will the base camp be to the set? Will you need shuttle vehicles of some sort? What about restroom facilities?

I was going through these questions in my mind regarding the planet location and the aforementioned 800 troopers in *Starship Troopers*. As I thought about setting up a feeding area, I realized that if I were to feed those 800 troopers, I was going to need restroom facilities for those 800 troopers. (What goes in must come out.)

In addition, it will be necessary to have a place for the actors and the extras to relax while they are not being filmed. The actors will often stay either on the set in their chairs or in their dressing rooms. The extras will usually bring their own chairs, but they do need some place to put them. On *The Anarchist Cookbook*, I noticed our extras lounging on the lawn of a house across the street from our location. We had neglected to arrange for a holding area for them and they were making do the best that they could. I knocked on the door of the house and when the homeowner answered, I arranged to rent his lawn. He was very gracious and at first refused payment, but I knew that having that many people sitting on your grass could result in damage to the lawn. For a very modest payment, we had a place for our extras, we created goodwill in the neighborhood, and we prevented a call later from the homeowner claiming damages for a worn lawn.

Are There Any Hazards?

This is a question that is not asked enough. Often the owners or tenants will not be concerned about hazards since they live with them everyday and are used to them. Look around and try to imagine what might go wrong. Some locations are obviously hazardous. Have you ever filmed in a working steel mill? I have. When the steel bars come out of the forge, they are so hot you cannot get within 30 feet of them, even long after they have ceased to glow. Sometimes the hazards are not so obvious.

One of the locations we scouted for *Iceman* was Churchill, Manitoba. We were scouting in the winter, and the day after we arrived, there was a 40-knot wind blowing and the temperature was 40° below zero. It doesn't matter if it was Fahrenheit or Celsius: 40° below is where the two scales intersect. Never having experienced such extreme cold, I asked the guide if there were any concerns he might have because of the temperature. He thought a minute and then pulled a wind chill chart out of his pocket.

"It says here that, exposed flesh freezes in 30 seconds," he announced. We stayed in that day.

Later that night after the wind had died down, a few of us were going

Fig. 10.1. A visitor to Churchill, Manitoba, browsing at the town dump.

to walk down the street to get some dinner. The guide told us to make sure that we made lots of noise as we walked between the trailers that make up the town.

"Why should we do that?" I asked.

"So you don't surprise a polar bear," he said. He explained that Churchill was on the migration route of the polar bears and that we were there at the time of year that they pass through town. In fact, I remembered seeing a *National Geographic* television special on the town of Churchill and the polar bear migration, and I recalled shots of houses torn open by hungry bears. Being the type of person who likes to be prepared, I asked the guide what I should do if I did surprise a polar bear. He told me that I should drop down on my knees, crouch down with my face against the ground, cover my head with my arms, and stay crouched without moving. I asked him what he thought the bear would do if I did that. He said that he thought the bear would probably sniff me and could roll me over a few times. I tried to picture myself in that situation and asked him if he knew of anyone who had ever tried that.

He thought a moment and shook his head. "Nope."

On the way to dinner that night, we sounded like Times Square on New Year's Eve.

Not all hazards on locations are as dramatic. If you are in a wooded area find out if there is poison ivy or poison oak present. Will you be near any wasp or bee nests? Poisonous snakes? Scorpions? Are you working near high drop offs such as cliffs or the edges of roofs? Are you near rapidly running water? Is there vehicular traffic going through the set? Movie crews are notoriously unaware of traffic dangers. If you see a group of people standing in the middle of a busy street obliviously talking, that is probably a movie crew on a scout.

Weather can create a hazard where none was apparent. On *Starship Troopers,* we had constructed our fort and were staging the large battle with the bugs outside of Casper, Wyoming, in a canyon called Hell's Half Acre. Miles away, a sudden rainstorm sent a raging flash flood through the canyon causing the crew to scurry for high ground and making the set unshootable for a week. Know where you are and what can happen.

It's the Question You Didn't Ask... or *Howard the Duck* and the Case of the Disappearing Swamp

There is a scene in *Howard the Duck* where Howard is flying over a marsh in an ultralight aircraft. To shoot this scene, we needed a marsh with a straight, smooth road along side it. We were going to hang the ultralight from the boom of a truck crane. With the camera mounted on the bed of the truck and Howard strapped in the ultralight, it would appear as though he were flying over the marsh in the background as we filmed him while driving down the road.

The location we found was perfect: a beautiful picturesque marsh with sky blue water punctuated by green clumps of tall grass. It was located in the Sacramento River delta on the northern edge of the San Francisco Bay. We found a levee bordering the delta with a nice, straight, smooth road running along the top. From the levee, it appeared that the marsh went on forever. On the location scout, the ranger in charge of the area was most cooperative. He even seemed a bit excited at the prospect of our shooting there. As the appointed day drew closer, I called the ranger several times and he assured me everything would be ready.

On the morning of the shoot, I drove up to the levee and parked. Most of the crew was there, but everyone seemed to be waiting for something. I saw the second unit director, Tom Wright, the assistant director, and the director of photography standing on the levee with their hands on their hips, staring out over the marsh. I wondered why they weren't setting up the first shot. I climbed up the levee, looking for answers.

"Why aren't you shooting?" I asked.

The director didn't say a word. All he did was point out toward the marsh. I followed his gesture and was stunned to see that the water wasn't there. Our beautiful marsh had become a sea of mud.

"Where's the water?" I asked.

"Exactly," said the director.

I saw the ranger standing uncomfortably a short distance away and I strode over to him. "Where's the water?"

"We drained it."

"When?"

"Last night."

"Why would you do that?"

"We always drain the marsh this time of year."

I was forcing myself to be calm and deliberate.

"Why didn't you tell us?"

"You didn't ask."

Fortunately, the California Highway Patrol officers that were with us that day were able to direct us to another levee that overlooked a part of the marsh that had not been drained.

No question is foolish. If you are going to shoot in a forest, you might ask, "Will the trees be here?" They might not.

Impact on the Local Area.

A large shooting company descending on a small town can seem like an invading army. You will fill the motels, jam the restaurants, throw the economy into convulsions, block the streets, and basically disrupt everything. Even a small, low-budget film has an enormous impact on the communities it films in. It is important to prepare the locals for the disruption and help them cope with this invasion. Having a film shoot in your town or area is a lot like having children: you have no idea what you're in for.

The first rule is to never minimize the impact in your presentations to the community leaders and/or property owners. Whatever their size, film companies are an inconvenience at best. If the local people are prepared and know what to expect, they will not feel misled. Be honest. Tell them the worse case, but then tell them how you can help them minimize the disruption. Reroute traffic and work with the local officials in addressing their concerns. As best as you can, schedule filming times so you do not interfere with rush hour or citizens trying to sleep. Be courteous, concerned, and listen. Listen to their complaints, anyone's complaints, and follow through in solving them. Keep your door open to the community and they will be much more apt to keep their community open to you.

John Carpenter's *The Thing* was partially shot outside a small town in northern British Columbia called Stewart. Stewart has the only glacier in North America that can be reached by trucks. The only way to get to Stewart is by 200 miles of logging roads, boat, pontoon plane, or by a plane small enough to land at the tiny airstrip. It is remote. We had wonderful cooperation with the townspeople and made strong friendships. When we were finished, I thought I would never see the place again. A few short years later, I found myself entering Stewart once more for *Iceman*. Because of their previous experience with me and the terrific crew we had on *The Thing,* the people of Stewart welcomed us back enthusiastically.

Dealing With the Property Owner And Tenants

We have addressed the need to determine who actually owns the property. Once you have identified the owners and made your arrangements with both them and the tenants, you should make sure that they all know why you chose the property, and make sure they don't destroy the very reasons that brought you there. Let's say that you have found a house that works as the hideout of the bad guys in your film. The lawn is overgrown, the house has needed paint for ten years, and the carport is visibly sagging—just what you were looking for. For many property owners, their first impulse is to cut the lawn, paint the house, and repair the carport. After all, the house is going to be in a movie and they want it to look its best. Besides, the extra funds that your rental is bringing in will finally make these things possible. Persuade them to do the repairs *after* you have finished. If you can, get them to postpone the repairs until after the release of the film in case you have to go back for reshoots or added scenes.

Making a deal for any property just takes common sense. You need to find the point at which the property owner feels justly compensated and the rental fits into your budget. Typically, a nice middle class house could go for $2,000 per day. A mansion might go for $5,000 per day. The key is defining what "per day" means. Early in my career on a picture entitled *All Night Long,* I made a deal that I grew to regret. We needed a house to serve as the home of the character played by Gene Hackman. We found a great house and the deal I made compensated the owners each day that we were present on the property. In addition, I agreed to repair any damage that the film crew caused. On the surface, this seemed fair. However, the art director had extensive cosmetic changes he wanted to make, such as painting a number of rooms. Based on the deal, we paid the rental fee for each day that we had a crew there prepping the house. We paid a higher fee for each day that we shot at the house, and finally we paid a wrap fee equal to the prep fee for each day we spent restoring the house. During the restoration, the homeowner pointed out damage that we had caused, so we spent more time repairing that. Of course, each day that we spent repairing things caused another day of rental. Then there was damage from the repair crews, or things weren't quite right based on the homeowner's opinion. It finally became clear that we were never going to be free of this location, and in addition, we would be paying for our captivity. I finally had to call in our attorneys to reach a settlement.

The homeowner should be justly compensated, but there needs to be an end to the process. The better way to structure a deal such as this is to agree on a fee per shooting day with the understanding that there will be *x* number of prep days and *y* number of wrap days. A rate for extra shooting days, if needed, should be agreed upon in the contract. Any damage noted after the shooting is completed should be negotiated to a cash payment that the property owner can then use to have the property repaired on his or her own time.

Also, it's possible to throw other items of value into the deal. If you are shooting at night and will make it difficult for the residents to sleep, offer to put them up in an inexpensive hotel or motel. If you need to paint the house, maybe you can use a color that the homeowner wants to keep, thus saving you the expense of repainting. If you need to spruce up the lawn, offer to leave the sod in place when you are done.

Don't forget the neighbors, since your filming can be almost as much of an inconvenience to them as it is to the owners of your primary location. Get them into the deal. Offer to rent space for actor dressing rooms (saving the rent on trailers). The neighbors might supply places to park vehicles or set up lunch tents. If you can include them, you will eliminate one more potential source of complaints.

When negotiating the fee for a location, it helps to keep it in perspective if you estimate what it would cost to rent a stage or a warehouse and build a comparable set. In some instances, it might actually be cheaper to build the set, especially if there are a large number of shooting days for that set. Most of the time, however, you will be shooting at a location for only one to three days. Over a short period, it is usually better to rent a location. If you are unable to get the price of the location down to an affordable level, you can always go somewhere else. Never believe that there is only one spot on Earth that will work. If you are ready to shift gears and go somewhere else, you can save your picture what could be a large overage.

Dealing With the Public

Any time you are shooting on location you will be dealing with the public. This can be pleasant and constructive if it is handled correctly. But first, a couple of tales of public interaction.

In the early 1970s, I was an assistant director trainee working on a movie of the week in a town in Louisiana . At that time, filming was rare outside Los Angeles and New York, and film companies enjoyed a bit of celebrity. We were shooting outside a state capitol building and the director was trying to find a good angle to shoot from. As he stared up at the building and moved around, he bumped into a parked car. This car was legally parked and the owner regularly parked there during work hours. The director muttered something about it being a shame that the car was there since it would have been a good angle, but took the camera crew to another spot to set up the camera. As we were finalizing the camera position, I happened to glance over to where the car was parked in time to see a tow truck driving off with the car trailing behind it as a uniformed policeman was waving to the driver. I ran up and asked why they had towed the car. He proudly told me that now we could put our camera there. The director did use that shot. However, I spent the next two hours finding out where the owner of the car worked, and when I finally tracked her down, I went up to her office and apologized for having her car towed. I explained what had happened and she was very gracious about it. The film company paid the tow charges and impound fees, and we provided a car and driver to take her to the impound yard.

There is a scene in *The Blues Brothers* where the bluesmobile (Jake and Elwood's car) leaps across the gap of a drawbridge while it is opening. This was filmed on a bridge in Chicago. Because of the placement of several cameras and because of safety concerns, traffic was restricted in the area around the bridge while we were filming at that location. Around mid-afternoon, I was chatting with one of the Chicago policemen who had been working with us that day when an extremely irate man came up to me and started shouting about how I was destroying his business. As I was attempting to calm the man down and understand what it was I had done to him, I noticed that the policeman had slipped away and I was on my own. When I got the irate man calmed down, he told me that he was the owner of a bar situated on the other side of the river near the bridge and he was losing $10,000 that day because we were keeping traffic away from the area. I was wondering if a neighborhood bar could really make that much money on a week-day while trying to think of a reliable way to check the veracity of his statements, when I saw the policeman returning. He walked up behind the man and gave him a good hard kick in the seat of his pants. (I thought *now* it was going to cost me $20,000!) Before the man could recover his composure, the policeman told him to get out of there before he ran him in for fraud. The alleged bar owner left as fast as he was able to. After he had gone, the policeman told me that he had gone to the bar to check the license of the bar owner which was required by law to be posted on the wall. He saw that the owner of the bar was a woman, and when he described the plaintiff to her, she said that he was the neighborhood drunk. She also said that her business hadn't been hurt at all by our filming. Moral: It'helps to have the police on your side.

Most of the people you come into contact with will be pleasant and interested in what you are doing. Some will not. A few will loudly proclaim their constitutional rights as U.S. citizens as they walk though your shot. (Be aware that the deliberate interference with a film company in an effort to stop the filming is considered restraint of trade and is illegal in many jurisdictions.) When asking for the public's cooperation, be polite but firm. Listen to any complaints and find a way to solve them. Treat each complaint as though it is very important. Don't be dragged into an argument. Be conscious of the public's needs, but also protect your right to work.

Night Shooting

Night shooting is probably the biggest source of complaints of any activity a shooting company may engage in. Imagine, if you will, having to wake up early the next morning after having a film company firing AK47s in the street all night with helicopters swooping low overhead. Night shooting is hard on the neighborhood and hard on your crew.

Film crews are much less efficient at night and this should be reflected in the way nights are scheduled. Everything takes longer. This is partially because of the extra lighting that must take place. However, it's also due to the debilitating effects a night schedule has on people. We are, after all, diurnal creatures.

One way of minimizing the impact of night shooting on both your crew and the neighborhood is to shoot a half day/half night schedule and spread the night work over several days. This way you can wrap each night around midnight and let everyone get a little sleep. Try not to switch from a day schedule to nights, and back to days, too often. Once you go into a night schedule, try to finish it. Switching back and forth plays havoc with crews. Eventually, if you switch back and forth enough, you will find that many members of the crew will become ill.

By contract, SAG actors must have twelve hours of rest between their dismissal one day and their call time the next day. Union film crews must also have eight to twelve hours of rest between calls (depending on the crewmember's job). Even non-union crews need to have some time to get themselves turned around. With this in mind, it is virtually impossible to turn a crew around mid-week. Always schedule your night work to end at the end of a week or before a holiday. That way, you can adjust everyone back to a day schedule over the idle days.

The Filmmaker's Code of Conduct

A code of conduct, originally developed for film companies shooting on location in California, has been adopted by cities and states around the world. A Google search on *'Code of Conduct' +film* will produce a long list of cities and countries that use it. Film companies, large or small, will find that adhering to the code will help smooth the way in their relationships with whatever community they may be filming in. The following represents the code as it appears, more or less, throughout the world:

1. *When filming in a neighborhood or business district, proper notification is to be provided to each merchant or neighbor who is directly affected by the company (this includes parking, base camps, and meal areas). The filming notice should include:*
   - *name of the company*
   - *name of the production*
   - *kind of production (e.g. feature film, movie of the week, TV pilot, etc.)*
   - *type of activity and duration (i.e. times, dates, number of days, including prop and strike)*
   - *company contact (first assistant director, unit production manager, location manager)*
   - *The Code of Conduct should be attached to the filming notification which is distributed to the neighborhood.*

2. *Production vehicles arriving on location in or near a residential neighborhood should enter the area at a time no earlier than that stipulated in the permit, and park one by one, turning off engines as soon as possible. Cast and crew shall observe designated parking areas.*

3. *When a production pass identifying the employee is issued, every member of the crew shall wear it while at the location.*

4. *The removal, moving, or towing of the public's vehicles is prohibited without the express permission of the municipal jurisdiction or the owner of the vehicle.* [It is wise to get this in writing.]

5. *Do not park production vehicles in driveways, or block driveways without the expressed permission of the municipal jurisdiction or driveway owner.*

6. *Cast and crew meals shall be confined to the area designated in the location agreement or permit. Individuals shall eat within their designated meal area during scheduled crew meals. All trash must be disposed of properly upon completion of the meal.*

7. *Removal, trimming, and/or cutting of vegetation or trees is prohibited unless approved by the permit authority or property owner.* [Again, get this in writing.]

8. *Remember to use the proper receptacles for disposal of all napkins, plates, and coffee cups you may use in the course of a working day.*

9. *All signs erected or removed for filming purposes will be removed or replaced upon completion of the use of that location unless otherwise stipulated by the location agreement or permit. Also remember to remove all signs posted to direct the company to the location.*

10. *Every member of the cast and crew will keep noise levels as low as possible.*

11. *Articles of clothing that do not display common sense and good taste should not be worn by crewmembers. Shoes and shirts must be worn at all times, unless otherwise directed.*

12. *Crew members shall not display signs, posters, or pictures on vehicles that do not reflect common sense or good taste (i.e. pin-up posters).*

13. *Do not trespass onto the property of neighbors or other merchants. Remain within the boundaries of the property that has been permitted for filming.*

14. *The cast and crew shall not bring guests or pets to the location, unless expressly authorized in advance by the company.*

15. *Make sure all catering, craftservice, construction, strike, and personal trash is removed from the location.*

16. *Observe designated smoking areas and always extinguish cigarettes in butt cans.*

17. *Cast and crew will refrain from the use of lewd or improper language within earshot of the general public.*

18. *The company will comply at all times with the provisions of the filming permit.*

11

The Day-Out-of-Days

Once the production board has been scheduled, the day-out-of-days report (DOD) is the very next item that should be created. A DOD is simply a chart of which days each actor works. Your casting director and producer will want to get the DOD from you as soon as possible. This is because they cannot begin making the cast deals or even know what actors may be available until they know what the dates are for each of the parts.

Figure 11.1 shows a DOD for the first twenty-six actors in *The Anarchist Cookbook*. Most computer scheduling programs will automatically create a DOD for you but they are not always as flexible as they should be. The examples in this chapter were created in Microsoft Excel®. Making the DOD in Microsoft Excel allows more control in how the report will appear and what information can be included in it. Filling out the report is simply a matter of copying down the information from the production board.

Across the top of the report is the general picture information similar to that which was put on the header board. Notice the date in the top right hand corner. Every document generated in the making of a film should be dated. This is because these documents are constantly revised and at some point, people often end up with two or more copies of the same document. If they are not dated, they may get confused as to which one is the most current.

Below the general information is a section showing the dates of the shooting period. The first item is the start date: May 23, 2001. Below the start date are a series of weekly divisions that make it easier to see how many weeks an actor will be working. Notice that the weeks start on

Wednesday. This is because our first shooting day was a Wednesday. An actor's work week starts on the day that he or she was hired. Therefore, if an actor was hired on Wednesday and worked through Friday, took Saturday and Sunday off, and finished on the following Tuesday, that actor would have worked one week.

Below the weekly divisions are monthly divisions, and on this film they are the months of May and June. Next comes a row showing the calendar dates for each day, whether it will be worked or not. In this case, the calendar dates run from May 21, 2001 through June 24, 2001.

In the row directly below the calendar dates is a row showing the day of the week for each produciton day. Again, notice all days are indicated, not just the work days.

Below the days of the week is a row showing the numbered shooting days, in this case days 1 through 24. The weekends and the one holiday are shown with grayed backgrounds. This is carried into the chart grid below making it easier to know where you are in the chart. The workweek on *Anarchist* was from Monday through Saturday, with Sunday designated as the off day. The holiday was Memorial Day on May 28.

Down the left side of the chart is the list of the cast with their identification numbers. This list is taken directly from the header board.

At the very bottom of the chart is a row labeled "Total # of Actors Working." This is the total number of actors who will be working on set each day. I like to include this because it makes it easy to see how many dressing rooms are needed on any particular day.

Abbreviations

The grid of the report is filled in with letter abbreviations that indicate what each actor is doing on each day of the picture. They are as follows:

- S Start. The first day of an actor's services.
- W Work. Any day on which an actor's services are required on set.
- H Hold. Any day on which an actor who has begun working on the picture is not required on set.
- F Finish. The last day of an actor's services.
- D Drop. The last day of the first period of an actor's services who will be picked up again later.
- P Pickup. The first day of an actor's second term of service.
- T Travel. A day on which an actor travels to or from a distant location.

Day out of Days

Title: The Anarchist Cookbook **Prod. Number:** **Date:** May 16, 2001

Producer: Robert Brown, Jordan Susman **Director:** Jordan Susman **UPM/Asst. Dir:**

Start Date: 23-May-01

Week # 1 | Week # 2 | Week # 3 | Week # 4 | Week # 5

ID	Month:	May											June																									Tvl	Start	DROP DATE	PICK UP DATE	Finish	Work	Hold	Total
	Date:	21	22	23	24	25	26	27	28	29	30	31	1	2	3	4	5	6	7	8	9	10	11	12	13	14	15	16	17	18	19	20	21	22	23	24								
	Day:	M	T	W	T	F	S	S	M	T	W	T	F	S	S	M	T	W	T	F	S	S	M	T	W	T	F	S	S	M	T	W	T	F	S	S								
	Shoot Day:			1	2	3	4		/	5	6	7	8	9		10	11	12	13	14	15		16	17	18	19	20	21		22	23	24												
ID	Character																																											
1	Puck		T	SW	W	W	W		/	W	W	W	W	W		W	W	W	W	W	W		W	W	W	W	W	W		W	W	WF	T				2	5/23	-	-	6/20	24	0	26
2	Double D			T	SW	W	H		/	H	H	H	W	W		W	W	H	H	H	W		W	W	W	W	W	H		W	W	WF	T				2	5/24	-	-	6/20	15	8	25
3	Johnny Black			T	SW	H	W		/	H	H	H	W	W		W	W	H	W	W	W		W	W	W	W	W	W		W	H	WF	T				2	5/24	-	-	6/20	17	6	25
4	Johnny Red								/			T	SW	W		W	W	H	W	W	W		W	H	W	W	W	WF	T								2	6/1	-	-	6/16	12	2	16
5	Karla								/			T	SW	H		W	W	W	W	H	W		W	W	W	W	W	H		H	WF	T					2	6/1	-	-	6/19	12	4	18
6	Jody								T	SW	W	W	WF	T																							2	5/29	-	-	6/1	4	0	6
7	Sweeney								/		T	SW	W	H		W	H	W	H	H	W		W	W	W	W	W	H		W	WF	T					2	5/31	-	-	6/19	12	5	19
8	Gin								/			T	SW	W		W	H	H	H	H	W		W	W	W	W	W	H		H	WF	T					2	6/1	-	-	6/19	10	6	18
9	Milo								/										SW	H	H		H	W	H	H	H	W		WF							0	6/7	-	-	6/18	4	6	10
10	Buck								/										SW	H	H		H	H	H	H	H	W		WF							0	6/7	-	-	6/18	3	7	10
11	Dale								/										SW	H	H		H	H	H	H	H	W		WF							0	6/7	-	-	6/18	3	7	10
12	Rich								/										SW	H	H		H	H	H	H	H	W		WF							0	6/7	-	-	6/18	3	7	10
13	Lawyer								/								SW	W	H	H	W		H	H	H	WF											0	6/5	-	-	6/14	4	5	9
14	Mr. Gold						SW		/	WF																											0	5/26	-	-	5/29	2	0	2
15	Officer Roger				SW	H	H		/	W	H	H	H	H		W	H	H	H	H	H		H	H	H	W	H	H		H	WF						0	5/24	-	-	6/19	5	17	22
16	Tour Leader								/																						SWF						0	6/19	-	-	6/19	1	0	1
17	Mrs. Gold								/	SWF																											0	5/29	-	-	5/29	1	0	1
18	FBI Agent sc. 224																															SWF					0	6/20	-	-	6/20	1	0	1
19	Security Guard																														SWF						0	6/19	-	-	6/19	1	0	1
20	Teen															SW	H	H	H	H	H		H	H	H	WF											0	6/4	-	-	6/14	2	8	10
21	Clean-cut Kid																							SWF													0	6/12	-	-	6/12	1	0	1
22	Guard sc. 52				SWF																																0	5/24	-	-	5/24	1	0	1
23	Manager sc. 76					SWF																															0	5/25	-	-	5/25	1	0	1
24	Japanese Girl											SWF																									0	5/31	-	-	5/31	1	0	1
25	Sweet Thing												SW	H		H	H	WF																			0	6/1	-	-	6/6	2	3	5
26	Waitress sc. 127																						SWF														0	6/11	-	-	6/11	1	0	1
	Total # of Actors Working:			1	5	3	3			5	2	4	9	5		9	6	5	8	3	8		8	8	7	10	7	7		8	8	4												

Fig. 11.1. A day-out-of-days report for ***The Anarchist Cookbook*** showing "Hold" days.

Not all of these abbreviations were used in *The Anarchist Cookbook* DOD because we did not have any drop and pickup deals. We will examine each of these designations in detail below.

Start, Work, Finish

An actor's start-work date is usually the first day that the actor appears on set. An exception to this would be an actor who has a contractual start date, but because of schedule changes does not actually report to set until later. That actor would still start on the original contractual date and would be shown on the report as *SH* for that day, which means the actor started on payroll but was not required to report to the set.

Every day that an actor is required on set is marked *W* for work. The last day an actor works on set is shown as *WF* which means the actor is finished on the picture. An actor who only works one day would be shown as *SWF* which means that the first and last days of the actor's term of contract are the same.

Hold Days

A *hold-day (H)* is a day on which an actor is on payroll but not needed on set. This is a result of the requirement by the standard Screen Actors Guild (SAG) agreement that actors be kept on payroll until released from the picture. This means that any actor who has started on the picture must be paid an eight-hour minimum day for any day the actor is on hold. Therefore, it becomes important that you minimize the number of hold-days that your actors have.

Hold-days are often unavoidable. Figure 11.1 show several examples of actors with more hold-days than workdays. The most grievous of these is character number 15, Officer Roger. He is shown working five days and on hold for seventeen. That means that Officer Roger will be paid the equivalent of twenty-two days for five days of acting. When confronted with a situation such as this, you should reexamine your schedule to see if switching the order of the shooting days will help.

There are exceptions to the hold rule. Films made under the SAG low-budget contract do not have to pay for hold-days. The actor is paid only for the days needed on set. If you are unsure that you need an actor on a specific day and you instructed that actor to remain "on-call," then you would pay the actor for a minimum day even if he or she did not work and even if you were working under the low-budget agreement. The logic behind this is that you have prevented the actor from working elsewhere by demanding that the actor remain available to you. Figure 11.2 shows the *Anarchist* DOD with the hold-days removed. Since *Anarchist* was made under the SAG low-budget agreement, the hold-days were not a factor. That is why it is okay for Officer Roger's situation to remain as it is.

Drop and Pickup

A way to help reduce the number of hold-days on a picture made under the standard SAG agreement is to use drop-and-pickup deals. Under the standard agreement, an actor on a theatrical film may be dropped from payroll and then picked up again, once on each picture, if there are ten days between the drop-date and the pickup date. (Television has slightly different rules.) These are calendar days and you can include weekends and holidays. If you exercise this option, the actor must be given a firm pickup date, and the actor would go back on payroll on that date whether you are ready or not.

In Officer Roger's case, this would still not help because the largest consecutive run of hold-days runs from June 5 through June 13, a period of nine days. However, we are so close to satisfying the 10-day rule that it may be worth reexamining the schedule to see if we can open up more space in Officer Roger's run. We could swap the tenth day with the eighth day. That would move Officer Roger's third workday closer to his second without causing any of the more expensive cast members in the top few rows to be extended. We could also swap the nineteenth day with twenty-second day. That would open up Officer Roger's down time even more.

Figure 11.3 shows the result in shifting the schedule in this way. The table below summarizes how many days each of the affected actors gained or lost.

Actor	Days Gained or Lost
Johnny Red	+1
Jody	+2
Milo	-1
Buck	-1
Dale	-1
Rich	-1

Day out of Days

Title: The Anarchist Cookbook **Prod. Number:** **Date:** May 16, 2001

Producer: Robert Brown, Jordan Susman **Director:** Jordan Susman **UPM/Asst. Dir:**

Start Date: 23-May-01

Week # 1 | Week # 2 | Week # 3 | Week # 4 | Week # 5

ID	Character	21	22	23	24	25	26	27	28	29	30	31	1	2	3	4	5	6	7	8	9	10	11	12	13	14	15	16	17	18	19	20	21	22	23	24	Tvl	Start	DROP DATE	PICK UP DATE	Finish	Work	Hold	Total
	Month:	May											June																															
	Day:	M	T	W	T	F	S	S	M	T	W	T	F	S	S	M	T	W	T	F	S	S	M	T	W	T	F	S	S	M	T	W	T	F	S	S								
	Shoot Day:			1	2	3	4		/	5	6	7	8	9		10	11	12	13	14	15		16	17	18	19	20	21		22	23	24												
1	Puck		T	SW	W	W	W		/	W	W	W	W	W		W	W	W	W	W	W		W	W	W	W	W	W		W	W	WF	T				2	5/23	-	-	6/20	24	0	26
2	Double D			T	SW	W			/				W	W		W	W				W		W	W	W	W	W			W	W	WF	T				2	5/24	-	-	6/20	15	0	17
3	Johnny Black			T	SW		W		/				W	W		W	W		W	W	W		W	W	W	W	W	W		W		WF	T				2	5/24	-	-	6/20	17	0	19
4	Johnny Red								/			T	SW	W		W	W		W	W	W		W		W	W	W	WF	T								2	6/1	-	-	6/16	12	0	14
5	Karla								/			T	SW			W	W	W	W		W		W	W	W	W	W				WF	T					2	6/1	-	-	6/19	12	0	14
6	Jody								T	SW	W	W	WF	T																							2	5/29	-	-	6/1	4	0	6
7	Sweeney								/		T	SW	W			W		W			W		W	W	W	W	W			W	WF	T					2	5/31	-	-	6/19	12	0	14
8	Gin								/			T	SW	W		W					W		W	W	W	W	W				WF	T					2	6/1	-	-	6/19	10	0	12
9	Milo								/										SW					W				W		WF							0	6/7	-	-	6/18	4	0	4
10	Buck								/										SW									W		WF							0	6/7	-	-	6/18	3	0	3
11	Dale								/										SW									W		WF							0	6/7	-	-	6/18	3	0	3
12	Rich								/										SW									W		WF							0	6/7	-	-	6/18	3	0	3
13	Lawyer								/								SW	W			W					WF											0	6/5	-	-	6/14	4	0	4
14	Mr. Gold						SW		/	WF																											0	5/26	-	-	5/29	2	0	2
15	Officer Roger				SW				/	W						W										W					WF						0	5/24	-	-	6/19	5	0	5
16	Tour Leader								/																						SWF						0	6/19	-	-	6/19	1	0	1
17	Mrs. Gold								/	SWF																											0	5/29	-	-	5/29	1	0	1
18	FBI Agent sc. 224																															SWF					0	6/20	-	-	6/20	1	0	1
19	Security Guard																														SWF						0	6/19	-	-	6/19	1	0	1
20	Teen															SW										WF											0	6/4	-	-	6/14	2	0	2
21	Clean-cut Kid																							SWF													0	6/12	-	-	6/12	1	0	1
22	Guard sc. 52				SWF																																0	5/24	-	-	5/24	1	0	1
23	Manager sc. 76					SWF																															0	5/25	-	-	5/25	1	0	1
24	Japanese Girl											SWF																									0	5/31	-	-	5/31	1	0	1
25	Sweet Thing												SW					WF																			0	6/1	-	-	6/6	2	0	2
26	Waitress sc. 127																						SWF														0	6/11	-	-	6/11	1	0	1
	Total # of Actors Working:			1	5	3	3			5	2	4	9	5		9	6	5	8	3	8		8	8	7	10	7	7		8	8	4												

Fig. 11.2. A day-out-of-days report for ***The Anarchist Cookbook*** without "Hold" days.

Day out of Days

Title: The Anarchist Cookbook | **Prod. Number:** | **Date:** May 16, 2001

Producer: Robert Brown, Jordan Susman | **Director:** Jordan Susman | **UPM/Asst. Dir:**

Start Date: 23-May-01

Week # 1 | Week # 2 | Week # 3 | Week # 4 | Week # 5

ID	Character	21	22	23	24	25	26	27	28	29	30	31	1	2	3	4	5	6	7	8	9	10	11	12	13	14	15	16	17	18	19	20	21	22	23	24	Tvl	Start	DROP DATE	PICK UP DATE	Finish	Work	Hold	Total
	Month:	May											June																															
	Day:	M	T	W	T	F	S	S	M	T	W	T	F	S	S	M	T	W	T	F	S	S	M	T	W	T	F	S	S	M	T	W	T	F	S	S								
	Shoot Day:			1	2	3	4		/	5	6	7	8	9		10	11	12	13	14	15		16	17	18	19	20	21		22	23	24												
1	Puck		T	SW	W	W	W		/	W	W	W	W	W		W	W	W	W	W	W		W	W	W	W	W	W		W	W	WF	T				2	5/23	-	-	6/20	24	0	26
2	Double D			T	SW	W	H		/	H	H	H	W	W		W	W	H	H	H	W		W	W	W	W	W	H		W	W	WF	T				2	5/24	-	-	6/20	15	8	25
3	Johnny Black			T	SW	H	W		/	H	H	H	W	W		W	W	H	W	W	W		W	W	W	W	W	W		W	H	WF	T				2	5/24	-	-	6/20	17	6	25
4	Johnny Red								/			T	SW	W		W	W	H	W	W	W		W	H	W	H	W	W		WF	T						2	6/1	-	-	6/18	12	3	17
5	Karla								/			T	SW	H		W	W	W	W	H	W		W	W	W	H	W	H		W	WF	T					2	6/1	-	-	6/19	12	4	18
6	Jody								T	SW	W	W	H	H		WF	T																				2	5/29	-	-	6/4	4	2	8
7	Sweeney								/		T	SW	W	H		W	H	W	H	H	W		W	W	W	W	W	H		W	WF	T					2	5/31	-	-	6/19	12	5	19
8	Gin								/			T	SW	W		W	H	H	H	H	W		W	W	W	H	W	H		W	WF	T					2	6/1	-	-	6/19	10	6	18
9	Milo								/										SW	H	H		H	W	H	W	H	WF									0	6/7	-	-	6/16	4	5	9
10	Buck								/										SW	H	H		H	H	H	W	H	WF									0	6/7	-	-	6/16	3	6	9
11	Dale								/										SW	H	H		H	H	H	W	H	WF									0	6/7	-	-	6/16	3	6	9
12	Rich								/										SW	H	H		H	H	H	W	H	WF									0	6/7	-	-	6/16	3	6	9
13	Lawyer								/								SW	W	H	H	W		H	H	H	H	H	H		WF							0	6/5	-	-	6/18	4	8	12
14	Mr. Gold						SW		/	WF																											0	5/26	-	-	5/29	2	0	2
15	Officer Roger				SW	H	H		/	W	H	H	WD																	PW	WF						0	5/24	6/1	6/18	6/19	5	4	9
16	Tour Leader								/																						SWF						0	6/19	-	-	6/19	1	0	1
17	Mrs. Gold								/	SWF																											0	5/29	-	-	5/29	1	0	1
18	FBI Agent sc. 224																															SWF					0	6/20	-	-	6/20	1	0	1
19	Security Guard																														SWF						0	6/19	-	-	6/19	1	0	1
20	Teen												SWD																	PF							0	6/1	6/1	6/18	6/18	2	0	2
21	Clean-cut Kid																							SWF													0	6/12	-	-	6/12	1	0	1
22	Guard sc. 52				SWF																																0	5/24	-	-	5/24	1	0	1
23	Manager sc. 76					SWF																															0	5/25	-	-	5/25	1	0	1
24	Japanese Girl											SWF																									0	5/31	-	-	5/31	1	0	1
25	Sweet Thing															SW	H	WF																			0	6/4	-	-	6/6	2	1	3
26	Waitress sc. 127																						SWF														0	6/11	-	-	6/11	1	0	1
	Total # of Actors Working:			1	5	3	3			5	2	4	9	5		9	6	5	8	3	8		8	8	7	8	7	7		10	8	4												

Fig. 11.3. The DOD report after swapping day 10 with day 11, and day 19 with day 22.

Actor	Days Gained or Lost
Lawyer	+3
Officer Roger	-13
Teen	-8
Sweet Thing	-2

At first glance, this seems to be a very positive change to the schedule. Nevertheless, several questions must be answered before the change is implemented. What is the financial impact? Does Johnny Red's daily rate wipe out any savings that might be realized? If he is making $8,000 per day, he's the one you should be trying to shorten. (Remember, Johnny Red is also on distant location and his living expenses must be figured into the calculation.) Are Johnny Red, Jody, and Lawyer available for the extra days? Are the locations and/or sets available on the new dates? Does the change in shooting order affect other schedule parameters? In other words, do certain scenes need to be shot before other scenes and does this change violate that need?

Travel

When on distant location, an actor is generally traveled the day before the actor starts and is returned home the day after the actor finishes. This is done even if the travel day falls on a weekend or a holiday which can be seen in the cases of Johnny Red and Jody in figure 11.1. Under the SAG agreement, an actor is paid an eight-hour minimum day for travel, even if it takes twenty-four hours to get to the destination. If the actor travels on a holiday or a weekend, the actor receives 1½ times the minimum day. If an actor is held on distant location over the weekend or on a holiday and the actor does not work, the actor is also paid a straight minimum day. Therefore, it makes sense to minimize the actor's time on location, even if that means traveling the actor on a weekend or holiday.

When making plans for traveling your actors, be sure that you provide time on the location for costume fittings and any hair work that may need to be done if those tasks cannot be done in the actor's home city.

12

The Printed Schedule

The printed schedule is how all the information from the breakdown sheets and the production board is disseminated to the cast and crew. It comes in two forms: the full shooting schedule and the one-line schedule. Although some assistant directors have started using just printed copies of the production board, the printed shooting schedules are more useful and convenient to use for shooting crews than copies of the production board.

The Full Shooting Schedule

Figure 12.1 shows the first two pages of a full shooting schedule. At the top of each page is the name of the project, the title of the document, and the date of issuance. Also notice that the pages are numbered. Each day begins with a banner announcing the number of the shooting day, the day of the week, and the date. Below the day banner are a series of lined-off sections. Each of these sections corresponds to a breakdown sheet and a strip on the production board.

The full shooting schedule contains all of the information from each of the breakdown sheets. Each of the lined-off sections begins with the name of the set, whether the scene is day or night, and the page count. On the next line are the scene numbers and the synopsis. Below these are the cast required for the sequence, the extras, and all the other categories from the lower portion of the breakdown sheet including miscellaneous notes. Note that the medium that the sequence was to be shot on is also listed in these examples. That was because *The Anarchist Cookbook* was to be shot using

May 16, 2001 **The Anarchist Cookbook** Page 1

Shooting Schedule

Shoot Day # 1 Wednesday, May 23, 2001

INT Computer Company	Day 2/8 Pgs.
Scene #: 155	*Puck's boss compliments him.*
Cast Members 1.Puck 27.Boss sc. 155 Extras 10 workers	Props computer keyboard computer monitor Standins Standin #1 Standin #2 Media 16.16 mm film
INT Computer Company	Day 1 Pgs.
Scene #: 160	*Puck gets an email from Jody.*
Cast Members 1.Puck Extras 10 workers	Props coffee computer keyboard computer monitor Standins Standin #1 Media 16.16 mm film
INT Computer Company	Day 1/8 Pgs.
Scene #: 163	*Puck continues to slave away.*
Cast Members 1.Puck Extras 10 workers	Props coffee computer keyboard computer monitor confetti party hat Standins Standin #1 Media 16.16 mm film
INT Computer Company	Day 2/8 Pgs.
Scene #: 169	*Puck call Johnny B names in an email to Jody.*
Cast Members 1.Puck Extras 10 workers	Props computer keyboard computer monitor Standins Standin #1 Media 16.16 mm film
INT Computer Company - Boss's Office	Day 1 Pgs.
Scene #: 161	*Puck tells his boss the reason for the party.*
Cast Members 1.Puck 27.Boss sc. 155 Extras 10 workers	Props coffee computer keyboard computer monitor confetti party hat Standins Standin #1

Fig. 12.1a. The first page of a full shooting schedule.

three different media, depending on the sequence: 35mm film, 16mm film with filters, and digital video (DV). At the end of the day there is an end-of-day banner repeating the day and date, and giving the total page count for the day (fig. 12.1B).

This version of the shooting schedule is usually issued only once, prior to the beginning of principal photography. Because of all the information that it includes, it is usually quite long. When the schedule changes, as it

May 16, 2001 **The Anarchist Cookbook** Page 2

Shooting Schedule

Standins
Standin #2
Media
16.16 mm film

INT Computer Company | Night | 1/8 Pgs.
Scene #: 162
Cast Members
1.Puck

Puck works late into the night.
Props
coffee
computer keyboard
computer monitor
confetti
party hat

Standins
Standin #1
Media
16.16 mm film

INT Computer Company | Night | 1/8 Pgs.
Scene #: 164
Cast Members
1.Puck
28.Carolyn sc. 164
Extras
10 workers

Puck is asleep. Carolyn tells him to go home.
Props
tray of food

Standins
Standin #1
Standin #2
Media
16.16 mm film

INT Computer Company | Night | 3/8 Pgs.
Scene #: 170, 171
Cast Members
1.Puck
28.Carolyn sc. 164
Extras
10 workers

Puck turns down an invitation from Carolyn to wait for an email from Jody.
Props
computer keyboard
computer monitor

Standins
Standin #1
Media
16.16 mm film

End Day # 1 Wednesday, May 23, 2001 -- Total Pages: 3 2/8

Shoot Day # 2 Thursday, May 24, 2001

EXT Neiman Marcus - Service Entrance | Day | 1 1/8 Pgs.
Scene #: 52, 53
Cast Members
1.Puck
3.Johnny Black
22.Guard sc. 52

Johnny B. hits the guard. Puck checks to see if he is okay.
Props
collapsible nightstick

Standins
Standin #1
Standin #2
Standin #3
Vehicles
SUV
Makeup
blood
Livestock
5 Minks
Animal Handler

Fig. 12.1b. The second page of a full shooting schedule showing the end of the first day.

inevitably will, a shorter version is issued known as the one-line schedule. Even after the one-line schedule is published, the full shooting schedule is retained by the cast and crew for reference because it has more complete information than the one-line schedule.

May 16, 2001 — **The Anarchist Cookbook** — Page 1

ONELINE SCHEDULE

SCENE(S)	I/E	SET DESCRIPTION	D/N	PAGES
Shoot Day # 1 Wednesday, May 23, 2001				
155	INT	Computer Company	(Day)	2/8
160	INT	Computer Company	(Day)	1
163	INT	Computer Company	(Day)	1/8
169	INT	Computer Company	(Day)	2/8
161	INT	Computer Company - Boss's Office	(Day)	1
162	INT	Computer Company	(Nigh)	1/8
164	INT	Computer Company	(Nigh)	1/8
170, 171	INT	Computer Company	(Nigh)	3/8
End Day # 1 Wednesday, May 23, 2001 -- Total Pages: 3 2/8				

Fig. 12.2. A portion of a true one-line schedule. This format is not very informative.

The One-Line Schedule

The one-line schedule gets its name from the idea that the information from each breakdown page or production board strip would take up only one typed line on the schedule. Figure 12.2 shows a portion of a true one-line schedule. As is apparent, this is not a very useful format because it leaves so much information out. A better solution is a modified version of the one-line schedule shown in figure 12.3. Like the full shooting schedule, each day is announced by a banner stating the shooting day number, the day of the week, and the date. Each breakdown page is lined off below this with only a few essential pieces of information included: the scene number, the set, day or night, page count, synopsis, and cast. This requires three lines, but it is still a great deal shorter than the full shooting schedule. Each day is then closed with an end-of-day banner as in the full shooting schedule.

Scheduling software makes all of this a great deal easier and more efficient. The next chapter will give a few pointers about using scheduling software.

The Anarchist Cookbook
ONELINE SCHEDULE

Page 1
May 21, 2001

Shoot Day # 1 Wednesday, May 23, 2001

Scs.	155	**INT**	**Computer Company** Puck's boss compliments him. Cast Members: 1.Puck, 27.Boss sc. 155	**Day**	2/8 pgs.
Scs.	160	**INT**	**Computer Company** Puck gets an email from Jody. Cast Members: 1.Puck	**Day**	1 pgs.
Scs.	163	**INT**	**Computer Company** Puck continues to slave away. Cast Members: 1.Puck	**Day**	1/8 pgs.
Scs.	169	**INT**	**Computer Company** Puck call Johnny B names in an email to Jody. Cast Members: 1.Puck	**Day**	2/8 pgs.
Scs.	161	**INT**	**Computer Company - Boss's Office** Puck tells his boss the reason for the party. Cast Members: 1.Puck, 27.Boss sc. 155	**Day**	1 pgs.
Scs.	162	**INT**	**Computer Company** Puck works late into the night. Cast Members: 1.Puck	**Night**	1/8 pgs.
Scs.	164	**INT**	**Computer Company** Puck is asleep. Carolyn tells him to go home. Cast Members: 1.Puck, 28.Carolyn sc. 164	**Night**	1/8 pgs.
Scs.	170, 171	**INT**	**Computer Company** Puck turns down an invitation from Carolyn to wait for an email from Jody. Cast Members: 1.Puck, 28.Carolyn sc. 164	**Night**	3/8 pgs.

End Day # 1 Wednesday, May 23, 2001 -- Total Pages: 3 2/8

Shoot Day # 2 Thursday, May 24, 2001

Scs.	52, 53	**EXT**	**Neiman Marcus - Service Entrance** Johnny B. hits the guard. Puck checks to see if he is okay. Cast Members: 1.Puck, 3.Johnny Black, 22.Guard sc. 52	**Day**	1 1/8 pgs.
Scs.	55	**EXT**	**Neiman Marcus - Service Entrance** Cops examine the crime scene. Cast Members: 22.Guard sc. 52	**Day**	1/8 pgs.
Scs.	44	**EXT**	**Restaurant** Puck and Double D pose as valets and steal an SUV. Cast Members: 1.Puck, 2.Double D, 40.Man #1	**Day**	2/8 pgs.
Scs.	44A	**EXT**	**City Street** Puck and Double D pose as valets and steal an SUV. Cast Members: 1.Puck, 2.Double D	**Day**	1/8 pgs.
Scs.	138	**EXT**	**Sidewalk** Cops questions the computer laden lads. Cast Members: 1.Puck, 2.Double D, 15.Officer Roger	**Day**	1 2/8 pgs.
Scs.	223	**EXT**	**FBI Building** Establish FBI.	**Day**	1/8 pgs.
Scs.	229	**EXT**	**FBI Building** Puck walks away from the FBI past the parking meters and Neiman Marcus. Cast Members: 1.Puck	**Day**	3/8 pgs.

Fig. 12.3. A more detailed and useful form of the one-line schedule.

13

Scheduling Software

Isn't There an Easier Way?

Of course there is; this is the 21st century. Production software actually began to be used in a broad way in the 1980s. At first, there were many competing programs, mostly written by film production people who had knowledge of programming. Among the programs available were *A.D. 80®*, *The Production Toolkit®*, and *Movie Magic Scheduling®* by Screenplay Systems, Inc. (now Write Brothers, Inc.). This last program became the defacto standard. It was modeled after the physical breakdown sheets and production board, and it allowed printing strips on special die-cut paper that could be inserted into plastic sleeves to create a production board. Screenplay Systems sold the program to Creative Planet who in turn sold it to Entertainment Partners (the publishers of *The Paymaster*). Entertainment Partners updated the program and renamed it *EP Scheduling®*.The major programs currently available are *EP Scheduling* and *SunFrog Film Scheduling®*, but there are a number of others on the market. See the appendix under "Sources of Supply" for contact information.

The Industry Standard

As noted above, *Movie Magic Scheduling* has become *EP Scheduling®*, and Entertainment Partners has improved the program substantially. However, it still has some quirks, though far fewer than before. Every assistant director or production manager has a list of items he or she would like changed.

One thing that I would like to see added would be the ability to link props or other items to individual roles or sets. For instance, it would be nice to add Sheriff Curry to a breakdown page and have his gun and holster added to the prop list automatically on each breakdown sheet that he appears on. Of course, you should be able to override this on a selective basis. Another thing that the old *Movie Magic Scheduling* program was able to do but the new EP version cannot was to create a category list on the production board similar to the cast list.* (See fig. 5.3 for an example of how Tim Allen's makeup was tracked in *Santa Clause 2*.)

Entertainment Partners' stated goal is to create and deliver the most stable and most advanced scheduling program in the market. Now that they have brought the old program into the 21st century, they are beginning to add enhancements and user requests such as those stated above. In addition, they are working with other software manufacturers such as Reel Logix (**http://www.reellogix.com**), Write Brothers (**http://www.write-bros.com**) and Final Draft (**http://www.finaldraft.com**) to increase the interaction among their respective products. Reel Logix has developed the Reel Production Calendar with which EP Scheduling is fully compatible, allowing you to import scheduling data into the calendar automatically. Write Brothers' Movie Magic Screenwriter and Final Draft's Tagger application allow direct import of script elements into EP Scheduling and onto the breakdown pages.

Methods of Data Entry

One of the most important functions of scheduling software is being able to sort the strips into a useful order. Therefore, the key to using scheduling software is in being organized in how you name things, especially sets. For example, let's assume that you have the following list of sets on various strips:

Ext. College Campus
Int. Laurie Smith's Bedroom
Ext. Quad

* As this book was going to press, Entertainment Partners announced a new release of *EP Scheduling* (build 4.1.163) that will address many of these issues including an element linking ability and the ability to create cast-like category lists for categories other than cast.

Ext. Athletic Field
Int. Classroom
Int. Physics Lab
Int. Smith House
Int. Living Room
Ext. Laurie's House

If you had the scheduling program sort the strips by set and then by Int./Ext., you would get the following list:

Ext. Athletic Field
Int. Classroom
Ext. College Campus
Int. Laurie Smith's Bedroom
Ext. Laurie's House
Int. Living Room
Int. Physics Lab
Ext. Quad
Int. Smith House

This is no help at all because this order would have you running back and forth between the college and the house. Let's rename the sets using a systematic naming scheme:

Ext. Athletic Field	–	Ext. College – Athletic Field
Int. Classroom	–	Int. College – Classroom
Ext. College Campus	–	Ext College – Campus
Int. Laurie Smith's Bedroom	–	Int. Smith House – Laurie's Bedrm
Ext. Laurie's House	–	Ext. Smith House
Int. Living Room	–	Int. Smith House – Living Room
Int. Physics Lab	–	Int. College – Physics Lab
Ext. Quad	–	Ext. College – Quad
Int. Smith House	–	Int. Smith House

Now, let's sort by set and then by Int./Ext. again, but this time we will sort on the new names in the right-hand column:

Ext. Athletic Field	–	Ext. College – Athletic Field
Ext. College Campus	–	Ext. College – Campus
Ext. Quad	–	Ext. College – Quad

Int. Classroom	–	Int. College – Classroom
Int. Physics Lab	–	Int. College – Physics Lab
Ext. Laurie's House	–	Ext. Smith House
Int. Smith House	–	Int. Smith House
Int. Laurie Smith's Bedroom	–	Int. Smith House – Laurie's Bedrm
Int. Living Room	–	Int. Smith House – Living Room

This is more useful. At least we now have all the College sets together and all of the Smith House sets together. By naming the sets in a consistent manner, starting with the general name and then adding the more specific information, the set list will sort into location groupings that can be easily scheduled.

You can carry this naming scheme throughout your breakdown pages in all the different categories. Let's consider locations. Perhaps your locations are in several different states. If you preceded each location's name with the state or general area that it was in, you would have some semblance of order after having the program sort by location. Don't list your locations as in the following list:

Zion National Park
Yosemite
Mojave desert
Bryce Canyon National Park

Instead, list them as follows:

Utah - Zion National Park
California - Yosemite
California - Mojave desert
Utah - Bryce Canyon National Park

Then if you sort on locations, you will get the following list:

California - Mojave Desert
California - Yosemite
Utah - Bryce Canyon National Park
Utah - Zion National Park

It is only logical that you should finish one state before moving off to the next. Stunt doubles should always reference the role that is being doubled (i.e. *Dbl Puck, Dbl Johnny Black*). Stunt players who are not doubling a specific role should be called *utility stunt*. If there are more than one, put down how many (i.e. *5 utility stunts*). Extras should always start with a number if you are speaking of more than one person (i.e. *2 pedestrians, 7 businesswomen, 25 party goers, 350 crowd*). Being organized and systematic in how you enter the information into the computer for the breakdown pages will save you vast amounts of time later.

Once the schedule is finished, you have the information necessary to create the budget. In Part III, we will go through each account in the budget for *The Anarchist Cookbook*. Before we do that, we need to decide what unions, if any, we will work with.

14

Unions

In the early days of Hollywood, there were no unions. Employees made the best deals that they could and often they were taken advantage of. There are stories of companies bringing cots onto the sound stages for the crew to sleep on for a few hours so they wouldn't have to waste time going home. However, unions soon began to form in order to protect the employees and to give them a unified voice in negotiations with the studios.

Some might argue that the unions' voice became too strong. In the early 1970s when the film unions were at the height of their power, I was a trainee on a Universal Studios film. It was raining very hard when we wrapped one evening, and since I had my car parked at the stage, I offered to give the script supervisor a ride to the production building (a distance of about one hundred yards) so that she would not have to walk in the rain. She gladly accepted and I did my good deed. The next day, I was informed that the film had had a grievance filed against it by the Teamsters Local because I had transported a crewmember in my personal car and, by contract, that duty belonged to the teamsters. The studio paid the fine without a fight. Today, that grievance would not have been filed, and if it had, it would be vigorously fought by the studio.

Anecdotes aside, the film unions provided a valuable service. They evened the balance of power between the studios and the crews, and they created a basic codified set of rules and working conditions under which labor peace has reigned, for the most part, for over half a century. Now the business is changing dramatically with studios seeking cheaper labor overseas in Canada, Mexico, Eastern Europe, Southeast Asia, Australia, and New Zealand. Large expensive pictures are routinely shot outside of the United States, and now many third world and developing countries have knowledgeable and experienced crews. Hollywood no longer has a lock on film production.

What does this mean for the low-budget film? It means that U.S. crews that would normally be out of reach are often willing to work on smaller pictures for less money. In May of 2001, I was preparing to shoot *The Anarchist Cookbook* in Dallas, Texas. The mainstay of the Dallas crews, *Walker, Texas Ranger*, had shut down. The SAG agreement was about to expire at the end of June and it was widely believed that there would be a strike. Consequently, film production had ceased. No studio was willing to start a production with the threat that it might be interrupted by an actors' strike. Everyone was out of work.

There was no way that the meager $2 million budget of *The Anarchist Cookbook* could afford to pay union scale rates and benefits. So I went to the various union crewmembers and honestly told them I could not pay them what they were worth, but would they consider working at reduced rates with us until something better came along? I fully understood that if something better did come along, that I might lose my crew and I would have let them go with my blessing. However, nothing did come along until we were finished shooting (there never was a strike), and *The Anarchist Cookbook* had the benefit of some of Dallas's best people.

I had been warned about the Dallas teamsters and I anticipated difficulties in dealing with them. Colleagues that had filmed in Dallas told me to avoid them if I could. However, the teamsters owned much of the equipment I needed and I simply did not believe that they would not appreciate a direct and honest appeal. I made an appointment to see the business manager of the local, and when the time came, I arrived with my budget in hand. I explained to him what the film was about and I showed him what I had available to make the film. I also told him that I needed their expertise and their equipment. Then I asked him how he could help me to make it all happen. His response was overwhelming. He gave us an extremely generous deal and cut their staffing requirement. The support our film received from the Dallas teamsters made it possible to shoot the film efficiently. The individual teamsters on our crew were most helpful and were always looking for ways to cut costs. They did not have to do any of this. They did it because they saw what we were trying to do and wanted to help.

The only union that you probably will have no choice about using is the Screen Actors Guild. Every professional actor in film belongs to SAG and that guild will fine any actor who works for a non-signatory company.

The fortunate thing about SAG is that they do have a low-budget contract (under $2 million) which gives a huge break on rates and actor carry requirements. If your film is budgeted for under $500,000, you can do even better. Many actors, even well known ones, welcome the chance to work on low-budget films because they are often character driven films with meaty parts. SAG will require you to post a bond with them amounting to the total of your cast budget. This is to ensure that the actors are paid what they are due. This bond will be returned to you after the end of principal photography and can then be applied to your post production expenses. Be sure to give SAG warning as you near the end of production so that you can get the bond returned promptly. If your film is bonded, or you have posted a substantial deposit with a payroll company, SAG will often reduce the bond that they require.

Negotiations

Whether you are using union crews or not, you will be negotiating with everyone you hire. More than likely, you will not be able to afford the level of compensation to which they are accustomed. Don't even try. Be honest with them and be prepared for them to say, "No." However, everyone wants something; money is not the only reason people take jobs. Try to get them to fall in love with your script. Show them how it will only take a few weeks. Find out what it is they want. Get on your knees and beg if you have to. You know you are asking them to work at a cheap rate and so do they. Be frank and be firm. Do not fall in love with someone and break your budget to get him or her. You cannot afford to do that. On *The Anarchist Cookbook*, the director and I were fully prepared to recruit film school students if we were unable to attract experienced crew people. It would not have been the same film, but it would have been shot regardless.

What About Non-Union?

Non-union crews typically work for union scale rates or less but without the fringe benefits such as pension, health plans, or vacation allowance. Just because a person does not belong to a union does not mean that he or she is inexperienced. People have many reasons why they do or do not join a union. I once asked a brilliant non-union special effects supervisor why he did not join the union. He told me that he saw no need to; he had all the work he wanted, he did not have to pay union dues, and he was able to command the salary he wanted. In addition, most of his contacts in the business were with non-union companies. He would have been relatively unknown in the union world.

Before deciding that you are not going to sign with a union, give the union a chance to tell you how they can work with your project. Most of the unions have realized that they need to make allowances for low-budget productions and have recently devised contracts that might make it possible for your picture to sign with the union and get the benefit of their members' experience.

Part III

THE BUDGET

15

AN OVERVIEW

What Is a Budget?

The first question you will be asked about a film project by any investor or financier is, "What will it cost?" Let's you and I make a sacred pact, right now, that we will never, ever blurt out a number when first asked this question. The first number to pass your lips will be what is engraved in stone and you will live with that number whether it is good or not. Do not answer until you have enough information to make a sound, well-informed estimate.

There are two types of budgets: budgets that are derived from the needs of the picture, and budgets that dictate what the needs of the picture will be. The latter are more common than the former. Typically, you are given a figure because someone says, "We have to shoot this picture for ***x***." ***X*** may be too much, more often it is too little, and rarely is it just right. In cases such as this, you first need to make a budget based on what the script requires and what the filmmakers want to do. Once you see how much over ***x*** you really are, you must then guide the filmmakers (or yourself, if this is your own project) through a series of choices in order to tailor the film to the budget. The following chapters will give you the background and the knowledge to do that.

A film budget is a guess, an estimate. It should be an educated and accurately derived guess, but nonetheless it is a guess. We expect more from it than we would from most guesses. We expect prescience. It is a guess that needs to be right. Can you completely anticipate every dime that you will spend in the making of a film? I have been doing this for over thirty years and have never been able to catch everything. Does this mean my pictures go over budget? Not at all. There are ways other than just blatantly padding the budget to make sure that your guesses are reasonably accurate. A curious thing happens when you are dealing with a spending plan as complex as a film budget. Most of the time, the areas that are overestimated equal the areas that are underestimated. Where this doesn't occur, there are methods of bringing the whole thing back on track. We will discuss these further, but first let's look at a general philosophy of budgeting.

Spend It All

Film budgeting is a zero-sum game. All the money budgeted should equal the money spent. But shouldn't you try to do everything as cheaply as possible? Well, you certainly should not pay more for something than it is worth, and you should definitely save money if you see an opportunity to do so. The goal is to use the money and resources that you have been given to create a product that represents the full value of what was allocated.

Let's say that I am a home builder and you come to me with the idea of hiring me to build your dream home. You want it just so, and to that end you have had plans drawn up showing how the home is to look and what rooms it is to contain. You expect this home to cost one million dollars and you caution me that you don't want any waste. You want me to be as thrifty and economical as possible. You add that you don't want the project to go one penny over budget. I agree to the job and assure you that you could not have picked a builder more fiscally responsible than me.

Months go by, and eventually I tell you that I am finished and that you should come see the result. As you get out of your car, you notice that the brick-paved driveway you requested is brick colored concrete. The fescue lawn is just dirt painted green. The tongue and groove wooden floors inside have been simulated with linoleum, and the light fixtures are just ceramic sockets with bare bulbs. None of the bedrooms have closets, they only have doors mounted on the walls, and some of the rooms don't even have any windows. You turn to me and I announce with a proud smile that on top of it all, I even saved you several hundred thousand dollars. Are you pleased? Are you thrilled? Are you becoming homicidal? The answers are no, no, and yes. You expected a million dollar house. What you got was a poor imitation that would not be worth what was spent on it. The fact that you got it for several hundred thousand dollars less than what you had planned to spend means nothing. Now, the money that was spent has been completely wasted.

A film is no different. When it has been determined to spend one million or a hundred million on a film, then that is what should be spent. It needs to be spent wisely, but it all should be spent and the value of that spending should be apparent on the screen. There is nothing wrong with saving money in any area, but then use that money to enhance the production in other areas. Do not penny-pinch just to save money. Get value for the budget and make it work for the film. This was a lesson that I learned early in my career.

The film was *Maxwell Smart and the Nude Bomb*. I was a brand new production manager and this would be the first film that I would do on my own. Universal Studios had great confidence in me and sent me up to meet the producer, Jennings Lang. Jennings was an old time Hollywood producer and was somewhat intimidating. He sat me down in his office and asked if he were to pull the plug on the picture today, how much did I think the studio would be out of pocket? I had no idea. Not wanting to appear ignorant, I said "About a million dollars." He looked at me for a second and agreed, and announced that we would therefore make the movie (he didn't want to waste the million he had already spent). Then he fixed me in his most withering gaze and sternly told me that I was not to let the movie exceed seven million by even one penny. I said "Yes sir!" and went off to get the ball rolling.

I was thrilled. At last, I was in charge of my own production. The director was a true gentleman in every sense of the word. On a scout, he might say that he would need thirty extras for a particular scene. I would say "You've got fifteen." He would accept that and make do. He never fought me or protested. In discussing the schedule, he might say that he needed a week to film a certain sequence, and I would say, "You've got four days." Again, he would take my pronouncements as gospel and adjust his shot list accordingly. Having seen other production managers deal with some extremely demanding and autocratic directors in the years leading up to this film, I suppose I was overcompensating. In any event, when I saw the final cut of the film, I realized that I may have hurt it. The director did the best he could with the resources that I provided, but the production value was not there. In scenes that were supposed to be in Washington D.C. (but were shot in Los Angeles), you can see palm trees in the background. Coverage of scenes was at times skimpy, and scenes with crowds of extras appeared a little bare. The film came in on budget and on schedule, but it had not been done in the best way.

The goal is to spend the money. Spend it all, but no more. Spend it so that you get the most production value for your dollars. It has been said of some production managers that they step over dollars to pick up nickels. This happens when the production manager is inflexible and blind to new ideas; when things are done because of policy or habit, not because it has been thought out and determined that this is the best way. When cell phones first began to be popular, many of the studios refused to reimburse cell phone calls except to a few important people such as the director or the director of photography. This made no sense. Imagine that you have sent a driver to a vendor to pick up something and you find that he could do another errand in the same area. Without the cell phone, you would try to page him on his pager. He would then have to get off the freeway, find a pay phone, and call in, wasting a great deal of time. That wasted time would cost far more than the reimbursement of the call on his cell phone. I was reimbursing cell phone calls long before I was officially allowed to.

How Many, For How Long, at What Rate?

Every line item in a film budget tries to answer these three questions. If you know the answers, you know what any given thing will cost. Your production board and schedule will give you the first two answers. That is the purpose of them. You can glance at the schedule or board and say, "I know I need the role of The Killer for 3 weeks and I only need one Killer." Or, "I see we need two fire trucks for three days." That's the easy part. Where most people stumble is in answering, "At what rate?" I will be giving you some guidelines in each account to help figure out what it will cost.

Details, Details, Details

The best budget is the most detailed budget. I am always suspicious when I see "Miscellaneous Expense" in a budget. It is either a pad, or the person who made the budget didn't think it through and has made a wild guess to cover any mistakes. Put down everything that you know. Add detail as you learn things. If you have some wild guesses, and every budget will, work to eliminate them. Research the costs and make those guesses as accurate as possible.

In the early 1990s, I was involved in the preparation of a film tentatively entitled *Anne Bonny*. The title role was a female pirate who roamed the Caribbean and the southeast coast of the United States in the early 1700s. The instructions to us, the filmmakers, were to bring the below-the-line costs in at no more than $50 million. The producer and I went off to do a preliminary budget, and the below-the-line costs came in at $52 million. When we showed the studio the budget, they felt that we were close to being able to meet the goal. They told us to keep working on getting the cost down and to continue scouting and preparing the picture.

Over the next few weeks, we scouted the southeast coast of the U.S., almost every island in the Caribbean, and visited sailing ships from Quebec south almost to the coast of Venezuela. We walked the decks of HMS *Rose*, *Old Ironsides*, imported Black Sea merchant sailing ships, and every historic skiff sporting a sail that we could find. We circumnavigated Jamaica, toured Nevis, circled Barbados, and explored the clear, rocky waters of Bridgetown Harbor. We walked the streets and wharf of St. George's in Granada and imagined it as 18th Century Charleston, South Carolina, and throughout all of this I compiled pages of notes about what the director wanted to do and what it would cost.

When we returned, the producer and I went at the budget again, and came up with a below-the-line cost of $55 million. The more we learned and the more detail we added to the budget, the more apparent it became that the costs were going up, not down. The studio was optimistic, they liked what the director told them he was going to do. They told us that they really wanted to make the film but we had to get the cost down to at least $52 million below-the-line.

Casting for a strong female lead who could "open the picture" started in earnest. I began discussions with a marine coordinator in England who started researching building the ships we needed. The discussions with the director continued, and the producer and director tried to find ways to reduce the costs. The film commissions of all the Caribbean nations that we visited sent us boxes of photographs and information on shooting in their countries.

Once again we produced a budget, and this time the below-the-line cost was near $60 million. The studio looked at us as though we had lost our minds and they shut the picture down. They were right to do so. If the costs were that difficult to control in the preliminary budgeting stage, they would have been impossible to control once the picture got under way. A picture often will live or die by the first number that is reported.

What went wrong? Two things. First, our original "wild" guesses weren't nearly wild enough, and second, we did not adjust the picture to fit with our resources. As they say, the devil is in the details. If we had not continually added details as we learned of them, we would have started the picture with a false idea of what it would have cost. The studio would have been misled, and we would have looked incompetent.

Background on *The Anarchist Cookbook* Budget

Throughout "Part III," I will use the budget of *The Anarchist Cookbook* as an example. The entire budget has been reprinted in the appendix. If you want to reference the film itself, it can be rented or bought through Hollywood Video, Tower Records, other video outlets, or online. *The Anarchist Cookbook* was filmed in Dallas, Texas, for just under $2,000,000. As we explore the details that make up the budget, I will explain the thinking behind each account, talk about the reasons for each line item, and point out ways to economize.

It is important that the reader understand the context in which this budget was created. Every budget is a product of its times and circumstances, and this budget is no different. The filmmakers were able to take advantage of a situation that will not be repeated often. Nevertheless, each project will have its unique opportunities, and the circumstances of this budget can serve as both a guide and an inspiration.

No one who worked on this film worked at his or her normal rate of pay. Every single person on this picture did us an enormous favor for which we were extremely grateful. We were able to employ talent and expertise far beyond our means. What were the circumstances that made this possible?

In the spring of 2001, the entire motion picture industry was bracing for a strike by the Screen Actors Guild. After months of negotiations, it seemed that no further progress was being made in the talks between the Association of Motion Picture and Television Producers (AMPTP) and SAG. The SAG Agreement was set to end at midnight on June 30, 2001. Since the studios did not want to get caught with films in production as the contract ended, they stopped initiating new projects which would run beyond the term of the agreement. This created a lack of work many months ahead of June 30, as if the strike had already begun.

In this context, we arrived in town and began to try to recruit both talent and crew. We approached experienced actors and crew in Los Angeles and Dallas who we knew would bring much expertise to the production. We could not pay them what they normally worked for, and we were frank about that. What we could offer was a chance to work on film that was both original and fun, and could possibly leave a unique impression on the industry. After reading Jordan Susman's script, most of the people we approached were both enthusiastic and ready to go. If the contract was settled, and the members of the crew were offered jobs at their normal rates, we were fully prepared to release them from any obligation to us. (Knowing this crew as I now do, I doubt we would have lost any of them unless it was due to financial hardship.)

What if we did not have this unique set of circumstances? When we began the budgeting process, we did not know we would be so fortunate. I was doubtful that we could get experienced crew to work for the rates we could afford. Our "Plan B" was to hire film school students in the crew positions and hope that their inexperience would be made up for by their enthusiasm.

Now let's go through *The Anarchist Cookbook* budget. Refer to the appendix for the complete budget. Please note that not all of the accounts and subaccounts from the Universal chart of accounts were used in the *Anarchist* budget. I have included in the discussion some of these accounts that are commonly used on other pictures.

16

The Top Sheet

The Header

The first page of the budget, known as the top sheet, serves as both a table of contents and a summary of the budget (fig. 16.1). At the top of the page in the center is the title of the picture and the name of the production company. Below that are two blocks of information on both the left and the right margins. On the left is listed the writer/director, the producers, the date the script was finalized, the date the budget was printed, and the revision number of the budget. The dates and the revision numbers are helpful when you have several copies of the budget and you are not sure which is the most recent.

As stated earlier, whenever you produce a document in connection with a film, it is vitally important to date the document. Very often documents are revised and people will end up with several copies of what appear to be the same document. The only way it is possible to determine the latest version is if they are dated.

On the right are listed the date of the beginning of principal photography, the anticipated date of completion of principal photography, how many days on stage and/or the various locations, and finally, how many weeks there are in the post production schedule. This header information varies with the requirements of the budget and the person creating it.

The Bottom Line

When you first hand a completed budget to an investor or financier, they ignore all of the above. The first thing they look at is the bottom line. It literally is the bottom line, at the bottom of the page where it says "Grand Total." This figure finally answers their major question: *what will the picture cost?* This budget's grand total is $1,994,188. This is not a random number. This number was deliberately arrived at in order to qualify for the Screen Actors Guild's Low-Budget Agreement. If you can stay under two million dollars, you get a huge break on the cast salaries and working conditions.

The bottom line number of a budget is known as the "negative cost" of the picture. The negative cost of a picture is the cost of producing the final cut film negative. Producing that negative is what the entire process is about. Of course, these days there may not be any camera negative if the film is shot on DV or with an HD video camera. Nevertheless, even in these cases, the final cut is scanned out to a master film negative before prints are made. We will go into this process in more detail in the post production discussion later. We will not escape using film entirely until digital distribution to theaters is commonplace.

How The Top Sheet Is Organized

The top sheet, and the entire budget for that matter, is organized by production level. The highest production level is "Above-the-Line." It is literally above the line if the line were drawn after the first five accounts in the budget. The "Above-the-Line" constitutes mainly the "talent" such as the writer, producers, director, and cast. In the *Anarchist* budget, these are accounts 803 through 810, if you include the fringe benefit account for the above-the-line labor. Fringe benefits are comprised of union benefits such as health insurance, pension, vacation, and holiday, plus any payroll taxes which may be applicable. The "Above-the-Line" costs in this budget are $451, 036.

The next production level is the "Shooting Period," or as it is called in this budget, "Production." This section covers all the costs in the preparation for shooting and the actual shooting period of the film, and it is comprised of accounts 811 through 849. This is where the majority of the money is typically spent unless there are some very high priced cast members inflating the Above-the-Line total. The production costs are $978,924, over half of the entire budget.

The "Post Production" level, accounts 851 through 860, covers the ex-

The Anarchist Cookbook
Freedonia Productions, LLC

Writer/Director: Jordan Susman
Producers: Brown, Susman, Greenspun
Script Dated: April 5, 2001
Budget Dated: 05/21/01
Revision #14

Start Principal Photography: 05/23/01
Complete Prin. Photography: 06/20/01
Dallas Local Location: 24 Days
Dallas Stage: 0 Days
Post Production: 16 Weeks

Acct No	Category Description	Page	Total
803-00	WRITING	1	20,000
805-00	PRODUCER & STAFF	1	72,277
807-00	DIRECTOR & STAFF	1	20,000
809-00	TALENT	1	295,855
810-00	**Total Fringes**	**3**	**42,904**
	Total Above-The-Line		**451,036**
811-00	PRODUCTION STAFF	3	95,440
813-00	CAMERA	5	75,543
814-00	ART DEPARTMENT	5	23,908
816-00	SPECIAL EFFECTS	5	1,800
817-00	SET OPERATIONS	6	66,032
819-00	ELECTRICAL	7	47,004
821-00	SET DRESSING	7	55,070
823-00	ACTION PROPS	8	24,228
825-00	PICT. VEH. & ANIMALS	8	6,100
829-00	EXTRA TALENT	8	40,820
831-00	COSTUME	9	39,395
833-00	MAKEUP & HAIR	9	18,500
835-00	SOUND	10	25,926
837-00	LOCATION	10	160,394
839-00	TRANSPORTATION	11	128,577
841-00	FILM & LAB	12	88,062
843-00	TESTS	13	1,100
847-00	SECOND UNIT	13	1,250
849-00	**Total Fringes**	**13**	**79,775**
	Total Production		**978,924**
851-00	EDITING & PROJECTION	13	78,500
853-00	MUSIC	14	75,000
855-00	SOUND (POSTPRODUCTION)	14	105,000
857-00	POSTPRODUCTION FILM & LAB	14	51,194
859-00	TITLES & OPTICALS	14	10,000
860-00	**Total Fringes**	**14**	**7,534**
	Total Post Production		**327,228**
861-00	INSURANCE	14	27,500
862-00	PUBLICITY	14	500
865-00	GENERAL EXPENSES	14	9,000
870-00	CONTINGENCY	15	200,000
	Total Other		**237,000**
	Total Above-The-Line		**451,036**
	Total Below-The-Line		**1,543,152**
	Total Above and Below-The-Line		**1,994,188**
	Grand Total		**1,994,188**

Fig. 16.1. ***The Anarchist Cookbook*** budget top sheet.

penses involved in converting the shot footage into a completed motion picture. Most of the spending in this area occurs after the production period has ended, hence the title of "Post Production." The total for "Post Production" in this budget is $327,228.

The last group of accounts is "Other." In some budgets, it may be known as "General Expense." These are miscellaneous and ongoing expenses such as insurance, office space, publicity, etc. These expenses are not typically confined to any of the other production levels. The total for "Other" in the *Anarchist* budget (accounts 861-870), is $237,000.

Contractual Charges

At the bottom of the top sheet, the contractual charges are listed. Contractual charges are expenses that are tacked onto the budget after the above and below-the-line expenses are totaled up. Usually they are based on a percentage of this total. In some instances, that total may have certain expenses excluded. At other times, a contractual charge may simply be a flat fee tacked onto the budget such as an overhead charge for the producing company.

The original *Anarchist* budget (fig. 16.1) does not have contractual charges, but I have shown in figure 16.2 what the top sheet would have looked like had we needed to include them. The two contractual charges I have added are a contingency and a bond fee. Notice that the original *Anarchist* top sheet also had a contingency and it was assigned an account number. The contractual charges in figure 16.2 do not have an account numbers and they are added at the end of the budget outside of any of the normal production level groups. The difference is in how these two contingencies are to be used, and that determination goes back to whether the picture is bonded or not.

To Bond or Not To Bond

That is the question. To understand what a film bond company or guarantor does, you must look at film financing from the perspective of the financier. If a bank lends you money to buy a new car and you default on your payments, the bank will simply repossess the car and auction it off to satisfy your debt. In this instance, the car is the bank's collateral; its insurance or guarantee that the debt will not go unpaid. What happens if a bank lends you money to produce a film and you take the money and run off to Brazil, or more likely, the film just doesn't get finished? How does the bank insure that the debt will be repaid?

The bank insists in its lending agreement with you that the film be bonded. A film bond is nothing more than a guarantee to the financier that a film will be produced and can be seized in case the filmmaker defaults and cannot pay back the loan. The bond company's responsibility

The Anarchist Cookbook
Freedonia Productions, LLC

Writer/Director: Jordan Susman
Producers: Brown, Susman, Greenspun
Script Dated: April 5, 2001
Budget Dated: 05/21/01
Revision #14

Start Principal Photography: 05/23/01
Complete Prin. Photography: 06/20/01
Dallas Local Location: 24 Days
Dallas Stage: 0 Days
Post Production: 16 Weeks

Acct No	Category Description	Page	Total
803-00	WRITING	1	20,000
805-00	PRODUCER & STAFF	1	72,277
807-00	DIRECTOR & STAFF	1	20,000
809-00	TALENT	1	295,855
810-00	**Total Fringes**	**3**	**42,904**
	Total Above-The-Line		**451,036**
811-00	PRODUCTION STAFF	3	95,440
813-00	CAMERA	5	75,543
814-00	ART DEPARTMENT	5	23,908
816-00	SPECIAL EFFECTS	5	1,800
817-00	SET OPERATIONS	6	66,032
819-00	ELECTRICAL	7	47,004
821-00	SET DRESSING	7	55,070
823-00	ACTION PROPS	8	24,228
825-00	PICT. VEH. & ANIMALS	8	6,100
829-00	EXTRA TALENT	8	40,820
831-00	COSTUME	9	39,395
833-00	MAKEUP & HAIR	9	18,500
835-00	SOUND	10	25,926
837-00	LOCATION	10	160,394
839-00	TRANSPORTATION	11	128,577
841-00	FILM & LAB	12	88,062
843-00	TESTS	13	1,100
847-00	SECOND UNIT	13	1,250
849-00	**Total Fringes**	**13**	**79,775**
	Total Production		**978,924**
851-00	EDITING & PROJECTION	13	78,500
853-00	MUSIC	14	75,000
855-00	SOUND (POSTPRODUCTION)	14	105,000
857-00	POSTPRODUCTION FILM & LAB	14	51,194
859-00	TITLES & OPTICALS	14	10,000
860-00	**Total Fringes**	**14**	**7,534**
	Total Post Production		**327,228**
861-00	INSURANCE	14	27,500
862-00	PUBLICITY	14	500
865-00	GENERAL EXPENSES	14	9,000
	Total Other		**37,000**
	Contingency : 10.0%		179,419
	Bond Fee : 3.0%		53,826
	Total Above-The-Line		**451,036**
	Total Below-The-Line		**1,343,152**
	Total Above and Below-The-Line		**1,794,188**
	Grand Total		**2,027,432**

Fig. 16.1. ***The Anarchist Cookbook*** budget top sheet with contractual charges added.

is to make sure that a film is delivered. The bond company does this by examining your schedule, your budget, and your choice of personnel. The bond company will decide if your shooting schedule is realistic, your budget is adequate to do what you want to do, and if you have personnel on the film with enough experience to know how to complete the film. If your production fails any of these criteria, they will refuse to bond the picture and the bank will deny you your financing.

Let's say that you passed inspection and the bond company agrees to guarantee the film. The bond company will then keep close watch over the production throughout the prep and shooting phases. It does this by requiring daily call sheets and production reports, weekly cost report estimates, and an occasional visit to the set. If you should begin to fall behind schedule, the guarantor will want to know how you are going to complete the film on time. You will do this by increasing your pace or eliminating scenes. If you should begin to stray over budget, the guarantor will want to know how you are going to make up the overage. You will do this by eliminating or reducing other areas of the budget. The bond company does not care how you do it; it is just guaranteeing the completion of the film.

Now we come to the contingency, which has been entered as a contractual charge. It is added to the budget for the sole use of the bond company if it should need to step in and complete the film. It is not there for the benefit of the filmmakers. If, for whatever reason, the bond company determines that the film is in danger of not being completed on budget and on schedule, it will take over the production, and it will complete the picture. The bond company has the power to fire whomever it needs to fire and replace whomever it needs to replace to make sure that the film is completed. Typically, among the candidates for replacement are the producer(s), the director, the director of photography, the assistant director and occasionally, but less likely, an actor or two.

It should be mentioned that bond companies would rather not have to step in. They would rather you finished your project on time and on budget. To that end, most will be more than willing to offer advice and support to make sure you succeed. They will cajole, threaten and coerce you into staying on the straight and narrow. Nevertheless, they are in business to make money, and they don't make money by letting films fail. Your film will be made, good or bad, with you or without you.

So, should you employ a guarantor? Only if your investors or financiers require it. To understand why, let's look at the consequence of adding a film bond to *The Anarchist Cookbook* budget. If you compare the bottom line of the top sheet in figure 16.2 with the top sheet of the original budget in figure 16.1, you will see immediately that the budget has grown from $1,994,188 to $2,027,432, an increase of $33,244. This will preclude our being able to work under the SAG low-budget agreement and will increase our cast expenses. Looking further, notice that since the contingency and bond fee represent money that is not available to make the film. We actually have only $1,793,187 available to make the film (the total of Above and

Below-the-Line) as opposed to $1,994,188, a decrease of $200,001. That is $200,001 that the audience will never see up on the screen. The cost of a bond is actually much greater than the 3%–6% of the budget that will be charged as a fee.

If you must bond your film in order to get it financed, try to exclude as much as possible from the calculations of the fee and contingency. For example, the script costs of $20,000 could have been excluded since that is a one-time fee and presumably the script is already owned by the production company. If the bond company had to take over the film, they would not have to rebuy the script and therefore it can be argued that the script cost should not enter into the bond calculations. There may be other expenses that you can successfully negotiate to have excluded, such as producers' fees or insurance premiums.

The Chart of Accounts

The account numbers I referred to earlier in this chapter are listed on the top sheet down the left side of the page. These are known as the major account numbers. They, along with their respective detail accounts, are known as the chart of accounts. The *Anarchist* budget uses the Universal Studios chart of accounts. Each studio has its own chart of accounts that ties into its broader accounting system. As an independent, I could have used any number of different charts of accounts. I chose Universal Studios' chart of accounts because I was familiar with it and it seemed to fit the project well.

Critical Assumptions

Often a page of critical assumptions precedes the top sheet. *The Anarchist Cookbook* budget did not have a page of critical assumptions, but an example of a critical assumption page from another film can be seen in figure 16.3. This sheet lists various assumptions upon which the underlying budget is based, such as the important dates of the picture, a summary of the schedule, and the rates at which the extras were budgeted. Next are a series of five notes explaining how the work week will be structured, that certain cast are not yet included, as well as living expenses for the cast, on what basis the crew will be paid, and which union agreements will be entered into. Below that is a list of people who will be housed "on location," with the understanding that all other crew will be from the area where the film will be shot.

A critical assumption sheet is often used to give a quick understanding of the critical factors that went into calculating the bottom line. Investors and financiers understand that if these assumptions were altered, it would change the bottom line.

Critical Assumptions
***The Loser* Budget 1.6** 2/23/2004

Based on script dated October 10, 2003.
Shot entirely on location in and around Wilmington, North Carolina.

Schedule:

Pre-production	3/14/2004-6/4/2004
Commence Principal Photography	6/7/2004
Wrap Principal Photography	8/9/2004
Post Production - LA	18 Weeks
Delivery	12/13/2004

Production Days:

45 Days	Shoot North Carolina (9 x 5 day weeks)
1 Day	Holiday (Independence Day)
46 Days	Total Days

Extras Budgeted:

Non-Union Standins:	180 Man/Days	$132/12 hrs
Non-Union Extras:	4,141 Man/Days	$87.50/12 hrs

Notes:

1. Schedule is in 5-day weeks.
2. Principal Cast not yet budgeted. All other cast budgeted at scale + 10% except for the parts of 8. Skeeter Burke, 10. Mr. Sanchez, and 27. Hot Blonde.
3. No living or travel expenses are budgeted yet for cast.
4. Crew is non-union with their rates based on the Southeastern Area Standards Agreement.
5. Unions: DGA, SAG, WGA

LA Personnel budgeted to be housed on Location:

Mr. Resola - Producer
Mr. Brown - Line Producer
Director
Production Designer
Director of Photography
"A" Camera Operator
Editor

Fig. 16.3. An example of a critical assumption sheet.

17

Methods of Entry

Column Headings

Before we get into the detail of the budget, we should discuss the types of entries we will be seeing. Most budget entries fall under one of three types: flat fees, weekly salaries, and hourly employees. Each of these differs slightly in the way the budget columns are used. The columns are labeled across the top of each detail page as shown here.

Acct No	Description	Amount	Units	X	Rate	Subtotal	Total
803-00 WRITING							
803-01	Writers' Salaries						

fig. 17.1. Budget column headings.

These headings are mostly self-explanatory, but they deserve a brief discussion. The *Acct No* (account number) is a three-digit number from the chart of accounts, such as "803," that is assigned to a particular charge. The detail numbers that follow the hyphen as in "803-51" are fairly consistent from major account to major account. For example, subaccount 51 is used for purchases in each of the accounts: account 803-51 would be used for purchases concerned with the script writing and 823-51 would be used for prop purchases. The *Description* indicates what expense the account is covering. The *Amount* is usually a number indicating how long something or someone will be used for, or how much of something will be used. *Units* denote days, weeks, feet, hours, etc. Occasionally the word "Allow" will be seen in this column. "Allow" just means that a lump sum has been allowed for an expense without having detailed exactly how much or how long it is needed. The **×** column is simply used as a multiplier. The *Rate* is the rate per unit based on the units noted in the *Units* column. When the *Amount* is multiplied by the **×** column and then multiplied by the *Rate* column, the result is placed in the *Subtotal* column. At the end of each detail account, a total of all the subtotals in that particular detail account is entered in the *Total* column.

Flat Fee Entries

Flat fees are the simplest type of entry. In a flat fee entry, a "1" is entered into the *Amount* column, the *Unit* is "Allow" or "Fee" or "Flat" (see fig. 17.2). The cost of the item being allocated for the entire show is entered under *Rate* and then the *Subtotal* is entered which is equal to the *Rate*.

Acct No	Description	Amount	Units	X	Rate	Subtotal	Total
803-00 WRITING							
803-01	Writers' Salaries						
	Jordan Susman	1	Fee	1	20,000	20,000	
	Total						20,000
Account Total for 803-00							**20,000**

Fig. 17.2. A flat fee entry.

Weekly Salaries

In a weekly salary or weekly rate entry, the number of weeks is entered in the *Amount* column, the *Units* are, by definition, weeks, the multiplier (×) is usually "1" but can be greater if more than one of the item is being used, and the *Rate* is the rate the item costs per week (see fig. 17.3).

Acct No	Description	Amount	Units	X	Rate	Subtotal	Total
809-01	Principal Cast						
	Cast #1	4	Weeks	1	8,750	35,000	
	Cast #2	4	Weeks	1	6,000	24,000	
	Cast #3	3.17	Weeks	1	10,095	32,001	

Fig. 17.3. Weekly salary entries.

Employees or equipment hired on a daily basis are done in the same way except the units are days and the rate is the daily rate.

Hourly Employees

Hourly employee entries are the most complicated since the number of pay-hours the employee will be paid for in a week must be calculated. Pay-hours are work hours with overtime added. To explain this more clearly, let's use an example from the *Anarchist* budget: the driver of the camera truck. The contract with the Dallas Teamsters stipulated that we would pay the straight hourly wage for the first eight hours of each day. Hours beyond eight hours would be paid at an overtime rate of one and a half times the base hourly rate. The following chart demonstrates what this means in terms of pay-hours:

Worked Hrs.		Overtime Multiplier		Pay-Hours	
8	×	1	=	8	
4	×	1.5	=	6	
12	Work Hrs.		=	14	Total Pay-Hours for 1 Day

As this chart shows, the first 8 hours of each day will be paid at the straight base rate. In this case, worked hours equal pay-hours. The next 4 hours will be paid at 1½ times the base hourly rate. Rather than multiply the rate times 1½, we multiply the work hours which gives us the number of pay-hours. Working 4 hours at the overtime rate of 1½ times the base pay rate is equivalent to working 6 hours at the straight base pay rate. This chart shows that working a 12-hour day with the overtime provisions in force is the equivalent of working 14 hours at the straight time rate. How many pay-hours does this equal in one 5-day week? We multiply the daily pay-hours times 5 days.

14	Total Pay-Hours for 1 Day
× 5	Days
70	Total Pay-Hours for a 5-Day Week

This means that if our driver works five 12-hour days, or 60 hours, he will actually be paid for 70 hours due to the overtime provisions of the contract.

The contract with the Dallas Teamsters further stipulated that a driver who worked on Saturday would be paid at the overtime rate of 1½ times the base rate for the entire day. In as much as the production would be working a 6-day week, we needed to know how many pay-hours we would be paying. We can use the same charts to compute the effect of the additional day.

Worked Hrs.		Overtime Multiplier		Pay-Hours	
				70	Pay-Hrs. for a 5-Day Week
12	×	1.5	=	18	Pay-Hrs. for a 6th Day
				88	Total Pay-Hrs. for a 6-Day Week

We now know that if we work our driver for six 12-hour days, or a total of 72 hours, we will pay the driver as if he or she worked 88 hours. We expected the drivers to work 12 hours each day during the prep and wrap periods, but what about when we are shooting? Our plan is to work a 12-hour day when we are shooting. This means that from the initial call time, to when all the equipment is put back in the trucks and the crew leaves the set, should be equal to 12 hours. The drivers will actually be working longer. They will be expected to have the trucks parked and open in the morning when the crew arrives, and they will need to drive the trucks to a parking lot at the end of the day. This means that they will be working a longer day than most of the crew. To be safe, let's plan on a 14-hour day for the drivers. How many pay-hours will this be equal to? We can use our same chart:

Worked Hrs.		Overtime Multiplier		Pay-Hours	
8	×	1	=	8	
6	×	1.5	=	9	
14			=	17	Total Pay-Hrs. for 1 Day
			×	5	Days
				85	Total Pay-Hrs. for a 5-Day Week
14	×	1.5	=	21	Pay Hrs. for the 6th day.
				106	Total Pay-Hrs. for a 6-Day Week

In the above chart, we have changed the hours worked so that they total 14 hours per day. This shows us that a driver working six 14-hour days, or 84 hours, will be paid the equivalent of 106 hours times the base hourly rate. In other words, the driver will be paid 106 pay-hours per week.

Now that we know how many pay-hours our driver will be earning, let's look at how the entry would appear in the budget (fig. 17.4). On the prep line, the employee will be working 0.2 weeks or the rough equivalent of one day. As we have seen above, the prep weeks will earn the drivers 88 pay-

Acct No	Description	Amount	Units	X	Rate	Subtotal	Total
839-03	Studio Drivers						
	Camera						
	Prep	0.2	Weeks	88	18.96	333	
	Shoot	4	Weeks	106	18.96	8,039	
	Wrap	0.2	Weeks	88	18.96	333	
	Holiday	1	Day	8	18.96	151	
						8,858	

Fig. 17.4. How an hourly employee, the camera truck driver, would be entered into the budget.

hours per week. The figure "88" is inserted into the multiplier column. The *Rate* column shows the driver's hourly rate. The *Subtotal* shows the result of multiplying the number of weeks (0.2) times the number of pay-hours per week (88) times the hourly rate ($18.96). Notice that the pay-hours per week have been raised to 106 during the shoot weeks.

18

Above-the-Line

This section of the budget covers most of the higher paying positions including the producer, the director, and the actors. On a union picture, most of the above-the-line employees are covered by guilds rather than unions, and most work on a flat fee or weekly based salary rather than an hourly wage.

Although a guild is a collective bargaining unit, it differs from a union in that it does not function as a hiring hall. In other words, you cannot call up the Writers Guild and say, "I need seven writers tomorrow at 6AM" as you can with the Grip union or the Teamsters union. You can ask the guild for a list of members who are available for work, and get their phone numbers or their agents' phone numbers.

800-00 Story & Other Rights

The Anarchist Cookbook was an original script written directly for the screen. It was not based on any other work.* (Although the book, *The Anarchist Cookbook*, was a major prop in the film, it is merely a collection of recipes for various nefarious concoctions and sets of instructions on how to make traps with punji stakes, etc. It should be noted that much of the information in the book is inaccurate.) Therefore, there is no money allocated to

* The production company's parent, Anarchy Movie Partners,LLC, did enter into an agreement with the publisher of the book, Barricade Books, for use of the title.

this account. If we were doing a picture based on Stephen King's latest novel, you would put the rights payment to Mr. King in this account as a flat fee entry. Likewise, if this were a film based on the life of an actual person, there would be a fee for that person, or his or her estate, entered here. These rights fees are completely negotiable and can run from a token payment of a dollar up to millions of dollars.

803-00 Writing

All script costs go here. The writer is getting a $20,000 flat fee for the script. Other costs that might go here are the writer's living expenses if he or she is housed away from home, typists, copying expenses, and research done by the writer. Each of those items would have its own sub account such as 803-30 for the living expenses.

803-01 Writers' Salaries

How much do you pay for a script? It is completely negotiable if the Writers Guild of America (WGA) is not involved. If the writer is a member of the WGA, then the producing company must become a signatory to the WGA contract in order to buy from that writer. The current minimums for a theatrical script for a picture budgeted under $5,000,000, written by a WGA writer (effective November 1, 2005 to October 31, 2006) are:

- Screenplay, including treatment $47,999
- Screenplay, excluding treatment $29,993

Of course, a WGA writer is always free to negotiate a payment higher than the minimums stated above. Scripts for studio films typically run in the low to mid six figures. Some scripts even sell for a million dollars or more.

803-04 Secretaries

At one time, writers wrote in longhand on yellow pads or they typed manuscripts on typewriters. Both the yellow pad pages and the typed pages were very messy and full of corrections. The writer's secretary then took these messy manuscript pages and typed them into a standard script format. Any writer's secretaries' wages would go here. If hired, the secretary is typically paid on a weekly basis which today runs around $750 to $1,000 per week. The writer, Mr. Susman, was his own secretary so no money was allocated here.

Due to the almost universal usage of computers and script writing software, writers are rarely given secretaries today. Most writers work at home and deliver their scripts on a computer disk in a file format that can be read by the producing company. The software takes care of putting the script into the standard script format.

803-05 Story Consultants

Let's say that you were writing a script about the US Navy's Top Gun Fighter School, and you employed an alumnus of the program to make sure that you had the proper flavor and procedures in all the written scenes. That person would be a story consultant and his salary would go here. This is different from the rights payments that would go into account 801 since you are not writing this person's story, but using him instead for verisimilitude. We did not use a story consultant on *Anarchist*.

Later in account 811, we will come across a similar line item under Tech Advisor. The difference is that the Story Consultant is used in the writing of a script while the Tech Advisor is used during the actual filming. There are no set prices for this position; it is completely negotiable.

803-08 Script Printing

This would be more accurate if it were called "Script Copying." Normally, a master copy of the script is printed out on a laser printer and then copies are made on a copy machine. Anticipate spending about $5 per script copy. In addition, there will be script page revisions that would be charged here. These will run about four cents per page. There is no money allocated here in the *Anarchist* budget because these costs were folded into the Office Equipment Rental costs in account 837-56.

803-30 Travel & Living Expense

If it were necessary to house the writer on location, his airfare, hotel, and per diem expenses would be coded here. Per diem expenses are monies given to an individual for daily expenses such as food, laundry, etc. In some charts of accounts, all of the above-the-line travel and living expenses are put into one account which is usually listed at the end of the Above-the-Line section.

The amount paid for per diem is open to negotiation. On high-budget films, above-the-line per diems can range from the SAG minimum of $60 per day to several thousand per week, depending on whether or not the production company is paying hotel expenses separately, what city the person is being housed in, and who the person is. Tom Cruise in London is going to command a great deal more money per week for living expenses than an unknown actor in Dothan, Georgia. On a low-budget film, especially a non-union low-budget film, you should negotiate the lowest possible amount that is fair. "Fair" means that the amount should pay for the person's reasonable expenses. It shouldn't cost him or her money to work on your film.

When budgeting airfares, writers are flown first class on pictures made under the WGA agreement. On a low-budget film, if you need them on location, they fly however you can get them to fly. Whatever class of airfare you are using, budget the amount that a ticket would cost if you called up the airline right now to buy a ticket to fly to your location tomorrow. In other words, do not budget cut-rate fares unless you are certain of being able to get them. If you book tickets far in advance in order to lock in a lower rate, I guarantee that the travel date will change and you will be paying penalty fees to the airline to change the ticket. Since Mr. Susman was also a producer on *Anarchist*, his travel expenses were covered under 805-30.

Hotels will often give you a generous discount if you can guarantee them a certain number of rooms over a specified period. *Always* ask for a discount.

803-40 Research

These are expenses that your writer may run up in researching the story. They can run from the cost of a few books, to a trip to Rome to see which way the Trevi Fountain faces. Discuss this with your writer before you hire him or her. Be clear who is responsible for what expenses. If you are paying for some research, make sure that the limits of what you are willing to pay for are clear. There were no covered research expenses on *Anarchist*.

803-51 Purchase & Supplies

Ink cartridges, paper, cover stock, brass brads, etc. Mr. Susman payed for his own writing supplies.

803-56 Rentals

Computer, copy machine, printer, software, etc. Mr. Susman provided his own equipment.

803-60 Miscellaneous

You will see miscellaneous accounts throughout this budget and other charts of accounts. Try not to use them unless you have something specific to cover that is not covered in any of the other detail accounts. If you have an item in your budget that reads "Miscellaneous—$5,000," you are sure to be questioned by any knowledgeable person reading it.

"$5,000? For what?"

"Um, for miscellaneous."

"Yes, I can see that, but what specifically are you anticipating?"

"Um, you know, stuff."

"What kind of stuff?"

"Um, unanticipated miscellaneous stuff?"

However, if your writer is only able to work while hooked up to an IV dripping Red Bull directly into his bloodstream, you could legitimately put something like the following into the Miscellaneous account:

803-60 IV hook-up for Red Bull drip........................$2,752

805-00 Producer & Staff

This account covers the producers, their staffs, and their expenses.

Title Inflation

Variants of the producing title seem to proliferate like acne on a teenager. They are "executive producer," "co-producer," "associate producer," "supervising producer," "line producer," "creative producer," and "assistant producer." All of these titles are used so loosely that they have almost lost their meaning. I will attempt to clear the fog.

In the early days of Hollywood, the producer was the person who was in charge over the whole course of the production. It would start with the producer working closely with the writer to develop the script. The producer would also hire the director and the other key members of the crew. It was the producer's job to shepherd the film through the prep, shooting, and post production phases. This person had to create a synergy among the film's various feuding forces in order to bring them together into a coherent and unified whole that would result in a successful picture that people would pay money to see.

Occasionally, an experienced producer would hire other producers to do the actual day-to-day, hands-on work while confining his or her own efforts to making the important deals on the pictures and securing their financing. When this person had several pictures going at once, each of which had an assigned producer who would keep him informed, then our godfather of production would often take the title of "Executive Producer." Today, television preserves this meaning of "executive producer" as exemplified by David E. Kelly (*The Law Firm*, *Boston Legal*, *Ally McBeal*) or Stephen Bochco (*NYPD Blue*, *Blind Justice*, *City of Angels*).

As films became more complicated to produce, producers would hire people to help. These aides might be given the title of "assistant producer" or "associate producer." If the aide was more experienced, he or she might be given the title of "co-producer" which would indicate someone of a status closer to the producer's own status. Currently in television, the associate producer is often the person who oversees the post production process.

Eventually, producers began to specialize. A producer might be very successful in finding story material, working with writers, making deals, and securing financing while not knowing the first thing about how one makes a film. These producers, while keeping the title of "producer," were categorized as "creative producers." Creative producers needed someone to handle the nuts and bolts of picture making. Thus was born the line producer. The line producer was usually an experienced production manager who was given a producing title in order to boost his or her authority, and often to soften any demands for a high raise in salary. On feature films, line producers have been credited as almost anything including "executive producer," "co-producer," and "associate producer." Sometimes the line producer will also be the unit production manager or the first assistant director.

In medieval times, philosophers debated about how many angels could dance on the head of a pin. How many producers does it take to make a motion picture? This is not supposed to be a philosophical question but it sometimes has a very surreal answer. The Academy of Motion Picture Arts and Sciences (who bring you the Oscar awards program each year,) recognizes only three producers per picture, regardless of how many can dance on the head of a pin. They instituted this rule recently when pictures were coming out with eight, ten, or more producing titles. Most of those producers had very little to do with the making of the film. Usually the actual hands-on activities of producing the film fall to no more than one to three people. Since the producer title is not covered by any union contract, it became misused by dealmakers who would give the title away in lieu of money or as an incentive.

The Producers Guild of America (PGA) has developed guidelines in an attempt to bring some order to the chaos by publishing definitions of the various producer titles. The PGA defines the producer of a film as an individual who receives the "produced by" credit.

> *The "Produced By" credit is given to the person(s) most completely responsible for a film's production. Subject to the control of the Owner (see Rules of Arbitration, section I.B), the "Produced By" would have significant decision-making authority over a majority of the producing functions across the four phases of a motion picture's production. Those phases are: Development; Pre-Production; Production; and Post Production & Marketing.**

The PGA then lists specific duties that the producer would be involved with during each of the aforementioned "four phases of a motion picture's production:"

- *Within the development process, the "Produced By" will typically conceive of the underlying premise of the production, or select the material. S/he also will select the project's writer, secure the necessary rights and initial financing, and supervise the development process.*

- *In pre-production, the "Produced By" will typically select the key members of the creative team, including the director, co-pro-*

---

*Producers Guild of America, "Producers Code of Credits," *Membership Roster 2004-2005*, 18.

ducer, cinematographer, unit production manager, production designer, and principal cast. The "Produced By" also will participate in location scouting, and approve the final shooting script, production schedule, and budget.

- *During production, the "Produced By" will supervise the day-to-day operations of the producing team, providing continuous, personal, and usually "on-set" consultation with the director and other key creative personnel. S/he also will approve weekly cost reports, and continue to serve as the primary point of contact for financial and distribution entities.*

- *For the last phase, post production & marketing, the "Produced By" is expected to consult personally with post production personnel, including the editor, composer, and visual effects staff. S/he is expected to consult with all creative and financial personnel on the answer print or edited master, and usually is involved in a meaningful fashion with the financial and distribution entities concerning the marketing and distribution plans for the motion picture in both domestic and foreign markets.**

The PGA has also issued guidelines for the issuance of all other producing titles as well. Based on the following, it appears that the line producer would receive the co-producer credit.

CO-PRODUCER

1. *The credit of Co-Producer is to be granted to the individual who reports directly to the individual(s) receiving "Produced By" credit on the theatrical motion picture.*
2. *The Co-Producer is the single individual who has the primary responsibility for the logistics of the production, from pre-production through completion of production; all Department Heads report directly to the Co-Producer.*

EXECUTIVE PRODUCER

1. *The credit of Executive Producer only shall apply to an individual who has made a significant contribution to the motion picture and who additionally qualifies under one of two categories:*
   a. *Having secured an essential and proportionately significant*

---

*Ibid.

part (no less than 25%) of the financing for the motion picture; and/or

b. Having made a significant contribution to the development of the literary property, typically including the securement of the underlying rights to the material on which the motion picture is based.

VISUAL EFFECTS PRODUCER

1. *The Visual Effects Producer reports directly to the individual(s) receiving Produced By credit on the theatrical motion picture.*
2. *The Visual Effects Producer has responsibility for the creative and business aspects of the motion picture in collaboration with the visual effects supervisor, director and the individual(s) receiving Produced By credit.*

ASSOCIATE PRODUCER

1. *The Associate Producer credit is granted solely on the decision of the individual receiving the Produced By credit, and is to be granted sparingly and only for those individuals who are delegated significant producing functions.*
2. *The Associate Producer is responsible for performing one or more functions delegated to him/her by the individual receiving the Produced By credit and the Co-Producer.*

PRODUCTION SUPERVISOR

1. *The Production Supervisor reports directly to the Co-Producer.*
2. *The Production Supervisor is responsible for the coordination and oversight of the production units assigned to him/her by the Co-Producer, including all off-set logistics, day-to-day production implementation, locations, facilities, equipment, budget schedules and personnel.*

POST PRODUCTION SUPERVISOR

1. *The Post Production Supervisor reports directly to the Co-Producer.*
2. *The Post Production Supervisor is responsible for the coordination and oversight of the entire post production process, but not primarily as a production company executive.* *

---

*Ibid. 20-21.

Today when the Academy Award is announced for best picture, who goes up on the stage to collect it? Only someone who has the "Produced By" credit on the picture, and the Academy will only allow up to three individuals to be eligible for this honor. Sometimes this has caused the producing title to be taken by the most powerful people involved with the picture, who may or may not have had anything to do with the actual making of the picture.

The producing fee is completely negotiable, ranging from a minimum fee to millions of dollars. Typically this fee is paid over the course of a film in installments. If the producer has worked during the development of the script, he or she will be paid a development fee prior to pre-production. The balance of the producing fee would be allocated through a typical payment schedule as follows: 20% of the fee spread over the prep period and paid in weekly installments, 60% spread over the shooting period and paid in weekly installments, 10% at the delivery of the director's cut, and 10% upon final delivery. This type of payment schedule gives the producer incentive to hurry the picture along to completion and allows the studio to cut their losses if the picture is cancelled at some point along the way.

805-01 Executive Producer

See the discussion above. *The Anarchist Cookbook* did not have an executive producer budgeted. Executive producers' salaries are very much negotiable and range from a token payment to millions of dollars.

805-02 Producers

The Anarchist Cookbook had a team of three producers led by its writer-director, Jordan Susman. All three were involved in securing financing, casting, and production of the film.

805-03 Associate Producers

There were no budgeted associate producers on *Anarchist*.

805-04 Secretaries

805-06 Assistants

Usually a producer has an assistant or secretary or sometimes both. Since this film had such a low-budget, we did without. With a larger budget, I would have expected to pay around $800 per week for an assistant or secretary.

805-30 Travel & Living Expense

No hotel was budgeted because the director's family owned an apartment building where we located our production offices. This allowed us to house the producers, the production designer, and the editor for free. This obviously was a large savings to the picture.

The per diem allowance was $30 per day. If you can't feed yourself in Dallas for $210 per week when you have a kitchen available, you have very expensive tastes. Mr. Susman did not take a per diem allowance.

The airfares are for tickets between Los Angeles and Dallas. The costs are so low because we did book the tickets in advance and we did get cut rate fares and simply did not change our plans. The one time that we had to change a ticket (a cast member's), we did end up paying a penalty. Another strategy was to use people's frequent flyer miles to buy some tickets.

805-50 Independent Producer Overhead

We originally had $10,000 budgeted here but later removed it in order to get down to under $2 million. The $10,000 was going to be used for operating expenses for the producing company. These expenses were covered eventually by savings we realized in the shooting period.

805-51 Purchase & Supplies

Videos, crew gifts, and anything else the producers buy. The *Anarchist* producers simply decided not to use this account.

805-56 Rentals

Mobile trailer on set, or anything else that the producers rent or is rented for them. The trailer is not necessarily a luxury. The producer needs an office on set where he or she can have meetings, make phone calls, and conduct business in privacy. A mobile trailer works well for this. On *Anarchist*, we did not feel we could afford a trailer so we held our meetings and made our phone calls in a borrowed room at that day's location or simply set up a few chairs under a tree not far from the set.

805-57 Wrap Party

In the past, this was a party given by the producer, or director, or both to show their appreciation to the crew. It has since been institutionalized and is usually attended by many people who are invited for various political reasons. It has become a running joke among the crews that they know very few people at the cast and crew wrap party. However, this can be an excellent way to show appreciation to someone who has helped the production.

Although we could not justify budgeting any money for a wrap party when we were struggling to get to an acceptable bottom line, we did manage to scrape together a small party in appreciation of the great job that the *Anarchist* crew did.

805-58 Entertainment

This is not what it sounds like. This money is used by the producer to take various people to lunch, dinner, etc. Sometimes a deal is easier to make if you have fed someone. Obviously, we did not entertain much.

805-60 Miscellaneous Expense.

You know how I feel about this. (See page 159.)

807-00 Director & Staff

The director is the captain of the ship. He may be Captain Bligh or Horatio Nelson, he may be brilliant, or he may be a fool, but he is the boss. The entire point of the budget and everyone mentioned in it is to help the director achieve his visualization of the film. Orson Welles described a film company as the biggest electric train set you could ever want. Imagine having a company of 50 to 200 people dedicated to achieving your vision of a film!

With this enormous power must come some care. Remember the old adage to "be careful of what you wish for because you might get it"? Sometimes a director's offhand remark becomes an unintentional order. I am reminded of a story about George Lucas on *Return of the Jedi*. Although Mr. Lucas was the producer and not the director of the film, it will serve to illustrate the point. It was the custom of the staff to accompany Mr. Lucas each day from our offices in the Kerner building to the projection room at ILM* next door to see dailies. We would leave the Kerner building, cross the parking lot, and enter ILM through the model shop. I always found the walk through the model shop as interesting as the dailies. It was fun to see the Death Star in the process of construction and various spaceships in different stages of creation. Since George Lucas is an extremely nice and considerate person, he felt bad about interrupting the model makers with our parade through their shop each day. On one trip through the shop he said, "Gee, I'm sorry we interrupt you guys every day. It's a shame there isn't a hall here so we wouldn't disturb you."

When we opened the door to the model shop the next day, it opened into a newly enclosed hall that went down one side of the model shop and completely shielded the model builders from our walk-through. They thought they were doing what Mr. Lucas wanted.

On another occasion on *Return of the Jedi* during the filming of the Ewok Forest in northern California, I heard someone on the radio who was at the top of the forested hill we were shooting at say, "George wants the pickup at the top of the hill RIGHT NOW!" I think the pickup truck broke the land speed record getting to the top of the hill. What the driver didn't know was that it was George Mauricio, the efficient and hard-working craft service key, and not George Lucas who needed the truck.

A movie company is not a democracy. Even the nicest directors and the best-intentioned crewmembers need to know this. On *Spaceballs*, I had just introduced the stunt coordinator, Dick Warlock, to director Mel Brooks, on Dick's first day on the show. Mel Brooks is a charming man

*Industrial Light & Magic—Lucas's visual effects company.

and he made Dick feel completely at home and comfortable—too comfortable. We were shooting a scene that involved the late John Candy, and John was having trouble with the delivery of a line. Dick watched John's efforts for a awhile, and sensing Mel's frustration, thought he could offer John a tip on how to get the line to come out right. After Mel cut the scene once again, Dick started to go over to John Candy while saying, "Hold on, Mel, I think I can do something."

"Stop!" Mel said. "This isn't the Directors Club! We don't all get a turn here!"

There can only be one director, unless you have a very tight and predetermined team such as Joel and Ethan Coen (*Fargo*), or Bobby and Peter Farrelly (*There's Something About Mary*). Ideally, the director has a clear idea of what he wants. Sometimes he doesn't. When that happens, the producer, production manager, assistant director, and department heads need to preserve the director's choices as long as possible.

807-01 Director

The director's fee is entered here. Typically it is a flat fee for the picture. In the *Anarchist* budget, the director was paid $20,000, about 1% of the budget. This was for an official preparation period of 8 weeks, 4 weeks shoot, and about 16 weeks post.

As stated earlier, the DGA rules at the time that *Anarchist* was made stated that any picture with a budget over $1,500,000 was a high-budget picture. Under this definition, *The Anarchist Cookbook* would be a high-budget film. As of July 1, 2004, the weekly salary of a director under the DGA contract is $13,358 per week. In addition, that director would be guaranteed 13 weeks of work (2 weeks prep, 10 weeks shoot, and 1 week cutting). Paying a director at scale under these conditions would mean paying the director $173,654. On *The Anarchist Cookbook*, this would have amounted to almost 9% of the budget.

Let's look at a real high-budget movie, say in the $100 million range. On this type of film, the director would be paid typically four to six million. Let's be generous and make it six million. That amounts to 6% of the budget. If huge, hundred million dollar productions that are paying huge over scale fees amounting to several million dollars are allocating 6% of their budgets to the director, does it make any sense for a small $2 million dollar production to allocate 9% of its budget to the director?

Since most independent and low-budget films are shot in far fewer than eight to ten weeks, and given that every dollar is precious in a budget that

Budget level	Director's Minimum	AD/UPM Minimums
Level 1 $1 million or less	No minimum salary	33% of scale. No production fee.
Level 2 >$1 million and <$2.5 million	No minimum salary	50% of scale. Production fee = $25/ week
Level 3 > $2.5 million < $3.5 million	$70,000	60% of scale. Production fee = $200/ week for ADs & UPMs, $150/week for key 2nd Ads.
Level 4A >$3.5 million < $5 million	75% of scale	70% of scale. Production fee = 70% of scale
Level 4B > $5 million < $7 million	75 % of scale	80% of scale. Prod. fee = 80% of scale.

Table 18.1. A summary of the Directors Guild new Low-Budget Agreement as of 2005.

small, there does not seem to be any compelling reason to sign with the DGA under this scenario. Pictures in this range are often written, directed, and produced by the same person. This person stands to benefit greatly if the picture is a success critically or financially. Limited resources are better allocated to putting a finer picture on the screen.

In recognition of these realities, the DGA has adopted a new low-budget agreement that provides breaks for films of four different budget levels. This new agreement has made it much more affordable for low-budget filmmakers to take advantage of the skill and experience of the DGA members, including directors, assistant directors (ADs), and unit production managers (UPMs). Table 18.1 outlines the pay rates for each level.

In addition to these breaks in rates, ADs and UPMs do not receive vacation pay, unworked holiday pay, dinner allowances, or extended workday payments at any of the levels. Completion of assignment pay is due only at levels 3 and 4. Other benefits filmmakers can receive under this agreement can be found at the DGA web site: **http://www.dga.org/index2.php3** . If your film has a budget of less than $500,000, you may be able to negotiate terms that are even more favorable. The DGA says that they will consider films under $500,000 on a case by case basis.

807-03 Dialogue Coach

In *Robin Hood: Men in Tights*, Mel Brooks makes a joke of the accent Kevin Costner used in *Robin Hood: Prince of Thieves*. Mel has Prince John (Richard Lewis) ask Robin (Cary Elwes) "And why should the people listen to you?"

Robin replies, "Because, unlike some other Robin Hoods, I can speak with an English accent."

If your Robin Hood does not actually have a proper English accent as Cary Elwes did, a dialogue coach can help. Dialogue coaches have helped American actors achieve respectable British accents (Gwyneth Paltrow in *Shakespeare in Love*), British actors achieve respectable American accents (Minnie Driver in *Good Will Hunting*), and earthbound actors achieve alien inflections (various Goa'uld in *SG1*, the *Stargate* episodic series). In addition to coaching actors on how to speak with various unfamiliar accents, dialogue coaches run lines and work on readings with actors.

There is no set rate for these services; negotiate the best price that you can. Usually it will be on a daily or weekly flat fee, depending on the length of engagement. In the past, I have paid approximately $60 per hour and was charged only for the time that the coach actually worked with the actors or was required on set. There is no dialogue coach in the *Anarchist* budget since all the Texan accents were genuine.

807-04 Secretaries

See the remarks under 805-04 Secretaries.

807-05 Choreographers

You would expect to hire a choreographer on a project with featured dance numbers, but they can also be needed even for scenes in which normal popular dancing is taking place in the background, such as a scene at a high school prom. You cannot assume that all of your extras are skilled dancers. Choreographers can also be useful in teaching an actor how to move in a certain manner whether it be graceful or clumsy. For example, if you are doing a pirate movie and your hero needs to move with a swash-buckling élan, a choreographer can put the swash in his buckle.

Again, there is no set rate for choreographers in that they are not officially covered by any union or guild agreements. Nevertheless, most professional choreographers are members of SAG and if you are signed with SAG, your dancers will be paid under the SAG contract. On a picture covered by the SAG Agreement, you should expect to pay no less than SAG scale for a dancer. Current scale rates for solo dancers were as follows:

Agreement	Daily Rate	Weekly Rate
Standard	$716	$2300
Low-budget	$504	$1621

807-06 Assistants

Not to be confused with the assistant director, the director's assistant is very similar to the assistant listed in the producer's account. As in that account, this position is more of a personal assistant and typically pays around $800 to $1000 per week at the studios. It is unlikely that a low-budget production would find a need for, or could afford someone in this position.

807-30 Travel & Living

The *Anarchist* budget has no money here since the director lived at his parents' home in Dallas during the shoot. His airfare was covered by frequent flyer miles and he decided to forego any per diem payment, preferring to use the money elsewhere in the budget.

On a higher budget picture, the director's per diem and hotel would often be covered by a combined weekly payment in the $1,500 to $2,500 range, depending on the location. On DGA covered pictures, the director must travel first class.

807-51 Purchases & Supplies

Anything that you anticipate that the director might need to purchase such as DVD purchases, books, etc. A small amount of money from a few hundred dollars to maybe $2,500 would suffice, depending on your needs and the size of your budget.

807-56 Rentals

Again, this would include things like DVD rentals, video equipment for his or her office or trailer, etc.

807-58 Entertainment

This would cover a dinner with investors or actors, crew gifts, or even a cappuccino at the local coffee house.

807-60 Miscellaneous

Whatever.

809-00 Talent

This account is often called CAST. As used here, TALENT commonly refers to the speaking roles in a film. This is in contrast to extras or atmosphere players who do not speak. More specifically however, this account includes people whose work would normally be covered under the SAG agreement. The SAG agreement covers performers, stunt performers, stunt coordinators, pilots of aircraft, dancers, and singers.

In addition, under special circumstances, SAG also claims puppeteers. This occurs when a puppeteer becomes a performer by virtue of creating a character. For example, Frank Oz would be covered under the SAG agreement if he were operating Miss Piggy in a film. Miss Piggy is definitely a character created and given life by Mr. Oz's performance. On the other hand, a puppeteer who has been assigned the task of pulling a lever to control the indentation of a bed in which the Invisible Man is reclining on is not creating a character or role, and therefore need not be covered under the SAG agreement (unless the bed becomes a character).

As stated above, when a person appears before the camera and utters a line of dialogue, that person is by definition an actor and covered under the SAG agreement. What about a principal performer who never speaks? An example of this would be *Gigot,* a film released in 1962 with Jackie

Gleason in the title role. The character Gigot is a mute. He never utters a word. Is this role covered under the SAG contract? Absolutely. It is the title role of the picture, it requires great acting abilities, and it is a role in which you would want an experienced and talented actor.

Why all this concern about the SAG agreement in a book which purports to be about low-budget films? It may be that SAG is the only union or guild with which you sign a contract, even though you are making a low-budget film. There a several advantages in signing with SAG: they have reasonable low-budget rates, practically all publicly known actors are members, and their by-laws prevent them from working on non-SAG productions. If you are only using friends and family in your film, and you are not planning to have any SAG members fill any of the roles, then you would not sign with SAG. Nevertheless, if you are planning to try to distribute your film to the public, the first question a distributor is going to ask is, "Who is in it?" Your answer to that question will tell the distributor if he has a chance of selling your film.

If you decide you are going to sign with SAG, the next decision you must make is which contract should you sign? SAG has six separate agreements under which you can hire their members. They have a contract summary on their web site detailing each of these agreements at **http://www.sag.org/sagWebApp/CMS/Content/Public/lowbudget.pdf**. The agreement that you qualify for will depend on the budget (i.e. negative cost) of your picture, the number of shooting days, and the manner of exhibition of the picture.

Although most of the agreements list a maximum amount for your budget, this can be extended if you meet certain diversity in casting requirements. These criteria are listed on the web site under the Low-Budget Agreement. They are as follows:

1. Fifty percent of the cast must be drawn from the following four groups: a) women; b) people over 60 years old; c) people who are disabled as defined by the Americans with Disabilities Act; and d) people of color.

2. Twenty percent of all actor workdays on the picture must be worked by people of color. People of color are those whose ethnic heritage is Asian/Pacific Islander, Black, Latino/Hispanic, and Native American.

Table 18.2 summarizes the requirements and basic performer pay rates of each of the SAG agreements. Regardless of the agreement you fall under,

Agreement	Budget Ceiling	Extended Ceiling[a]	Exhibition Requirements
Basic	Unlimited	N/A	Unlimited
Low-budget	$2,500,000	$3,750,000	Initial theatrical realese.
Modified Low-budget	$625,000	$937,500	Initial theatrical release.
Limited Exhibition Ultra Low-Budget	$200,000[b] $500,000[c]	N/A	Extremely limited. No paid theatrical exhibiton.
Experimental Film	$75,000	N/A	Film festivals, Academy screenings, & other limited venues. Must obtain consent of performers.
Student Film	$35,000	N/A	Limited to classroom, student film festivals, & Academy screenings.

Source: Screen Actors Guild Film Contracts Digest, http://www.sag.org./sagWebApp/CMS/Content/Public/lowbudget.pdf.
a Extended budget ceiling applies if the film qualifies under diversity in casting. For requirements to qualify, see text.
b Excluding deferred payments.
c Including deferred payments.
d Compensation is determined by the nature of distribution beyond allowed distribution.

Table 18.2. Summary of the various Screen Actors Guild Agreements.

it is important to get the details of that agreement from SAG. Be sure to read the most recent contract summary at the above mentioned web site.

Once you have decided which agreement you will be working under, it is important to contact SAG as soon as possible after your budget is finished in order to get things started. SAG suggests no less than one month in advance of filming. In reality, you need all the time you can garner to get the paperwork filed and the picture cast. You cannot make official offers to SAG actors unless you are a signatory to the agreement. After you sign, SAG will require you to post a bond equal to your cast budget that they will hold in escrow in an interest-bearing account until all the actors have been paid all monies due. For cash flow purposes, this money will not be available to you during the shooting period, but you should have it back

Performer Compensation		Consecutive	
Daily Rate	Weekly Rate	Employment	Comments
$695	$2,411	Hold days are paid.	
$466	$1,620	Only on overnight locaiton.	Must be shot entirely in U.S.
$248	$864	Only on overnight location.	Must be shot entirely in U.S.
1 day = $100 2 days = $200 3 or more days = $225 plus $75 for each day		Not required.	Intended for workshop or training settings. Must be shot entirely in U.S.
Deferred.[d]		Not required.	Intended for workshop or training settings. Must be shot entirely in U.S.
Deferred.[d]		Not required but perfomers can accept other employment during production.	Producer must be a filmmaking student enrolled in an accredited institution. Producer must own the film. Total shooting days ≤ 20.

in your possession soon after you wrap principal photography in time to apply it to your post production expenses.

809-01 Principal Cast

As can be seen in the first three sub-accounts under Talent, actors are roughly divided into Principal Cast, Supporting Cast, and Day Players.

Principal Cast is where you put your over-scale, run-of-the-picture players: usually the lead parts and the occasional expensive cameo appearance. Principal cast deals are usually for the run of the picture and paid on a weekly basis over the proposed shooting period. In the *Anarchist* budget, the parts of Puck and Double D are for the full length of the schedule. Johnny Black's deal was for three weeks and one day. All are over-scale.

How much do put in for each part? This is governed by who you want for the role and how badly they want to do the role. It is not necessarily a measure of the actor's popularity, success, or ability, although all of those traits are also factors. Some actors have one quote for big budget studio pictures, and another quote for small independent pictures. Perhaps the actor simply likes working on small independent pictures. All of the main actors in *The Anarchist Cookbook* are talented, in demand, work professionally, and normally earn much more than what they were paid on this film. They did the film because they wanted to do it.

So back to the question, "How much?" You must put in this account what you can afford and then make offers. You will soon find out if your script is attracting the actors that you want. Normally, the actors that you will be seeking in order to add a "name" to your film will not read the script without an offer on the table. They simply do not have the time to waste reading scripts that will not be funded.

Once an actor is interested, his or her agent will begin the bargaining process. Remember, the agent's responsibility is to get as much as possible for the client. You need to establish a limit beyond which you will not go. The only possible way to make a film for a given price is to be prepared to say "no" and walk away. Once the agent feels that point has been reached, you will make the deal if the actor really wants to do the picture.

The Anarchist Cookbook had a cast list that was really too large for a picture of its budget size. For that reason, the amounts for the over-scale actors are less than what normally would be paid.

It is wise to have an over-scale deal include reasonable overtime (12-hour days) and looping days. Sometimes it's even possible to persuade the agent to throw in a few "free" days. "Free" days are not actually free; you do pay for them within the over-scale rate. Agents like them because the actor's overall picture deal is divided by fewer days to get a daily or weekly quote. As long as this does not cause an actor's rate to go below scale if the rate was divided by all days worked, this is perfectly legal.

The last line in account 809-01, *No. of checks*, is there to calculate the payroll company's fee. For the above-the-line accounts, the payroll company is paid at a flat fee per check as opposed to the .25% of gross pay used below-the-line. On *Anarchist*, this fee was $7.50. This is to the production's advantage for anyone making more than $3000 per week. To figure the total payroll fee for the account, the number of weekly payroll periods are added up and multiplied by $7.50. We used 13 weeks rather than 12 because one of the actors was going to be paid over five weeks instead of four.

809-02 Supporting Cast

This is also called Weekly Cast in some charts of accounts since these cast members are usually employed by the week. In the low-budget contract, the daily rate is $504 for an 8-hour day with time and a half after 8 hours and double time after 12. The weekly rate is $1752 for five 10-hour days with time and a half after 10 hours and double time after 12. In the standard contract, the daily rate is $716 for 8 hours with time and a half after 8 hours, and double time after 10 hours. The weekly rate is $2483 for a 44-hour week with double time after 10 hours worked on any one day, and time and a half after 44 hours worked during the week, less any daily overtime paid. (See table 18.2.)

In both contracts, the weekly rate is just under 3½ times the daily rate. Because of this rate structure, it makes sense to hire actors on a weekly rate if you need them for three or more consecutive days. Even if you are paying an actor over-scale, the overtime provisions make the weekly contract an attractive choice.

The Anarchist Cookbook budget has five actors in the Supporting Cast account, all of whom were paid over-scale rates. Since the rates are for five 10-hour days, there is a chance that overtime will be required. This is covered by the line labeled "Overtime." It has been set arbitrarily at 20% of the total weekly cast budget. An alternative way of covering this expense would be to budget each player at 12 hours every day. This would needlessly tie up funds in this account since it is unlikely that each actor would work 12 hours each day of their term of employment.

809-03 Day Players

This account covers actors hired on a daily basis. In light of the previous discussion about putting actors on a daily contract if they work three or more consecutive days, it may seem strange that there are actors in this account hired for four and five days. This is because they were needed on non-consecutive days and were not paid for the intervening hold-days. All of the actors in this account were hired for low-budget scale plus 10%. The extra 10% is for the actors' agents.

809-05 Stunt Coordinator

The stunt coordinator is usually an experienced stunt performer (stunt player) who has specialized in planning stunts for films. Proper planning is a key prerequisite to achieving stunts safely. I once interviewed a stunt coordinator who bragged to me that he had broken every bone in his body at one time or another. This is not the guy you want to hire. You want the guy who makes it *look* like he broke every bone in his body, but walked away unscathed.

A good stunt coordinator plans every aspect of the stunt work in a film meticulously, from selecting the doubles to planning each performer's move during the stunt. Well-planned stunts are risky, but safe. The risk has been assessed by all parties involved and precautions have been taken to minimize that risk. The stunt performers are skilled, highly trained, in superb shape, and they must have complete trust in the stunt coordinator's judgment. Before a stunt is photographed, the assistant director calls all the cast and crew together on the set, and the stunt coordinator goes through the sequence in detail so everyone knows what to expect. If, just before the take, something changes, then the assistant director needs to bring everyone back and have the stunt coordinator go through what has changed to make sure that there is no misunderstanding.

I did not work on the picture nor was I present on the set, but I was told the following story by someone who was there. A certain well-known volatile director was filming a sequence that required a number of stunt performers to fall into a tank of water. The stunt performers were to drop from a large box suspended twenty-five feet above the water's surface when the bottom of the box opened up. The director was dissatisfied with the first take, and at the last moment before the second take, ordered the box to be raised up another twenty-five feet. This was done without reconvening everyone, and therefore the stunt players were not aware of the change in height and were not prepared for the higher fall. The result was several broken arms and legs. They were lucky no one was killed.

The low end for an experienced stunt coordinator today is around $3500 per week. The high end can be $7500 per week or more. You must pay a stunt coordinator working under the SAG agreement a minimum of $1140 per day, or $4500 per week, to avoid overtime payments. When you get into the range above $12,000 per week on a SAG picture, the stunt coordinator is usually also serving as a second unit director. Be sure to give the coordinator adequate time to plan the stunts and cast the doubles.

The Anarchist Cookbook had no stunts to speak of, and therefore had no money in the stunt accounts. The only action that came near to being a stunt was when Puck hits Johnny Black with a frying pan. After discussing the scene with the actors, it was felt that we could make it appear that Johnny Black was hit when, in actuality, the frying pan never came too close to him.

809-06 Stunt Players

Actors don't perform their own stunts for the same reason that they don't make their own costumes: we can hire other people who can do it better. That is not to say that there aren't many skilled actors who want to do their own stunts, and sometimes they do. Nevertheless, there are usually many really good reasons not to let an actor perform his or her own stunts.

Skill. An actor who has spent a career learning to become a very skilled actor, usually has not had the time to learn and maintain the physical skills needed to be a stunt performer.

Safety. A stunt performer is almost always able to perform a stunt with less risk to himself and the other performers.

Financial Considerations. If your actor should be injured in the performance of a stunt, you risk shutting the company down and throwing a lot of people out of work, not to mention risking the completion of the film.

A stunt can be as simple as someone falling down or being hit with a break-away chair, bottle, etc., or as complex as a 200-foot high-fall from a bridge. It was during the filming of such a high-fall that I met AJ Bakunis. AJ called himself "America's Number One Fall Guy," and he would give out T-shirts with a silhouette of himself falling upside down through the air. He had made a specialty of high-falls and was one of a very few people who were available for such work. We were in Utah filming a picture called *The Car* about a devil car that went around the southwest running over people. (Motivation didn't seem to be very important to this story.)

In one particular scene, AJ was a bike rider pedaling across a two lane bridge stretched across a gorge that was about two hundred feet deep. The script called for the car to run into AJ, knocking both him and the bicycle off the bridge. All the shots leading up to the stunt had been done and we were setting up for the fall itself. The stunt was to be filmed from several angles by about five cameras. The action called for AJ to stand on the railing, toss the bicycle off the bridge, and to follow it in a head first dive, landing on a 30 by 40-foot air bag resting on the sand below.

I saw AJ standing at the takeoff point on the bridge and walked over to him. He was tossing pebbles, one by one, at the air bag below. I looked

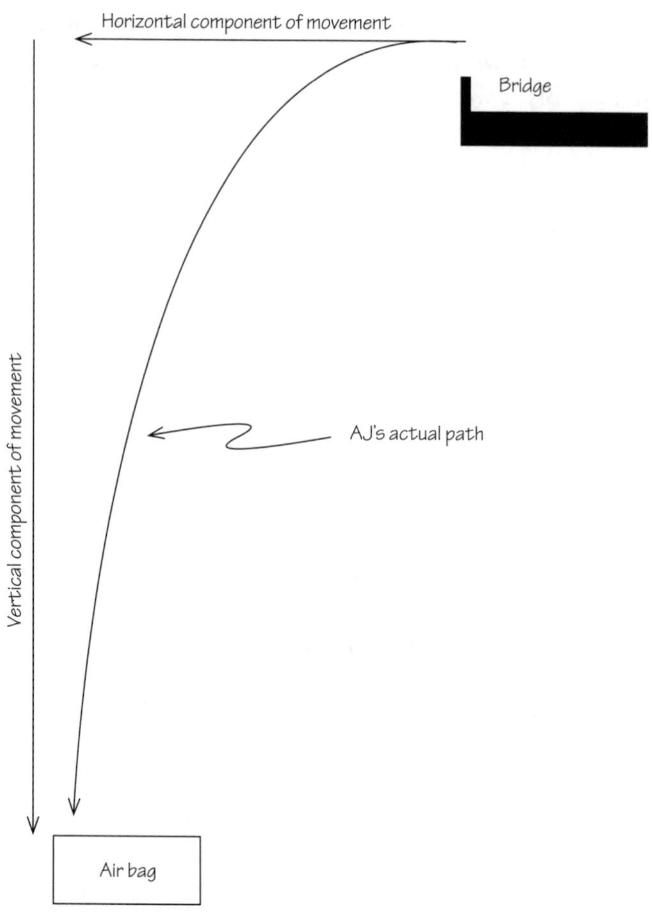

Fig. 18.1. The path of a falling body describes a parabola.

over the rail and saw the bag, which looked like a postage stamp. I asked him what he was doing and he said he was trying to judge how much he should push off from the bridge when he fell. Too much push and he could overshoot the bag, not enough and he might fall short. When a body falls from a height, there are two components to its movement: the downward acceleration caused by gravity, and the constant horizontal movement imparted by whatever force moved the body off of its elevated support. As the body falls, its path actually follows that of a parabola, since the horizontal component of its movement continues steadily throughout the fall, as the downward component steadily *increases* in velocity at about 32ft/sec^2 or 9.8m/sec^2. (See fig. 18.1.) When AJ said he was ready, I wished him luck and moved off the bridge to one side of the gorge to watch.

All the cameras were rolling and the director called action into the walkie-talkie. AJ tossed the bike and leaped. I started a stop watch I was holding. It seemed like he fell forever, and as he fell, I was afraid that he might overshoot the bag. As he neared the end of the fall, he tucked his head and legs, rolled onto his back, and hit the bag with his hips right at the far edge. According to my timing, it took him six seconds to hit the bag. A huge cheer rose up from the crew and the cameras were cut.

Later, I walked up to AJ to congratulate him on the success of his stunt. I told him that on his way down I thought he was going to over-shoot the bag.

"Really?" he said. "I thought so, too."

"You did?" I was flabbergasted. "What went through your head?"

"Well, I noticed that there was a lot of soft sand around the bag and I figured I would be all right."

If my timing of AJ's fall was accurate and he truly did fall for six seconds, he was going about 77 mph when he hit the bag. If he had hit the sand instead, I don't think he would have been "all right."

I tell this story to illustrate what goes into the makeup of a person doing extreme stunts. There is some science, some art, and a peculiar psychology. By "peculiar psychology" I mean that AJ truly did not believe he would be hurt or killed if he missed the bag. I guess a person needs a mindset like that to jump off a bridge into a tiny air bag 200 feet below. It is not something that I would attempt, but then, I know what would happen to me if I hit the sand instead of the bag.

High risk stunts must be evaluated by someone other than the stunt performer. An example of a stunt gone horribly wrong when it was not vetted by another expert in the field also involved AJ. The filming took place in Atlanta, Georgia, and AJ was to crash through a window a few stories up and land on his air bag. At the time, AJ felt that he was in competition with another high jumper named Dar Robinson. I was not working on this film, but the story related to me was that AJ wanted to go off the roof of the building instead of the lower floor in order to beat a record set by Dar. To protect himself from the high impact, AJ used two bags, a small one inside a larger one. These bags are made from a strong vinyl impregnated cloth, and are kept inflated by fans blowing into the bag through special fittings. When the stunt performer hits the bag, vents that are held shut by Velcro® burst open, allowing the bag to deflate in a controlled way, and thereby safely absorb the impact. When AJ hit the outer bag, the seams of the bag ripped open. Because of these rotten seams, the outer bag did not slow his fall by much. When he hit the inner bag, it was not enough to safely decelerate him and he sustained massive internal injuries. AJ died later in the hospital from this fall.

When tragedies like this occur, the refrain "it's only a movie" comes to mind. No film is worth risking someone's life. This particular incident was a result of AJ's choice, but he should have had better or more insistent advice.

Stunt players are hired either daily or weekly at stunt performer minimums. The daily minimum is the same as performer's scale in both the low-budget and standard contracts. The weekly minimum is slightly higher than the performer's rate in the SAG Basic Agreement ($2666 per week for a stunt player as opposed to $2483 per week for a normal actor). They are usually given a stunt adjustment after performing the stunt, the amount of which depends on the difficulty and danger of the stunt, and how often they were required to perform it. On particularly dangerous stunts like AJ's high-fall on *The Car*, the adjustment is usually negotiated beforehand and an agreement reached as to how much additional money will be added to the adjustment for each additional performance. The adjustment becomes part of the stunt performer's base rate in calculating overtime for the day. The adjustment might range from a few hundred dollars to many thousands. If I remember correctly, AJ got $7,500 for jumping off that bridge.

809-07 Stunt Equipment

This account covers the rental of items such as harnesses, trampolines, ratchets, air bags, pads, and many other tools that stunt performers own and use in the performance of their stunts. On a typical film with an average number of stunts, $2,500 to $5,000 should be sufficient.

809-10 Looping & Expenses

Once again on *The Car*, there was a scene in which the car runs over a hitchhiker played by John Rubinstein, grandson of the famous pianist Artur Rubinstein, (and a skilled musician and composer himself). John is sitting by the side of a desert road playing a French horn, when he sees a cloud of dust in the distance.

"A ride!" he says. He starts imagining who it is that is rocketing toward him to take him away from his roadside bivouac. He fantasizes that it is a beautiful woman who will stop for him and they will go off to romantic adventures together. As the cloud of dust draws nearer, he puts away his horn, holds out his thumb, and gets ready for the love of his life. Unfortunately for him it is the Car. The car is clearly visible now, and John stretches out his thumb even further. The car is approaching at a high rate of speed, and without even tapping the breaks, it runs over him, stops, backs up over him, stops, goes forward over him again, and roars off. CUT.

The next scene shows the local sheriff and his deputies at the scene. James Brolin (Wade) roars up on his motorcycle and approaches John Marley (the Sheriff) and Ronny Cox (Luke). Luke is facing camera, center screen, and holding the flattened French horn with both hands like a platter. The Sheriff is on one side of the screen in profile and Wade saunters up and enters the other side of the frame opposite the Sheriff.

Wade asks, "What happened?" The Sheriff goes through a brief recapitulation, and all the while Luke is still center screen holding the flattened French horn.

Finally the Sheriff says, "Luke, you'd better get on the *horn* about this."

In dailies we all fell on the floor laughing—all but the director, that is. He was irate. "Why didn't someone catch this when we were filming it?" he demanded. I knew right then that we would have had a hit if only it had been a comedy.

Sometimes you just don't see, or hear, these things until they are on the screen. That's what looping is for. On the looping stage, John Marley re-recorded his line, substituting the word phone for the word horn, making the line much less hilarious. Sometimes the location you are filming at makes it impossible to record usable dialogue, such as filming in a steel mill, or a boiler factory, or next to a freeway. It is possible to loop whole scenes or even whole movies. The Italians do it all the time.

The process is called *looping* because in the past the dialogue editor actually used to form the piece of film into a loop which would run continuously through the projector. Prior to the actual line, the editor would punch holes in three frames spaced 24 frames apart. On the soundtrack, the editor would put three beeps alongside the three punched frames so that the actor would see flash…flash…flash along with hearing beep…beep…beep…and then the line. This was all designed to help the actor say his line in synchronization with his image on the screen. Today, the loop of film has been replaced by digital video and computer controls, and the process is known as ADR for Automated Dialogue Replacement.

809-12 Cast Training

Do your cast members need to learn to ice skate, handle a weapon, play a musical instrument, ride a horse, dance, handle lab equipment, or any other skill to make them look convincing? Then you need cast training. For only $19.95... (Sorry, too much cable TV.) Nevertheless, this is where those expenses go.

On *Starship Troopers*, we needed to turn our group of actors and extras into convincing military units. For a week prior to filming, we actually put them through a "boot camp" conducted by our military tech advisor, Dale Dye. (See the discussion of account 811-06 Tech Advisors.) The boot camp was held at the bottom of Hell's Half Acre, a rugged canyon outside of Casper, Wyoming, where we staged the large bug battles. (I think the "recruits" came to believe that the place was named appropriately.) The expenses of running the boot camp were considered cast training. Actual expenses on your picture depend on what it is you want to train the cast to do. Some research about experts in the field should uncover the costs.

The *Anarchist* budget has no money here since our cast was able to mimic pseudo-anarchist, slacker behavior without prior training.

809-15 Casting Directors

This is who will help you cast your movie. The goal here is to hire Matt Damon just after he completes *Good Will Hunting* but before it is released. That way you can hire him for next to nothing and then reap the benefits when he becomes a huge star just before you release your picture. To do this, the casting director makes it a regular duty to see new films, independent theater productions, and to conduct thousands of interviews. A good casting director can also persuade a well-known actor to reduce his or her fee for a challenging role that might garner an Oscar nomination.

Casting directors are paid a flat fee plus expenses per picture. You can get a small independent film cast for $15,000 to $25,000, depending on the number of roles to be cast. Casting for larger budget films typically will cost $35,000 to $75,000.

The casting director will send out scripts or *sides* (pages of scripts) to various agencies and publicize that the picture is looking for cast. They know which big stars like to do independent movies (it isn't all about the money, you know), and who represents them.

809-16 Casting Asst. & Expenses

A casting director usually has one or more casting assistants who help them contact actors, schedule readings, and handle candidates when they arrive at the casting office. The assistants usually make from $800 to $1,500 per week depending on their experience and what casting director they are working for.

Expenses can include, but are not limited to, office rent, telephone expenses, office supplies, video tape purchase, video equipment rental or purchase, postage, courier services, DVD rentals or purchases, theater tickets, and meals. If you contemplate casting in another city, you should include airfare, hotel, and meals during the out of town casting for the director, casting director, casting assistants, producer, and anyone else involved. In addition, be aware that if you cast someone from another city, you will probably have to pay for that actor's airfare, hotel, and living expenses while working on your film.

809-30 Travel & Living Expenses

If you are signed with SAG, members of SAG must be flown first class, if available. SAG also stipulates the amount you must pay for per diem when housing an actor overnight. As of this writing, it is $60 per day. That is broken down into $12 for breakfast, $18 for lunch, and $30 for dinner. Obviously, any actor is free to negotiate higher rates and you are free to say "No."

809-40 Star Perks

Perk is short for *perquisite*: "An incidental payment, benefit, privilege, or advantage over and above regular income, salary, or wages." (*Webster's Encyclopedic Unabridged Dictionary of the English Language.*) The Star Perks account is where you put those expenses that are over and above what is normally required. For example, the SAG contract states that you need to give an actor a dressing room. This normally consists of a honeywagon room (see 839-56 Studio Vehicles), or a two or three room trailer, or at the higher end, a single room trailer. If your star requires a 50-foot pop-out trailer that becomes a small version of the Taj Mahal, then the cost of that perk would go here.

Other items might be personal assistants, personal costumers, makeup artists, hairdressers, security, exercise trailers, personal chefs, special foods, or any other item that is out of the ordinary and meant for one particular actor. These items are put above-the-line in the cast account because they truly are part of the cost of hiring particular actors. I once did a film in which the budget went from $7 million to $14 million when the lead actress was replaced by another well know actress. Only $4 million of the additional $7 million was paid directly to the replacement; the rest went to star perks.

The long-suffering cast on *The Anarchist Cookbook* received nothing that could be called a perk. The contracts were negotiated, however, to give all the actors perks if any one actor received a perk. This is called a *favored-nations clause.* In other words, everyone is on an equal footing. No one is getting an advantage that the other actors do not have. This takes the competition out of the perk arena and makes life easier for everyone on a low-budget film. Remember that under this type of agreement, if you weaken and give something to one of the actors, you have to give it to them all.

809-49 Insurance Exams

As part of your insurance package, you will have coverage on certain members of the cast and essential crew (see the discussion on 861-01 Cast Insurance). One of the requirements of the insurance company will be to have the covered cast take a medical examination. In the past, if the doctor could actually detect that the actor was breathing, the actor would pass. Today, insurance companies are much more careful and require doctors to discover any pre-existing conditions that might affect the filming. The cost of those exams, both for cast and essential crew, goes here. A typical exam costs $200 in the doctor's office. It might cost twice that if you require the doctor to go to the actor. We expected to pay for 10 exams on *The Anarchist Cookbook.*

809-60 Miscellaneous Expense

The star perks account covers most of the items that might go here. If there is a cast expense that has not been covered in any of the other accounts, put it here, but make sure it is clearly defined.

810-00 Above-the-Line Fringe Benefits

The *Anarchist* budget was set to print the fringe benefits and payroll taxes at the end of each production level. The expenses reported here are for the above-the-line accounts only. Of course, the percentages used represent those in effect at the time the picture was shot.

Typically, the fringe benefit calculations and payments are handled by the payroll company (and I strongly urge you to use a payroll company). They can advise you as to what the current percentages are and they are knowledgeable on all the intricacies of the law in the various states, and the various union contracts.

On this picture, the fees paid to the writer, director, and producers were not fringed. This is because those individuals had what are known as loan-out corporations. A loan-out corporation is a legal entity that loans the employee's services to the picture. This means that the employee is actually employed by the loan-out corporation, and the corporation invoices the picture for those services. The loan-out corporation is responsible for all payroll taxes and income tax withholding. However, the production company still must pay any union benefits required. For that reason, the actors who owned loan-out corporations still needed to have SAG fringes applied to their wages.

Technically, the fees paid to loan-out corporations are considered accounts payable as opposed to payroll. Nevertheless, they are usually still processed through the payroll company so that the individuals will be covered by Workmen's Compensation Insurance, and their union fringes, if any, can be managed. For this purpose, the payroll company will give you special start paperwork for loan-outs and time cards for those employees.

I must point out one more advantage to using a payroll company. If you are shooting later in the calendar year and some of your employees have worked on other productions that used the same payroll company that you are using, they may have already hit their ceilings on some of the payroll taxes, and you will not be charged for them. This can be a considerable savings.

The following explanations are given in the order in which the expenses are listed in the *Anarchist* budget account 810-00. Be sure to always check all percentages and ceilings with your payroll company.

FICA or Federal Insurance Contribution Act

This is the social security tax that politicians fight over continually. An amount equal to 6.2% of the employee's gross wages is deducted from said wages and, together with another equal amount from the employer, is sent in to the Social Security Administration. The cost to the picture is the matching 6.2% of the employee's gross wages. As of this writing, this tax is limited to the first $90,000 of each employee's gross wages, although the ceiling can increase on a yearly basis.

FUI or Federal Unemployment Insurance

Sometimes referred to as FUTA, this is calculated at 0.8% of the first $7000 of the employee's gross wages.

SAG

Currently, the Screen Actors Guild pension, health and welfare benefit is 13.8% of the first $200,000 of the actor's gross wages. When we made *Anarchist* in 2001, it was 11%.

Medicare

This is another federal tax. It is calculated at 1.45% of the employee's gross wages with no ceiling.

CA SUI or California State Unemployment Insurance.

Every state has a similar tax and they all differ as to what percentage they charge. Your payroll company can give you the current rate for your state. The rates are subject to change frequently. We paid 5.4% of the first $7,000 of the employee's gross wages. As of this writing, California's state unemployment insurance tax has risen to 6.2% of the first $7,000 of gross wages.

ATL Check Fee

As explained earlier in the discussion under 809-01 Principal Cast, the payroll company charges a $7.50 fee per check for the higher salaried above-the-line employees instead of a flat percentage of .025% of the gross wages. In the *Anarchist* budget, there were 70 weekly checks written at a fee of $7.50 each for a total above-the-line payroll fee of $525. This was well worth the expense. You are not just paying for the actual writing of the check, but for all the payroll calculations, union fringe payment management, and their advice and expertise.

TX WC or Texas Worker's Compensation Insurance

This insures the employees for job related injury or disability, and is something of a protection for the production company against getting sued. It is required in every state. Usually it is provided by private insurance companies, but in certain states, namely North Dakota, Ohio, Washington, West Virginia, Wyoming, Puerto Rico, and the Virgin Islands, it must be purchased from a government agency. Again, your payroll company can handle the details. The percentage of gross wages paid changes every year depending on the payouts made the previous year. We paid 2.87% of gross wages. This applies only to employees hired in the state of Texas.

TX SUI or Texas State Unemployment Insurance

See the discussion above under CA SUI. We were charged 6.27% of the first $9,000 of the employee's gross wages.

CA WC or California Worker's Compensation Insurance.

See the discussion above under TX WC. This is one of the reasons Arnold Schwarzenegger ran for governor of California. In 2001, we paid 2.45% of gross wages of employees hired in California. As of this writing, it has risen to 5.89% of gross wages.

19

The Shooting Period

This section of the budget begins the below-the-line aspects of the production and covers the actual filming of the picture. These expenses are usually spent mainly during the preparation and shooting periods, hence the name. Some charts of accounts will call this the Production Period.

811-00 Production

The production account is concerned primarily with the management of the picture.

811-01 Production Manager

The production manager, more formally known as the unit production manager (UPM), is the person charged with the day-to-day operations of planning and shooting the movie. If your director is a member of the DGA, then the production company must be signed with the DGA, and the production manager and assistant directors must be members. If the production company is not signed with the DGA, then members of the DGA are forbidden by their by-laws from working for you in DGA covered capacities.

If the director is the captain of the ship, then the unit production manager is the commander. He or she is in charge of the day-to-day logistics and workings of the company, the hiring of the crew, the tracking of the progress and costs of the picture, and the remedies to be employed to return a picture to the budget or schedule if it has strayed.

As one of the first people hired, the unit production manager will prepare a production board and a preliminary shooting schedule, from which he or she will create a preliminary budget. This is sometimes done with the assistance of a production accountant. The preliminary board and budget are crucial in that often the decision of whether to make the film or not will rest on the result of the preliminary budget.

A formal listing of the unit production manager's responsibilities would include:

- Coordinating, facilitating, and overseeing for the production unit all off set logistics, day-to-day production decisions, locations, budget, schedule, and personnel;
- Preparing or coordinating the budget (studios have budget departments and estimators);
- Overseeing the preliminary search and survey of all locations, and the completion of business arrangements for the same;
- Assisting in the planning and preparation of the production to insure continuing efficiency;
- Supervising completion of the Production Report for each day's work;
- Coordinating arrangements for the transportation and housing of cast, crew, and staff;
- Overseeing the securing of releases and negotiating for locations and personnel; and
- Maintaining a liaison with local authorities regarding locations and the operations of the company.

A key position with such heavy responsibility does not come cheaply. *The Anarchist Cookbook* was fortunate to only pay $1,500 per week during prep and wrap, and $1,800 per week during shoot. The DGA scale is quite a bit higher: in town, $3928 per week during prep and wrap, with a shooting fee added during the shooting weeks of $850 for a total of $4748 per week. On distant location with a six-day week, you will pay $5501 for prep and wrap. During shooting, the shooting fee of $1015 brings up the weekly rate to $6516.

The DGA has joined with the other motion picture guilds and unions in formulating a low-budget wage scale. See table 18.1 for a summary of the rates allowed under this agreement.

811-02 First Assistant Director

The first assistant director (1st AD) runs the set. A good first assistant director keeps the crew informed as to what is coming up next, keeps the director informed as to where he or she should be at any moment during the day, and keeps the set running in the most efficient way possible. Along with this, a good assistant director creates brilliant background action that doesn't detract, but rather enhances the foreground action, solves crew problems on the spot, has several solutions for problems that no one even knows about yet, makes every actor feel like the star, and is able to think fast and react immediately. On a movie set, time really *is* money. If I walk onto a set and feel the urge to start telling crew members what to do, then the assistant director is not doing his or her job.

Let's look at a few items from a formal list of duties of the first assistant director:

- Organizes pre-production, including organizing the crew, securing equipment, breaking down the script, preparing the strip board and a shooting schedule. During production he assists the Director with respect to on-set production details, coordinates and supervises crew and cast activities, and facilitates an organized flow of production activity.

Once the assistant director comes on a film, the UPM will turn over all prep period activity scheduling to him or her. The 1st AD normally will prepare a calendar which is published at least once per week showing what is happening and with whom.

- Prepares a new breakdown and production board, and prepares a shooting schedule keeping within the time limitations imposed by budget, cast availability, and the requirement of complete coverage of the script.

The goal at this point is for the 1st AD to create an efficient and realistic schedule that addresses the concerns of the actors and various departments while staying within the time and money resources available. This is not an easy task.

- If delegated by the UPM or in his/her absence, the 1st AD oversees the search, survey, and management of locations as they might affect the production. The 1st AD must be sent to each location site sufficiently prior to commencement of photography to adequately perform his/her duties.

The first assistant director needs to know exactly what he or she will be dealing with on each location: noise, extras holding, feeding areas, access, etc.

- Checks weather reports.

It is vital that the company is not surprised by the weather but is able to adjust to the weather in order that shooting is not delayed.

- Prepares day-out-of-day schedules for talent employment and determines cast and crew calls.

The day-out-of-days must be done as early in the prep period as possible so that the cast deals can be made. Cast and crew calls are determined each day for the following shooting day.

- Supervises the preparation of the call sheet for cast and crew.

All information on the set flows from the first assistant director and this is one of the most important pieces of information that must be disseminated each day: "What are we doing tomorrow, where is it, and what time do we show up?"

- Directs background action and supervises crowd control.

All those people you see walking around in movies that have no lines have been given direction by the first assistant director; even crowds on city streets or in auditoriums, or the other drivers around your stars during the driving shots.

- May be required to secure minor contracts, extra releases, and on occasion, to obtain execution of contracts by talent.

Actors often are given their contracts to sign when they report to the set for the first time. This is handled by the first assistant director and his or her staff.

- Supervises the function of the shooting set and crew.

The primary and most important function of a first assistant director's job is to make sure that the company continues to shoot and make progress regardless of what may happen. Any delay can mean scenes in the movie will never be shot, costs will go up, and the director will not get the film he or she is expected to deliver. The 1st AD is normally found a few steps from the camera and rarely leaves that position during the entire day. Even during lunch, the 1st AD is often involved in meetings. When a trip to the restroom is absolutely required, the second assistant director will step in to fill the vacancy.

The DGA scale rates for first assistant directors are as follows:

	In Town (5 Days)	Location (6 Days)
Weekly Salary	$3734	$5222
Shooting Fee	691	850
Total Weekly Salary	$4425	$6072

The Anarchist Cookbook was not made under the DGA agreement. Fortunately, we found a non-union assistant director for whom we paid $1,200 during prep and $1,500 during shooting.

811-03 Second Assistant Director & Trainee

As the title implies, the second assistant director (2nd AD) assists the first assistant director. A 2nd AD's duties go further, however. In addition to helping the first assistant director with the background players, disseminating information to the cast and crew, and occasionally stepping up to the camera to allow the 1st AD to go to the bathroom, the 2nd AD is responsible for wrangling the cast, dealing with the paper work, and keeping the production office up to date with what is happening on the set.

Again, looking at a formal list of duties, the second assistant director is responsible for:

- Preparing the call sheets, handling extras requisitions and other required documents for approval by the first assistant director, the unit production manager, and/or the production office.

- Preparing the daily production report and end of day paperwork.

The production report is a legal document which records what happened on each shooting day. It is the second assistant director's job to see that it is filled out correctly.

- Distributing scripts and script changes (after shooting has started) to cast and crew.

- Distributing call sheets to cast and crew.

- Distributing, collecting, and approving extras vouchers, as well as placing adjustments as directed by the first assistant director on the vouchers.

- Communicating advance scheduling to cast and crew.

- Aiding in the scouting, surveying, and managing of locations.

- Facilitating transportation of equipment and personnel.

I am reminded of a true story of a second assistant director back in the 1970s who was trying to get his crew all shipped back to the studio. The company had bussed the crew out to a location in the desert north of Los Angeles, and since it was a union crew, everyone was on the clock until they were dropped back at the studio where they had reported that morning. The 2nd AD was rapidly filling up the various vans, cars, and buses, and rushing all the personnel into whatever vehicle was available. He finally got the last person into a vehicle and sent it on its way to the studio. He took a deep breath and gazed at the empty landscape with the satisfaction of a job well done. It was then that he realized he had also dispatched the last of his vehicles and he had no ride for himself. It was a long, lonely, ten-mile walk to the nearest town that he made that night in the chill desert air.

- Seeing to the execution of minor cast contracts, extra releases, and on occasion, securing the execution of contracts by talent.

As stated earlier, the cast will sometimes not receive their contracts for signature until their first day of work. It will usually fall to the second assistant director to see that the contracts are signed. If an extra is upgraded to a speaking part during the day, the 2nd AD is responsible for having the extra's contract executed also.

- Coordinating with the production staff so that all elements including cast, crew, and extras are ready at the beginning of the day, and supervising the wrap at the studio and on location (local and distant).

This is a constant ongoing conversation that the 2nd AD has with the production office to make sure that everyone is in sync as to what is needed the next day. Also, the 2nd AD remains at the set until everyone has gone home.

- Signing cast members in and out (SAG time sheets).

As part of the cast wrangling duties, the second assistant director makes sure that the cast members sign the Exhibit G sheet each day (fig. 19.1). The Exhibit G sheet is a record of the actors' times for the day and is required by SAG. It is also the 2nd AD's duty to notify the first assistant director if a cast member or an extra is late or missing.

- Maintain liaison between UPM and/or the production office and the 1st AD on the set.

Since the unit production manager cannot be on the set all day, it is the 2nd AD's responsibility to call into the office to update the UPM as to the day's progress or lack thereof.

- Assist the 1st AD in the direction and placement of background action and in the supervision of crowd control.

This is where the second assistant director actually gets to direct.

- Supervise and direct the work of any trainee or intern assigned to the picture.

#17

Exhibit G

SCREEN ACTORS GUILD PERFORMERS PRODUCTION TIME REPORT

Picture Title______________________________

Company______________________________Prod. No.__________Date__________Contact__________________Phone No. (   )__________

Shooting Location ______________________________Is Today a Designated Day Off? * Yes___ No___ MP___ TV___ MOW___ Industrial___ Other_______

Please Complete in Ink

WORK - W START - S REHEARSAL - R HOLD - H FITTING - FT TEST - T TRAVEL - TR FINISH - F					WORK TIME			In / Out	MEALS				TRAVEL TIME						Wardrobe	Forced Call	
									1st Meal		2nd Meal										
CAST	MINOR?	CHARACTER	W S R TR FT H F T	Report Makeup Wdbe.	Report on set	Dismiss on set	Dismiss Makeup Wardrobe	ND Meal	Start	Finish	Start	Finish	Leave for Location	Arrive on Location	Leave Location	Arrive at Studio	Stunt Adj.	Minors Tutoring Time	No. of Outfits Provided	MPV'S	PERFORMER'S SIGNATURE

*THIS REFERS TO THE TWO (2) DAYS (ONE (1) DAY ON OVERNIGHT LOCATION) WHICH PRODUCER CAN DESIGNATE AS DAY(S) OFF FOR THE PRODUCTION FOR WHICH PERFORMERS ARE NOT PAID CONTINUOUS EMPLOYMENT.

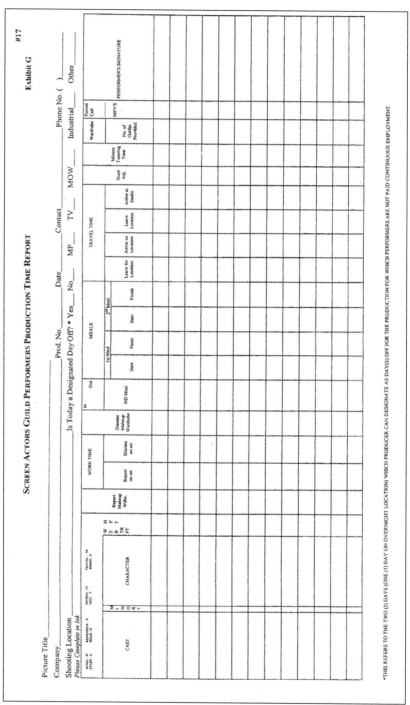

Fig. 19.1. An example of a production time sheet (Exhibit G) supplied by the Screen Actors Guild.

The Assistant Directors Training Program is a joint program of the DGA and the Association of Motion Picture and Television Producers (AMPTP) to create an entrance into the business for qualified people who want to become assistant directors. It is an extremely competitive program, but it is worth applying for should a person want to go in this direction. When you become a trainee, it is like being a production assistant with a future. Once you complete the training program (400 days of working on feature films and television shows), you are admitted to the DGA as a second assistant director. For more information on the program and its requirements, go to the web page at **http://www.trainingplan.org**.

The DGA has the same sort of two-tier rate scale for the second assistants as they do for the first assistants.

	In Town (5 Days)	Location (6 Days)
Weekly Salary	$2,430	$3,395
Shooting Fee	513	671
Total Weekly Salary	$2,943	$4,066

The DGA also has lower rates for 2nd second assistant directors and additional second assistant directors, but you must hire a key second assistant director first.

The Anarchist Cookbook second assistant director made $1,000 per week during prep and shoot.

811-04 Script Supervisor

The script supervisor is responsible for keeping an accurate log of every shot made, and watching for continuity mistakes. If you see an actor in a film pickup a glass in his right hand and then see a cut to a new angle with the glass in his left hand, you have seen a continuity mistake. Films are full of them and some film viewers take great delight in pointing them out to the filmmakers. It is the duty of the script supervisor to catch them when they happen on the set so that the director, if he or she chooses to, can retake the shot with the continuity goof corrected. Sometimes the director will decide not to correct the mistake if it seems to be something that will not be noticed and the company is short of time. Nevertheless, someone is sure to notice.

The other part of the script supervisor's job, that of keeping an accurate shooting log, actually takes up most of his or her time. The script supervi-

CR B10/SR7 TK 1: 16 COMP (2) 11 COMP (3) 7 COMP (HAIR - 80MM / IN GATE) (FALSE START) OKAY BY BROWN	5/29 150 CU OF BALL HITTING HOLE CAM TILTS ↑ TO REVEAL PUCK + DAD	SU 11 - 70MM - CHOC 2 - 85 N9
B10/SR7 TK 1: 38 COMP (3) 42 COMP (SERIES ON LINES)	150A MS PUCK HOLDS FLAG — LOOKING @ DAD — FOR VO ; COVERS LINE 9-10	12 CL nd 35MM CR
B10/SR7 TK (1): 31 COMP SERIES ON LINES 9-10 (2): 20 (FRAME — NOT AS GOOD)	5/29 150B MWS OF PUCK w/ FLAG LOOKING @ DAD FOR VO ; COVERS LINE 9-10	13 11 MM - CHOC - 85 N-9
CAMERA RELOAD TO CR B11		
B11/SR7 TK (1): 50 COMP	5/29 150C MWS OF DAD PUTTING (LOOKING CL)	14 - 25MM
B/11/SR7 TK (1) 30	5/29 150D MS DAD - SAME AS (150C)	15 - 70MM
B/11/SR7 TK (1): 35 COMP * (2): 42 THEY EXIT FRAME CL (3): 45 (NOT GREAT) FOR SOUND * (4) 43	5/29 150E MWS (2SHOT) PUCK ; DAD — PUCK MISSES — COVERS LINES	SU 16 [CL ← CR]
B/11/MOS TK (1) TAIL SLATE	5/9 150F 11 GOLF CART 2 CUTAWAY SHOTS — BIRDS 3 CUTAWAY OF GOLF COMING CLOSE (SERIES) (3 CUTAWAYS) GOING AWAY → COMING BACK	SU 17 - MNG 18
B11 TK (1) SERIES (2) - TALKING - SERIES	150G * SHOOTING ↓ OF CU OF HOLE	19

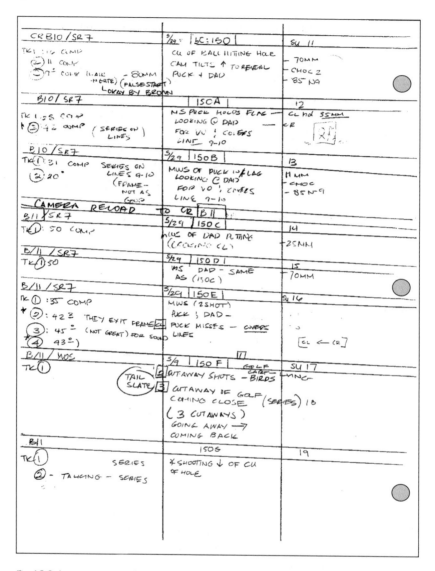

Fig. 19.2. A script supervisor's notes on the coverage of the script page opposite.

sor works from a current copy of the script which includes all revisions. At the end of each day's shooting, the script supervisor makes copies of the pages that were shot that day with the notes from that day's shoot. At the end of principal photography, the script supervisor turns in the entire script to the editor and this becomes the editor's index as to what was shot.

In figures 19.2 and 19.3, I have reproduced the script supervisor's notes

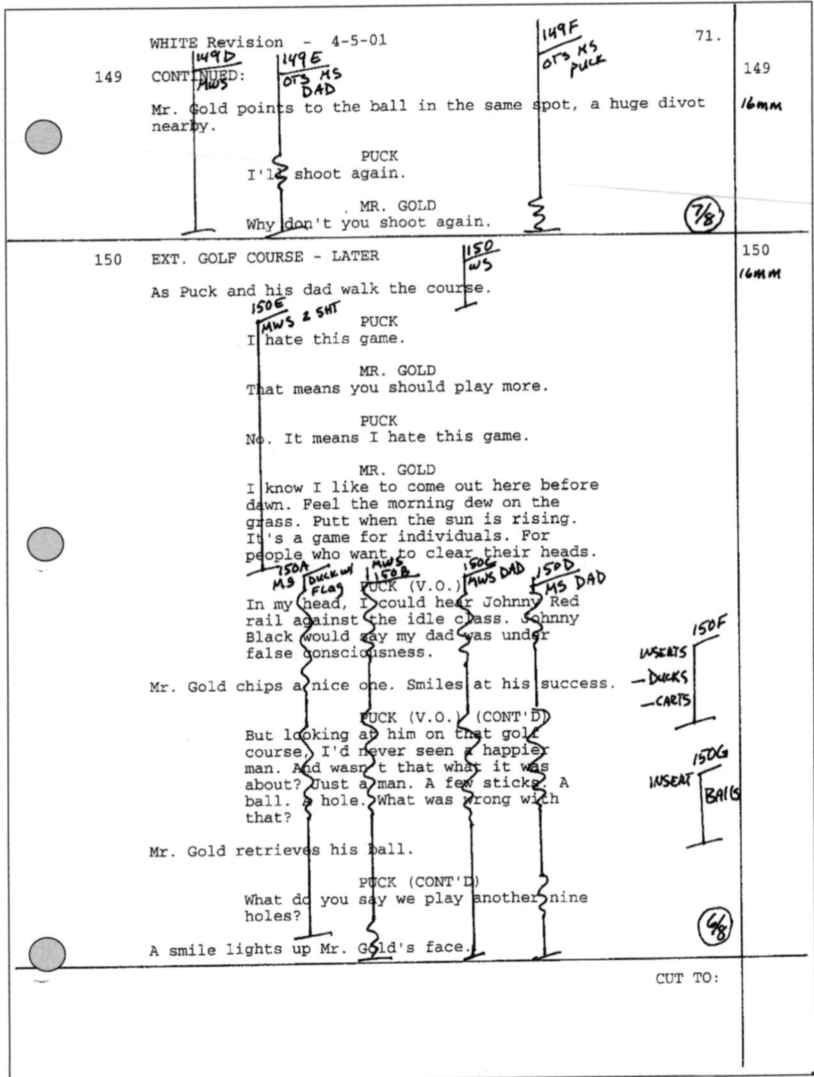

WHITE Revision - 4-5-01 71.

149 CONTINUED: 149

Mr. Gold points to the ball in the same spot, a huge divot nearby.

PUCK
I'll shoot again.

MR. GOLD
Why don't you shoot again.

150 EXT. GOLF COURSE - LATER 150

As Puck and his dad walk the course.

PUCK
I hate this game.

MR. GOLD
That means you should play more.

PUCK
No. It means I hate this game.

MR. GOLD
I know I like to come out here before dawn. Feel the morning dew on the grass. Putt when the sun is rising. It's a game for individuals. For people who want to clear their heads.

PUCK (V.O.)
In my head, I could hear Johnny Red rail against the idle class. Johnny Black would say my dad was under false consciousness.

Mr. Gold chips a nice one. Smiles at his success.

PUCK (V.O.) (CONT'D)
But looking at him on that golf course, I'd never seen a happier man. And wasn't that what it was about? Just a man. A few sticks. A ball. A hole. What was wrong with that?

Mr. Gold retrieves his ball.

PUCK (CONT'D)
What do you say we play another nine holes?

A smile lights up Mr. Gold's face.

CUT TO:

Fig. 19.3. A script page showing the script supervisor's markings.

and markings as they would appear in the script that the script supervisor keeps. It may all look a bit daunting at first, but we'll go through these pages in detail.

As can be seen in figure 19.3 the scene we will be talking about is Scene 150 with Puck and his father on the golf course. In figure 19.2, starting at the top, are the notes that were made during the shooting of this scene. At the top of the page in fig. 19.2 near the left hand margin is a cryptic notation "CR B10 / SR 7." This means that the following shots are on the tenth roll from camera B and the seventh sound roll. In the middle of the page at the top, we see the date (May 29, written as "5/29") on which the shots were done, the camera used (B camera), and the scene number (150). On the far right is a note describing this as the eleventh camera setup for the day ("SU 11").

Under this heading information, we see the list of takes for setup number eleven. The camera rolled three times: take number one was complete and lasted 16 seconds; take number two was also complete and lasted 11 seconds; and finally, take number three was complete and lasted 9 seconds, but a hair was noticed in the camera gate after the take was finished. The director of photography determined that it had not impacted the image area of the film. Take number three also had a false start and was shot with an 80mm lens as opposed to the 70mm lens used for the other two takes. Takes number two and three were marked to be printed.

In the center of the page is a brief description of what the shot looked like. It was a close-up of a golf ball hitting the cup, and the camera tilts up to reveal Puck and his dad. On the right side of the page are notes pertaining to the camera: a 70mm lens was used (except for take #3), along with a chocolate 2 filter and an 85 N-9 filter.

If you look at the page from the script in figure 19.3, you can see a vertical line in the upper center of the page marked "150 WS." This shows what part of the script was credited as being shot 150, and that it was a wide shot. As you can see, the script describes a shot of Puck and his dad walking. Instead, the script notes tell us that it was a close-up of a ball that became a two-shot of Puck and his dad when the camera tilted up.

The next setup, setup #12, was shot 150A. It was a medium shot of Puck looking at his dad while holding the cup pennant. There is even a little sketch of the shot on the right (looking rather like a Chinese ideogram) of Puck holding the flag and looking camera right. The notes say that the shot was to be used for the voice-over sections of the scene, and it covers voice-over lines 9-10 starting with, "In my head..." and ending with, "...What was wrong with that?" Looking at the line representing 150A, we see that it was a medium shot of Puck and the flag. The squiggly parts of the line indicate that those parts of the script were not on-camera in the shot. In other words, we don't see Puck saying the voice-over lines. The other thing to note is that Mr. Gold's smile is not in this shot. It will have to be covered in other shots.

Going back to the notes (fig. 19.2), we can see that there were two takes and take #2 was the only one printed. It lasted 42 seconds. Also, the director had Puck do a series of different readings of the line, "What do you say we play another nine holes?". The shot was done with a 35mm lens on the camera.

Shot 150B, setup #13, was a similar shot only it was done with a 17mm lens on the camera. The director did not like the framing as well as in shot 150A. After take #2 of this shot, the camera had to reload with new film, roll #B11.

Shots 150C and 150D were of Puck's dad putting, looking camera left, and smiling. Shot 150C was a medium-wide shot taken with a 25mm lens, and shot 150D, a medium shot, was shot with a 70mm lens. Notice on the script page that the lines for these two shots extend down through Mr. Gold's smile (meaning we actually see him smile in these two shots).

Shot 150E, setup #16, actually comes before shots 150-150D in the script. These shots are numbered in the order in which they are made, not in the order they are in the script or in the order that they will necessarily be in the completed film. Shot 150E is basically a medium-wide two-shot covering Puck and his dad's dialogue at the beginning of the scene. It appears that the action proceeds from right to left during the shot (small diagram on the right hand side of the notes page). Take 3 was not great for sound; probably an airplane flying over interfering with the dialogue.

Shots 150F and 150G, setups #17, #18, and #19, were a series of inserts used for cut-aways. These types of shots are useful to editors trying to change the pacing of a scene.

The script page reveals two other pieces of information. This scene was shot on 16mm film. This was a stylistic choice of the director. The plan was to use normal bright 35mm film for the fun, carefree world of Puck and his "anarchist" friends; flat, grainy, dead looking 16mm film for Plano, Texas (hence the chocolate filter); and DV footage for when the anarchists went into action. The other thing that is noted on the script page is that the script supervisor planned to take credit for 6/8 of a page when Scene 150 was completed, shown as (6/8).

Good script supervisors earn every penny of their money. Union scale for an experienced script supervisor is currently $29.20 per hour with time and a half after the first six hours of the day, although many of them make considerably more than the scale rate. We paid our standard department head rate on *The Anarchist Cookbook* which was $1500 per week. Did we get a good deal? Let's examine it.

Since a union script supervisor gets time and a half after 6 hours, and double time after 12 hours, a twelve hour day would amount to 15 pay-hours. However, script supervisors need time after wrap each day to copy their notes for the editor, so that usually adds an hour to their day, which is a double time hour. So then the script supervisor's 13 hour day would be

17 pay-hours [(6 × 1) + (6 × 1½) + (1 × 2)]. This becomes 85 pay hours for the week (5 x 17 phrs/day) or $2482 for the week (5 × 17 × $29.20).

But wait, that's not all: we were shooting 6 days per week. On the sixth day, union script supervisors make time and a half for the first 12 hours, and three times the rate after 12 hours. So, for a sixth 13-hour day, a union script supervisor gets (12 × 1.5) + (1 × 3) or 21 pay hours. Add that to the 85 pay-hours for the first five days and you get 106 pay-hours for the week. This would work out to $3,095.20 for a six-day week (106 × $29.20). I would say that our script supervisor graced us with an enormous gift of her time as did all the crew on *Anarchist*. We could not have made the film that we did without such generous and skilled help.

811-05 Location Manager

The location manager is responsible for finding the locations, making the deals, and supervising the company's interaction with the locations. All contact with each location should go through the location manager. It is confusing for people outside the business to have to deal with a dozen different people from one company. Going though the location manager allows him or her to develop a relationship with the property owner, and allows the location manager to head off conflicts in scheduling time at the location for the various departments. The location manager works closely with the production designer and/or the art director in selecting the locations. A good eye for architecture and style is just as important as the more practical aspects that were mentioned in Chapter 10, "Locations." On the west coast, location managers are members of the Teamsters Union. However, in New York they are part of the Directors Guild. On both coasts, location managers are paid by the week. An experienced union location manager makes $2,250 in Los Angeles plus a $60 per day car allowance. Location managers will usually also negotiate a box rental which can include camera equipment, a computer, digital imaging software, and a printer.

On *The Anarchist Cookbook*, we paid our standard department head rate of $1,500 per week to the key location manager. Because the entire film was shot on practical locations, we also provided for additional location assistants and a location production assistant at rates from $100 to $250 per day.

811-06 Tech Advisors

Technical advisors can be invaluable in giving a film authority and believability. On *Hollow Man*, we used a tech advisor to help the actors feel comfortable in the lab and with the lab equipment. On *Robin Hood: Men In Tights*, we used tech advisors to teach the extras and the actors how to handle the weapons. On every police show I am familiar with, tech advisors are used to help the director stage realistic scenes involving police procedure. Our tech advisor on *S.W.A.T.*, Randy Walker, had been a S.W.A.T. officer in the Los Angeles Police Department. He was very knowledgeable about S.W.A.T. procedures and weapons and Mr. Walker helped the director achieve the realism he was looking for. The "harpoon" device, which Colin Farrell supposedly invented and used in the film to pull the wall out at a barricaded suspect's house, was actually invented by Mr. Walker during his S.W.A.T. tenure.

A good tech advisor has to use considerable judgment and discretion. It is not simply a job where you go around imposing your knowledge on everyone in the film. Sometimes the truth is not dramatically exciting. A good tech advisor must realize that he or she is working on a fictional film, not a documentary. It is enough to make the reality of a situation known to the director.

Sometimes directors will choose to ignore the tech advisor for dramatic purposes. This was brought home to me on *Airport '79 – The Concorde*. I was in a meeting with the director and several other people in which various scenes in the movie were being discussed. One scene in particular bothered me and I mentioned it to the director. The scene in question was the one where the Concorde's engines shut down in flight and the airplane immediately begins a vertical dive to the earth. Although exciting, I knew as a private pilot that the plane would actually just drop its nose slightly and begin a controlled descent. Seeing that one of the more exciting moments in the film was being threatened, the director made it abundantly clear that I should stick to my production management duties.

Tech advisors are not covered by any union contracts and therefore they may be hired at whatever rate you can negotiate with them. A common rate is $2,500 per week. Most often you do not need them for the entire shooting schedule. We had no need of a tech advisor on *Anarchist* since the actors all seemed to have a fair grasp of anti-social and criminal behavior without any coaching (having seen it in many other movies).

811-07 Production Coordinators

These are truly the unsung heroes of the motion picture business. The production office coordinator (POC) runs the production office, hires the assistant production coordinator, the production secretary, and the office production assistants (PAs). In addition, the POC gathers and distributes reports from the set, script revisions, handles purchase orders for various departments' equipment orders, approves office supply orders, keeps track of film purchases, tracks the film inventory, has the production report and call sheet typed and distributed, coordinates and checks to make sure that third parties such as the caterer know where to report for the next day's shooting, handles all travel arrangements, negotiates hotel rates, soothes cranky cast and crew and helps them with whatever problem they may have, and basically carries the entire production on his or her shoulders. When not involved with the above, the POC is the production manager's right hand and works closely with the UPM in an effort to catch the endless things that can and do go wrong.

No low-budget film can afford to pay these selfless people what they are truly worth, so I will relate what is being paid and what we paid. The union does not list a minimum rate; the rate chart only says "As negotiated." However, on a union film shot in 2005, Columbia Pictures budgeted $1,900 per week for 5 days in town. *The Anarchist Cookbook* paid $700 for a six-day week.

A larger production will often employ an assistant production coordinator (APOC) to help with the demands of the office. *The Anarchist Cookbook* could not afford an APOC, but the same Columbia picture referenced above paid $1,300 for a five-day week. Had *Anarchist* used an APOC, we would have probably paid about $600 for a six-day week.

A production secretary is helpful regardless of the size of production in order to answer phones and generally take some of the burden off of the POC. The union film cited above paid its production secretary $900 for a five-day week, whereas *Anarchist* paid $500 for a six-day week.

811-08 Production Accountant & Assistants

The production accountant pays the bills, tracks the costs, and supervises the payroll. Once each week, the UPM and the production accountant should sit down together and go through each line in the budget, determine how much has been spent and how much will be needed to finish the picture. This is called an *estimate to complete*. This is how you will know if you are under or over budget, and where you might have savings. (See Chapter 22, "Tracking The Film's Progress".) This position is so important that you should get the most experienced accountant you can afford. Union accountants start at $2263 for a five-day week. On *Anarchist*, we paid $1200 for a six-day week.

On really large, complicated shows, your accounting staff might consist of six or seven people including the production accountant, an assistant accountant, a payroll clerk and a few second assistants, and file clerks. A production accountant usually has at least an assistant accountant and a payroll clerk. Union assistants start at $1,268 for a five-day week, while studios are currently paying 2nd assistants around $1200 per week, and payroll clerks $1,400 per week. *Anarchist* could not afford an assistant which put a much greater burden on our production accountant. We did hire a payroll clerk who we paid $800 for a six-day week.

811-09 Production Assistants

On union films, companies have to be careful not to use production assistants in jobs covered by union contracts. On non-union independent films, production assistants do everything including helping out in the office and acting as "gofers," assisting in handling extras, and/or helping out various departments as additional man-power. Often companies will have a group of office PAs, and another group of set PAs. It is a great learning position, but I caution anyone from trying to make a career of it. You are capable of much more. However, for the independent producer, production assistants usually make up an enthusiastic and ready supply of labor. On large Hollywood films, PAs make from $100 to $130 per day depending on experience. On low-budget independents, the rate is usually closer to $100 per day.

811-12 Pre-production Breakdown

In the early stages of planning a film, or before someone tries to raise the money to make a film, it is necessary to do a preliminary production board and a budget. The breakdown process was covered in "Part II" of this book. All costs related to this early breakdown and budget would go into this account. Studios allocate $2,500 to $7,500 to this expense, depending on how detailed the budget is and how much time is involved. More complicated budgets or extensive revisions will cost more. A low-budget film could follow the *Anarchist* example and put in $1,500, or you can do it yourself and save the money.

811-13 Script Timing

Script timing, another early planning stage process, means having a script supervisor estimate the finished screen time of the picture based on the shooting script. Although you can roughly figure about a minute of screen time per page, a script supervisor can be much more accurate. You will very quickly know if your script is too long or too short. Most low-budget features try to aim for somewhere in the vicinity of 100 to 120 minutes. *The Anarchist Cookbook*'s running time is 101 minutes according to the DVD case.

How does a script supervisor accomplish this estimate? He or she will sit down with the script and a stopwatch, read the dialog aloud, and even act out the action while timing each scene. The result will be a timing report which will summarize each scene and show its length in minutes and seconds. This report can be very helpful in determining what scenes to eliminate if cuts must be made. It is better to cut a scene before filming it than to waste money that will never appear on screen. Nevertheless, if the timing comes out to just a little longer than what you hope will be the final running time, it's not a bad thing. This will give you a little room to make pacing adjustments when editing the film.

A script timing typically costs from $600 to $800. If the final running time of the film is not critical, this is not an essential item.

811-35 Teacher / Welfare Worker

See "Working with Minors" in Chapter 9. If you are employing minors in your film, hire a studio teacher. Period. I cannot emphasize this enough. In Los Angeles, union teachers make $36.76 per hour on union pictures, and $43.45 per hour on non-union pictures. Why more on non-union pictures? Because the rate hike is an attempt to compensate the teacher for the fact that fringe benefits are not being paid into the union on a non-union picture. Regardless of the cost, studio teachers are worth every penny you pay them. This is not an area where you should try and save money. Studio teachers are discussed in more detail in Chapter 9.

811-51 Purchases

In the *Anarchist* budget, a token $500 was put here as an allowance toward whatever purchases might be necessary such as a production board or strips. We actually never charged any expenses against this account and it therefore became a $500 savings.

811-56 Rentals

No money was allocated here in the *Anarchist* budget. Any production office equipment rentals that we may have incurred were charged to office equipment rentals in account 865-57. One item that might be included here would be the accounting computer system.

811-58 Car & Box Rentals

If the production manager or anyone else in the production department had a deal that included a car allowance, it would be put here. It usually amounts to $150 per week. No one in production on *Anarchist* had a car allowance.

Since everyone in an office situation usually needs a computer to work with these days, a box rental for the employee's computer is usually allowed for. Typically it is $50 per week. Since computer prices have fallen so drastically, on a longer film production you could buy computers for people instead of giving them a box rental and you would come out ahead. For that reason, longer pictures will often cap the computer rental at $600 to $1,000 per picture per person.

811-40 Miscellaneous Expense

Since there were no additional anticipated expenses that were not covered in any of the other sub-accounts, no money was allocated here.

813-00 Camera

This is where all the planning and expense to put an image on film (or on a video chip) comes to fruition. Everything that you do goes toward arranging the people and objects before the camera. Decisions made in this area will affect your final product more than any other area.

This is the moment to decide whether you will be shooting on film or video. As mentioned in Chapter 2, DV can save you a lot of money if your film is to be released on DVD. In April of 2000, the *Los Angeles Times* carried a story entitled, "In This Day and Age, Everyone's a Director." It told of a sophomore in high school who wrote, shot, directed, and edited a two-hour action-adventure movie called *Stealing Can Be Murder*. It went on to say that his total cost was $130. This was a film using a $3,000 consumer DV camera.

The mainstream version of this high school kid is Robert Rodriguez, director of *Sin City*, *Once Upon a Time in Mexico*, and the *Spy Kids* films. He does it all—but with a 24P high-definition video camera instead of a consumer DV camera. DV is fine for DVD, internet, or any other form of home video. But the standard for high resolution video to be released in theaters is 24P. Both Sony and Panavision currently have excellent 24P cameras available. Michael Mann and George Lucas are just two of the better known directors moving into this new medium. Michael Mann used Hi-Def video throughout his film *Ali*, while George Lucas shot most of the recent *Star Wars* episodes on Hi-Def.

But what about quality? Isn't there something about film that 24P can't reproduce? Well, yes, there is. 24P cannot handle the same wide latitude of exposure that film can. That means, in a sunny outdoor shot, you are going to lose detail in either the shadows or the highlights. This situation is 24P's weakest area. Nevertheless, properly lit, 24P can be gorgeous. The staff at Panavision sat me in a room and showed me footage shot by one of Hollywood's most talented directors of photography, Alan Daviau. Mr. Daviau shot the exact same scenes on both 24P and the new Kodak Vision 500™ stock under a variety of conditions, ranging from tungsten lit interiors to sunny outdoors. They did not tell me which was which until I had viewed all of the footage and made my preferences known. In every case, I preferred the 24P shots. They looked richer to me and seemed to have colors that were more vibrant with more contrast.

I think the explanation is that even though 24P can only record a limited latitude of exposure, what it does record is stretched over the entire latitude of the print stock, giving you a rich and vibrant image. The lesson here is that video must be lit well. It's true that you can go out on a downtown street at night and shoot your heart out with 24P. But if you want it to look great, you had better light it well, or it will look like an episode of *Insomniac with Dave Attell*.

813-01 Director of Photography

The director of photography (DP) has more to do with how your film will look than any other person on the crew. Choose wisely. If you are shooting video, it would be best to get a DP who is experienced in lighting for video. When interviewing DPs, discuss with them how you want the film to look and listen to their ideas. Like finding your soulmate, you'll know when you meet the right one.

There are two different styles of working among DPs: the American style and the European style. The European DPs are often called *lighting cameramen*. This goes to the heart of the difference. European DPs take a more hands-on approach to lighting. They will actually call for specific lamps to be placed in specific positions. American DPs will often delegate more to the gaffer (or Chief Lighting Technician). They will discuss with him what sort of lighting effect and lens stop they are looking for and leave it up to the gaffer to deal with the specifics. These distinctions are, of course, stereotypes. I find many DPs combine aspects of both styles.

Current union minimum for DPs is $80.67 per hour or $5,646.90 for five 12-hour days. Most DPs work for over-scale rates, at least $6,000 per week. On *Anarchist* we paid $2500 for a six-day week due to the generosity of our DP. Be sure to schedule adequate preparation time, usually one to two weeks, for the DP to scout the locations with the lighting and grip keys.

813-02 Camera Operator

Union camera operators make a minimum of $49.59 per hour which comes to $3,471.30 for five 12-hour days. A way of saving money in this department (on a non-union film) is to have your DP also operate the camera as we did on *Anarchist*. Had this not been the case, we probably would have paid about $1500 for a six-day week. Nevertheless, we did allow for a few days of a steadicam operator at $500 per day.

813-03 First Assistant Camera

In *War of the Roses*, there is a shot which starts close on Michael Douglas's finger as it traces a path around the rim of a wine glass. At a certain moment, the camera racks focus to reveal Kathleen Turner in the background leaning on the railing of the second floor balcony. The scene is shot in extremely low light making the depth of focus in the close-up on the finger only millimeters long. The shot never loses focus even though the first camera assistant, Alan S. Blauvelt, had to continually adjust the focus as Michael Douglas's finger traced the rim of the glass. This is an excellent example of the art of what the British call the *focus puller*. To appreciate the skill required, it is necessary to realize that Alan was not looking through the camera or at a monitor. He was continually estimating the distance between the film plane and the object being photographed—by eye.

The first camera assistant is also responsible for maintaining and keeping track of the camera equipment, getting unneeded equipment off of rental, arranging for additional camera equipment such as special lenses or filters, keeping a shot log for the director of photography, hiring additional camera assistants and loaders as needed, and generally running the camera assistant crew.

In Los Angeles, scale for the first camera assistant is $36.02 per hour or $2,521.40 for a five-day, twelve-hour per day week. On a show with specialized equipment such as anamorphic lenses, the scale rises to $43.10 per hour or $3017 for a similar week. This is called the *tech rate*. Be advised that an experienced first camera assistant can earn as much as $10 per hour above the lower scale. On *The Anarchist Cookbook* with our compressed wage scale, we paid the first camera assistant $1500 per six-day week in recognition of his large responsibilities. We also allowed three days prep for him to go through all the camera equipment to make sure that it was all in proper working order, shoot lens tests, and load the truck. The wrap day is so that the camera equipment can be checked back into the rental house and any discrepancies can be immediately dealt with.

813-04 Second Assistant Camera

As you might expect, the second camera assistant assists the first camera assistant. In addition, the second camera assistant fills out the lab reports for the exposed film, loads the camera magazines in the absence of a loader, brings the needed lenses and filters to the camera from the truck, and keeps track of how much film stock is on hand, ordering more when needed. In addition to all of this, the second camera assistant is usually the person who holds the slate up in front of the camera, yells "Marker!" and then slaps the sticks together.

The current scale rate for a second camera assistant in Los Angeles is $33.16 or $2,321.20 for a week of five twelve-hour days. An experienced second camera assistant can demand an over-scale rate equal to that of first camera assistant scale. On *Anarchist*, we paid $900 for a six-day week. We added a day of prep and a day of wrap so that the first camera assistant would have some help with the equipment check out and check in.

813-05 Extra Camera Operators
813-06 Extra Camera Assistants

These accounts are where you would put additional camera crew for those days when you are shooting that spectacular stunt sequence.

813-07 Still Photographer

When you are thumbing through the reviews and ads for movies in the newspaper, your eye is often drawn to pictures which appear to be printed frames from the movie. These are rarely taken from the filmed footage, but instead are still shots taken by a still photographer. Movies are about people in motion and with an exposure time of 1/30th of a second for each frame, the subjects of each frame are often blurred. This motion blur is actually desirable in that it helps the illusion of motion and keeps the subjects from strobing. On the other hand, a still camera shooting alongside the motion picture camera can use a wider lens opening, faster film, and faster shutter speed to stop the subject's motion. This makes for a much more appealing publicity or ad photo. These still shots are taken by the unit still photographer.

On a union picture, a still photographer is part of the required staffing. They are part of Camera Local #600 and currently make a minimum of $43.11 per hour ($3,017.70 per five-day week) for a normal still photographer and $49.59 per hour ($3,471.30 per five-day week) for a portrait photographer. On *The Anarchist Cookbook,* we could not afford to hire a still photographer, so as a producer wearing many hats on this film, I filled in as best as I could. Obviously, the best photographs result when you have a professional still photographer in this position rather than an amateur such as me. Nevertheless, part of producing a low-budget film is making trade-offs to live within limited resources.

813-08 Loader

The camera loader is an entry-level position to the camera department. The loader's duties are to assist the camera assistants and to keep the camera magazines loaded with film. A loader can really streamline a shooting company, especially when you are shooting a lot of film. Union loaders currently make $28.39 per hour or $1,987.30 for a five-day week. This was a luxury we could not afford on *Anarchist.*

813-11 Loss & Damage

It used to be the case that studios would not let you budget for loss and damage. They said it was as if you were planning to damage the equipment. Nevertheless, accidents do happen and the occasional lens or filter will get broken so it is prudent to allow a token sum here. If a really expensive item is damaged, such as a camera or telescopic lens, the production's insurance policy will cover the costs less the deductible. On *Anarchist,* we put $1,500 in this account. Of that, we spent only $584.

813-51 Purchases

In the camera department, this money goes toward purchasing Sharpie markers, chamois for the camera eyepiece, and rolls of tape (film stock has its own account). It has always struck me as strange that the camera assistants cover the cameras in tape to insure that the magazine doesn't pop open or a stray light leak doesn't fog the film, even though Panavision will spend millions of dollars designing and producing the most advanced motion picture cameras in the world. I guess you can never be too secure, and the cost of a few rolls of tape is far preferable to losing a magazine full of exposed film. We allotted $500 to this account.

813-56 Rentals

Other than labor, this is where you can spend big money in the camera department. A fully accessorized Panavision camera package with a full set of lenses, filters, and backup camera bodies can easily reach $25,000 to $30,000 per week. The main camera package on a studio film is usually $18,000 to $22,000 per week. Depending on how busy they are, the camera rental houses will sometimes discount their rates, especially to low-budget films.

On *The Anarchist Cookbook*, we had a fairly unique situation in that the director wanted to shoot on different media or stock depending on the content of the scenes. We used regular 35mm color film during the happy days in the communal houses, as well as for the other normal scenes of real life. We used consumer grade DV for those times when the anarchists went into action and for Johnny Black's documentation of their activities. When Puck gets exiled to house arrest in Plano, Texas, we used grainy 16mm film with a coffee filter. The director said he wanted it to look like bad porn.

Shooting in all these different modes meant renting different equipment. Our normal 35mm camera was a Panavision PFX-M Millennium Camera. On the steadicam, we used a Moviecam Compact 35mm camera (also from Panavision). For the 16mm shooting in Plano, we used an Arri 16 SR3. Finally, for the DV sequences, we used a Sony DCR-VX1000 and sometimes its Canon equivalent. The DV footage looked so good that we actually had to degrade the image in the transfer process to get the look that the director wanted.

The budget shows how much we allotted for each of these items. Altogether we had budgeted $43,725 for camera equipment and we ended up actually spending only $34,061, a savings of $9,644. This shows the importance of working with your vendors and pushing for the very best possible deal.

813-58 Box Rental

Often camera assistants will want to receive a box rental. The box can consist of the assistant's tools, camera filters, rolling carts, tripods, or almost anything else that you might need in a camera package. I don't mind the camera assistant trying to pad his or her income, but I insist that a few rules are followed. I will not pay more for an item than I would need to pay to rent it for from a rental house. If the total rental comes to 50% or more of the purchase price, I may elect to purchase it with the idea that I would sell it at the end of the picture. If the item is part of the normal rental package, then I expect the rental package to be reduced to cover the box rental. Finally, I will not rent something that there is no need for. For example, I once had a camera assistant include a rain housing in his box rental on a picture that was to be largely shot on stage. His argument was that the rain housing was a part of his box and that it might be needed on one of the few days we had exterior. Of course, the rain housing was going to be available at all times on the truck. I told him that if the need for it arose, I would pay for it on the day it was used. Otherwise, whether it was on the truck or not, it I would not be paying for it.

Camera operators also occasionally ask for a box rental. An operator's box usually consists of a fluid camera head. This is reasonable since you want the operator to be working with a head that he or she is familiar with and that has been set up to the operator's specifications.

813-60 Miscellaneous Expense

There was nothing to add that wasn't covered in the normal accounts.

814-00 Art Department

Sometimes this account is referred to as SET DESIGN since that is the art department's primary function. Depending on the picture, the art department can oversee several other departments such as props, set dressing, and even costume.

814-01 Production Designer
814-02 Art Director & Assistant

This title, production designer, does not actually exist in the contract for Local 876, the west coast art directors' union. The titles that do exist are art director, assistant art director and visual consultant. In fact, if you want to credit an art director as production designer, you must petition Local 876 for permission. (It is routinely granted.) So why is production designer in the budget? George Orwell said it best in *1984*: Title Inflation. Just as experienced unit production managers prefer *production manager*, experienced art directors want to be called *production designer*.

1984's title inflation made a big deal out of nothing jobs or made sinister responsibilities seem benign. In contrast, production designer actually does have legitimate meaning in the way it is used in the business beyond simply dressing up the art director title. An art director may be concerned solely with the design and construction of the sets. The look and/or modification of locations are also often included. The title of production designer implies that the art director has taken on the additional responsibility of the look of the picture as a whole. As stated above, this can include the choice and/or design of props, set dressing, costume, and their visual effect on each other. Nevertheless, all good art directors have considered these elements regardless of their title.

Currently, an experienced union art director or production designer earns $2,750.86 minimum for a five-day week. There is no overtime since they are hired on an *on-call* basis. Most experienced art directors and production designers make at least twice that. Often on large extravagant studio pictures, a production designer will make $7,500 to $10,000 per week.

On *The Anarchist Cookbook*, we added to our normal department head rate and paid the art director $2,000 per week. He truly deserved much more, but generously agreed to work for this amount.

814-03 Set Designers

These are the people that produce the working drawings for the construction of the sets. Normally they are put in the budget for a specific number of weeks. Most of their time is spent in the prep period, but they can overlap into the shooting period depending on what the production's needs are. On a large studio film, there might be three or more set designers employed for a period of 10 to 15 weeks each. They would start as soon as a concept for the sets is ready. Since *The Anarchist Cookbook* had no stage sets, we did not need to hire any set designers.

Hollywood union set designers are classified into different pay scales based on how experienced they are. Currently, a Leadman Set Designer earns $42.11 per hour. They are usually employed for ten hours per day which equals 55 pay hours per week. This comes to $2,316.05 per week. Set designers are often hired on a weekly basis. In this case, you must give the set designer at least three day's notice before laying him or her off. The benefit to the show is a lower rate, such as $39.875 per hour or $2,193.13 per five-day week.

814-04 Illustrators & Graphic Artists

Production illustrators are the people who draw the storyboards. Storyboards are sketches of various of the various camera angles used to cover a scene. These are most useful in complicated visual effects sequences or in working out an action sequence. A series of storyboards allows everyone to understand what will be seen on screen.

We did not use a storyboard artist on *The Anarchist Cookbook*. However, we did hire a graphic artist to paint the graffiti on the walls of the communal house nicknamed Sam. We got a huge bargain from a very talented artist who did it for the fun of it. We paid $500 per week for two weeks.

Union production illustrators make a minimum of $438.65 per day or $1,934.33 per five-day week. Again, if you hire them on a weekly basis, you must give at least three days' notice before laying them off.

814-05 MODEL MAKERS

Model makers are needed when the director requires a model of the set so that the blocking can be planned before the set is built. The director can use a small periscope viewer to see the model from the perspective of a camera on the set. These models are based on the blueprints of the set plans and elevations, and are usually made of ¼-inch foam-core.

Model makers are also necessary for special types of photography using foreground miniatures. In this day of expensive computer generated effects, this trick is used far too infrequently. It was used to good effect in Mel Brooks's *Robin Hood: Men in Tights*. Near the beginning of the film, Robin swims from the Middle East to England. As he drags himself onto the beach, we see giant letters perched on the cliffs overlooking the beach in the manner of the Hollywood Sign spelling out "England." This was achieved through the use of a foreground miniature. See figures 19.4-6. The model maker cut the letters out of ¼-inch foam-core, glued them to a rod, and added model train foliage. We then set the rod up in front of the camera so that the letters appeared to be on the top of the cliff.

I saw this technique used in another instance in which a number of horsemen were riding away from the camera and disappeared inside a distant castle's walls. The castle was actually a miniature suspended a few feet in front of the camera in such a way that it appeared to be resting on a distant hill. As the riders rode away, they seemed to ride into the opening of the castle wall and disappear behind it.

Model makers are represented by the same union that represents set designers. Minimum union scale for a leadman model maker is $42.11 per hour if hired on a daily basis, or 39.875 per hour if hired on a weekly basis. A 50-hour week would come to $2,193.13, the same as a leadman set designer.

We had no reason to hire a model maker on *The Anarchist Cookbook*. If we had, we would have looked for an art student or some such person that we could afford.

814-06 Production Assistants

In the Art Department, production assistants are used to research visual reference and perform regular gofer duties. On *Anarchist,* we hired a production assistant for the art department at $100 per day or $600 per six-day week.

814-11 Blueprinting

Although we had no stage sets on *Anarchist,* we did require some blueprinting for work that we did in the communal houses. It used to be that the blueprints would be made by a blueprinting service which required that the drawings be left for a period of time. Now, the production usually rents a non-ammonia blueprinting machine and keeps it in the art department for use at any time. We budgeted $1,000 for all blueprinting expenses. We did not spend any money in this account.

814-15 Stock Units & Backings

Some charts of accounts put this item under set construction. This account covers the rental of stock units such as fireplaces, stairways, arches, etc. It also covers backings. Backings are large painted or photographic images that are hung on a set to give a background to views outside of windows or doorways. On *Child's Play 3* when we moved our forest onto a stage, we covered the stage wall with a forest backing which could be glimpsed beyond the trees and shrubs that had been set up on the stage. This prevented the camera from seeing the stage wall and enhanced the illusion that we were actually in a forest. It used to be that all backings were painted by scenic artists who specialized in painting background scenery. They could be as simple as a black velour backing to simulate a night sky, or a piece of canvas painted sky blue to simulate the daytime sky outside a window, or as complex as a painting that might have a cityscape or country view painted in such detail that the camera sees it as though it were the real thing. Actually, there is much less detail than you might think. These backings tended to be rather impressionistic and relied on the viewer's eye to supply a lot of the detail.

Other tricks were used to make backings look even more real. Night backings sometimes had miniature lights attached to them which were made to twinkle like stars. On *The Hindenburg,* the sea backing that hung

Fig. 19.4. The author and a member of the art department adjusting the miniature foliage glued to the rod holding the England sign.

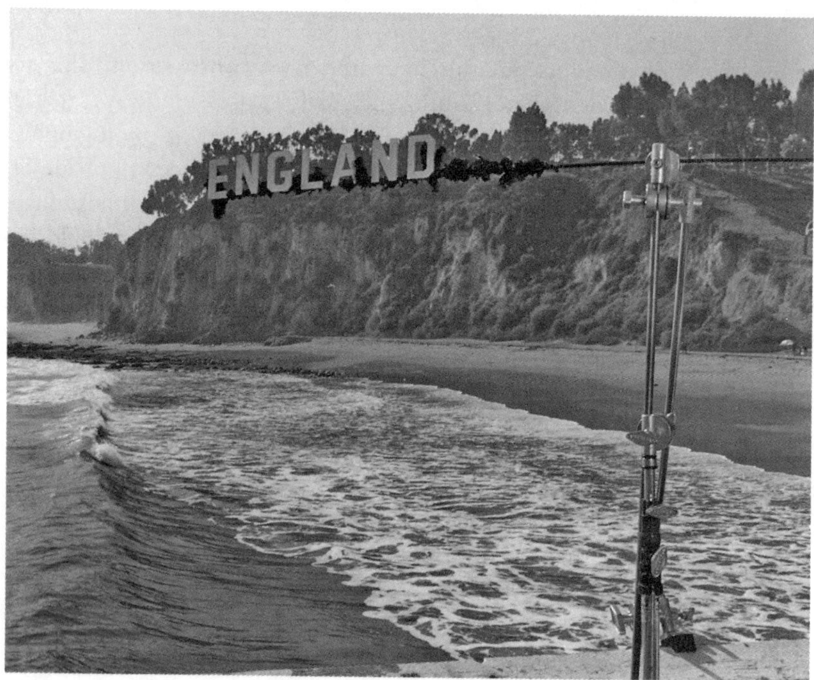

Fig. 19.5. The England sign showing the rod being held by a C-stand.

Fig. 19.6. The England sign foreground miniature as it appeared in ***Robin Hood: Men In Tights***.

outside the airship windows had small pieces of cellophane glued to the water areas so that when they were blown with a fan, they reflected the stage lights the way actual waves might reflect the sunlight. When a cityscape backing was used in a night scene, the windows of the buildings would be painted with translucent paint and there would be lights mounted behind the backing that would shine through the painted windows making them look real.

Eventually, large photographic transparencies were developed which could be lit from behind. These were called *translights* and could provide any background that could be photographed. This obviously saved a great deal of labor. Nevertheless, they have not completely replaced painted backings since sometimes you need a backing of a view that doesn't actually exist and so it cannot be photographed.

With no constructed sets, we had no need for backings on *Anarchist*. If we had wanted to rent one, we probably would have had to pay a rental fee of $2,500 to $7,500 per week, depending on the size and complexity of the backing. If at all possible, I would have tried to make do with a simple day or night sky backing since these costs would have been beyond our budget. If you require a backing to be specially created for your picture, the backing companies will often do it for half the normal rate if they get to keep the backing at the end of photography.

814-51 Purchases & Research

Although this sometimes goes toward professional research services, this is usually needed for books that the art director will buy as reference. Often the art director will want to add these books to his or her personal library. You can relieve the picture of some of the cost by selling them to the art director for 50% of their cost if he or she is willing; or, you can just give them to the art director for a job well done. On *The Anarchist Cookbook*, we allotted $250 to this account.

814-56 Rentals

In the art department, this would cover the rental of drawing tables, copy machines, special lamps, and any other equipment they may require. On *Anarchist*, we used sweat shop tactics and made them work on their laps.

814-58 Car & Box Rentals

Typically, a production designer or art director would get a car allowance, especially on a picture with many locations. On *Anarchist*, we originally had $125 per week budgeted for the art director's car allowance. Instead, we rented him a car since he was from Los Angeles and we were working in Dallas. That cost was put into the transportation account.

We did allow the art director a computer box rental at $50 per week. Sometimes set designers or illustrators will get a box allowance for graphic equipment or a computer.

814-60 Miscellaneous Expenses

Nothing required here.

815-00 Construction

This is where all set construction costs go. Under the original plan, *Anarchist* was not to have any stage sets, so we did not budget any money here; (a decision we later regretted). We did have some money in 837-01 for "location modifications and restoration" and this was used to pay for changes to the two communal house sets. The reason I say we regretted not having some set construction money was because of a scene that took place in the attic of the house called Son of Sam. The house had an attic and we figured we would just shoot the scene in the actual attic. This turned out to be a bad decision not only because of the difficulty of getting crew and equipment up into the attic, but because an attic, in Dallas in June, can reach temperatures well above 100° Fahrenheit. It would have been so much more efficient and comfortable to have rented a warehouse and built the attic set there. To redeem myself in the eyes of the cast and crew, I rented a portable air-conditioning unit to provide some relief, but it never really got comfortable.

815-01 Construction Coordinator

This is who runs the construction crew. The construction coordinator comes up with a budget for the sets once the art director settles on a set list and an approach. A good construction coordinator can save a picture hundreds of thousands of dollars simply by making wise choices in materials and finding ways to give the art director the look that is desired without spending huge sums on expensive items. For example, Masonite can be painted to look like marble, brick facades can be created with vacuum-formed plastic, and naturalistic rock formations can be carved out of large blocks of Styrofoam as was done in the bug tunnel set on *Starship Troopers.*

On a large union picture, the construction coordinator might be hired as early as ten weeks before principal photography starts. He or she will probably stay on through the second week of wrap. Union scale is $2,061.47 for a five-day week, although most experienced coordinators will make around $2500 per week. They will also rent you a trailer with all their power tools included for about $2,000 per week. Had we needed a construction coordinator on *Anarchist*, I probably would have tried to find someone for around $1,250 per six-day week.

815-02 Constuction Foreman

The positions listed here are usually the general foreman, paint foreman, and labor foreman. In addition, if the work requires it, you can also list a metal foreman and plaster foreman. Job titles in the film business are traditional and are not necessarily politically correct. Suffice it to say that one of the best general foremen I ever worked with was a woman. She is now an excellent construction coordinator.

The general foreman, also known as the propmaker foreman, is in charge of the propmakers. Outside of the film business, you would call propmakers carpenters. These are the crewmembers that make the walls of the sets and do most of the basic building tasks. The paint foreman obviously is in charge of the painters and will get a box rental to provide spraying equipment, air compressors, brushes, and rollers. The labor foreman runs the utility labor crew. These are the crewmembers that keep the stage or shop space clean, and take care of the general labor needs on the construction crew. The labor foreman also is in charge of the tool room, checking the tools in and out, and keeping them in good repair. If you have any welding needs, the metal foreman will run that crew. If you are doing any plaster work or masonry, such as plaster moldings or "pointing up" Styrofoam rocks, the plaster foreman would oversee that work. The table that follows lists the foremen and their current minimum hourly rates.

General Forman	$35.03 per hour
Paint foreman	$35.04 per hour
Labor foreman	$27.74 per hour
Metal foreman	$35.03 per hour
Plaster foreman	$34.11 per hour

A construction crew typically works for 10 hours per day. This has proven to be the most efficient day. Eight hours is really too short and the crew's efficiency starts to fall off past ten hours.

815-08 Construction Labor – Local
815-25 Construction Labor - Distant

These two accounts cover all the labor costs for the propmakers, painters, laborers, welders, and plasterers in town and on distant location. Hollywood uses a 70/30 split for labor and materials in estimating sets. For example, if you have a set that you will be spending $30,000 to construct, it is expected that 70% of the cost of the set, or $21,000, will be labor and 30% of the cost of the set, or $9,000, will be materials. On a low-budget film where you are not paying high salaries and union benefits, the split might be more in the range of 60/40 or even 50/50. This is important to know because you must remember to apply a fringe rate to the labor portion of the costs. Even on a non-union picture, labor will have around 18% payroll taxes applied. On union workers, combined fringe benefits and payroll taxes together can be as high as 28% to 32%.

There is a bit of a disconnect between how set construction is budgeted and how the money is spent. Producers like to see the budget entered per set. In other words, they like to know that the Int. Living Room will cost $50,000, and the Ext. Alley set will cost $27,500 (in labor and materials). The reason for this is the producer wants to know what will be saved if the Int. Living Room or the Ext. Alley set is eliminated. He or she thinks, "The living room costs $50,000. If I eliminate the living room set I will save $50,000."

On the other hand, the construction coordinator knows that a particular picture has, say, 23 sets that must be ready to shoot at various points spread throughout the shooting schedule. The reasoning goes somewhat like this: "I have to build 23 sets and have them ready at various times throughout our eight week schedule. I can probably handle this with a crew of about 10 propmakers, 5 painters, and 7 laborers. This will keep everyone busy at an efficient pace and *I can hang on to my crew throughout.* The labor should cost about $150,000 plus fringe." The italics express the coordinator's main concern. At a time when skilled labor can often be in high demand, once the coordinator gathers a crew, he or she does not want to lay them off until the job is done.

Now, let's assume that the producer is successful in persuading the writer to eliminate the living room. The production manager rushes in to tell the coordinator that the living room is gone and to reflect the savings in the construction cost reports. What is the construction coordinator left with? A hole in the work schedule. To save the $50,000, the coordinator must lay off everyone in the construction crew for the period of time that would have been spent building the living room. At the end of that time, the entire crew must be rehired, or a new crew must be found if the original crew has gone on to another job. This is a nightmare, especially if there are numerous productions vying for a limited labor force, or if the construction is taking place on a distant location.

Experienced construction coordinators can swing with the punches and will find a way to make it work. Nevertheless, it is important to realize that what may appear to be a substantial savings may not be much of a savings at all.

815-11 Loss & Damage

This does not cover normal wear and tear. If the motor windings on a router burn out because it is an old router and has reached the end of its useful life, then the construction coordinator should replace the tool with an up-to-date one at his or her cost. That is part of what you are paying a box rental for. (If you rent a car and the motor falls out on the freeway, you expect the rental car company to provide a replacement immediately.) However, if a company truck backs over the router, then you should expect to replace it at the company's expense. A token amount is sufficient here, perhaps $500 to $1,500 depending on the size of the budget.

815-29 Striking – Local
815-31 Striking – Distant

Striking is the removal and disposal of sets after they have been photographed. There are two types of striking: dead strike, and fold & hold. Fold & hold is covered under 815-35.

Dead strike is what you do when you will never need the set again. It can be as brutal and direct as running a skip loader over the set and shoveling it into a dumpster. In recent years, studios and independents have become more sensitive to the enormous waste the industry creates and have begun recycling the materials used in sets. They have set up programs to recycle the huge amounts of lumber which used to be simply thrown away. The lumber is sent to woodchip product manufacturers to be turned into chip board, paper, MDF (medium density fiberboard), and other similar products. Sometimes it is cleaned up by having the nails removed and sent to third world countries as construction lumber. (It is illegal to resell it for construction purposes in the U.S.) Even Styrofoam, that nemesis of most city recycling programs, can be recycled. On *Starship Troopers*, the manufacturer that supplied all the Styrofoam for the bug tunnels took it all back in the end and recycled it.

Striking (labor and materials) is typically budgeted at 10% of the construction costs (labor and materials). Sometimes this works, sometimes it doesn't, but it's a good place to start. The labor would consist of mostly laborers with a few drivers. If there is metalwork in the set, that would be broken down by metalworkers. Striking materials would actually cover heavy machinery rentals, dumpsters, and special tools.

One way that I have used to save on strike costs is to trade the materials in the set for the labor of striking the set. In other words, allow an individual or group to keep all the materials that they can salvage as long as they clean up the site and leave it in the same condition that you found it in. The groups that might be interested would include churches, service clubs, and other community organizations. Be sure that you are covered for any liability that would be incurred if someone was hurt dismantling the set. This approach works best on distant location or areas outside of Los Angeles. In Los Angeles, I once sold a number of set pieces of a science fiction movie to a paintball park with the understanding that they would furnish all labor and transportation to strike the set. On *S.W.A.T.*, we bought an L-1011 aircraft minus the engines and wings from the plane graveyard at Mojave, California. We had them quarter the fuselage lengthwise and we trucked the pieces to a site north of Los Angeles where we had prepared a concrete pad and supports. At the end of filming, we sold the reassembled fuselage to the landowner for a price that was a fraction of what it had cost us. He, in turn, planned to rent out the plane as a filming location.

Sometimes it doesn't work out. On *Robin Hood: Men in Tights*, we were approached by a restaurant that wanted to buy the castle wall and gate that we had built on a tract of land in the Antelope Valley. In that instance, I had to turn them down since the set was not built to withstand weather. It would have fallen apart after a rain or two.

815-34 Restoration – Sets

This account can be used to itemize costs involved in the re-erection of stored sets, or the refurbishing of standing sets. Most often, these costs are just included in the construction labor and purchases accounts.

815-35 – Fold & Hold

When you have a set that you may want to use again, either for a sequel, another movie, or in post production for added shots in your current movie, you go through the *fold & hold* process. This involves carefully taking the set apart by taking down the wall flats, staircases, fireplace mantles, ceilings, and other pieces of the set, stacking them in compact units, and delivering them to a warehouse for storage. Western Studio Services in Los Angeles stores sets for productions and they add to their warehouse space every year. There are acres of sets that are being stored that will never be used again…ever, but what a collection! (I think that I'm getting an idea for a movie: sort of *Night of the Living Dead* meets *Tomb Raider*.)

Typically, what happens as you start to finish shooting sets on your movie, the director thinks maybe there will be other shots needed and doesn't want to strike them. You think "The stage rental is killing me. I need to get off this stage." So you offer to fold and hold the set. This seems like a reasonable compromise and the director agrees to it. The sets get stored and forgotten since the people involved with storing them are off the picture long before the decision is made not to do any added scenes. So the sets sit in the warehouse, collecting money for the storage company and dust for anyone who eventually shows up to claim them. Do you remember the final shot in *Raiders of the Lost Ark*? I think they could have shot that in a set storage warehouse.

The fold and hold process can be useful when done with some thought. After *Spiderman* principal photography was finished, I came on to the picture to handle the post production shooting and added scenes. When that was finished, it was decided to store certain specific sets because it was assumed that a sequel would be made. The director knew exactly what would be needed. We stored the Int. Aunt May's House (including Int. Peter's Bedroom), Int. Mr. Jameson's Office, parts of Int. Osborn Mansion, and the alley where Spiderman first kisses Mary Jane. All of the sets were used in the sequel and the production saved a considerable amount of money by not having to rebuild them.

815-51 Purchases

This is the materials part of labor and materials. The account is usually input by set showing the full price of each set and taking 30% (or whatever percentage you are using) of the full price as the cost of materials for each of the sets. Using the example of the Int. Living Room set from above, it would appear as follows:

Description	Amount	Units	×	Rate	Subtotal
Int. Living Room	30	%	1	50,000	15,000

815-52 Greens Purchase

The term *greens* encompasses all plants used on the set, both real and artificial. It also includes grass mattes, sod, and dirt. Depending on the type of sets you are constructing, this account can range from nearly the full cost of the sets, in the case of a forest set, down to a small amount for house plants. The money in this account is usually entered as an allowance.

815-54 Backing Rental & Purchase

See the discussion above under "814-15 Stock Units/Backings."

815-55 Trash Removal

All construction activity generates a large amount of trash. Typically, the construction coordinator will rent dumpster bins which will be delivered to the stage or the location and which will be emptied periodically. Normally, the charge is for a certain number of trips to empty them. Your local waste disposal company can give you prices for the size bin you are ordering.

815-56 Rentals

This is where you would put the allowance for heavy equipment rentals such as construction cranes, graders, skip loaders, man lifts, and any other items you might need to rent from third parties.

815-57 Platforms

This would cover the cost of building camera platforms that are not part of the set.

815-58 Car & Box Rental

The construction coordinator will usually have a car allowance. Often the vehicle is the coordinator's pickup truck for which the production will pay $250 per week. In addition, the coordinator will get around $2,000 per week for a tool package and trailer. Some even have an additional office trailer that they will use as the construction office.

The other box rental that is usually found here is the one for the painter foreman. That tends to go for $350 to $500 per week and includes the compressors and all the spraying equipment that will be needed.

815-60 Miscellaneous

Any items that do not fit above can be put here, but be sure to describe them explicitly.

816-00 Special Effects

Along with the normal rain, wind, smoke, and fire, these folks are almost always asked to do things that have never been done before. Every picture brings new challenges to them. On *Hollow Man* when the invisible Sebastian gets up off of his hospital bed, we see the depression that he is making in the bed flatten out and disappear as he apparently rises. This was accomplished by the special effects crew, and I can pretty much guarantee that they had never done that before.

The same gap between budgeting methods and how money is spent that was discussed above regarding set construction budgeting also exists in the budgeting of special effects. The studios and/or producers like to think about the costs in distinct gags like the "freeway pileup" or the "apartment fire." The effects coordinator is thinking about how much labor he or she needs over how many weeks to accomplish the job in the most efficient way. If you eliminate the "apartment fire" do you save the $25,000 that was budgeted for it? Probably not entirely.

You may not need an effects crew with you throughout the shooting schedule. We did not on *Anarchist*. Using the information on your shooting schedule, you can see when you will be filming scenes that involve special effects, so count the days and budget accordingly. On *Anarchist*, we determined that we would need an effects crew on three separate shooting days. By hiring only for those days, we saved an enormous amount of money. Another benefit is that you will be able to pay a little more per day and buy the production a more experienced crew.

In planning for special effects days, the weather can become a factor. Many productions determine that if it starts to rain, they will just shoot in the rain. That's fine, and it is wonderful that the director is able to be so flexible and accommodating. But what happens when you are in the middle of the coverage on a scene that you started shooting in the rain and the rain stops? Nothing you shoot after that will match. It will look strange if the wide master is shot in a downpour, and when you go in close on the actors there is not a drop of rain in sight. One way to remedy this situation is to be prepared to create rain. That means a special effects crew equipped with rain towers and a water source. If you have an effects crew with you every day, you don't need to worry. However, if you do not have them with you all the time, then it might be wise to build in a few days' labor for rainy days.

816-01 Effects Coordinator

Also known as the special effects supervisor, on a big effects picture, this person might be overseeing the work of 20 to 50 effects technicians. The special effects coordinator is responsible for conceiving, manufacturing, and rigging (setting up) all the special effects gags or tricks. Union scale for this position is $35.16 per hour which translates to $2,461.20 for five 12-hour days. On studio pictures, this position can command $50 per hour or $3,500 per week for an experienced coordinator.

If you have pyrotechnic gags in your picture, the effects coordinator must have a license to possess and use explosives. It is important to check local laws regarding this. The effects coordinator is responsible for adhering to all laws and should obtain all necessary permits. Whatever you may be planning, there is probably an AMPTP safety bulletin outlining safe practices. These can be found online at **http://www.csatf.org/bulletintro.shtml**.

On *The Anarchist Cookbook*, the limited amount of special effects work that we had allowed us to schedule all of it over three shooting days. We added one day to allow the effects coordinator to collect the items that would be needed and to do some limited preparation. We found an experienced person with an explosive license for $400 per day. Our total expense for this person was $1,600 plus payroll tax. This was the extent of our special effects crew since the things we were doing did not require any additional help.

816-02 Operating Labor

This is where the effects technicians working on the shooting company are put. If the effects coordinator is not able to be on set due to preparation of future gags, this group is run by a key effects technician who should also have an explosive license. Union scale for this position is $35.03 per hour if the effects coordinator will be on set, or $35.16 per hour if not. On a studio picture, the key effects technician can make $40 per hour or more.

The rest of the set crew can be made up of special effects technicians. Union scale for technicians is $30.56 per hour. Studios usually end up paying these people around $35 per hour.

On a non-union picture, they will cost whatever you can persuade them to work for. Nevertheless, remember that you are paying for technical skill and experience, and entrusting the safety of actors, stunt players, and crew to them. In addition, you are expecting them to keep you free of violating state and federal laws. If that were not enough responsibility, you expect the things that they do for you will work the first time and every time. When you can afford it, they are worth a few extra bucks.

816-05 RIGGING & STRIKING LABOR

These people are interchangeable with the set crew except that this is the labor preparing the gags in the effects shop and setting them up on the set. In addition to the special effects technicians, usually a laborer or two is included to keep the shop clean and to assist the technicians. Often, in the spirit of the budget disconnect discussed above, the money in this account is listed per gag. A better way of budgeting it might be to determine how many people in the shop are needed for how long and list each person you plan to employ.

816-11 LOSS & DAMAGE

The comments above under "815-11 LOSS AND DAMAGE" for set construction apply here also. If you have a lot of special effects work, you might put in $1,500 to $5,000. Our exposure here on *Anarchist* was minimal and we put no money in this account.

816-19 MANUFACTURING LABOR & MATERIALS

This is where you could allow money for the special effects crew to make specialized props. For instance, the large machine in *Hollow Man* that the scientists used to irradiate the serum, which turned Sebastian invisible, was built by the special effects crew. Other items that might go here would be effects manufacturing done by outside contractors.

816-19 Load & Unload Labor

This account is a vestigial remnant of the days when studios employed crews to load and unload the trucks going out and returning from locations. Think of it as being similar to the human appendix and ignore it.

816-51 Purchases

All purchases necessary to accomplish the special effects gags go here, including explosives. If you are using pyrotechnic effects, be sure to get price quotes because they are expensive. Our needs were minor on *Anarchist*, so we just put a token amount in this account.

816-56 Rentals

This can cover everything from specialized equipment, to construction cranes, to shop space. Generally, the effects coordinator will come with a set of tools that you will rent in the same way that the construction coordinator does. Often the tools will be in a trailer which you will also rent. These items are usually put in the box rental account below. Be sure you know what items are included in the tool inventory since any items not included will have to be rented separately. Items that are typically not included in the box rental are such things as large wind machines (both gas powered and electric Ritters), specialized block and tackle mechanisms, and hydraulic pumps. Again, *Anarchist*'s needs were minor and we put only a token amount here.

816-58 Box Rental

As mentioned above, this is where the special effects coordinator's tool rental would go. Typically it runs about $2,000 per week. Even at this rate, you are getting a bargain. You could manufacture an automobile from scratch with the tools that are usually included.

Occasionally, a car allowance is also included similar to the construction coordinator's allowance. It often runs around $250 per week. In addition, there may a trailer which may be rented separately from the tool package. There was no need for an extensive tool package on *Anarchist*.

816-60 Miscellaneous Expenses

Special effects miscellaneous can include shop utilities, outside contracts, and any other unusual expenses not covered above.

817-00 Set Operations

This account contains the labor, rentals, and purchases for the general operation of the shooting company, including the grip crew. The grips are responsible for all equipment on which the camera is mounted such as the dolly, cranes, and cablecams. Grip crews also build camera platforms, move set walls in and out of the set, hang backings, and erect and maintain all diffusion materials which are not attached to a lighting instrument, such as free standing gels, silks, reflectors, and flags. On union shows, the grips, instead of the construction crew or laborers, perform the fold and hold operations if a set is to be stored once it has been shot. According to Wikipedia (**http://en.wikipedia.org**) the term *grip* comes from circus and vaudeville crews, and refers to the bag or grip that they carried their tools in.

817-01 First Company Grip

The first company grip, also known as the key grip, is in charge of the grip crew. These folks take great pride in being able to put a camera anywhere. To do this, they have a large arsenal of equipment ranging from dollies to cranes, to cable-cams, to platforms, and truss rigs. They can attach a camera directly to a vehicle or make it possible to dolly around a moving car.

Union key grips earn no less than $34.54 per hour, which translates to $2,417.80 per five-day week, and often command as much as $38-40 per hour. On *Anarchist*, we paid our standard department head rate of $1,500 per six-day week. In addition, our key grip served as the dolly grip saving us from hiring an additional person.

You will need to give your key grip enough prep to allow proper scouting of the locations and the loading of the equipment truck.

817-02 Second Company Grip

In addition to being the second person in charge of the grip crew, the second company grip is responsible for the equipment: ordering it, its maintenance, and returning all of it in good condition to the vendor. Occasionally, this position is called the best boy grip. I assume this comes from the time when film crews were strictly all male and the key grip picked the most reliable and best of all his boys to be his assistant and manage the equipment. And yes, there are female best boys too. Women in this position have been credited as best boy.

Union scale for the second company grip is $31.28 per hour or $2,189.60 per five-day week. Usually, they are paid on a par with the dolly grip ($32.39 per hour). They can command up to $35 per hour. On *Anarchist*, we paid our standard second position rate of $200 per day or $1,200 for a six-day week. Usually, it is helpful to have the second company grip start at about the same time as the key grip so that they can consult with each other on the location scouts.

817-03 Crane/Dolly Grip

As the position title implies, the dolly grip handles the operation of the dolly and a crane, if one is being used. A large camera crane will often require two crane grips, one positioned at the camera end of the crane and one positioned at the opposite end.

A word of caution is in order whenever a camera crane is in use. They are essentially large levers and can act like a catapult. When the camera is mounted on the crane arm, and the operator and assistant are seated on it, the arm is balanced by the use of lead weights being placed on, or by mercury being pumped to, the opposite end of the arm. This allows the grip to achieve a state of neutral balance in the arm thus making the arm easier to move. If any weight is suddenly removed without the arm being locked and rebalanced, the weighted end will crash to the ground while launching the camera and any persons on the opposite end of the arm into space, resulting in either death or serious injury. No person or object should be placed on, or removed from, the crane arm without the expressed permission of the crane grip. This is essential for the safe use of the camera crane.

The dolly grip must be skilled in the operation of both the dolly and any crane you anticipate using, and in being able to smoothly start and stop the dolly on a preassigned mark. In addition, the dolly grip will direct the laying and leveling of track for either the dolly or crane.

Union dolly grips earn no less than $32.39 per hour. As noted above, our key grip on *Anarchist* handled the dolly.

817-04 Company Grip

Also known as hammers since that used to be their principal tool (it is now the cordless drill used as a screw gun), company grips make up the bulk of the grip crew. These crewmembers move the set wall, set freestanding diffusion, and build the camera platforms.

Union grips earn no less than $29.90 per hour or $2,093 for a five-day week. They are usually paid the scale rate, but on rare occasions, get a dollar or two per hour above scale. On *Anarchist*, we paid our grips $1,000 for a six-day week. Based on federal labor rules and assuming six 12-hour days, this would work out to about $11.37 per hour.

817-05 Rigging/Striking Labor

On pictures with a larger budget and more complex lighting setups, a rigging crew can be an efficient way to save time for the shooting crew. If you have a stage set or a location that will be lit with many hanging instruments and diffusion, it will save time to have that equipment placed before the shooting crew ever arrives. Likewise, this same rigging crew can strike the equipment and return it to the vendor once the shooting crew has left.

A rigging crew is led by a key rigging grip who is assisted by a rigging second grip. The crew itself is made up of rigging grips who may be hired as needed on a daily basis. If your picture is going to have a rigging crew, it is important that the key rigging grip be available during prep for the location scouts.

The Anarchist Cookbook did not have the resources or the need for a rigging crew. As noted in the budget, the shooting crew lit the sets each morning and struck the equipment once each set was finished.

817-07 Craft Service Labor

To fully understand this account, some historical perspective would be helpful. When I first entered the business in the early 1970s, the craft service person was the extra hand. At a time when strong labor unions guarded each of their duties and defined responsibilities zealously, the craft service person was the one employee, other than the producer, who could pitch in wherever needed. If horses were being used that day, the craft service person made sure that their droppings were kept cleaned up. If the sound crew needed help managing their cables during a moving camera shot, the craft service person would jump in. If the special effects crew needed someone to fan bee smoke from one side of the set, they would give the craft service person a large paddle to start fanning.

Since craft service people were not always busy, they would sweep the stage, and also keep a small cart to one side of the set with an urn of coffee and a box of glazed donuts. During the day, the crewmembers would drop a dime in a cup kept on the cart if they wanted a cup of coffee, or a quarter if they wanted a glazed donut. The money was used by the craft service person to buy the next day's coffee and donuts. This idyllic situation had been the practice long before I entered the business and seemed destined to never change.

Then one day, an actor, a producer, or a director stopped by the craft service cart and thought, "We have donuts…why can't we have a bag of bagels, too?" At that moment, I am sure that some film company executive, alone in his office, felt a disturbance in the force.

The craft service person, being accommodating and wanting to please, brought in a bag of bagels with the glazed donuts. Then someone asked for cream cheese to go with the bagels. Someone else asked if some fresh fruit could be part of the offering. Another person asked if there could be bowls of chips in the afternoon. Soon the poor craft service person had to go to the production manager for some money to fulfill all of these requests. Other shows heard about what was being done on this show, and soon craft service people across the city were setting up banquet tables to hold all the snacks that were being offered. The crews gradually began to gain weight. The production manager pulled his hair out trying to cover the expense; it had grown to $100 per day.

It wasn't long before the craft service table had lunch meats for sandwiches, cereal for breakfast, and all sorts of hot goodies the craft service person would create throughout the day. The studios pleaded with the production managers to try to keep it down to $500 per day. Craft service people bought and outfitted trailers that they rented to the studios. These were fitted out with refrigeration units, cold cut storage, drawers & cabinets to contain more groceries than a 7-11. Satellite dishes appeared on the top of the trailers to feed the ever-sophisticated video systems that ran nonstop inside the trailers. Businesses sprang up to supply ready-made platters of snacks that the craft service person could just unwrap and serve. The cost crept up to $750 per day. Entire flu epidemics were spread through open bowls of chips. The Los Angeles County Health Department began issuing citations to craft service people and shows that were not serving all this food out of licensed kitchens. The snack portions were required to be individually wrapped. Soon craft service people were required to be licensed food workers.

Then one day on *Dracula: Dead and Loving It*, our craft service person came into my office. He seemed uncomfortable but I encouraged him to tell me what was on his mind.

"We have horses working on stage tomorrow," he said.

"Yes, we do," I responded.

"Well, you need to get an additional craft service person."

"Why?" I asked, "I have you. Is everything okay?" I thought that maybe he had some health difficulty.

"Yes, I'm okay," he said, "but I can't be sweeping up horse poop one minute and making sandwiches the next."

I was stunned. He was right, of course. I hired an extra craft service person for the following day to keep the horse poop swept up.

Time marched on. On *Starship Troopers* the craft service costs had risen to $1,000 per day. We shot for 120 days. So that means we spent $120,000 on snacks. On a recent show which shall remain nameless and on which I was not the production manager, they were spending $3,500 per day. On a 120-day picture, this would be more than 2% of the gross national product of Tuvalu. For snacks.

The final irony is that nowhere in the craft service union's contract does it mention food or food preparation. I have asked the craft service union's business agent where it is going. He had no idea. The union does not know how to respond. They have tapped into a wildly successful job category that really isn't theirs and they are reluctant to give up any possible areas for jobs. Recently, the craft service local was folded into the grip local, which would have made sense thirty years ago. Now it is like having the teamsters represent Wolfgang Puck.

There is some justification for providing snacks, although perhaps not at quite the level discussed above. Production companies ask their crews to work long hours at what can be, at times, extremely strenuous and perhaps dangerous tasks. Who would begrudge a lamp operator, stuck 50 feet above the ground in a Condor basket all night, a cup of hot chocolate or a bowl of hot soup; or a candy bar and a soda for a grip, who has just carried a camera crane piece by piece down the face of a cliff to the beach below? Who wouldn't want to reward the crew that defied all predictions of not being ready on time for that crucial sunrise shot, with five gallons of ice cream or fifteen pizzas? I believe eventually a happy medium will be found. (And before you begin to think I am being too harsh about feeding the crew, lunches are budgeted separately under 837-09 Meals/Catering.)

The craft service person is usually in at the earliest makeup call so that the actors and makeup people can have a cup of coffee first thing, and usually doesn't leave until everyone else does so that the location or stage is left free of trash. If you are paying your craft service person by the hour, you should budget him or her for 13 to 14 hours per day. Current union minimum for this position is $25.40 per hour. On *Anarchist*, we paid a flat rate of $720 per six-day week: another gift from a generous crew member.

817-08 Greensperson

If you have sets that have a lot of greens, it might be good to have someone whose sole responsibility is to attend to them. This would include placing them for camera as well as watering them and making sure they get enough sunlight to survive, if they are alive. On *Anarchist*, we did not have enough greens to justify hiring someone in this position. What greens we did have were covered by props and set dressing.

Union minimum for a greens foreperson is $32.12. If we had needed someone, we would have paid around $750 for a six-day week.

817-10 Standby Painters

In *The Parent Trap* (1998), there is a scene where the two twins are putting rocks in the backpack of their dad's girlfriend. The spot where the director wanted to shoot the scene was in front of a large boulder. Unfortunately, the boulder was covered in graffiti. If we sand-blasted the graffiti off, it would have left fresh rock that would not have looked at all natural. I asked the park ranger if we could paint over the graffiti and she agreed to let us do it on the promise that we would remove our paint when the scene was finished.

Our standby painter went to work and when he was done, you could not tell that there had ever been any paint on that rock. He had the color and texture down perfectly and he had even added painted lichen to blend into the painted areas of the natural rock. The park ranger was amazed and asked us to leave our painted cover-up on the rock. I had to tell her that we used water-based paint so that we could clean it up easily and that after the first rain it would wash away.

These highly skilled craftspeople are essential to a movie set. They blend the seam in a wall that has been removed and then replaced, they can turn plywood or even cardboard into beautifully grained mahogany, and they add the finishing touches to a set that make it look real, such as smudges near the light switches and nicks on the baseboards.

On *Anarchist*, we could not afford to hire a standby painter and people from the art department covered those duties. Union standby painters get no less than $32.12 per hour but more often are paid the journeyman signwriter rate of $36.13 per hour.

817-11 Loss & Damage

Items that might be damaged in this account include grip diffusion such as flags, nets, and silks. Normal wear and tear are to be expected, but occasionally these items may get ripped, torn, or dirty. We allowed for $500 here on *Anarchist* and actually spent $851, putting us $351 over in this account.

817-16 First Aid & Expenses

Hiring someone in this category is mandatory on union pictures and I highly recommend it on all pictures. The first aid person is not there just to treat trauma in case of an accident. On *Anarchist*, the first aid person was watching for people who were becoming dehydrated in Dallas's summer heat and making sure that they got plenty of fluids and electrolytes. In freezing weather, the first aid person watches for signs of frostbite or hypothermia. Typically, the person hired as a set medic is a registered nurse or EMT. A movie set can be a dangerous place and being prepared goes a long way toward preventing serious injury.

Union first aid people make no less than $27.35 per hour. We paid $1,200 per six-day week on *Anarchist*. Typically, the first aid person will have a box or kit you need to rent which will be covered in 817-58. In addition, there will need to be money for expendable supplies such as aspirin, bandages, swabs, etc. We allocated $500 on *Anarchist* and spent $593.

817-51 Purchases

Items that will get charged here will include tape, clothespins, rope, lumber, screw gun bits, dry wall screws, and gels (both hard and soft). On *Anarchist* we allocated $3,000 for the show and spent $4,832.

817-52 Craft Service Purchases

Here it is: the dreaded sinkhole of the budget. (See the discussion under 817-07 Craft Service Labor.) On a small crew of 30 to 50 people, you should try to keep it down to around $500 per day. That's what we tried to do on *Anarchist* and we ended up spending an average of $626 per day. Most of that was for water, which *is* important.

There are a few things you can do to help yourself here. First and foremost, make a deal with a bottled water company or a soft drink company. I have found that they will often give you regular shipments of drinks for a mention in the credits or use of their product in the film. Don't put out a lot of food just before lunch. Otherwise you will find that the crew is eating craft service for lunch and your costs will skyrocket. Talk to the craft service person about how much you want to spend and track the costs to make sure that he or she is following your request. Encourage your craft service person to make soups in bulk, especially for night shooting. Buy as few prepared platters as possible. They are expensive.

The *Anarchist* budget indicates that the $500 per day was to include the occasional second meal. This was unrealistic since maintaining a supply of bottled water, cold drinks, and the normal snacks took up that amount of money. A second meal is called for when the company is working past 12 hours. It is appreciated by the crew and really does help their efficiency to bring in some food as that twelfth hour starts rolling by. Pizzas, Chinese, or a big pot of spaghetti all work well. Sometimes it even makes sense to go down to the nearest fast food place and pick up 50 hamburgers. Just be sensitive to any people on your crew who may be vegetarian or have other special food requirements. Often the second meal may cost $200 or more all by itself, but it is money well spent.

817-56 Grip Rental

No, you are not going to rent grips. This is for renting grip equipment. Items that might be included would be flags, diffusion, nets, and frames to put them on. Even on a major feature, you can get a fairly complete grip package for around $3,500 per week. On *Anarchist*, we budgeted $1,400 per week. The dollies and cranes would be additional. Dollies go for around $750 to $1,200 per week. We set aside $3,000 for a crane. We thought we would use it for three days but ended up using it only for two. For the entire account, we only spent $10,098, a savings of $2,102.

817-58 Box Rentals

The key grip will get a box rental to cover his tools and specialty items. On major features, key grips are getting around $500 per week. We paid $200 per week. Painters typically get $150 to $350 per week, depending on how much equipment they have. Craft service will get $500 and up, depending on how elaborate the setup is. Be sure you are not renting more than you really need or want. First aid typically gets $50 to $150 per week for a box rental that will probably include first aid supplies and an oxygen unit.

819-00 Electrical (Set Lighting)

In many respects, the set lighting account mirrors the set operations account, or more specifically, the set lighting crew mirrors the grip crew. Both crews are headed by a key who is assisted by a best boy. On larger pictures, they each tend to have four to five additional members on their crews. Even on low-budget pictures, they tend to have the same number of people in each of their crews. Each of the levels of compensation are usually the same from lighting to grip, and the company that rents you your lighting equipment will probably be where you get your grip equipment.

The set lighting crew is also called the *electric crew* or collectively the *electricians*. This is somewhat a misnomer. They are not electricians in the sense of someone who is knowledgeable about house wiring, although they may be. Their connection to electricity is that it powers their lighting instruments. Often this power comes from a generator mounted on the tractor that pulls their equipment trailer, or one that is towed behind a smaller 10-ton truck. They know how many amps of power they need to light a set, how to balance the load on a generator, and if need be, how to tap into the wiring of a building. Electricity and their lamps are merely tools of their trade, which is to light a set in such a way as to evoke the mood and effect that the director and DP are trying to achieve, while supplying enough light so that an image registers on the film. Of all the crew, except the camera crew, the set lighting crew's work impacts the quality of the captured image the most.

819-01 Chief Lighting Technician

Also known as the *gaffer*, the chief lighting technician is the boss of the lighting crew. The term gaffer comes from the use of a long pole or gaff by which they adjusted the lights in the early days of film. Outside of film, *gaffer* is also a term applied to any leader of a group of workers. The gaffer works closely with the director of photography. Depending on the way the DP likes to work, the gaffer may light the set independently with only the barest of direction ("I'll be shooting at *f*2.8. Keep it low key and let the shadows fall off to black."), or he may simply facilitate the DP's wishes ("Give me a 10K over here and flood it out."). Most working relationships between the DP and the gaffer fall somewhere in the midst of these two extremes, with the DP using the gaffer's experience and creative ideas to help arrive at the director's vision of what the scene should look like.

Union gaffers make no less than $34.54 per hour. Note that this is the same as the minimum for the key grip, and like the key grip, can command as much as $38 per hour or more. Typically, productions pay the key grip and the gaffer the same rate. On *Anarchist*, we paid our gaffer our department head rate of $1,500 per six-day week. Be sure to allow enough prep time for the gaffer to scout all the locations and sets with the DP.

819-02 Assistant Chief Lighting Technician

Also known as the *best boy*, this person is the immediate boss of the lamp operators and is responsible for the ordering, maintenance, and return of all lighting equipment. It is very important that this person be organized and methodical with the vendor paperwork since lighting instruments are extremely expensive. Even the light bulbs (known as globes) can be several hundred dollars each. Another reason to double check all return paperwork is that some studio lighting departments are not very accurate in determining whether you have returned specific pieces of equipment. I had one studio's lighting department try to charge me for equipment that was allegedly lost, only to find out that we had returned the equipment and it had then been checked out to another show entirely.

Union scale for the best boy is $31.28 per hour. Occasionally, they will get a few dollars over scale. At any rate, the electric best boy and the second grip usually receive the same rate of pay. As with the second grip, we paid $1,200 per six-day week on *Anarchist.* Your gaffer will likely want the best boy on the scout so schedule adequate preparation for both the scout and loading the equipment truck.

819-03 LIGHT TECHNICIANS

Also known as *lamp operators,* the lighting technicians make up the set lighting crew. They handle the lighting instruments, cable, and any diffusion attached to the instruments. A typical crew strength on a mainstream feature film is four to five lamp operators each day, with an allowance made for extra man-days for night shooting or larger sets. On *Anarchist,* we budgeted for two lamp operators each day, with an allowance of fourteen additional man-days.

Union lamp operators earn $29.90 per hour. If you are using a dimmer board, the operator will make $30.56 per hour. On *Anarchist,* we paid our lamp operators $1,000 for a six-day week.

819-05 RIGGING & STRIKING LABOR

As was noted in the discussion of set operations, sometimes it is useful to have a rigging electric crew to pre-light and strike sets. The crew would consist of a rigging gaffer, a rigging best boy, and a few rigging electricians. They would be paid what their equivalents on the grip rigging crew are paid. We did not have a rigging crew on *Anarchist.*

819-06 GENERATOR OPERATOR / POWERHOUSE

On a union picture, you would need a member of Local 40 of the United Brotherhood of Electrical Workers (UBEW) to run a towed generator, or a teamster to run a generator mounted on the tractor of a semi. The Local 40 operator would make $31.67 per hour. On *Anarchist,* our set lighting crew would start the generator each morning and check on it at various times during the day.

819-11 Loss & Damage

Since the lighting instruments and globes are so expensive, it makes sense to put a little money here. On *Anarchist,* we put $2,500 since that was the deductible on our equipment insurance.

819-51 Purchases

Items that might be purchased under this account would include rolls of gel ($200 per role), tape, clothespins, clamps, black wrap (black aluminum foil), rope, WD-40, and a few pairs of leather gloves. We set aside $3,000 for set lighting purchases on *Anarchist.*

819-52 Globes & Carbons

The title of this account is somewhat anachronistic in that the carbons that are referred to were used in a lamp that is not used much any more: the arc lamp. In an arc lamp, a carbon electrode was brought near a copper electrode. The resultant electric spark, or arc, created a brilliant white light that was used to fill in shadows in bright sunlit shots since the color temperature of the light from an arc lamp was very close to sunlight. In practice, the arc in the lamp would consume the carbon electrodes and they would have to be replaced frequently. Today, HMI lights have now largely replaced carbon arc lamps and it is no longer necessary to purchase cases of carbon electrodes.

Nevertheless, globes can still be an expense. Most rental houses today will include globe burnouts within the rental price of the lamp. If you have such an arrangement with the rental house you are using, your lighting crew will save all burnouts so they can be returned to the rental house. This proves that you have not gone off and sold perfectly good globes, and then claimed that they were burned out.

819-56 Rentals

With the advent of HMI® lights, Kino Flo® fluorescents, and other specialty lamps, this account can become astronomical. With three fully rigged stages on *Starship Troopers,* we were paying up to $75,000 per week in lighting equipment rental. The way to control costs in this account is to stick with normal old-fashioned tungsten lamps, don't leave excessive equipment hanging on unused sets, and ask the DP to explain to the lighting crew that it will not be expected that they have every new gadget.

On *Anarchist*, we budgeted $3,800 per week for a total of $15,200. We actually spent $16,688 resulting in an overage of $1,488. Fortunately, we only spent $1,505 in account 819-51, giving us a savings of $1,495 with which to cover our overage.

819-58 Box Rental

The gaffer will usually have a box rental that covers specialty items and tools. On major features, this box rental, like that of the key grip, can be up to $500 per week. On *Anarchist*, we paid $200 per week.

821-00 Set Dressing

Although *Showgirls* was not a box office success, the video sales and rentals were fantastic. This is due, I am sure, to the efforts and talent of the set dressing department. I am joking, of course, but there is a scene in the film set in the showgirls' dressing room involving a monkey. The monkey in and of itself is not important. The interesting point of this scene is what the set dresser did with each of the girls' makeup stations. Each station reflected the personal life and personality of each of the girls. There were snapshots pasted around the mirrors, notes from friends tucked here and there, goofy little trinkets that were given to them by someone, and other items placed in special spots, each of which was deemed important to that character for one reason or another. It was possible to walk by each of the stations and learn a great deal about the person who used it. None of this actually registers in detail with the audience, but the overall effect is to lend a great deal of realism to the set.

Along with the carpet, the drapes, and the furniture in sets, set dressers or decorators supply the details that surround us and fill our living spaces. From the manila folders carelessly strewn across the police captain's desk to the choice of spices in the kitchen cabinet, all were carefully chosen and placed by the set dressing crew. Technically, any object in a set that an actor does not handle is set dressing.

There are gray areas where an object could be either a prop or set dressing, such as a refrigerator in a kitchen set that is opened by an actor. Is it set dressing or a prop? What about the saloon chair that the bad guy breaks over the head of the hero; set dressing or prop? In the first instance, since a refrigerator is a normal part of a kitchen, the set dressing crew will probably supply it. In the second instance, since the chair has to be made out of special materials and be designed to break easily without harming the actor, it would be supplied by the prop department. Nevertheless, it is important that the set decorator and the propmaster agree on who will be responsible for each of the items in each set so that none is overlooked.

821-01 Set Decorator

On a low-budget production, it is especially important that your set decorator be resourceful. Set dressing can be found at swap meets, thrift stores, and garage sales, as well as prop rental houses and department stores. Your set decorator should also be knowledgeable about the styles of furnishings that would be appropriate for your picture's setting.

Union set decorators make no less than $2,117.71 for a five-day week. An experienced set decorator on a union picture can cost a good deal more. On *Anarchist*, we paid our department head rate of $1,500 for a six-day week. A set decorator and crew will need several weeks prep to locate the set dressing, and will need at least a day or two on each set to dress it.

821-03 Swing Gang

The swing gang makes up the set dressing crew. These crewmembers move all the set dressing onto the sets and later move it off. The swing gang gets its name from the fact that they usually did their work at night, on the *swing shift*, when the shooting crew had left the stage and gone home. Because they deal in a lot of heavy furniture, it is customary to hire them in even numbers so that you can always have a swing gang member on each end of a heavy piece of furniture. They are customarily led by a leadman. This is one of those titles in film which has not yet been converted to the more politically correct leadperson; but don't take offense, like the general foreman mentioned earlier, one of the best leadmen I ever worked with was a woman. In addition to bossing the swing crew, the leadman keeps track of all the set dressing paperwork such as purchase orders, rental return slips, and tracking of inventory. On *Anarchist*, our set dresser functioned as her own leadman due to our tight budget.

Union scale for swing gang members $28.58 per hour and they are usually paid at scale. On *Anarchist,* we paid our two swing gang members $750 each for a six-day week.

821-11 Loss, Damage, & Cleaning

Set dressing can be expensive and accidents do happen. It is wise to put a little money here. We allocated $2,000 to this account.

821-51 Set Dressing Purchases & Rentals

As mentioned above, set dressing can be expensive. It depends on what sort of sets you are dressing. Offices can be surprisingly expensive. If you are on a limited budget, try to pick locations that you do not have to dress. Mel Brooks was always on the lookout for live flowers on his sets. His final instruction to the set decorators that worked his pictures was "No live flowers! Ever!" This is because they have to be replaced everyday to keep them looking good. If you are staging a wedding, or even worse, a funeral scene, for a week with lots of big expensive bouquets costing several hundreds or thousands of dollars each, imagine what the bill will be. If you must have flowers, one way around this is to use silk flowers or even plastic. On film, it will not be apparent, and you only have to buy them once. Another method to help alleviate set dressing costs in general is to have a sale at the end of the film to sell whatever you had to purchase. Giving a 50% discount usually gets many people interested and every penny you get back helps to offset any expense or overage you may have incurred.

On *Anarchist,* our sets were not very expensively dressed and we did take every advantage that we could of what was already present at our locations. We budgeted $33,825 for this account and spent $33,423 for a savings of $402.

823-00 Action Props

George Lucas shot *Return of the Jedi* in both England and the United States. Jabba the Hutt's barge hovered above the sarlacc pit monster in the sand dunes of Buttercup Valley, California, a short distance west of Yuma, Arizona. Lucas had asked for a dress rehearsal to take place the day before filming was to begin so that he could see that everything was as it should be. All the cast and extras were in costume and arrayed on the deck of the barge, each in his or her specific place. Princess Leia, a little embarrassed to be so scantily clad, was chained at a spot near where Jabba would be. Luke Skywalker paced the deck and played with the camera. Han Solo chatted with some of the stunt players. C-3PO relaxed near Artoo who squatted in mute readiness. Jabba's henchmen were decked out in their finest. The crew stood ready.

Onto the deck strode Lucas like the Admiral of the Fleet with the director, the production staff, and the director of photography trailing in his wake. Lucas nodded approvingly at Princess Leia, discussed a few details of the scene with the director and Luke Skywalker, looked over the side of the barge to the sarlacc pit, and then came to a sudden halt in front of a pig guard who was nervously trying to maintain his sense of military bearing while clutching his weapon close to his armored chest.

Lucas snatched the weapon from the startled pig guard's hands and said to the rest of us, "A pig guard would never use this weapon!" He put the hapless guard's weapon down next to a pile of other strange looking props, grabbed another weapon, and held it up for all to see.

"This is what a pig guard would use!" and he slammed the weapon into the guard's waiting hands. All of us mentally slapped our foreheads and thought, *Of course! Why didn't we see that?*

Even if you never have to arm a pig guard, props can take on enormous importance. Alfred Hitchcock spoke of the *McGuffin*, the thing everyone in a film is after. The McGuffin was the driving force behind the plots of his films such as the Maltese falcon in the film of the same name. Sometimes the McGuffin was an ideal or a concept, but often it was an actual thing—a prop. A talented director is able to invest such great emotion into a simple prop that the audience will hold its collective breath every time it comes on screen: think of the timer counting down near the end of a James Bond film, or a golden, inscribed ring that would determine the fate of Middle Earth, or maybe a box of chocolates that contains the meaning of life.

And what is a prop? As discussed above in the section on set dressing, a prop is any object that the actors handle. A sword mounted on the wall above the mantle is set dressing. If the hero grabs it to run the villain through, then it's a prop. With all this in mind, choose your propmaster carefully.

823-01 Propmaster

When I started in the film business, my first film job was on *The Hindenburg*. The propmaster, Bob Murdock, was a World War II combat veteran who had flown P-38 fighters in Europe. He had crashed three times in combat and always went back for more. During the prep period, he would have show and tell sessions with Robert Wise, the director, so that Mr. Wise could approve, disapprove, or comment on the props. I followed along behind the director on one of these inspections where Bob had all the props that would be used on the Zeppelin set laid out on display. There was Zeppelin china, mail with Zeppelin stamps, 1930s German currency, pencils embossed with the Zeppelin logo, Hindenburg stationery, Cuban cigars from the 1930s, and anything else that could possibly have been on board the *Hindenburg* on its final voyage. I thought I was touring the Smithsonian Museum. Of course, Mr. Wise loved everything that had been presented. He complimented Bob and then left.

As soon as the director was gone, I looked around for Bob but he was nowhere to be seen. I asked the assistant propmaster if he knew where Bob was.

"Oh, sure, he's out behind the stage," he said. I asked him why Bob was behind the stage.

"He's throwing up. He always does that after a show and tell."

This was the same man who would do strafing runs through blizzards of anti-aircraft fire on Nazi airfields. It was then that I realized what a perfectionist Mr. Murdock was, but he had more to teach me.

I am ashamed to admit it now, but during the shooting period when I got bored, I tried to see if I could get a rise out of him. I would run up to the prop truck in a highly agitated state and say something like, "Quick, Bob! Mr. Wise needs a crystal ball and a long-stemmed red rose! Now!"

He would say "Just a minute," and go into his truck. Seconds later, he appeared on the tailgate with the crystal ball and a long-stemmed red rose. I never once stumped him. No matter how ridiculous my made-up requests were, he was always able to produce the item.

Bob Murdock was probably the best propmaster I have ever known. I am not suggesting that propmasters should get so stressed that they throw up, but his total dedication to making every prop the right one, his thoroughness, his extreme attention to detail, and his professionalism (not to mention his sense of humor,) all conspired to put him in the propmasters' hall of fame in my eyes.

Union propmasters make no less than $34.54 per hour and often more. On *Anarchist*, we paid our propmaster our standard department head rate of $1,500 for a six-day week.

823-02 Assistant Propmaster

A propmaster typically works with one to two assistant propmasters. With a large cast or on a day with a large extra contingent, there may be even more prop assistants, especially if there is a scene involving food such as in a restaurant, or other prop-heavy scenes such as an airport terminal or train station.

Union assistant propmasters make no less than $30.55 per hour. We paid $750 for a six-day week on *Anarchist*. We also never had more than the one assistant propmaster.

823-51 Purchases

The amount of money that you put into this account depends entirely on what type of show you are doing and what props you need. When a propmaster starts on a picture, one of the first things to be done is a prop breakdown and a budget. Until then, it is best to do an initial estimate based on the script breakdown. On *Anarchist*, we budgeted $10,000 for both prop purchases and rentals, and spent $11,463. Compare this with $775,481 budgeted for purchases and rentals on *S.W.A.T.* (many firearms and much blank ammunition), and $47,000 on *A Lot Like Love* (a romantic comedy with many walk-and-talk scenes). We did not budget a separate loss and damage allowance.

823-58 Car & Box Rental

When Bob Murdock would disappear into his truck to get whatever strange and desperately needed object I dreamed up, he would go to his boxes. A propmaster's boxes are literally his or her stock in trade. They are put together over a lifetime of collecting and often have been handed down through several propmasters. When a propmaster retires, there is usually quite a competition among young aspiring propmasters to buy the old veteran's boxes.

Along with the odd artificial long-stemmed rose and crystal ball, there are usually extensive collections (both period and modern) of eye glasses, watches, lighters, cigarette cases, rings, jewelry, binoculars, pistols, knives, pens, currency, bottle openers, typewriters, and countless objects I cannot even begin to list. On a major feature film, a propmaster's box might rent for $800-$1,000 per week. On *Anarchist*, we paid $120 per week.

We did not offer a car allowance to our propmaster, but on some film projects, the propmaster does receive one. It can run from $125 to $250 per week and often will only be for the prep and wrap periods (with the assumption that it is only during those periods that the propmaster will need to drive around town to the various vendors).

825-00 Picture Vehicles and Animals

At first glance, this may seem an odd pairing. When you learn that they are together because the teamsters handle both on a union show, it makes more sense. But then another question arises: Why do teamsters handle both picture cars and animals? Teamsters handling picture cars makes sense. Cars are motor vehicles and teamsters drive motor vehicles. But why animals? Teamsters have been America's freight haulers for longer than there have been motor vehicles. It used to be that the teamsters' sole job was to drive freight wagons pulled by teams of horses or oxen. That is why we call them teamsters. In the early days of film, wagons and teams were often called for. Who better to handle them than teamsters? They were the logical choice. As the film unions were organizing, the Teamsters Local claimed jurisdiction over not just domesticated animals, but all animals on a set. Today, the Teamsters' Local 399 contract lists twelve separate categories for animal wranglers and/or handlers:

ramrod – arranges for and coordinates all the animal work on a show.

wrangler gang boss – runs a crew of wranglers.

wrangler – handles large domestic animals.

driver/wrangler – can handle and transport 2 or less horses.

wrangler (pickup) – handles horses or cattle in dangerous situations such as stampedes.

wrangler (braider) – specializes in braiding manes & tails of horses.

trainer (domestic livestock) – first trainer hired, gangboss.

trainer (stable) – trains large domestic animals (usually horses).

wild animal trainer – specializes in training wild animals.

wild animal handler – cares for and provides non-domestic animals (including insects).

dog trainer – specializes in training dogs and cats to perform specific actions.

dog handler – cares for and provides dogs and cats.

825-01 Picture Vehicles

Any vehicle that appears in front of the camera, in picture, is a picture vehicle. This covers vehicles ranging from a donkey cart to the USS *Enterprise* to the *Concorde.* A helicopter that appears on-camera is a picture vehicle. A helicopter that is used to get the camera high in the air for an aerial point of view is a camera platform and is budgeted under Set Operations.

Sometimes what appears to be a picture vehicle might actually be a set. For example, Int. Submarine – Forward Torpedo Room is probably going to be a stage set because (1) getting access to an actual submarine will be very difficult, and (2) trying to squeeze an entire film crew and its equipment into the forward torpedo room of an actual submarine will be very problematic. Filming Ext. HMS *Queen Mary* would be a location (if you were shooting in the Los Angeles area) because the *Queen Mary* is fixed on pilings in Long Beach Harbor, and it functions much like any other piece of real estate.

The normal items in this account will be cars and trucks of various descriptions. Prices can range from $30 per day for an extra's or a crewmember's car, to $1,000 or more for high-end luxury or sports cars. Antique automobiles and trucks are more available than you might think, but they can still rent for several hundred dollars per day.

If your scene calls for wrecking the vehicle, you will have to buy it. By getting creative, you can limit your expenses here also. On *The Blues Brothers,* we bought seventy-five police cars that were being phased out from the Chicago Police Department. With the help of a body shop that was running twenty-four hours per day, we wrecked those seventy-five police cars five to ten times each. Flood damaged cars can sometimes be obtained for a fraction of their original price. In the case of brand new flood damaged vehicles, the manufacturers usually will want the car returned or proof of destruction furnished so that they know that the vehicle has not been sold. If the car does not have to run but must just blow up, you can go to a junk yard and buy a body without the engine for a small portion of what a functioning car would cost. Many of those great looking luxury cars in films that go off cliffs, only to explode in a giant fireball, could not have been driven five feet.

Another source of vehicles is product placement. A number of car manufacturers lobby vigorously to get their vehicles into films and will even let you destroy the vehicle if they feel they will get sufficient positive exposure.

General Motors has been especially aggressive lately in getting their vehicles into high profile films. A good example of this would be *S.W.A.T.*

The original *Anarchist* picture vehicle list consisted of the following:

10 ND cars	bus	Milo's car
10 new cars	cop car	pickup truck
5 ND cars	golf cart	roller coaster
7 unmarked cars	Jody's BMW	SUV
8 cop cars	log ride	Sweet Thing's car

(*ND* means *non-descript.*)

Of these, our final budget only listed "8 cop cars," "bus," and "cop car." The golf cart came with our location fee to the golf course, the Log Ride was eliminated, and the roller coaster came with our location fee to the small amusement park we shot at. We anticipated getting all of the other vehicles gratis by using crewmembers' personal vehicles. It turns out that we were overly optimistic. Although our crewmembers were extremely generous with the use of their vehicles, we ended up having to go to third parties and atmosphere players for some of our needs. With $3,000 budgeted, we spent a total of $6,873 giving us an overage of $3,873.

Other subaccounts that we did not use but you might want to set aside some money for include PICTURE VEHICLE MODIFICATION & RESTORATION, and MECHANIC.

825-10 ANIMALS

As noted earlier, just because you only have one dog in your script does not mean that you will only use one dog in filming the scenes. It all depends on what you want the dog to do. It is always best to let an animal trainer read your script and submit a bid while suggesting the best approach. You will be amazed at what you don't know about animals.

I was doing a preliminary board and budget for a feature film based on the *I Dream of Jeannie* television series. There was a scene in which the evil king of Opolis summons kings, sultans, and princes of the surrounding kingdoms. They all meet at the Xerxes Gate in all of their finery. "All of their finery" included caravan animals: elephants, camels, donkeys, and horses. Since I had limited experience with elephants, I called up an animal trainer and asked if I could get a number of elephants together for this scene, and what would it cost? He told me that he thought he could put together a group of five Asian elephants, and that they would cost $1,200 each per day.

"Why five?" I asked. "Why not seven or ten?"

"Well," he explained in a manner one might use with a particularly clueless person, "If you put a bunch of elephants together that don't know one another, they'll fight. Five is the largest number of elephants in Los Angeles that have all been introduced to one another."

Oh. Who would have thought that elephants only like to hang with their buddies?

Our need for animals on *Anarchist* was a bull and some chinchillas. The script originally called for minks but we found that no one in the Dallas area farms minks, but they do farm chinchillas. Chinchillas are cuter and nicer anyway. We allowed $500 for cattle and $1,000 for minks/chinchillas.

Trained dogs typically go for around $200 per day. Horses are a little more. A cat would be around $50 per day. And camels? Camels go for $500 each per day. Other costs that you may want to include in your budget are expenses for feeding and stabling, transport, and vet service.

825-12 WRANGLERS & HANDLERS

When you have animals, you need someone to handle them, train them, and take care of them. On *Anarchist*, we allowed for 4 days of wranglers/handlers at $400 per day. The union hourly rates are as follows:

Ramrod	negotiable
Wrangler Gang Boss	$29.78
Wrangler	$27.53
Driver/Wrangler	$28.30
Wrangler (Pickup)	$41.53
Wrangler (Braider)	$34.80
Trainer (Domestic Livestock)	negotiable
Trainer (Stable)	$38.12
Wild Animal Trainers	$38.12
Wild Animal Handlers	$33.08
Dog Trainer	$33.08
Dog Handler	$27.53

How do you know how many wranglers or trainers is enough? It's always best to ask. One wrangler can handle five horses as long as you have experienced riders to put on them. If you want an animal, such as a dog, to go from point A to point B you need a minimum of two trainers, one where the animal starts (A) and one at the animal's destination (B). One bug wrangler can handle hundreds of roaches. Each camel needs a separate handler and seven trainers can handle five Asian elephants who have all been previously introduced.

If you want to be able to put the disclaimer at the end of your credit roll that "no animal was harmed in the filming of this motion picture," you must contact the American Humane Association (**http://www.americanhumane.org**) and let them monitor your filming. Along with giving you bragging rights and heading off any public disgust over the mistreatment of animals in your film (no audience wants to think that their entertainment came at the cost of suffering or death of an animal), the American Humane Association can help you find ways to get your shots while keeping the animals safe. I have always found them extremely helpful and resourceful. They also have a set of guidelines on their web site to assist you in your planning and use of animals in film. It is especially important to have them present if your film depicts the harming of an animal. They are experienced in making the most gruesome scenes safe for the animals involved. I strongly urge any filmmaker planning to shoot scenes with animals to contact the American Human Association.

829-00 Extra Talent

Extras are performers who appear before the camera but who do not have lines. If you are signed with SAG, you may or may not have to hire extras under the SAG agreement. If you are shooting in the New York zone (within a 300-mile circle of Columbus Circle including New York City, Boston, Philadelphia, or Washington DC), or in the Los Angeles zones (Los Angeles, San Francisco, Sacramento, San Diego, Las Vegas, or Hawaii), and you are a signatory to the SAG agreement, you must give preference of employment to extras who are members of SAG. If you are operating under the SAG basic agreement in the Los Angeles or New York zones, the first forty-five extras you hire on any given day must be members of SAG. If you are operating under the SAG low-budget agreement, the first thirty extras that you hire on any given day must be members of SAG. Obviously, SAG extras hired under any SAG agreement must be paid minimums in accordance with that agreement. Any extras that you hire on any given day beyond the minimum number required can be hired as non-union extras. (See the discussion under "809-00 Talent" for an understanding of the various SAG agreements.)

If you are filming anywhere else in the U.S. other than the zones defined above, you can hire all of your extras as non-union extras without regard to SAG minimums or rules. This is what we did on *Anarchist* since Dallas is not part of either of the above-mentioned zones.

829-01 Stand-ins

Stand-ins are the people that the DP and the gaffer use to stand in place of the actors when they are lighting the set. A good stand-in watches the rehearsal and learns the actor's blocking or movements so that the DP will be able to light the critical positions the actor takes during the scene. This is not an easy job and requires some concentration on the part of the stand-in.

If money is plentiful, you can plan to have one stand-in for each major actor in a scene. I find a good rule is to budget four stand-ins for every shooting day of the picture. If you are shooting on a low-budget, two stand-ins per day should be sufficient. That just means in the more populated scenes, each stand-in will have to cover more than one actor.

The SAG minimum under the basic agreement for stand-ins as of July of 2005 was $137 for eight hours in the both the L.A. and N.Y. zones. In the L.A. and N.Y. zones, the stand-ins will be the first extras hired toward the thirty or forty-five extras quota.

Since all the extras on *Anarchist* were non-union, we were able to pay our two stand-ins $100 per day or $600 for a six-day week.

829-02 Extras

The extras are typically listed as a total for each shooting day of the picture. In addition, this account would normally have been split into union and non-union categories. As can be seen in the budget, if *Anarchist* had been required to hire union extras, we could have used non-union extras only on days 9, 10, 11, 12, 14, 17, and 18 since our first thirty extras hired would have had to be under SAG. Since we had two stand-ins every day, any day we needed twenty-eight or more extras would have satisfied the quota.

The minimum for SAG extras is $122 for eight hours. On *Anarchist* we paid our extras (all of whom were non-union) $60 per day. When setting the rates that you will pay for non-union extras, be careful not to set them too low or you will find that it is difficult to get and keep the people that you need. Even the most naïve non-union extras eventually realize that it's not all autographs and sunglasses and that, in fact, it can be downright boring.

There are other strategies for attracting large crowds and keeping them with you throughout the day without paying them. One method would be to raffle off nice prizes at intervals throughout the day such as MP3 players, televisions, PDAs, video cameras, etc. In addition to the prizes, you should provide a box lunch for the extras and plenty of water and soft drinks.

Regardless of whether your extras are union or non-union, there are certain amenities that you should provide. You need a holding area or a place for the extras to wait until they are needed. It should be comfortable, out of the sun and weather, and secure from anyone not affiliated with the project. Folding chairs should be provided so that the extras have a place to sit. The extras should be able to leave personal belongings in the holding area without fear of them being stolen. You also need a feeding area. The feeding area and the holding area can be the same place. There should also be adequate restroom facilities. Often in stadiums or similar situations, the seats the extras occupy for filming become the holding and feeding areas. Nevertheless, they still need a place to be able to go to get into the shade.

When you have a large area to fill with people, you should consider alternatives to hiring large crowds. Cardboard cutouts of people actually can be used very effectively in large shots, especially areas in scenes where the crowd is seated. Another method that is used successfully is to hire a small fraction of the people actually needed and then duplicate them throughout the scene through computerized visual effects. When using this method be sure to get an accurate estimate of the costs so that they can be compared to other strategies. One drawback to this method can be seen in the film *Gladiator*. A few hundred extras were costumed and photographed in a stadium setting. The visual effects people then placed numerous copies of the crowd section in the shots to fill the coliseum seats. One particular extra can be seen standing with his arms pumping up and down in a "V." He is visible in at least three different locations and it can be quite distracting once you become aware of him. The lesson here, if you are using this method, is to make sure that no one extra is overly conspicuous in actions, dress, or any other manner.

If you are calling for extras with special abilities such as dancing, horseback riding, weaponry, or any other special talent, you can be sure that every extra who shows up will tell you that he or she has been doing it for years. This may be an outright lie so be prepared to test them. Otherwise, you may end up wasting a lot of time when you are shooting. On *Robin Hood: Men in Tights*, we needed extras who could ride horses well and competently handle a bow and arrow. We held interviews one day in which the prospective extras had to demonstrate their ability to ride for our stunt coordinator, and exhibit their ability with a bow and arrow for our armorer.

829-15 Fittings & Interviews

The Screen Actors Guild requires that you pay a two-hour minimum if you call SAG extras in to be interviewed or to fit them for costumes. If an extra is required to remain for an *interview* beyond two hours, you are required to pay in two-hour increments for each additional two-hour period or fraction thereof. If a *fitting* goes beyond the initial two-hour period, you are required to pay in half-hour increments for each additional half hour or fraction thereof. For example, an SAG extra making $122 for eight hours makes $15.25 per hour. For either an interview or a fitting lasting two hours or less, the extra would be paid $30.50 (2hrs × $15.25). If the *interview* lasted two hours and forty-five minutes, the extra would be paid $61 (2 × 2hrs × $15.25). If the *fitting* lasted two hours and forty-five minutes the extra would be paid $45.75 ((2hrs × $15.25) + (2 × .5hrs × $15.25)). Once you've fitted a SAG extra, you have guaranteed him or her at least one day of work whether the extra is eventually used or not.

If you are using SAG extras and you expect to be fitting or interviewing them, estimate how many will be going through each process and enter the money accordingly. It should not be necessary to budget for more than the two-hour minimum for each extra. If you are interviewing or fitting a large number of extras, stagger the times so that you are able to finish with them within the two-hour minimum.

If you are not planning on fittings, interviews, or you are exclusively using non-union extras, you can ignore this account as we did on *Anarchist.*

829-20 Atmosphere Cars

Extras are generally paid $30 per day for their cars if they are used in picture. This is an inexpensive way to obtain picture cars for such situations as parking lots, parked cars on the street, or cars seen in the background in moving shots or in drive-bys. I commonly extend the $30 per day payment to crewmembers whose vehicles are used in picture also.

It's a good idea to keep a record of who owns each vehicle in the picture. During post production on *Showgirls*, it was decided that an additional shot was need of our actors driving down the main strip in Las Vegas. Unfortunately, the car that would be in background of that shot was a very conspicuous VW Bug. We were able to contact the extra that owned the vehicle, but when we contacted him, we found that he had sold it. Fortunately, we were able to track down the new owner and he agreed to supply the car to us for the additional shot. Had we not been able to track down the owner, we would have had to rent another VW Bug and paint it to match the original one.

On *Anarchist*, all of our picture car needs were covered in the picture car account. Therefore, we did not put any money in this account.

829-39 Extras Casting Service Fee

Someone needs to find the extras, accept applications, maintain a database of the extras (preferably with pictures), and make the calls to tell them when and where to show up. You have two choices on how to approach this. One is to go with an established extras casting agency. The most famous one in Hollywood is Central Casting. They have been around since the early days of the film business. They typically charge the production 10% of the gross wages of the extras for their services. They can supply both union and non-union extras, and they have vast databases of every type of extra you would ever want to use, including unusual types such as little people, amputees, acrobats, tattooed gang members, etc. Some directors have complained that the established casting houses always give them the same people, and that there is a "look" to professional extras that detracts from the realism they are trying to create. Personally, I have had very good experiences with the established houses, and there is a benefit to using professional extras who know what to do.

The other route is to hire someone to function as your extras casting director. If the combined salaries and fringes of the extras casting director and assistant plus the office they work out of, add up to less than 10% of the gross wages of the extras, then this might be the way to go. Directors who complain about the established houses often say that they get a better "look" from an independent extras casting director. Some independents have personal databases that they maintain and draw from. If you go this route, be sure to give the extras casting office a phone number distinct from that of the production office. Otherwise, your production staff will be doing nothing but answering calls from prospective extras.

On *Anarchist*, we went the way of the independent casting director. On a strictly monetary basis, this was not the best choice since 10% of our extras gross wages (including stand-ins) was $3,522 and the total of the salaries of the extras casting director and assistant alone was $5,600. Nevertheless, because we were filming on location in Dallas, it was our only choice at the time.

829-60 Miscellaneous Expense

If you were using SAG extras, some expenses that might go here would be additional payments to extras for getting wet, working in smoke, special abilities, and supplying additional costume changes. We did not need this account on *Anarchist.*

831-00 Costume

One day when I was a young DGA trainee at Universal Studios, I was given an envelope by the head of production and told to take it up to the Wardrobe Department. When I got there, Pete Saldutti, the head of the department, asked what he could do for me. I told him that I had been instructed to take this envelope to Wardrobe and that was why I was there.

He fixed me in a withering gaze and said, "Young man, what you have at home in your closet is wardrobe; these are costumes."

He obviously made a great impression on me since I have never forgotten the incident. However, most film budgets call this account Wardobe. I have changed it to Costume in deference to Mr. Saldutti.

You can actually require your actors to show up in their own clothes and not provide costumes at all. Most productions do not chose to do this, since they have more control over the look of the characters if the production provides the costumes. In addition, with a long running part, it is impractical to require an actor to get his or her clothes cleaned each night and it is risky to trust that an actor will show up in the correct outfit. This is not to say that an actor never provides a personal article of clothing to be used as a costume. But in those instances, the piece of clothing is turned over to the costume department at the end of each day and it is managed by them.

831-01 Designer / Supervisor

Some charts of accounts separate these into their own accounts. Universal Studios' chart of accounts combines them. It is convenient that they are combined here in that it lends itself to a discussion of whether you need both of these people on every film. My opinion is that you do not.

Almost all studio films employ a costume designer and they all employ a costume supervisor as well. Costume designers design costumes. This includes all aspects of a costume from its appearance to the materials it is made from. So when do you need a costume designer? The answer is when you have costumes that need to be designed, specifically, on period pictures, science fiction pictures, or any picture in which the costumes are not present day clothing bought off a department store rack. A designer's taste in choosing clothing off a department store rack can be wonderful, but a costume supervisor with a good eye can buy clothing equally well.

Occasionally, a picture set in the present needs special costumes designed for such things as dream sequences or for special needs where a costume has to function or malfunction in a specific way. But if you are simply clothing actors in present day dress, you can do it with a costume supervisor.

A costume supervisor creates the costume budget, runs the costume department, chooses the costumers, supervises the making (they call it building) of the costumes, oversees the fitting of actors and extras, keeps track of all rentals and purchases, and oversees the wrapping and storage of the costumes at the end of principal photography.

Often a good costume supervisor saves you a ton of money. On *Hollow Man*, we needed to create several total-body covers of bright green spandex for Kevin Bacon so that the visual effects house could easily select his image in a scene and substitute background in its place, thus making him invisible. The effects house said that we had to buy our spandex from one specific supplier who was charging $200 per yard for it. The effects house's reasoning was that they knew that this one supplier dyed his spandex to the exact color and wavelength needed by their computer systems. They did not want to have problems simply because we decided to use an inferior spandex.

Our costume supervisor, James W. Tyson, found what he claimed was the identical cloth at a downtown wholesaler for about 10% of the cost. We first appealed to the effects house to see if they would allow us to go to the wholesaler. They refused, not wanting to risk working with an unknown material. We then tried to bargain with the original supplier to lower the cost since we found the same thing for so much less. He also refused our request since he knew that the effects house would back him. He claimed that the material might look similar but it actually reflected a slightly different wavelength of light.

Jim Tyson then suggested that I ask the effects house to test two samples of spandex, one from the $200 per yard batch, and one from the wholesaler, so that they could choose the best material for their needs. With nothing to lose, we did just that. We gave them the two unidentified samples to test, and they chose the wholesaler's cloth. It was actually better, as well as being much cheaper, and we cut our expenses considerably.

Union costume designers make no less than $1,967.65 per five-day week, and they usually make much more. For a well-known designer, a salary of $4,500 to $7,500 per week would not be out of line. At the higher end, we are talking about Academy Award winners. The union rate for assistant costume designers is $1,612.07 per five-day week. Union costume supervisors make no less than $31.084 per hour. An experienced costume supervisor can make $35 to $38 per hour.

On *Anarchist*, our costume designer was also the costume supervisor, and she had no assistant. We paid the designer/supervisor $1,500 per week.

831-06 Costume Labor

There is normally a women's costume labor account and a men's costume labor account. We combined the two accounts into just one costume labor account because we only had one costumer and a PA. On a larger, union show, there might be a women's key costumer, a men's key costumer, and two to four additional costumers depending on the size of the cast and the requirements of the show. In addition, there would be additional man-days budgeted for days with large crowds or a large number of cast. A union key costumer makes no less than $30.28 per hour, and a costumer makes $27.81 per hour.

On *Anarchist*, we paid our one costumer $1,000 for a six-day week and the PA was paid $600 for a six-day week.

831-10 Cleaning & Dyeing

The costumes should be dry-cleaned each night after they have been worn, and dry-cleaned once more during wrap. This is easily several hundred dollars per day. Sometimes you can make a deal with a dry-cleaners to give you some sort of bulk rate. Over the 24 budgeted days of *Anarchist*, our cleaning was budgeted at an average of $125 per day. Of the $3,000 budgeted, we actually only spent $2,208.

One way to keep costs down is to buy or rent a washing machine and dryer. The washing machine can also be used for any dyeing that may be needed, but I have had costumers ask for a separate machine if they plan to do a lot of dyeing. Costumes are dyed not just to change their colors but also to give them a worn or aged look. Sometimes they are dyed in order to soften overly bright colors or to tone down white shirts.

831-11 LOSS & DAMAGE

If you are renting many of your costumes from a costume house, you should probably put some money here. Invariably, costumes are damaged or misplaced. Sometimes they are damaged because of requirements of the scene. Sometimes the costume rental house claims that you have not returned an item.

Here is another place that your costume supervisor can save you some money. One costume house in Los Angeles was known to check items out under one name and check them back in under another. This would result in the item showing up as missing. For instance, they would check a blouse out as "one chartreuse blouse" and check it back in as "one green blouse," and then they would charge the production for the chartreuse blouse they showed as never having been returned. An alert costume supervisor will catch this and make sure that the returned items are properly credited. The more modern costume houses are now bar coding their costumes so that this will not happen.

831-19 MANUFACTURING LABOR & MATERIALS

If you plan to make some or all of your costumes, you would put the labor expenses for the tailors and sewers, and the expenses for the materials of the costumes in this account. *Anarchist* did not manufacture any costumes.

831-51 PURCHASES

This covers all costume purchases. Sometimes this account is broken up by individual characters in the cast with the expenses for each listed separately. In the *Anarchist* budget, we just entered an allowance for all the purchases and rentals. We only spent $16,813 of the $17,000 budgeted. This savings was the result of the diligence of our costume department.

831-56 Rentals

If you are listing rental expenses separately, they would go here. As in purchases, this account is often listed by character. In the *Anarchist* budget, rentals are covered in the purchases account. (See above.)

831-58 Car & Box Rentals

Often the costume designer, supervisor, and key costumers will get both car and box rentals. The car allowances range from $125 to $150 per week. Sometimes the key costumers' car allowances are paid only during prep. The box rentals on a studio picture can range from $75 to $150 per week. Sometimes the key costumers are paid their box rentals only during the actual shooting period. On *Anarchist*, we paid our designer/supervisor a box rental of $50 per week for every week she was on the picture.

833-00 Makeup and Hair

Whether you want to turn Charlize Theron into a homely, lost soul as was done in *Monster*, or make the beautiful people in your film like Charlize even more beautiful, or depict a gruesome and disfiguring wound, the makeup artists and hairdressers are the magicians who make it happen. One of the great realizations I had upon getting into this business was how ordinary many of the "beautiful people" look before they go into makeup. This is why the actors have a great interest in who will do their makeup and hair.

On the first day of shooting on my very first film, *The Hindenburg*, I was assigned to meet Anne Bancroft at 5AM in the makeup department at Universal Studios. I was to make sure that she arrived on time, check to see if she needed anything, wrangle up some breakfast and coffee for her if she wanted it, and get her transported to her dressing room once she was done. I was twenty-seven years old, had seen *The Graduate* about six times, and now I was going to greet Mrs. Robinson. I was just a little excited.

Her car pulled up in front of the building, the driver got out and came around to the near side of the car. When he opened the door, out stepped Anne Bancroft, the woman whom I thought was the sexiest woman alive. She was wearing a bulky turtleneck sweater and jeans. I was transfixed. As I held the door for her, I must have been staring, because she looked at me and said in her Brooklyn accent, "So wadda ya want at 5AM, glamour?" I felt I had died and gone to heaven.

833-01 Makeup Artists
833-02 Additional Makeup

The normal structure for this department is to have a key makeup person who acts as the head of the department, and then to add additional makeup artists as the show requires. Very often a show will carry the key plus one additional artist, with a provision for additional makeup artist days. If an actor requires a specific makeup artist in his or her contract and that artist will only be working on that actor, the requested makeup artist is considered a star perk and the money for that is put above-the-line in the Talent account.

Union makeup artists earn no less than $39.63 per hour, with the head of the department making $43.75 per hour. Makeup artists who are in high demand can make $50 per hour or more. On *Anarchist*, our makeup artist who functioned as the head of the department made $1500 for a six-day week. We also budgeted for an additional makeup artist for one and a half weeks at $1,000 per week. In fact, we needed more days than that and this account went slightly over budget.

833-03 Body Makeup

If you have scenes with nudity or low-cut and revealing costumes, you might want to add some money here. Body makeup artists specialize in covering birthmarks, tattoos, and other blemishes that might distract from the intention of a scene. Usually a female body makeup artist is used with female actors and a male is used with male actors. Why an actor would get a tattoo is beyond my understanding. It is like someone owning a classic car and sticking STP® stickers all over it. It is not always easy to cover tattoos without it being apparent.

The makeup local no longer has a category specifically for body makeup artists and so their rates are the same as for a normal makeup artist. We did not need a body makeup artist on *Anarchist*. When body makeup was needed, our normal makeup artists covered it. If we had thought we might need it, I probably would have put in an allowance of $1000.

833-05 Hairstylists
833-06 Additional Hairstylists

These accounts invariably parallel the makeup artist accounts (833-01 and 833-02) in rates and numbers of employees. As with makeup personnel, hairdressers requested by stars are often put in the Talent account Above-the-Line as a star perk. The only difference is in the union rate for a hairstylist which is $34.56 per hour as opposed to $39.63 per hour for a makeup artist. In practice, makeup and hair are often paid the same rate.

On *Anarchist*, our hairstylist budget was exactly the same as the one for makeup artists. In the end, we actually had a small savings in this account.

833-10 Makeup Supplies

This money is for purchases of makeup, sponges, brushes, and the wipes that are used to apply it. In addition, you might find the makeup artists buying special lotions and emollients, especially if latex appliances are being attached to an actor's face. Special effects makeup can be irritating or even damaging to a person's skin when used on a consistent basis.

Makeup is expensive. On a recent studio film I was on, we budgeted $450 per week for makeup supplies, with a like amount for hairdressing supplies, and we ended up going $2500 over budget in the two accounts. This is not always the fault of the makeup artists. There are times when actors insist on a specific expensive makeup or have special skin requirements. The best thing to do is to make sure the department head keeps you informed as to how well the department is keeping to the budget. Also insist that purchase orders be used for all makeup purchases. If need be, tell the vendors that you will not honor any invoice that is not accompanied by a valid purchase order number. On *Anarchist*, we budgeted $925 for makeup supplies and spent $1762, an overage of $837.

At the end of the show, do not be surprised if you are asked to approve a purchase order for a large makeup purchase when principal photography is finished or nearly so. This stems from a practice that is increasingly being criticized by the studios. When a makeup artist is hired for your show, he or she will arrive with a makeup kit or box full of makeup. During the run of the show, the department members will replace items through purchases charged to this account as those items are consumed. At the end of the show, the makeup artists will want to restock their boxes to their previous levels.

On the surface, this may seem fair. Nevertheless, every picture's requirements are a little different, and what was necessary on one show may not be necessary on another. From the studio's point of view, the makeup artists are renting their boxes of makeup (which they obtained on their previous show) to the studio, and are then having the studio buy the items to go into the box. The studios feel that it would cost them much less if they were simply to provide the makeup artist with a makeup kit.

The makeup artists say that there is much more to their makeup kits than the makeup that the productions buy for them. I have asked makeup artists to give me an inventory of what I was renting from them. Apart from makeup which the makeup artist did not buy, the inventories list items such as tweezers, razors, airbrushes, artists' brushes, sponges, and of course, the actual box itself. Hairdressers have a more impressive list consisting of, among other things, hair dryers, curling irons, curler sets, scissors, and electric shears.

The reality of the situation is that the makeup artists are not renting anything that could not be purchased for a few hundred dollars. Their kit rental is nothing more than an extension of their salary. Because of this, I have begun refusing to pay for items that are permanent additions to their kits. When the construction coordinator burns out a router, I do not replace it. That is why he is getting his tool rental. It should cover normal wear and tear on his equipment. The same principal should apply to a makeup artist who is allegedly renting me a makeup kit. (See below 833-58 BOX RENTAL.)

833-12 HAIRDRESSING SUPPLIES

Hairdressing supplies consist of hairspray, shampoos, rinses, dyes, paper for hair rollers, perm solutions, and various other hair products. The comments above regarding makeup supplies apply equally to hairdressing supplies. In addition to the items noted above, I have seen scented candles, decorations for the makeup trailer, and other equally irrelevant items in both this account and in makeup purchases. I am told that much of these latter purchases are necessary to enhance the mood of the actors. Okay…

Usually on major features, this account is given the same amount as the makeup purchases account. As mentioned above, on a recent feature we budgeted $450. On *Anarchist*, we put $925 in this account as we did with makeup purchases. We actually spent $1122, an overage of $197.

833-51 Wig Purchases & Rentals

You may have a character, male or female, in your film whose hair length changes at some point in the picture. You have two choices in how to deal with this. If your actor already has the longer length hair, simply schedule the scenes with the long hair first, then you can cut his or her hair and shoot the scenes with the shorter length hair. This approach has a few drawbacks: 1) your actor may not have the longer length hair; 2) you may not be able to schedule the scenes in that particular order; 3) your actor may not want his or her hair cut; and 4) you may need to do an added shot from a long-hair scene after you have cut the actor's hair. The second and better approach is to use a wig or several wigs. A well-made, human hair wig can cost $1000 to $5000.

Another reason you may need to purchase or rent a wig is if you need to match a stunt double's hair to that of the actor. In this situation, it is best to use a synthetic wig, which will cost around $100 to $200. No wigs were needed on *The Anarchist Cookbook.*

833-52 Appliances

This is not for toasters and dishwashers. Appliances are pieces, usually made of foam latex, that are applied to an actor's face to change its shape. Some examples of this are appliances to change the shape of an actor's nose or facial structure: Mr. Spock's pointy ears, and almost everyone's makeup in *Sin City.*

When estimating this account, be aware that foam latex appliances are essentially destroyed in the removal process at the end of each day, so they will need to be continually made throughout the filming. Depending on the film's needs, this account can run into several thousand dollars or more. It is always best to get an estimate from a makeup appliance maker. *Anarchist* did not use any makeup appliances.

833-58 Box Rental

The makeup artists and hairdressers that are in high demand can command $500 to $750 per week for their boxes. (See 833-10 Makeup Supplies for a discussion of makeup kits.) A more common box rental rate for a head of department is $150 to $250 per week. Additional makeup artists and hairdressers will get $25 to $30 per day. On *Anarchist,* we paid our makeup and hair people $25 per day for their kits which is still a good figure on a low-budget film.

835-00 Sound

The production sound account is one of the more straightforward accounts in a film budget. Everything in the account is geared toward obtaining the best production soundtrack possible. The better your production soundtrack is, the less ADR you will have to do. (See 809-10 LOOPING & EXPENSES.) This will save money during post production. Therefore, it makes a great deal of sense to pay for the best mixer that you can afford. And when the mixer tells you that he or she needs to wait until an airplane has flown far enough away to no longer be a factor, it makes sense to heed the warning. Factors that will affect the quality of your production soundtrack are

(1) location—don't pick a location next to a freeway or a boiler factory;
(2) actor volume—advise your director to encourage the actors to speak loud enough to overcome background noise; and
(3) extra cameras—don't shoot tight and wide in the same take—it makes microphone placement problematic—one of the angles (probably the close up) will not have the proper mike presence.

835-01 MIXER

More formally known as the production sound mixer, the mixer's sole responsibility is to record the best soundtrack possible, or to be more specific, to record the best production dialogue track possible. Most directors prefer to use the line readings recorded during the filming of a scene if possible rather than a line reading added later in ADR.

Scale for union production sound mixers is $55.27 per hour. In the union's rate book, this is known as the Y-1 rate. Most work at the scale rate. A week consisting of five twelve-hour days would cost approximately $3,868.90. On *Anarchist*, our mixer generously agreed to work for $1800 for a six-day week.

835-02 Boom Operator

The boom operator is the person holding the microphone over the actors' heads by means of a fishpole. Scale for union boom operators is Y-8 or $37.45 per hour. However, most work above scale at the Y-4 rate, which is $42.75 per hour. Our boom operator on *Anarchist* worked for $1500 per six-day week.

835-03 Recorder / Cable Person

On a union production, the cable person is a mandatory position. On a smaller, non-union production, it's possible to do without. The cable person's duties include technical maintenance of the equipment, microphone placement, and managing the microphone cables during moving camera shots. A cable person's presence will speed up a sound crew and make them more efficient, but it may be more than you can afford.

Union cable persons work at the Y-6 rate of $37.45 per hour. Since this is the same as the boom operator's rate, cable persons can fill in and hold a second boom when needed. On *Anarchist*, we did not use a cable person and instead used a two-person crew.

835-04 Playback Operator

There are two types of playback: audio and video. They are each used in entirely different circumstances. In *Dracula: Dead and Loving It*, there is a ballroom dance scene in which extras and cast members are dancing. In order to get them all dancing to the same tempo, a prerecorded music track was played while each of the shots of the dancing was taken. This made it possible to cut from one angle to another without sudden changes in tempo or rhythm. If it is not possible to play music while filming because you are trying to record dialogue during the scene, then a click track is used. A click track plays a regular beat of clicks or low frequency thumps that can be easily filtered out of the production soundtrack in post while still keeping the dancers in sync. The other normal time to use audio playback is when you have a performer lip-synch to a prerecorded track. Sometimes you get an unusual situation that only audio playback can solve. On the *Child's Play* films, Brad Dourif prerecorded all of Chucky's lines, which were then played back on stage during filming so that the puppeteers could synchronize Chucky's mouth to the words Brad spoke.

The obvious place where video playback is used is when a television is seen onscreen with content on the screen. In addition to this, almost every instance of computer displays, instrument readouts, or medical monitoring displays uses prerecorded video feeds. This provides much more control over the display than if you are depending on a computer program to do what you want, when you want. If a television that uses a cathode-ray picture tube is used, the video material must be converted to 24 frames per second (fps) standards to match the film rate. If a flat screen or LED screen is being used to display the image, then standards conversion is not necessary.

Union playback operators make no less than the Y-7 rate of $37.45 per hour. Some demand the Y-4 rate of $42.75 per hour. On *Anarchist*, we needed two days of video playback for scenes in which we had a television playing or a computer being operated. We budgeted $2000 in this account and we spent $2800.

835-12 Transfer Dailies

This account pays the costs of transferring each day's soundtrack from ¼-inch audio tape, or DAT, to magnetic film. If you are only posting digitally, then you only need to transfer the soundtracks to digital files. On *Anarchist*, we put the transfer money into account 841-05 and I will go into further detail when I discuss that account.

835-51 Purchases

Purchases in the sound account are generally for dry cell batteries and ¼-inch audio tape or DAT. On a low-budget film, $15 to $20 per day should be sufficient.

835-56 Rentals

Normally the soundmixer will own the equipment needed to record the production soundtrack. On studio films, the rate they charge currently is around $1800 to $2200 per week. On *Anarchist*, our mixer asked us for only $1200 per week because he knew how limited our budget was.

Sometimes the mixer will also be able to rent walkie-talkies to the production. On *Anarchist*, we rented them from our mixer and paid $6 per week for each walkie-talkie. Audio equipment houses in Los Angeles will rent them for $10 to $15 per week.

Audio and video playback equipment rental will also be put in this account. Depending on how elaborate the set-up is and how many feeds are needed at the same time, video playback equipment can run from $850 to $2000 per day. On *Anarchist*, we were able to rent our equipment from the video playback operator for $300 per week. Audio playback equipment can run from $350 to $800 per day.

837-00 Location

The location account can be one of the largest in a budget. It encompasses all expenses pertaining to shooting on location, whether local or distant. The definition of a distant location is any location where you house and feed the cast and crew. Even if you do not move the production to a distant location, you may have individual members of the cast or crew who will be housed. Cast expenses will go above-the-line in the cast travel account, while all below-the-line expenses will go here.

When should you use a location and when should you use a stage set? Several factors enter into this decision. Let's look at the advantages and disadvantages of each. Stage sets have several advantages. They are easy to control, they are not affected by weather or sunlight, and they are closed to the public. The downside of stage sets is that you have to build whatever you are going to shoot, and they are expensive to rent. On the other hand, locations give you tremendous production value for very little money. Imagine trying to create the lobby of a high-rise office building on stage. It would be very expensive. The negative side to locations consists mostly of the reverse of the stage set pluses: they are difficult to control, they are affected by weather and sunlight, and they are usually open to the public. In addition, locations must be rented from their owners and tenants, deals must be struck with nearby neighbors, trailers, trucks and drivers must be hired, and the cast and crew must often be fed a catered lunch. See "Location or Stage?" in Chapter 10.

The deciding factors are usually cost and efficiency. Let's say you need an Int. Living Room set for fourteen days and the choices are to build it on stage for $50,000 or rent a location for $2500 per day. That makes it easy to choose, doesn't it? While you are counting the thousands of dollars you anticipate saving, give a thought to efficiency. Will it take the crew a great deal longer to shoot the scenes on the location than it would on stage? How long will you need the location? Will the scenes take a day or two weeks? Fourteen days at $2500 per day adds up to $35,000. Add in the extra drivers and equipment, and you might find the stage more affordable. Each set must be considered on its own with all factors weighed before making a final decision.

837-01 Site Fees & Rentals

This account covers not only site fees paid to property owners and/or tenants, but also filming permit fees paid to governing bodies that have jurisdiction over whatever sites you may be considering. Film permits can be issued by town or city governments, state governments, the federal government, including such departments of the state and federal governments as the National Park Service, National Forest Service, and the Department of Defense.

The most accurate way to budget this account is to list all fees for each location. However, you may not know what the details are when you are creating the budget. Another way to estimate the costs are simply to budget a certain amount for each day's shooting. On *Anarchist*, we budgeted $2000 per day and finished well within our budget. Yet on a recent studio feature, we budgeted $10,000 per day and found that amount to be accurate for that picture.

Other items in this account in the *Anarchist* budget deserve an explanation. "Modifications and Restoration" ($40,000) was the money that essentially ended up being our construction account. Since we planned to modify the houses we were shooting in extensively, we had set this money aside. "Clean out attic" was used to hire laborers to clean debris out of the attic we were going to shoot in and to try to remove as much dust from the area as possible. "Set Chairs" was money used to rent folding chairs to put in the extras' holding areas.

837-02 Police / Firemen / Watchmen

Police and firefighters are usually stipulated by the jurisdiction issuing your shooting permit. A good rule of thumb is to count on using two motorcycle officers for each day you are on public roads, and to plan on hiring a fire safety officer or fire safety advisor when you are shooting in brush areas, or in a building that is open to the public while you are filming. Other times that normally require a fire safety officer would be anytime the production is filming with pyrotechnic effects. In Los Angeles, off-duty police officers assigned to a motorcycle cost $44.61 per hour and they are usually given $50 per day for their motorcycles. Los Angeles uniformed fire safety officers earn $64 per hour. Both the police and the fire safety officer will want to see your filming permit, and either can officially stop your filming if they believe you are not abiding by its restrictions.

Set security guards or night security guards are often overlooked but necessary. They are usually hired through a private security service and can cost from $12 to $20 per hour with the higher rates reserved for armed guards. It is not necessary to hire armed guards unless you are filming in a war zone. I recommend against it. I never thought that anything I had on a movie set was so important that it was worth shooting someone. I would rather the guard be alert and aware of what is going on, and if something suspicious is observed, a call should be made to the police and/or someone on the production staff. When hiring guards at the above rates from a security firm, the hourly rate is usually applied around the clock at straight time, regardless of how many hours have elapsed since an individual started work.

837-03 Scouting

Before you can shoot a location, you must find it. This is done through a process called *scouting*. In England, you would go on a recce (pronounced *recky*, it is derived from the word *reconnoiter* or perhaps *reconnaissance*). It normally begins with a set list created from the script breakdown. The location manager and the production designer search out and find likely locations for each of the sets. When they have narrowed the list of locations down to three or four for each set, they take the director on a tour of them. At that time, the director either selects one of the locations or tells the location and art departments to keep looking.

Once the list has been narrowed down to the few that the director will see, the production manager and line producer should also see them. This is important so that production can be sure that each location has the elements needed. Along with the parameters discussed in Chapter 10, each of the following items should be considered.

Suitability. Presumably this has been judged by the production designer who has made sure that each location works for the scene.

Access. This is of prime importance. If the location is difficult to get to, or you are unable to park the equipment trucks reasonably close, it will delay the filming. Is there security in place, such as at an airport terminal, that the crew will have to negotiate when entering or exiting? Can the camera truck and generator be brought within a suitable distance?

Holding area. Is there a place for the extras to sit while they wait?

Feeding area. Is there a place for tables and chairs if you are catering lunch?

Rental Fee. Is the fee within the limits of the budget?

Odd restrictions. Are there rules or regulations that will cost money or time?

Noise. Is the location reasonably quiet? Is it under the flight path of an airport, or near a freeway?

Neighbors. Are the neighbors difficult? Do they object to the production's use of the property? Will they allow their property to be used for equipment or light placement?

Weather. What is the norm for your location at the time of year you are shooting? What are the extremes? Rain, wind, flash flood, hurricanes, tornadoes, bizzards. Is this the year the 17-year locusts will hatch? Plan for the unexpected.

Once the locations are picked, certain key crewmembers are taken on a tour of the sites so that they will be prepared for them. This is called the tech scout. It usually happens within two weeks prior to principal photography and can include as many as 25 or 30 crewmembers on a large company. At a minimum, the tech scout should include the director, DP, production designer, location manager, gaffer, key grip, assistant director, and the production manager. Some producers also like to be included. If there is a line producer on your picture, he or she should definitely be there. If you have the money and space, you could include the keys of other departments such as sound, props, special effects, and add the best boys from grip and electric and the rigging keys if possible.

This account is meant to cover all costs incurred in scouting. When deciding how much money should be allocated to this account, you must have an idea where you will be looking. (The salaries of the people on the scout are covered in their respective labor accounts.) Will you be traveling to other states? Will there be hotel expenses? On *Anarchist,* we knew that we would be shooting in and around Dallas so we only put enough money in this account to pay for a few scouting lunches and some photographic coverage ($500).

837-05 Travel Fares

Normally on a show that involves distant locations, this account would list all the below-the-line personnel that would be traveling, with an amount for each their airfares. The only below-the-line crewmembers traveling on *Anarchist* were the production designer, the editor, and the assistant editor. The production designer was originally from Dallas and agreed to combine his work on the picture with a planned trip home, so we hired him as a local and did not incur any expense for his travel. The editor and assistant editor decided to drive out to Dallas from Los Angeles, so we budgeted $500 for each of them for gasoline and motel expenses.

837-07 Hotels

The production designer lived at his parents' house, and the editor and the assistant editor were housed for free in an apartment house owned by the director's family. Otherwise, this account would have listed each out-of-town crewmember, with an amount for each night they would need to stay in a hotel. If you do use a hotel, always ask for a discount.

837-08 Living Expenses / Per Diems

Our three out-of-town crewmembers were each given $30 per day for food and expenses. This was a compromise with the production designer even though he was hired as a local. After all, he really was from Los Angeles.

837-09 Meals / Catering

If you are really hunting for money, you can simply break the crew each day for a set amount of time, say an hour, and have them go find their own lunches. However, it is often more efficient to cater a lunch each day. This will insure that they are all back on time, and if you are shooting at odd times of the day or night, or in areas where there are no restaurants, you know that the crew will get fed. Standard meals in Los Angeles are running from around $13.50 per plate to about $16.00 per plate with most caterers charging $15 per plate. Some caterers who service primarily big productions with huge stars charge as much as $25 per plate. For the per-plate price, the caterer will usually provide a walking breakfast (such as a burrito, or plate of bacon and eggs) in the morning, as well as a hot, sit-down lunch in the middle of the day. Be sure to check out how many choices of entrees are being offered and make sure you will be getting a varied menu. Crews tire quickly of the same food menu every week. Also make sure any extra charges, such as those for ice, propane, gasoline, tables, chairs, and anything else related to catering, are clearly spelled out. On *Anarchist*, we put in $12.50 per plate per day for meals, with an extra $1000 allotted for ice, water, propane, etc. In addition to the per plate charge, you are often required to carry the cook and helpers on your payroll.

837-10 Entertainment / Gratuities

At one time, this account could have simply been labeled "Bribes." This was where the money was put to pay off neighbors who ran their stereos full blast while you tried to shoot, or who began to mow their lawns, or do any number of things to try and disrupt your filming. Obviously, the more these payments were made, the more disruptive certain people became. In Los Angeles, it is now illegal to interfere with a film company that has the proper permits. It is considered restraint of trade. Nevertheless, there are times when you have not anticipated the inconvenience you may truly cause someone, and it's good to have some money here for those instances. In addition, there are times when it would help the location manager to be able to take a property owner out to lunch to try and close a deal. On *Anarchist*, we had no money here and we did not need any.

It should be noted that it is a federal criminal offense for any American company to bribe a foreign official. Any such act can subject the company, the officers of the company, the employee who commits the act, and the supervisor of the employee to federal prosecution.

837-15 Film Shipping

If you are on a distant location and you are shooting on film, you need to get your film to a lab each night. Depending on where you are in relationship to the lab, this can run from $100 to $500 per day. We budgeted $200 per day on *Anarchist*. The shipping is normally done over-the-counter on a major airline. There must be someone on the other end to pick up the film and let you know if there are any problems. Don't forget to add money for dailies to be shipped back to the location if you will be viewing film dailies. The shipping of DVDs or video tape will be less but could still amount to approximately $25 per day or more if sent by an overnight service. Check the carrier's web site for current pricing.

837-16 Baggage & Equipment Shipping

It is best to try to get your equipment in the place where you are filming. If it is not available, then you must ship it in, and you should compare the slower but lower cost of ground-shipment (by truck) with the speedier but higher cost of air-shipment. Keep in mind that during the period of shipping, you will be paying rent on the equipment. I have investigated using trains for shipping large bulky items in the past, but have found rail shipping so arcane and unreliable for film purposes that I have never used it. Rail is okay if the items shipped do not have to arrive at a specific time, a rarity in film production. On *Anarchist*, we allotted $500 as an allowance. We spent $1109.

837-18 Mileage & Parking

On union pictures, if the crew is required to report to a local location, they are paid mileage consisting of 30¢ per mile. This is calculated on the round-trip distance between the production's base of operations and the location. On a non-union project, it all depends on the deal you have with your crew. Whatever your deal is, you will have to provide parking for the crewmembers' cars near the location. In addition, there will be mileage reimbursements requested in petty cash envelopes by certain members of the crew such as location scouts, etc. On top of this, add in parking for your trucks on shooting days and on the weekends. On *Anarchist*, we budgeted $2500 for this account but we spent $6332. We simply under-estimated the cost of parking in the Dallas area, and the amount we would be spending in mileage.

837-30 Location Restoration

In addition to their rental fees, most property owners ask only that their property be returned to them in the same state that you found it. If you damage something, you need to either repair it, or give the property owner compensation so that the owner can repair it. Along with inadvertent damage, you might have painted rooms, uprooted plants, or made other deliberate changes that must be rectified. On *Anarchist*, we allotted $1000 here but only spent $297.

837-51 Purchases

Location purchases can be almost anything that the use of a location requires you to purchase. On *Anarchist*, the items charged here were six pop-up canopies to shelter equipment from the sun and rain. Other items wrongly charged to this account were a location fee (837-01), an added second day at another location (837-01), and postage used by the location department (837-54). Even with the misallocated charges, we spent only $1602.67 where we had allotted $3000.

837-52 Office Rentals

Since we had the use of several apartments in the complex owned by the director's family, we did not need to rent offices. We only added money here to pay for a cleaning service ($1000). The cleaning service actually cost only $450. If you rent a warehouse for your stage sets, often warehouses come with offices built in. If you are on a distant location and housing a large crew in a hotel, the hotel will often give you the use of several rooms or a banquet room to use as offices gratis. Sometimes you simply have to rent a separate space. If you need to do this, check out areas of the city or town that are not in high demand and you will find lower prices.

837-54 Phone & Postage

Watch out for this account. It can consume a huge amount of money, mostly through cell phone reimbursements. Before you hire your first crewmember, you need to develop a policy for cell phone reimbursements and that policy should be clearly stated on the deal memo that the crewmembers sign. A policy that I have found to be workable recently is to agree to reimburse whatever percentage of the crewmember's phone bill is equal to the percentage of minutes claimed as business calls. This encourages people to take out appropriate cell phone plans without using up all their included minutes. If someone has an inexpensive plan such as $10 per month for 30 minutes and every call afterwards is $1 per minute, I will encourage the crewmember to get a better plan. If he or she declines, I will offer a Nextel phone rented by the production. If the employee declines that offer, I will refuse to reimburse his or her calls.

The pitfall in postage is the danger posed by overnight services. Sometimes crews will get so used to everything having to be rushed that FedEx becomes the standard method of sending documents. I once had a casting office send me their invoice by FedEx, the cost of which they had included in their invoice. I deducted the charge. I certainly had no interest in their bill getting to me overnight. FedEx and the other overnight services certainly are necessary at times, but often the material does not have to arrive overnight, or it can be sent by email or fax. It is best to have all requests for overnight shipping be routed through the production coordinator so that some control can be maintained.

On *Anarchist*, we had $6000 in this account and spent $16,063. Most of the large expenditures were for FedEx, cell phone reimbursements, phone installation, and courier charges. This is a place where you can bleed money and it justifies extra attention.

837-56 Office Equipment Rental

Office equipment consists of copy machines, office furniture, lamps, fax machines, and answering machines among other items. Always compare the rental cost to what the expense would be if you simply bought the item. Keep in mind that it's often quite easy to sell items you have purchased at a 50% discount at the end of production, thereby reducing the final cost. On *Anarchist*, we budgeted $2000 and spent $2758.

839-00 Transportation

The amount of equipment that you carry will determine how expensive this account is. If everything can fit into a couple of U-haul trucks, you may not need to use teamsters. In that situation, crewmembers would drive what few vehicles you have. On the other hand, if you need a 10-ton truck or tractor-trailer semis, you will want to use properly licensed professional drivers and that means teamsters. In addition to the equipment trucks, keep in mind whether or not you will be using dressing room trailers and a honeywagon (a tractor-trailer truck housing dressing rooms and crew restrooms). This may also mean signing with the teamsters since these vehicles are not only specialized equipment which should be handled by a knowledgeable driver, but they are also heavy, towed vehicles requiring specific license ratings. If you do decide to sign with the teamsters, set up a meeting as early as possible. Be honest, explain your financial circumstances and your goals, and ask how they can help you do it. (See Chapter 14.)

There are certain strategies that can save you an enormous amount of money, especially when using union drivers. If the company will be at one specific location over several days, lay off some drivers for that period. If a truck is not moving, it does not need a driver. You do not necessarily need a driver for every vehicle. You may be able to shuttle drivers back and forth in order to move less urgently needed vehicles. Use dressing room trailers rather than motor homes. The trailers can be towed by stake-bed trucks. Once the trailers are parked, the stake-beds then go to work shuttling equipment on the location. In addition, dressing room trailers come in two, three, and four room versions as well as singles. By using a favored-nations clause in your cast contracts, you can put all of your actors in multi-room trailers or a honeywagon. If you are shooting long days and moving to a new location each night, use a move crew. A move crew is a fresh crew of drivers who come in on straight time after the company wraps, and who move the trucks to the new location. This way you don't have your day crew of drivers moving the equipment while earning heavy overtime and losing needed sleep. In addition, you can do this with many fewer drivers than the company normally carries since the move crew has an 8-hour shift to move all the trucks. Three drivers and a shuttle van can move a large number of trucks in eight hours.

839-01 Transportation Coordinator

This is the manager of the transportation department. The coordinator's responsibilities include making an initial budget, managing the equipment and labor efficiently, and seeing to the day-to-day transportation needs of the production company. In addition, the coordinator, or someone whom he or she designates can oversee the selection and procurement of the picture cars. This is a vitally important position since the transportation coordinator will be in charge of one of the larger budget accounts on the picture. Fill it with someone who is knowledgeable and trustworthy.

In Los Angeles, Teamsters Local 399 represents motion picture drivers. The current rates that have been established in negotiations between Local 399 and the AMPTP will be the rates that I quote for union drivers. The rate for transportation coordinator is left up to negotiation between the individual and the production company. It is usually set up as a weekly on-call salary. On *The Anarchist Cookbook*, part of the help that the Dallas teamsters gave to us was to not require a coordinator but have those duties assumed by the transportation captain.

839-02 Transportation Captains

On a large picture, the coordinator would remain in the production office most of the time while two transportation captains would handle matters on the set. Having two captains is especially helpful when the company is moving between locations in the course of the day. With two captains, one can be dispatching equipment from the finished location, while the second captain can direct the trucks where to park at the new location. If your transportation department is small, then this sort of organization is not necessary. You might use a coordinator and one captain, or just a captain as we did on *Anarchist*.

In Los Angeles, union captains get $32.55 per hour. On *Anarchist*, we paid our one captain $23.62 per hour. This was the rate that the Dallas teamsters had set for the captain. In addition, the Dallas teamsters generously agreed that our captain could drive a working truck (thus saving us an additional driver). Normally, captains do not drive working equipment but instead usually drive a car solely for their own transportation.

Note that the captain was budgeted for 113 pay-hours per week. This was in anticipation that the drivers would normally be the first people on the set in the morning and the last to leave at night, and that they would work 14 hours per day on a six-day week.

839-03 Studio Drivers

In a full chart of accounts, there is an account called 839-04 Location Drivers in addition to this one. On a project that involves a distant location, location drivers would refer to any drivers hired on the distant location, and studio drivers would be those hired at your home base. In as much as *Anarchist* was shot solely in Dallas and all our drivers were hired in Dallas, we put all drivers in the Studio Drivers account.

As you can see in the budget, the drivers make a variety of rates depending upon what vehicle the individual is driving. On *Anarchist*, the Dallas drivers ranged from $18.96 to $23.32 per hour. The current scale rates in Los Angeles are broken out in Table 19.1. Notice that the cook-driver and the catering helpers are included in the driver list.

839-12 Repairs / Maintenance

There should be an allowance here for washes, windshield wipers, and minor repairs. On *Anarchist*, we allocated $2500 here and spent $2671.

839-14 Pickups, Taxis, Etc.

If you plan to shoot in New York City, this account would need to be substantial since you would probably be relying on taxicabs or car services for airport pickups and other shorter trips. We really did not plan to use them in Dallas and therefore did not allocate any money here.

839-23 Gas & Oil

This should cover all your fuel and oil needs. If you are traveling a long distance, you will need to increase this account accordingly. On *Anarchist*, we shot 25 days with a prep period of four weeks and a wrap period of one week. Our most distant location was a small amusement park in the Fort Worth Stockyards. All other locations were in the greater metropolitan area of Dallas. We budgeted $10,000 here and spent $8978. Of course, fuel was less expensive during the summer of 2001 than it is now. On a recent studio picture budgeted in the $30 million range that I managed, we spent $94,525 on gas and oil.

839-24 Tolls & Permits

If you are sending your trucks into other states, you may incur toll fees if your trucks are not licensed to operate in the other states. If you will be using toll roads during your filming, you will obviously need to put money here. On *Anarchist*, we put $1000 here and only spent $243.

839-51 Purchases

Purchases in transportation might include road flares, tire chains, traffic cones, and honeywagon supplies. We allocated $500 here on *Anarchist*, but we did not charge anything to the account.

Vehicle Description or Position	Rate/Hr
Drivers of autos, station wagons, minivans with 9 or fewer passengers, motorcycles	$17.00
Experienced drivers of the above vehicles	$22.71
Drivers of vehicles requiring a Class C driver's license (crew cabs, 5-tons, pickup trucks)	$24.06
Drivers of vehicles requiring a Class B driver's license (water trucks, maxivans with 10 or more passengers, busses, dump trucks, 5-ton crew cabs, crew cabs towing trailers under 6,000 lbs., motor homes)	$26.24
Drivers of vehicles requiring a Class A driver's license (vehicles towing trailers over 6,000 lbs., cranes, heavy earth moving equipment, honeywagons, cook/drivers)	$28.30
Mechanic	$29.84
Drivers of camera cars or Chapman cranes	$32.55
Drivers of production vans (tractor trailer with mounted generator)	$33.23

Table 19.1. Los Angeles Teamster Rates

839-54 Location Self Drives

This account covers rental cars for crewmembers who are being housed away from their homes. On *Anarchist*, we had to cover three rental cars and we allocated a total of $2550. The rate we used, $150 per week, was too low, and we ended up spending $4276.

839-56 Studio Vehicles

Just as in the labor accounts, equipment is divided into studio and location vehicles. On *Anarchist*, we only used the studio vehicle account. Because we were so limited in our budget, we tried to keep the vehicles down to a minimum. The following will explain the reasons for using each vehicle.

Camera truck. A small cube van should be sufficient. It is helpful to have a darkroom built into the truck to facilitate loading and downloading of camera magazines. If a darkroom is not available, all the loading and unloading will have to be done in a changing bag.

Grip/Electric truck. This was a 5-ton truck. When renting any truck for production, it is a good idea to get one with a liftgate. It is especially important for grip and electric crewmembers since they may be working with large, heavy items such as the camera dolly or large lighting instruments. Ideally on a low-budget film, you want to put both departments in one truck. On studio films, sometimes we will have two 50-foot semis for each department. The reason for this is that the keys never want to tell the DP that they do not have some piece of equipment that he has asked for. In turn, the DP never wants to tell the director that he or she is unable to do something because of lack of equipment. That is why so much equipment is carried on a large studio film. If they make it, it's on the truck. Therefore, the way to control the amount of equipment you will be carrying and, by extension, the number of trucks you will need, is to reach an understanding with the director and DP as to what items are truly going to be needed. If some esoteric and expensive piece of equipment is needed for some particular shot, then rent it for that day. Don't carry it on the truck for the entire shooting period.

Costume (Wardrobe) trailer. This was a small 28-foot trailer fitted out with racks so that the costumes could be hung up for transport and storage. Your costume supervisor will be able to help you decide on the minimum space needed. This trailer was towed by the stake bed truck that the driver captain was driving.

Props/Special Effects truck. These two departments seemed to be able to coexist peacefully on one truck. This was a typical truck that you might rent from Ryder or U-haul.

Honeywagon. The honeywagon is a truck about 28 feet long pulling a trailer of about equal length. Built into the honeywagon are six to eight dressing rooms, plus a men's and a women's restroom. The company that you rent the honeywagon from will provide the driver, who will go onto your payroll. Notice that we had an additional honeywagon budgeted for one week. This was in order to handle additional cast on certain days.

Set Dressing 5-ton truck. The set dressing department uses this truck to fetch and return all the furniture and other set dressing you will need. It should start at about the same time that your swing crew starts, and will stay on until the swing crew has finished wrapping.

Stake Bed truck. This is the vehicle driven by our driver captain and also pulled the wardrobe trailer. Once the wardrobe trailer was parked, the stake bed became a utility truck for the use of any department that needed it.

Maxivan. This is used to pick up actors from their hotel and return them at the end of the day, to pick up people from the airport, to follow the camera car with crewmembers when doing moving shots on a road, to scout locations, and to perform any other jobs in which people have to be transported.

Once production started, I realized that I needed two other vehicles. One was a makeup trailer, the other was a fuel truck. It turned out that it simply was not practical or efficient not to have a place to do the actor's makeup. Having a dedicated trailer where the makeup and hair people can leave their equipment set up saves their time and reserves the actors' dressing rooms for their own use. The vehicle I chose to pull the makeup trailer was a fuel truck. A fuel truck is simply a large pickup that has been fitted out with tanks and pumps in its bed. Having a fuel truck greatly simplifies keeping all the vehicles and generators fueled. Instead of having the driver of each vehicle search out a gas station at the end of the day when the driver is earning overtime, the fuel truck brings the fuel to each of the vehicles during the normal day. This can save at least an hour on each driver each day.

839-58 Cranes & Insert Cars

An insert car is synonymous with a camera car. It is a heavy duty pickup truck outfitted with speed rail to allow the mounting of a camera, and various towing attachments to allow the towing of trailers or picture cars. The driver of such a vehicle needs to be conscious of what is going on around the camera car at all times. Camera cars are inherently dangerous and are often overloaded by productions by allowing too many crewmembers to ride on the camera car during the shots. If makeup and hair people, props, special effects or any other crewmembers need to accompany the unit during the shooting of a moving vehicle, then they should follow in a van. Only the minimum people required should be on the camera car, such as the director, assistant director, script supervisor, camera operator, camera, assistant, and DP. The sound mixer will often ride in the cab of the insert car next to the driver.

Camera cranes also demand respect and certain precautions. Once the camera is mounted on the crane arm and the camera operator and assistant have been seated, weight is added to the opposite end of the crane arm to balance it. By balancing the arm, one crane grip can easily move the camera and crew that are riding on the crane. If you are using a camera crane, no one should get on or off the crane without the crane grip's permission. If someone should step off the crane once it is balanced, the crane becomes a catapult. If a person needs to get off the crane or a piece of equipment must be removed from the crane, the crane grip must rebalance the arm before the person or item is removed.

On *Anarchist*, we allowed $7500 for two days of crane use and a few days of a camera car. We only spent $4599.

841-00 Film & Lab

This is the account where all expenses for film and processing during the shooting period go. Post production has its own film and lab account. If you are shooting on 24P video (HD) or DV, you will not have to put any money here. For films without a theatrical release that will be distributed digitally, either by DVD, broadcast/cable, or on the internet, I recommend against using film. (See Chapter 3.) The drawback to shooting HD or DV when you have a theatrical release is that most theaters in the United States do not have the ability to project digital media. This requires a film print release, which means you will have to scan the digital image out to film to make your internegative. That can be expensive. Both the theater owners and the studios would like to switch over to digital projection; the sticking point is who will be stuck with the bill for the new equipment. Nevertheless, digital projection is the direction in which the industry is heading, and in the not too distant future, digital video may become the medium of choice for the low-budget film. It is worth exploring. (See the discussion in this chapter under 813-00 Camera.)

841-01 Raw Stock

If you do decide to shoot on film, you will need to purchase raw stock. The emulsion should be decided in consultation with the DP and the director. On *Anarchist*, the director had made a stylistic choice to shoot the happy, "normal" anarchist life on bright, beautiful 35mm color stock. The scenes during Puck's house arrest in Plano, Texas, were to be shot on 16mm stock with a brown (coffee) filter. In addition, those scenes were to be made as grainy, boring, and dull as possible with flat camera angles and an absolutely still camera. He said he wanted it to resemble badly shot pornography. When the anarchists went into action, the scenes were to be shot on consumer DV. (As mentioned earlier, we actually had to degrade the DV image in post production in order to achieve the look that the director was aiming for.)

The Eastman Kodak Company currently charges about 62¢ per foot for their 35mm Vision® stock. Sometimes deals can be made. On a recent studio film, a major film manufacturer sold us their stock at a price that was essentially their cost to manufacture. They simply wanted the prestige of having their film used on the project. It never hurts to ask.

Another money saving source of film stock would be the various film stock resale companies. On a large feature, there are often 100 to 200 feet of unexposed film left on a reel. Rather than risk running out of film in the middle of a take, the camera assistants re-can these *short ends* and the production company will sell them along with their excess full cans to a film stock reseller. These resellers in turn offer the stock to the public at much reduced rates. Not everything they sell is less than 200 feet. You can actually get unopened, full, 400-foot or 1000-foot cans. Most of the resellers test the stock that they sell to make sure that it is not defective and that it has been stored properly.

Judging how much stock to purchase is another issue that must be determined. If you do not know your director's rate of shooting, a good rule of thumb is to budget 5000 feet of film per day. If you will be carrying a second camera, another 2500 to 3500 feet of film per day for the second camera is usually correct. On *Anarchist*, we budgeted 5000 feet per day for nineteen days. This was determined by counting the number of days in the schedule on which we were shooting scenes that were to be filmed on 35mm film. In addition, we also budgeted 1700 feet of 16mm film for each of the six days that we expected to use that stock. The difference in footage per day is partially because 16mm film runs through the camera at 36 feet per minute where 35mm film runs at a rate of 90 feet per minute. Altogether, we budgeted $52,438 for stock purchase and we spent $55,892.

841-02 Negative Development

On most film projects, you will develop 90% of the film stock that you purchase. The other 10% ends up being thrown away as waste or becomes short ends. If you are purchasing 5000 feet of film per day, then you will process or develop 4500 feet per day (90% × 5000 ft.). That is how we budgeted the processing for the 35mm film on *Anarchist*. We planned to buy 10,200 feet of 16mm film stock, so 90% of that would have been 9180 feet. In the budget, the 16mm footage to be developed was rounded off to 9000 feet.

On *Anarchist*, we were paying 11.5¢ per foot for processing both 16mm and 35mm film. Check with your lab for exact prices. It is wise to shop around since labs can vary in their pricing. Because we used more stock than anticipated, we also went over in this account: $13,403 spent as opposed to $10,868 budgeted.

841-03 Positive Prints

Once each day's footage has been developed, the shots marked as prints by the director will be printed onto print stock. These make up the dailies that are projected and viewed each day. On average, your printed footage will be about 70% of the purchased stock. Having budgeted 5000 feet of 35mm raw stock to be used each day on *Anarchist*, we would have expected to print about 3500 feet each day (70% × 5000 ft.). Again, it is wise to check with your lab for current prices. At the time of the *Anarchist* shoot, our lab was charging 25.179¢ per foot for *one-light prints*. A one-light print is a print of your negative that does not incorporate color correction. If you are going to print your dailies, this is the least expensive way to do it.

If you look at account 841-03 in the *Anarchist* budget, you will see no entry in this account, instead it was covered under 841-06 Videocassettes. This was because we did not plan to print our dailies, but instead look at them on video tape. Were we shooting the film now, we would receive our dailies on DVD. We made this decision to save money, but it is risky. There are imperfections that can occur on film that will be invisible on a video image of the frame, but will stand out like a neon sign on a projected film image. This is because the resolution of DVD or VHS video tape is so much less than that of a projected film image. Focus is especially difficult to judge on video, whereas an out-of-focus shot will be immediately apparent on film. Forego film dailies at your own risk. Nevertheless, we did save $31,785 by doing this.

841-04 ¼" Sound Stock

This is where we put the money for the DATs (digital audio tape) used by our production sound mixer: one DAT cartridge each day. DAT makes a lot of sense now that films are edited digitally so often. DAT recordings are already in a digital format. At the time, DAT cartridges were $15 each. Today, they can be bought for $3 to $5 in quantities of 10 or more.

841-05 Sound Transfer

This account covers the expense of transferring the production sound to magnetic film. This is necessary when film dailies are made. Although we budgeted $7391 here, we did not do any transfers because we did not print our dailies. The entire amount was a savings. The footage was based on the amount of film printed plus 15% for additional transfers.

841-06 Videocassettes

Telecine is the digitizing of the dailies into files that can be used in the digital editing process. These files can then be transferred to video tape or to DVDs for viewing. We anticipated putting 100,000 feet through this process. The other lines in this account are discussed below.

"Key number prep" refers to the cost of reading and indexing the edge numbers that are printed on the negative film. These numbers are correlated with the video and audio timecode during the transfer. This will allow the filmmaker to shoot on film, edit digitally, and match back to the camera negative to enable release in any format. With the newer stocks, Kodak has begun putting machine-readable bar code on its negative film, which allows this process to be automated.

"Video stock" for the DV camera was used in those shots that were to be shot on DV.

"Tape stock" money was used to purchase the VHS cartridges that were used to view the dailies.

"Telecine 16mm" was the money used to digitize the 16mm film that we shot.

Having budgeted $16,005, we actually spent $22,527. This was partly due to an extra day of shooting, and partly due to shooting more footage per day than anticipated.

841-51 Polaroid Film

Up until recently, Polaroid film was used for documenting sets, set dressing, costumes, props, actors' makeup and hair, and for script continuity. Every department had a Polaroid camera, and we would buy the film cartridges by the case; that was the situation on *Anarchist*. Now, many crewmembers are using digital cameras. Although it is no longer necessary to buy film, this money is now spent on color printer cartridges and photo paper. Sometimes I think it was cheaper with the Polaroids because of the high expense of color printing cartridges and photo paper. With $1000 budgeted, we only spent $866.

843-00 Tests

The tests that you may need to pay for include those requested by the DP such as photographic, film emulsion, and lighting tests, as well as costume, makeup, and screen tests for actors. The chart of accounts provides for expenses related to talent, crew labor, purchases, rentals, film, and miscellaneous—all the items you would need to pay for to shoot the test. If certain crewmembers such as the DP, gaffer, key grip, etc., are already on payroll because they have started their prep period, there is no need to add them to the test account.

843-51 PURCHASES
843-56 RENTALS

On *Anarchist*, we expected only to shoot some very brief tests having to do with how DV shots would look in the final film prints so we only budgeted $500 in purchases and $600 in rentals. Our lab put the video images through the post production processing gratis. Of the $1100, we only spent $893.

845-00 Facility Expenses

This account is used for studio offices, phone, postage, messengers, stages, dressing room rental, parking at the studio, and other facility charges. As stated earlier, we did not use a stage, and our offices cost us nothing since they were located in an apartment complex owned by the director's family, so we did not need to budget any money here. If you are renting stages, be sure that you are aware of all the potential additional charges such as power, custodial services, utilities, stage manager, grip and electric studio best boys, and studio guards.

847-00 Second Unit

This account resembles the entire budget squeezed into one account. It contains sub-subaccounts for director, talent, production staff, camera, etc. just like the full budget contains subaccounts for each. If you are going to have an extensive second unit, then you should itemize the expenses here just as you have done for the film as a whole in the rest of the budget.

847-13 Camera

This was the only second unit subaccount that we used on *Anarchist*. This was because our second unit consisted only of crewmembers who were already accounted for in the rest of the budget, except for an additional camera assistant. Therefore, it was only necessary to budget the camera assistant that we would hire. This second unit was used to obtain establishing shots of Plano and a few drive-bys.

20

Post Production

Post production can be broken down into two paths, one for picture and one for sound (see figure 20.1). The picture path starts with the original footage from the camera, whether it is film or video. Film footage must be put through a telecine process if you are using digital editing. This is done from the original camera negative and results in digital image files that can be manipulated by Adobe Premier®, Apple Final Cut Pro®, or the Avid® editing system.

If you are not using a digital editing system but are cutting on film, you will be cutting and splicing together printed footage made from each day's negative. This is called the *workprint.* If you are not printing dailies, but are editing electronically, then the cut of the film resides in the editing computer and as a *decision list.* Using the decision list or the workprint as a guide, the negative cutter then cuts and splices the negative to conform to the existing cut of the picture. If you are shooting only digital video, there will be no negative to cut.

Once the negative has been cut, it is sent to the lab, which then makes an *answer print,* also known as a black-track answer print since it has no soundtrack at this stage. (If there is no negative, the timing process described below in the rest of this paragraph is done electronically on specialized video timing equipment before the video image is scanned out to film.) In making the answer print, the lab has a color timer view each cut and adjust the printing lights so that there are no jarring changes in color from one shot to another. For example, if a scene took all day and into the late afternoon until just before sunset to shoot, the shots made toward

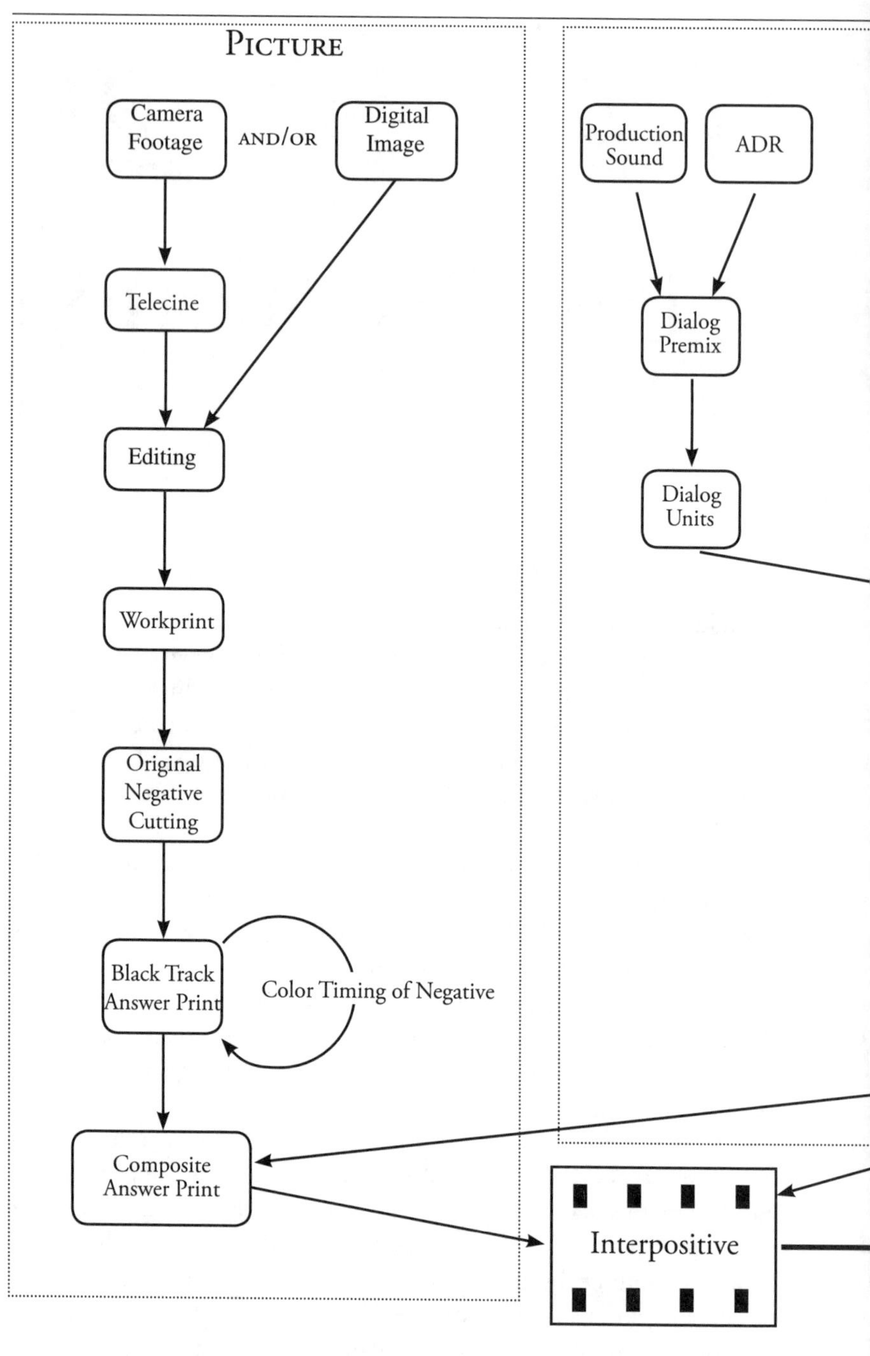

Fig. 20.1. The post production process.

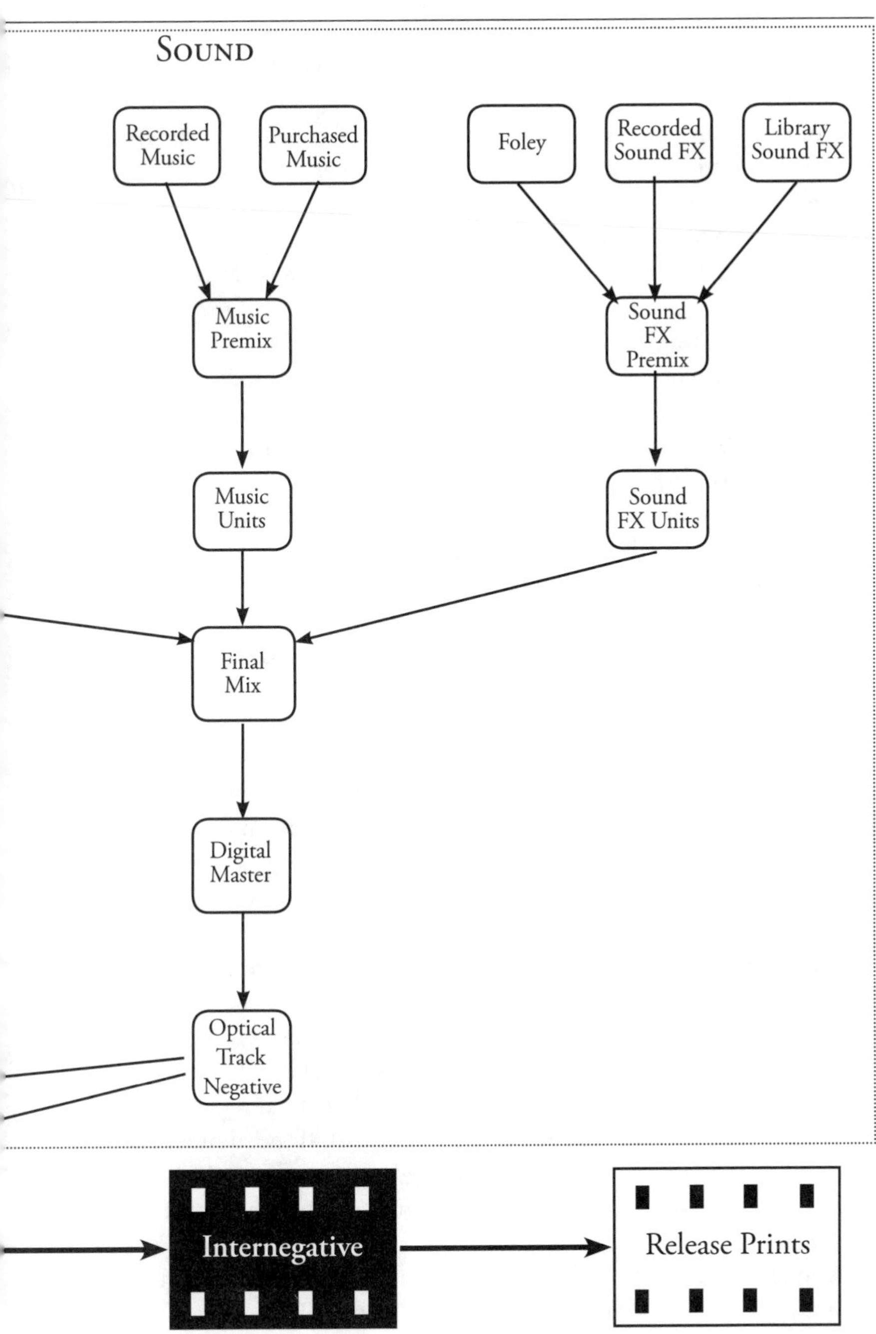

Sound
Recorded Music
Purchased Music
Foley
Recorded Sound FX
Library Sound FX
Music Premix
Sound FX Premix
Music Units
Sound FX Units
Final Mix
Digital Master
Optical Track Negative
Internegative
Release Prints

the end of the day will have a definite orange cast to them because of the change in the quality of sunlight throughout the day. The color timer compensates for this by increasing the cyan component of the printing lights and/or decreasing the magenta and yellow components. After the timer is satisfied with the chosen printing lights, an answer print is made to show to the filmmakers for their approval.

If the filmmakers disagree with some of the choices made by the color timer, adjustments will be made and another final answer print will be struck. Normally, the lab will indulge one set of changes. If the filmmakers are still not satisfied and the lab believes that they have done everything the filmmakers have asked for, the lab may begin to add additional charges for more changes. In order to lower costs, some labs have begun making single frame blowups of each of the cuts in a film for the first viewing by the filmmakers, thereby saving the expense of printing the entire film. The final answer print will have the soundtrack added and can be used to exhibit the picture. It will never look better than this.

The sound path is, in itself, made up of three paths that converge to create the soundtrack of the movie: dialogue, music, and sound effects. The sources of the dialogue track are the production sound recordings made when the scenes were shot, and other recordings made through the ADR process. These are combined and their relative volume levels set in the dialogue premix.

The music track is made up of purchased tracks of previously recorded music such as music from commercial albums (also known as needle drop), and music recorded specifically for the film in a scoring session. Like the dialogue track, the various music sources sometimes are mixed together in a music premix.

The third path, sound effects, has three sources other than the production sound recordings made during the filming of the scenes. Since production sound recording is optimized to record the actors' voices, it is not the best way to supply sound effects to a film. Often the sounds never actually occur during filming. For example, when a car squeals out of a parking lot, the tires may not make any noise at all. If the filmmakers want a tire squeal, it is much easier and more effective to add it in the effects track than to spend a lot of production time to make the actual tires on the car squeal.

A sound effect such as a tire squeal would probably be obtained from a sound effects library. Sound effects editors usually have a large library of useful sound effects that can dropped into a film in the appropriate places. A few years ago, every time I saw a film with a western landscape, I think I heard the same hawk screech. That hawk screech has been in more films than Kevin Bacon has.

Another source for sound effects is foley. *Foley* is the process in which sound effects are created and recorded in real time and in synchronization with a projected scene. For example, if a stunt person crashes through a window in a scene, the foley artist will drop a box of glass shards on the floor of the foley studio at just the right moment so that the crash of the glass is recorded in sync with the breaking of the window on the screen. Foley artists are also called foley walkers. This is because they often walk on various surfaces in sync with an actor on the screen to make the proper sound of someone walking on pavement, or on gravel, or on dirt, or on whatever the surface was in the scene.

The third source of sound effects is recorded sound effects often created by a sound designer. Sound designers are a creative and imaginative lot. When George Lucas needed a sound for R2D2, he turned to his favorite sound designer, Ben Burtt. Ben created that sound as well as the sound of the light sabers, TIE fighters, and even Darth Vader's breathing, among many others in the *Star Wars* movies. Anytime that Ben came across an unusual sound he would record it, manipulate it, and eventually it would become the sound of some strange alien creature. No one knew what these things sounded like until Ben Burtt created the sounds.

Once the sound effects from all the various sources are collected, they are mixed down into a few sound effects units in a sound effects premix. A sound effect unit used to be a reel of magnetic film; now it is more likely to be a CD.

The final mix is where all of the tracks, dialogue, music, and effects are combined together by the re-recording mixers into one soundtrack. A digital master is made from that soundtrack. The digital master is then used to create the optical track which exists in the form of a film negative. The optical track negative is used to print the soundtrack onto the final answer print.

If you were only going to exhibit your film a few times, this is where the process would end. You would simply use the final answer print for exhibition. However, if you need to strike a number of release prints, there are a few more steps to take in order to preserve your original negative. A film negative will wear out after a certain number of prints are made from it. In addition, there is always the danger that the negative may be damaged by the printing equipment. For those reasons, you need to create a number of copies of the negative from which to make the release prints.

These copies of the original cut camera negative are called *internegatives* since they are negatives that exist in the process between the original negative and the final release print. To make the internegatives, you must first make an interpositive since printing from a negative creates a positive print. The optical track negative is printed onto the interpositive along with the picture image, thus marrying picture and sound for successive generations. The interpositive is very similar to the final answer print except it is printed on film stock that exhibits a lower contrast. This is because each successive generation of negative-to-print tends to add contrast, and the lower contrast of the interpositive stock helps to compensate for this.

Each internegative can make around 100 release prints before showing signs of wear. Once an internegative wears out, another can be struck from the interpositive. A standard theatrical release for a mainstream film in the U.S. is approximately 2500 to 3500 prints. If a day-and-date release is planned (opening throughout the world on the same day) as was done for *Spiderman,* in an effort to beat the film pirates, you will need approximately 15,000 prints. As a contrast, *The Anarchist Cookbook* total release print run was—two.

851-00 Editing & Projection

Sergei Mikhailovich Eisenstein is credited with being the father of modern editing techniques or montage. Prior to Eisenstein, editing was just a way of joining together pieces of film that were shot separately into a coherent whole. Scenes were acted before the camera as though the actors were on stage and the camera was the audience. Each scene was a single shot. Once shot, the scenes simply had to be spliced together into the proper order. Eisenstein explored how the placement of different shots made from various camera angles affected each other and the meaning of the cut sequence as interpreted by the audience. Another early Russian cinema experimenter, V.I. Pudovkin, describes in his book, *Film Technique and Film Acting,* how he first became aware of this magical power of film:

> *Kuleshov and I made an interesting experiment. We took from some film or other several close-ups of the well-known Russian actor Mosjukhin. We chose close-ups which were static and which did not express any feeling at all—quiet close-ups. We joined these close-ups, which were all similar, with other bits of film in three different combinations. In the first combination the close-up of Mosjukhin was immediately followed by a shot of a plate of soup standing on a table. It was obvious and certain that Mosjukhin was looking at this soup. In the second combination the face of Mosjukhin was joined to shots showing a*

> *coffin in which lay a dead woman. In the third the close-up was followed by a shot of a little girl playing with a funny toy bear. When we showed the three combinations to an audience which had not been let into the secret the result was terrific. The public raved about the acting of the artist. They pointed out the heavy pensiveness of his mood over the forgotten soup, were touched and moved by the deep sorrow with which he looked on the dead woman, and admired the light, happy smile with which he surveyed the girl at play. But we knew that in all three cases the face was exactly the same.**

Today, this technique (*montage*) is exploited to its fullest. The pace of the cutting and the sophistication of the audience have given rise to a grammar of film editing that can cue an audience into a character's emotion or attitude with a speed that is unparalleled in the history of storytelling. Our audiences instantly "get it." At the center of this magic act is the editor.

851-01 Film Editors

When I produced my first film, I knew very little about post production. Ed Warschilka, the editor on that film, was a seasoned veteran and a very patient man. He gave me my education in post production. The editor's primary responsibility is to cut the picture. He or she understands the processes, what is required, what is missing, and what is possible. The editor shepherds a film through the post production process, is aware of how all the parts are coming together, and where the bottlenecks are. And if your editor is as patient as mine was, you will get an education along the way.

Usually a film will have one editor with a staff of a few assistants and perhaps an apprentice. On large and very complex films, sometimes a second or even a third editor is brought in to cut specific sequences. In those cases, the additional editors will also have an assistant or two working with them. Union editors on an independent feature currently make $2458.85 per week minimum. Most editors make considerably more than scale at the studios, but there are editors who enjoy working on smaller independent films and they will often give you a break on their rate if they really like the project. Alan Bell, our editor on *The Anarchist Cookbook*, was an experienced and well-known editor who did the project because he liked

*Pudovkin, V.I., *Film Technique and Film Acting*, 168.

the script and the writer-director. Without his resourcefulness and dedication, we would have been hard pressed to finish the film.

851-02 Assistant Film Editors

The assistant editor is chosen by the editor. Usually the assistant is someone the editor has worked with before. The assistant runs the cutting room, interacts with the lab and visual effects houses, schedules screenings, in some cases, loads the digitized picture files into the Avid or other electronic editing system, organizes printed dailies or other clips, searches for stock footage, and generally assists the editor in the cutting of the film. Often, an editor will give an assistant a scene to cut in order to help train him or her. In fact, many assistants are ready to cut film long before they are actually allowed to do so. This can be a source of inexpensive and knowledgeable editors for low-budget films. Many a low-budget film has been cut by an editor who works as an assistant in the union world and who is looking to get a credit as a full-fledged editor.

Union minimum for an editorial assistant is $1395.58 for a forty-hour week. Editors usually work at least a ten-hour day, so a union editorial assistant would make $1615.96 per week for 50 hours. As can be seen by the budget, our assistant editor on *Anarchist* gave us a huge break.

851-03 Apprentice Editor

This is an entry-level position that the editor's union has set up, much to their credit. Very few Hollywood unions give much encouragement to people seeking entry or even provide a mechanism by which to accomplish it.

Union apprentice editors make $26.748 per hour when hired on a weekly basis (a guarantee of 48.6 hours per week). This is by no means inexpensive. Nevertheless, it is an opportunity for a producer of a union show to hire a person who can be very knowledgeable at a discount rate, while at the same time, providing an opportunity to someone trying to break into the business.

On *Anarchist*, our editorial team was limited to an editor and an assistant so we did not hire an apprentice.

851-04 Post Production Supervisor

Most low-budget films do not need someone in this position. The producer can handle much of what this person would do, and the editorial team can deal with the rest. A post production supervisor is concerned with scheduling mix rooms, ADR, following up with the lab and visual effects house, and generally keeping the post schedule on track. We did not use a post production supervisor on *Anarchist*. If you plan on hiring one, rates can vary from $1000 per week and up.

851-05 Projectionists

If your editor is cutting a workprint and you want to project versions of the cut at various times, or view other printed footage, you need to put some money here. The cost could be $100 to $200 per screening. On *Anarchist*, the negative was put through telecine and the director viewed the editor's work on the editing machine, so we never had anything to project until the answer print.

851-05 Coding & Miscellaneous Editing

Coding is the printing of edge numbers on the workprint. If you have no print, there is no coding cost. Normally this is handled by renting a coding machine for a few hundred dollars per month, and having the assistant editor use it to code all printed footage that comes into the editing room.

Miscellaneous editing is any editing cost not covered elsewhere in this account. As in other miscellaneous accounts, if you are adding something here, be explicit.

851-07 Sound Effects Editing

This subaccount covers the labor to cut all the sound effects in preparation for the sound effects premix. This would include library effects, recorded effects, and foley. The sound effects editor is responsible for making sure that all sound effects needed for the picture are gathered and cut into the sound units which will be used in the premix. Union sound effects editors earn $1,796.50 for a weekly guarantee of 48.6 hours, or $36.965 per hour.

Most low-budget films find that it is better to negotiate a contract with a post production sound company to handle all post production sound matters. This is economical since the post production sound company can combine the requirements of your picture with those of other pictures it may be working on, and thus achieve an economy of scale. For example, you may need an effects editor to work sporadically over a period of several weeks. If you were to hire independently, you would need to maintain this person on salary during that entire time. A post production sound company can move that editor to other projects, allowing you to split that person's cost with those other projects. On *Anarchist*, these costs were covered under account #855-06.

851-09 ADR Editing

The ADR editor supervises the ADR recording sessions, and cuts all resulting recordings into the dialogue units that will be used in the dialogue premix. This can also be included in a post production sound package.

851-12 Negative Cutting

A word about *picture lock*, *final cut*, and *director's cut* is appropriate here. A locked picture is one in which the visual aspect has been edited into its final form; no more editing of the sequences will occur. Once the picture is locked, it is turned over to the post production sound crew. The *final cut* of a picture is the final edited form of the film once a soundtrack has been added to the locked picture. The *director's cut* is the edited form of the film that the director approves of. This may or may not be the final cut. A director with *final cut* in his or her contract gets to determine the final edited version of the film. (On films made under the DGA basic agreement, the director's cut is considered the director's version of the edited visual element without the final mixed soundtrack. It is usually completed within ten weeks of the finish of principal photography.)

In earlier days, it was difficult for even well known directors to be granted final cut. Director Billy Wilder would at times cut takes in the middle of an actor's speech since he knew exactly how the film would be put together and where he wanted to cut to a new camera angle in the final edited version. By doing this, he made it almost impossible to cut the film any other way than how he intended it to be cut. Today, most directors have final cut in practice even if it is not in their contract.

Once your picture has been locked, it's time to cut the negative. (In practice, this usually occurs after the final mix.) This is a traumatic time for your director. To understand why, you need to know a little about the negative cutting process. It is the negative cutter's job to conform the negative to the workprint. This is done by matching the edge numbers on the workprint with the corresponding sections of original camera negative. If the project has no workprint and is being edited electronically, the editing software will generate a decision list, which is a list of edge and frame numbers referring back to the original camera negative. Using these code numbers, the negative cutter cuts and splices together the original camera negative into an exact copy of the finished cut. The splicing method used on negative stock is called a *hot splice*, and it is this splice that causes your director so much anxiety. When making a hot splice, the negative cutter scrapes the emulsion from a part of the end frame of one piece of film so that it can be overlapped and cemented onto another piece of film. This process destroys a frame that can never be regained. Negative cutting is a very unforgiving business. After the negative is cut, if the director wants to lengthen a particular shot, it can no longer be done without a noticeable jump in the image. That is why the director will be so reluctant to lock the picture. The director knows that he or she must be absolutely certain that the cut is what is wanted and cannot be improved. What artist is ever satisfied? Leonardo DaVinci continued to work on the *Mona Lisa* throughout his life.

The cost of negative cutting is still $1100 to $1200 per 1000-foot reel for normal dramatic film. Costs can run higher on films with higher than normal cuts per reel or on films with special needs. If your picture is expected to run for 100 minutes, then you will have a film that is 9000 feet in length (35mm film runs at 90 feet per minute). Theoretically, this would fit on nine 1000-foot reels if it could be arbitrarily divided between the reels. However, it is necessary to split the film between reels at points that are appropriate and less noticeable, such as at the end of a scene or on a shot that is held for a period. This facilitates the switching over from one projector to another when each reel is mounted separately on a two-projector system. The safest bet is to budget for 10 reels of negative cutting. That would make the negative cutting cost on your picture run about $11,000 to $12,000. *Anarchist*, which was 104 minutes in length, spent $10,569.

851-15 Post Shipping & Messenger

There will always be a need to ship film reels, video tape or disks, or other items during post. On *Anarchist*, we budgeted $500 and we spent $334.

851-34 Continuity Expenses

One of the items that will be required by a distributor as part of your delivery documents will be a Dialogue Continuity Script. This is a transcript of all dialogue and text from the final cut version of the film, which is used in the preparation of foreign language dubs or subtitles. These continuity scripts are prepared by freelance people who specialize in this work.

This cost was not originally included in the *Anarchist* budget since we thought this would be a distribution expense. We ended up spending $475. The film was considered dialogue heavy but we received a discount based on an agreement our distributor had with the person generating the continuity script.

851-51 Purchases

This would include markers, tape, reels, cores, cans, printer cartridges, paper, and any other items that the editorial staff may need. We budgeted $500 and spent $564.

853-00 Music

What you spend on Music depends entirely on the nature of your soundtrack. If you have an original score recorded by an 80-piece orchestra over several days, and you throw in a few Beatles songs, you can spend $3 to $4 million or more in the blink of an eye. The other extreme is the route John Carpenter took in one of his early films where he scored the film himself with an electronic keyboard, playing with one finger, and the entire score went something like *dink, dink, dink, dink*... So how do you figure out what to budget here? The easiest way is to do as we did on *Anarchist* and say, "I'm spending $75,000 and will take whatever kind of score that buys me." I do not recommend this. (Do as I say, not as I do.) The better method is to understand all the expenses that will make up the cost of scoring your picture, and to understand what you need the music to do for your movie.

There is not a more magical moment than when you first see your film with a musical score. After months of working with a film, and during all that time you've only heard the production track with the images, the first time you see it with music it becomes an entirely new film. You will see layers of meaning and emotion that you never knew were there, even if you directed it. In our brains, the area that interprets music is closely linked to the emotional centers. In a film, music guides us. It tells us when to feel sad, scared, happy, or anxious. It can emphasize the action, or it can comment on the action and create irony. It is rarely neutral, and it does all this quite often without our being aware of it.

When the feature film comedy *MASH* was first previewed, no one laughed. This was in 1970 at the height of the Vietnam War. Although *MASH* was set in Korea during the Korean War, the parallels were too strong and the subject too real for Americans to laugh at it. Then the director, Robert Altman, added the song *Suicide is Painless* over the main titles. Suddenly the film became hilarious. The song told the audience that it was okay to laugh. *MASH* became a huge hit and it spawned an extremely successful television show (*M*A*S*H*) that lasted for eleven years.

Your choices of sources of music are well defined. There is the original score written by a composer specifically for your film, there is prerecorded music or songs, also known as needle-drop, and there are musical performances, in-studio or out, that you or your sound crew record. So that you may more fully understand the choices available and how you may be able to work them into your budget, we will ignore the lump-sum approach that was used in *The Anarchist Cookbook* and discuss each of the music subaccounts in detail.

853-01 Clearances

Some budgets refer to this as music rights. This account covers the license fees you must pay for pre-existing music. This includes both published and unpublished music that was created independently of your picture. It does not matter if it is instrumental, vocal, or a combination of the two. There are two types of licenses you must purchase for each piece of music you wish to appropriate and use in your film. These are known as *synch* and *master* licenses.

The term *sync license* is short for *synchronization license*. This is negotiated with and paid to the copyright holder of the music for the privilege of using that piece of music in the synchronized soundtrack of a motion picture or video production. The copyright holder is generally the publisher or author of the music. (You might have to deal with Michael Jackson for the sync license to a particular Beatles tune, since he bought the copyright to a large part of their work.)

A master license gives you the right to use a recording of a particular performance of a piece of music. In other words, the right to have access to and the use of a particular finished master recording of a performance. Performance here can mean any recordable rendering of the music. It can be a recording of a live performance given in front of thousands, or an in-studio recording made for a record album, or a recording of your uncle singing *I Gotta Be Me* in the shower. This is paid to the performer or performers.

If you have a character who is humming *I Feel Pretty* in your film, you only need a synch license. Your actor is the performer and is being paid to act in your film already. The synch license fee that you negotiate would be split between the estate of Leonard Bernstein (music) and Stephen Sondheim (lyrics).

If you decide that the humming isn't working and you want to use a recording of the Rolling Stones singing *Gloria* instead, then you need both a synch and a master license. The synch license fee would be paid to whoever owns the copyright to *Gloria*, while the master license fee would be split among Mick Jagger, Keith Richards, Ian Stewart, Charlie Watts, and Bill Wyman (the performers).

If a piece of music is in the public domain, you do not need a sync license to use it, but you will still have to pay a license fee to the performers if you are using previously recorded material. Be careful that what you assume is in the public domain actually is. Have you ever wondered why you so seldom hear the song *Happy Birthday* in films? Surely, this is in the public domain. It is sung everyday at thousands of children's birthday parties throughout the United States. If you assumed that, you would be wrong. The melody of the song was composed by Mildred J. Hill of Louisville, Kentucky, in the late 1800s. The lyrics were written by her sister, Dr. Patty Smith Hill, who was professor emeritus of education at Columbia University. The song was first published in 1893, but was not copyrighted until 1935. The copyright was then renewed in 1963. In 1988, Warner Communications bought all the assets of Birch Tree Group, Ltd., including the copyright to *Happy Birthday*.* If my understanding of the current copyright law is correct, filmmakers will have to obtain a sync license from Warner Communications for the use of the song *Happy Birthday* up through the year 2010. After that, I predict a rash of birthday films.

I strongly urge you to hire an experienced music supervisor to handle the securing of all necessary music licenses for your film. A music supervisor will know who controls the rights to the songs you want to use, and can negotiate the fees. If a song is too expensive, the supervisor will be able to suggest lower priced substitutes. On *Anarchist*, our total combined sync

* *Time* 133, no. 1 (January 3, 1989): 88.

and master license fees cost $43,800. The least expensive were tracks that were bought from Megatrax, a music syndicate. A Megatrax track typically cost us $600 total for the sync and master licenses together. Our most expensive song cost $2000 for the sync license and $2000 for the master license adding up to a total fee of $4000 for the song. Usually, the total license fee is divided evenly between the master and sync licenses.

When negotiating master and sync licenses, know what you are buying. What you want is unlimited use in the soundtrack in any medium, both known and unknown, throughout the universe. That is not a joke. That is the actual wording you should seek. Some licensors may try to limit your use to a certain number of screenings or theaters. Resist this. Another tactic they may use is to charge you an additional fee as the revenues for the picture grow.

In other words, they may charge you $1000 for the initial use, and then another $1000 once the picture has grossed $5,000,000, and another $1000 once the picture has grossed $10,000,000, etc. Again, you should try not to encumber the future earnings of your picture. Remember, you have the upper hand: you can always say no. Another strategy is to charge extra for out-of-context use of the music. An example would be if you were to have 30 seconds of a song in your soundtrack but wanted to use the whole song in the trailer; that would be out-of-context use. You might be unable to avoid that restriction. Almost all your music licenses will state how long the piece of music you are licensed to use can be. It can go on anywhere from a few seconds to the entire piece. Usually, shorter segments cost less, so it's good to know approximately how long of a segment is needed.

In addition to being willing to walk away from a deal, there are other money saving strategies. There are a huge number of unknown but very talented bands and single musicians in the world who would jump at the chance to have the exposure a motion picture could bring them. Some of them would be willing to license their compositions and performances for very little money to get that exposure. If a tune you have found is too expensive, you could have your music supervisor look for something else that is similar. As a last resort, and if you have a composer on the picture, you can ask the composer to write you something that has a similar effect. (Even big studio pictures do this.)

853-02 Song Writers

Studios will occasionally commission a songwriter to write a title song that will play over the main or end credits as was done in *MASH*, cited above. Another instance might be if the plot of the picture requires a song for some reason. Sometimes a song can be an intrinsic part of the script as in *There's Something About Mary* where the two singers served as a type of Greek chorus, commenting on the action by way of the song they were singing.

If you need to budget for a songwriter, be aware that the cost is completely negotiable. It depends on who the songwriter is, his or her level of renown, the complexity of what you are asking the songwriter to do, and as always, how badly you want the songwriter and how badly the songwriter wants the job. The cost can range from nothing, to a token payment, to tens of thousands of dollars and up.

853-03 Composer

A composer who writes a musical score specifically for your picture is a wonderful luxury. Major motion picture composers make several hundred thousand dollars per picture, but there are many talented composers whom you can probably afford. The *Anarchist* music track was structured so that the purchased songs carried most of the picture and we only needed specific short cues for the rest. This was accomplished by our very able and talented composer, Josh Kramon, who charged us a very reasonable price since he was not scoring the entire picture.

If you do hire a composer, make sure that you are benefiting from his or her talent as much as you can. I have seen many directors on many big studio movies plead for a high priced composer and then not let the composer contribute all he or she can to the picture. What often happens is that during the editing process, the editor has taken music from other films and incorporated it into a temp music track so that the director can fully appreciate the way the film will look and sound. The director falls in love with the temp music, and when the composer finally arrives the director says, "We really like our temp track, can you write something that sounds like that?" The fact that you do not hear more often of directors being bludgeoned with a ream of notation paper speaks only to the general restraint of composers as a class of people.

853-04 Music Supervisor

As stated before, I am a big believer in the use of a music supervisor in general and for low-budget films in particular. A music supervisor will provide you with an estimate of what he or she thinks the purchased music will cost, will be able to make innumerable suggestions for music tracks you can purchase, will negotiate the purchase price of music licenses, will steer you toward composers that fit within your budget, and will act as your guide in putting your music track together. A music supervisor will cost anywhere from a few thousand dollars to $15,000 or $20,000.

853-05 Arrangers

An arranger will take a previously written tune, and will create and write out the parts for the various instruments. Usually on low-budget films, this is part of the service that a composer will furnish. Some composers work with arrangers and some do not. You might also need an arranger if you have written a melody and you want it orchestrated to use in your music track.

853-06 Copyists

A copyist will take a score written by a composer and copy out the parts for the various musicians. At one time this was normal practice, but since the advent of electronic keyboards and computers, the parts are usually printed out by a computer.

853-07 Prescore Musicians

These are musicians hired to play music prior to the shooting of a film. An example of where this might be necessary would be if you needed to playback an original piece of music during the filming of a scene for timing purposes, such as in a dancing scene or if a singer is singing on-camera. Prescore musicians are paid at the same rates that underscore musicians are paid.

853-08 Underscore Musicians

Underscore is instrumental music played during a film as differentiated from singing or music that comes from a visible source in the film. Underscore musicians are simply musicians hired to play the score of a movie so that it can be recorded. There are few groups of musicians in the world as impressive as the musicians who play and record film scores. When the musicians arrive at the beginning of a session and once their instruments are tuned and they are ready to play, the composer or the composer's assistant hands out the sheet music. The composer will have the orchestra run through the piece once or twice, stopping only to go over difficult or tricky passages, and then they record it. The music that you hear in the theater is often only the second or third time any of the musicians have ever played it. As one who suffered through agonizing hours of practicing piano and violin, I can tell you that to witness this is truly astounding. The reason for this remarkable efficiency is that scoring sessions are expensive and every minute counts.

Members of the American Federation of Musicians (AF of M) are hired for a minimum of three hours. A musician earns from $251.86 to $289.67 for a three-hour session depending on how many musicians are hired as outlined in the following table.

Number of Musicians	3-Hour Session Rate/Musician*
35 or more	$251.86
30 to 34	264.44
24-29	277.03
23 or less	289.67

The more musicians in the session, the lower the pay rate. When using ten or more musicians, one of them is designated the leader and receives double the pay rate. A scoring day usually consists of two three-hour sessions within an eight-hour span of time. The seventh recording hour earns the musicians a 20% increase in rate. Work after the eight-hour span earns the musicians a 50% to 100% premium depending on whether the work is before or after midnight. If part of the eight-hour span is between midnight and 8am, you will pay a 65% premium. Work on a sixth or seventh consecutive day will cost a 50% premium. Now, multiply that by 80 to get an idea of what a full orchestral scoring session might cost. I'll give you a hint; for two three-hour sessions of an 80-piece orchestra during normal business hours, it will cost you $40,801.32 plus 4% vacation pay for a total cost of $42,433.37 per day. On top of that, add a 10% pension benefit. Of course, there are ways to cut that down. A 35-piece orchestra will cost

*These rates were due to change in August, 2005. However no new rates had been announced by the time this book went to press.

$18,859.28 per day. Add the 10% pension and it comes to $20,745.21. But don't despair, the AF of M has a low-budget agreement.

The AF of M defines a low-budget theatrical production as one whose final estimated cost does not exceed $29,500,000. Under this agreement, a musician earns $174.44 for a three-hour session regardless of how many you hire and there is no vacation pay. If you hire ten or more musicians, one of them is designated the contractor or leader and is paid at double the rate. In addition, all the musicians would receive the normal AF of M fringe benefit of 10%. With this in mind, that 35-piece orchestra cited above would cost $12,559.68, plus pension, for a total of $13,815.65, a savings of $6,929.56.

Keep in mind that if you sign an agreement with the AF of M, their agreement covers copyists, orchestrators, and arrangers also.

853-15 Music Editors

The music editor's ultimate responsibility is to prepare the music tracks for the temp dub, premix, and final mix. In addition, if you have hired a composer, the music editor will work closely with the composer in the timing of the music tracks as well as how they will synchronize with the picture.

Union music editors make $43.57 per hour. If you are not signed with the union, then you may be able to find someone with some experience for around $2000 per week. The music editor is usually hired once the picture has been locked, but before the spotting session where the placement and nature of the music cues are discussed.

853-30 Purchases

Purchases in this account can include cores, reels, tape, blank CDs, and editing supplies. An estimate of $500 should be sufficient.

853-30 Travel and Living Expenses

These costs would include the cost of per diem allowances, hotel, and airline tickets for musicians, vocalists, the composer, songwriters, etc.

853-53 Video Dupes (Cassettes)

This account is specifically to provide video tape or DVD copies of the cut film for the use of the composer, the music editor, and the music supervisor. Since copies can be taken right off of the Avid or other editing system, the cost consists only of the media that you are using, whether it be video tape or DVDs. On most low-budget films, $100 or even less would suffice.

853-56 Rentals & Cartage

When you hire musicians for a scoring session, many of them turn up with their instruments, such as the piccolo player, the violinists, and the French horn player. I have even seen string bass players lugging their instruments to the recording stage. Nevertheless, with some instruments, it would simply be impractical for the musician to be required to bring the instrument along. Examples would be pianos, percussion sections (including such items as kettledrums), and vibraphones. In those instances, your music contractor or leader will arrange for the moving of the instruments by an instrument cartage company. These companies specialize in the moving and setting up of orchestras and bands, and may even rent the instruments to you. (I have always thought it interesting that musicians such as violinists take great pride in their instruments and make the choice of the instrument a very personal part of their performance, whereas pianists must make do with whatever instrument is provided to them.) Instrument cartage is not simply freight hauling. Instruments need special handling and some, like the piano, must be retuned professionally after they are moved. Other instruments, such as those in the percussion section, involve complicated setup. Your music contractor or leader will be able to give you an estimate of these charges.

853-57 Music Recording Stage

Music recording stages or scoring stages come with technicians to handle the recording of the music and the projection of the film or video. The book rate on most scoring stages is $900 per hour. This can be negotiated down depending on how busy the stage is and how flexible you can be in scheduling. The low end is probably in the $500 to $800 range. Using those figures, a two-session day of scoring would cost $3000 to $4800.

Setup time must be added to this. An 80-piece orchestra will take a full day of setup and will cost approximately $1000 to $1500. A small 20-piece group would take much less setup and would cost $300 to $500.

853-60 Miscellaneous

One cost that might go here is food for the scoring session. Yes, craft service has even invaded the scoring stage. Coffee, juice, bagels, etc. are customary and a small amount of money should be set aside for it.

855-00 Sound (Post Production)

The job of the production sound mixer is to record a clean dialogue track during the filming of the scenes. All other sound is added in post production. As in the music account, there is an easy way to budget this account, and then there is the detailed way. The easy way is to throw a sum of money in as the total post-sound cost and hope that you can find a sound effects house that can deliver a soundtrack for the money that you have in the account. For a studio film, $150,000 is considered the minimum amount you can spend and still have a halfway decent soundtrack. Many films budget $200,000, $250,000 or more. The feature film *S.W.A.T.* spent over $200,000 on temp dubs alone.

On *The Anarchist Cookbook*, we realized early on that we could only afford $105,000 for the soundtrack and that we would have to fit into that figure. Fortunately for us, we found a dedicated and highly talented supervising sound editor, Rob Nokes, who believed in the film and stopped at nothing to deliver a quality soundtrack to us within our limited resources. We were the beneficiaries not only of Rob's skill but also of his many contacts in the world of post-sound. Without his campaigning and his calling in of many personal favors, we would have been hard pressed to produce our soundtrack for that budget, not to mention having an Academy Award winning mixing team do our final mix.

Even though the *Anarchist* budget lacks detail in the post-sound account, it is important to understand what the various subaccounts cover, so we will discuss each of them in detail.

855-02 Dubbing Stage

Also known as a mixing stage, or more formally a rerecording stage, the dubbing stage is where the soundtrack premix and final mix are done. (The words mix and dub are used interchangeably.) A dubbing stage is actually a theater with a mixing console placed in the middle of the seats. Although a film soundtrack can be mixed in a room that is just large enough to contain the mixing controls and allow for the projection of the picture, most filmmakers prefer to mix their pictures in theaters that will duplicate the space in which the audiences will view the film. This allows for better judgment on the part of the mixers in adjusting the relative volumes of the various tracks.

Mix rooms come with a crew usually consisting of three rerecording mixers and support personnel. Normally there is a dialogue mixer, music mixer, and sound effects mixer, although sometimes this will be reduced to just two mixers. The support personnel consist of a projectionist (whether you are projecting video or film), and a machine room technician. The machine room is where the various sound units are mounted on playback machines that are controlled by the mixing console, and the mixed digital track is recorded on either magnetic or optical media.

There are three types of mixes: temporary mix, premix, and final mix. The temp mix is usually made for previews of the film in front of recruited audiences who are then asked to give their opinions of the film. A temp dub can consist of temp music borrowed from other films or commercial recordings. This is done without seeking licenses for the use of the music since it will not be part of the final soundtrack and is not exhibited before a paying audience. The reason temp music is used is because at this stage, the composer has not had a chance to finish the score or the final music has not been selected. Similarly, the dialogue track and the effects track may or may not be in their final form. For example, there may be unintelligible parts of the dialogue that the dialogue editor plans to replace. Many of the sound effects may be from the production track or may be slapped together from less than ideal sources. Needless to say, the preparation and recording of a temporary track takes a great deal of time and money from the preparation of the final version of the film, and this is time and money that does not add to the final product. Beware of tying up your post-sound crew with too many temp dubs.

The premix is used to consolidate all the various units of the dialogue, music, and effects tracks, and to work out problems presented by each of the tracks separately. On a studio film, this can take from two to four weeks. A low-budget film should aim to complete the premix in one to two weeks. Since your picture probably consists of five 2000-foot reels, doing the premix in five days is probably optimistic. Six days is probably more realistic on the low end.

The final mix is where all three tracks (dialogue, music, and effects) are blended into one track and a digital master is made. During the final mix, the filmmakers have the option of giving a direction to various sounds--in other words, making them seem like they are coming from a specific place in the theater. Studio films usually complete their final mix in two to four weeks. A low-budget film could do it in two or less if the soundtrack is not too complicated.

Mixing rooms can be rented for about $450 to $650 per hour, depending on the size of the theater. A standard day is 9 hours long, not counting the lunch break. This works out to $4050 to $5850 per day. A ten day final mix can cost from $40,500 to $58,500. This is why it is often a good idea to inquire about package deals that include mix time, foley, and editorial sound services. Packages can range from approximately $50,000 and up, depending on the complexity of the film. I recommend giving a few post production sound houses your script and post schedule, and have them supply you with bids.

855-03 ADR Stage

Also known as a looping stage, the ADR stage is where unintelligible or badly recorded lines of dialogue can be replaced and where crowd noises for party scenes or other groups can be recorded. (See 809-10 Looping & Expenses.) Most ADR rooms with a mixer and recordist usually cost about $325 per hour with a nine-hour day being standard. That works out to $2925 per day. A low-budget film should try to keep looping to two or three days maximum. The best way to save money in looping is to hire the best production mixer that you can afford and to choose your locations carefully, keeping in mind what sort of noise is in the area. If you are shooting next to a freeway or a busy intersection, you will be spending time on the looping stage.

855-06 Sound Effects Package

If you were to make a package deal with a post production sound house, this is where you would enter the cost. As stated earlier, this can run from about $50,000 to the-sky's-the-limit. You can actually get a pretty amazing soundtrack for $150,000 all in. Solicit bids from various houses, let them know what your limitations are, and get their help in designing a sound package that you can afford. Be sure that you get an itemized list as to what exactly the package includes.

855-07 Foley Effects Recording

Foley recording is the art of creating and recording sound effects such as the rustle of clothing, footsteps, and breaking glass in synchronization with a picture. It was invented by Jack Donovan Foley, one of the more remarkable men in motion picture history. For a brief history of his amazing career, visit **http://www.marblehead.net/foley/**. Since the production mixer's primary responsibility is to record the dialogue, incidental sounds are not usually recorded in an optimal way. Many sound effects can be purchased from sound effects libraries, but it is difficult to find exactly the right footsteps at exactly the right pace to match an actor's walk in your film. For these reasons, foley is essential to a quality soundtrack.

A foley stage is one of the strangest places you might encounter in the world of post production. It is a soundproofed room with projection capabilities. Part of the floor is divided into one-square yard sections, each of which contain different surfaces such as dirt, gravel, cement, tile, etc. Elsewhere in the room you may see boxes of broken glass, metal scraps, chains, creaky rocking chairs, hammers, slabs of meat, boards of various thicknesses, and innumerable other strange items. These are used by the foley walkers to create the sound effects to accompany the various actions and events on screen. To get an idea of some of the tricks that they perform and the devices that they use to make the sounds, visit the web page at **http://www.irasov.com/WTAD/foley.htm**.

Foley stages usually rent for $350 per hour, and that includes usually two foley artists and a recordist. An eight-hour day is standard, which works out to $2800 per day. The number of days depends on how many cues there are, and that depends on the type of film that you have made and how detailed you want to make the track. Five days of foley is not uncommon.

855-12 Tape Transfers

In the past, this account covered transferring sound from ¼-inch tape to 35mm magnetic film stock. Mag film is rarely used these days since most systems have gone digital. The advantage of mag film was that it was driven by sprocket holes just as regular film was, and therefore it was easy to keep in synch. Now with digital media, the synch problem is solved with time code laid down on the media whether it is magnetic or optical. This account is now used to cover the costs associated with the transfer of soundtracks from one medium to another, such as from a hard drive to CDs or CDs to DAT, etc. I recommend talking to your editor or sound effects house to determine what you should budget here. The costs can range from a few thousand dollars to tens of thousands.

855-51 Purchases

Purchases in post production sound can range from magnetic tape, CDs, and editing supplies to coffee for the sound editors. Again, talk to your editor or post production sound house.

855-56 Rental & Cartage

Rental items may include the software program ProTools, editing equipment, hard drives, and the use of a sound effects library. Costs can be wide ranging depending on your needs.

855-58 Geographic Separation Master

Better known as a music and effects master, an M&E is used by the distribution company to replace your dialogue track with a track in a foreign language. In other words, an M&E is simply your soundtrack without the dialogue. The cost of this is essentially the cost of the media that it is recorded onto, and the cost of the labor to make whatever adjustment must be made. Sometimes new sound effects must be added if essential sounds from the production track were eliminated along with the dialogue. I have seen this account budgeted for as much as $1000 per reel. You should be able to do it for less. If you never intend to distribute overseas, you do not need to incur this cost at all.

857-00 Post Production Film & Lab

This account covers all costs pertaining to purchasing film stock, and normal laboratory work during the post production period with the exception of titles, visual effects, and editorial optical effects such as fades, dissolves, and wipes.

857-03 Stock Shots – Purchase

Stock shots are previously filmed shots that you purchase from a stock shot library. If you have a television in a scene and the television is showing a program, the money to license that program would be placed here. Similarly, if you need to establish in your film that the scene has moved to Paris but you do not have the resources to go there and film, you can purchase stock establishing shots of Paris that can be directly cut into your film.

Make sure you know what format the shots are being offered in and that the format is compatible with your film. If you shot on DV and are never printing, you should get the shots delivered to you in the DV format, not 35mm film negative. Likewise, if you are shooting in 35mm, you don't want the shots delivered to you in DV or digibeta (a high-definition video format). The only exception to this would be if you are planning a digital intermediate in which you will process the entire film, or a large part of it, through high-definition video. This process is still so expensive that it is out of the reach of low-budget films.

The Anarchist Cookbook had a television playing in a few scenes and we needed to buy programming to play on the TV. We allowed $25,000 for this but only spent $8700.

857-06 Tape to Tape Transfers

This covers the costs involved in transferring footage from DV to digibeta, or between any other formats. *Anarchist* budgeted $2500 and spent $2891.

857-07 Lab Special Handling

If you expect to be asking the lab for special procedures such as pushing stock in the developer, eliminating the bleaching stage in the printing process, desaturating the color, etc., those costs would go here. On *Anarchist*, we knew we would have to scan our DV footage out to 35mm color negative so we allowed $6000 here. Our actual costs were much greater: we spent $10,460.

857-08 Videocassettes / Tape

Your editor will have to make tapes of the cut footage for the use of the composer, sound effects editor, and others. These dupes can be made directly off the editing machine (Avid or even a personal computer), so the only cost would be the tape cassettes or DVDs. On *Anarchist*, we budgeted $250 and spend only $32.

857-09 Reversal Dupes

Back in the old days before electronic editing and video tape, if you wanted to give a copy of the workprint to someone such as the composer, you would make a low cost reversal dupe of the workprint. Fortunately, this no longer needs to be done. Now you would simply make a video dupe from the editing computer.

857-17 Optical Soundtrack

If you will be distributing your project on film and once the digital master of your soundtrack has been recorded in the final mix, an optical soundtrack is made on 35mm negative film. The final product of this procedure looks like a clear piece of 35mm film with a black squiggly line down one side. This will be combined with the original cut negative to make your interpositives. The cost of this is based on the length of your film. *Anarchist* was approximately 10,000 feet in length and we were quoted a rate of $0.458 per foot for a total cost of $4580. We actually spent $4385.

857-40 Answer Print

The answer print is the print that the lab will make after the color timer has finished making all the adjustments to the printing lamps. (See the discussion at the beginning of this chapter.) Be aware that if you send the film back to the lab too many times to correct problems, they will start to charge you additional amounts for each print. The lab's contract should be clear as to how many answer prints you get. The best thing to do is to make sure you point out all the problems that you have with the printing lights the first time that you view the answer print. Often this process starts with the color timer making color-corrected 8 x 10 color stills from each cut in the movie, and by this means, giving you a preview of what the finished print will look like. Very often this is sufficient, and the next thing that you see will be a color print of your movie that looks the way you want it to look. A composite answer print is the final answer print with the soundtrack added.

The lab on *Anarchist* quoted us a cost of $1.2864 per foot of cut negative. With an estimated length of 10,000 feet, that would be $12,864. Our actual cost was $9,608.

857-41 Interpositives & Internegatives

Some distributors will require you to supply a certain number of interpositives and internegatives as part of the delivery requirements. If you are only making a few prints, this is not necessary. If your distribution is larger, then it makes sense to make interpositives and internegatives. As discussed earlier, an interpositive is a print made from your original cut negative on low contrast stock from which several internegatives can be made. An internegative is a negative made from an interpositive from which release prints can be made. This protects your original cut negative from wear and tear, and accidental damage. Both interpositives and internegatives cost approximately $1.00 per foot of original cut negative. Be sure you need to make these before you commit to them.

857-45 Protection – YCM

Color film dyes will fade with time. In order to guard against this and preserve a film for future generations, YCM protection prints are made. The YCM protection prints are three separate black and white prints of your negative made respectively through three separate color filters: yellow, cyan, and magenta. These black and white negatives can later be printed onto color stock, again through their respective color filters, enabling a fully reconstituted color print of the film. The cost of YCM protection masters is about $3.00 per foot of original cut negative. Few low-budget films can afford this unless the film turns out to be a big hit.

858-00 Visual Effects

Visual effects is the manipulation of the photographic image after it has been shot. This is such a large and complex subject that entire books have been written on visual effects alone. Many visual effects can be created on the computer system that you are using to edit your film. That is why *The Anarchist Cookbook* budget does not have this account listed. We had two visual effects in the film. In one of the shots, Puck is sitting and working at his desk in normal time while all around him the people in the office are sped up. The light changes as though the sun drops to the horizon and the daylight fades. Our editor, Alan Bell, was able to create this effect on his computer system by combining two different shots. In the other shot, a police car drives up and parks in front of Puck's parents' house in Plano, Texas. As the police car moves across the screen, it sucks the color out of the image. Again, Alan did this on his computer.

Today, if you can imagine it, you can put it on film. Often you will see visual effects in a movie without knowing that what you are watching does not, nor did it ever exist. Visual effects are not always about space aliens and exploding planets. Sometimes it is simply removing support wires, or telephone wires, or a jet contrail from the frame (about $2500-$7500). Sometimes it involves replacing part of the frame with a painting. These are known as matte shots. If you saw *The Patriot*, you saw many matte shots. One that springs to mind is Charleston harbor crowded with sailing ships.

In *Jurassic Park* when the young girl is being lifted up out of the kitchen to the floor above, the actress's face was put onto the stunt woman's body in the shot looking down on her while the raptor snaps at her from below. In *Titanic* as the ship tilts stern high, the people running in panic and falling into the sea in the wide shot are all computer generated. In *Master and Commander*, the men at the top of the mast in the opening shot were nowhere near the sea when that shot was made. In *Gladiator*, the Coliseum and the people sitting in the stands were all added digitally. The set was built only up to about ten to twenty feet high. If you look closely at the wide shots of the people cheering in the stands, you can see one particular extra who is pumping both arms up and down above his head in about three different places in the stands.

How do you determine what visual effects will cost you? On big studio features like *Starship Troopers* or *Hollow Man*, I have found that it works out to about $100,000 per shot. You have four hundred visual effects shots? Better set aside $40,000,000. As techniques become more sophisticated, these costs will come down. Often you can do it yourself or very inexpensively as in the shot described above from *Anarchist.* (See "Shooting the Locket Sequence in *Robin Hood: Men In Tights*" in the appendix to learn how a visual effects sequence was done with nothing but low-tech film school tricks or techniques.) If you need to include one or more visual effects shots in your film, send your script to several visual effects houses and ask them to bid on the work. Be sure they know that you are a low-budget film and that your resources are limited. Often they can suggest ways that you can lower your costs.

859-00 Titles & Opticals

Titles can generally be divided into main titles and end titles. The main titles typically are constrained by the contracts with the various people who appear in the main titles. Often actors' contracts will state whether they are above or below the title, whether they have a single card or they share a card, where they appear (first, second, third, last, etc.) in the list of actors in the main titles, and whether they have any special designation such as "and introducing" or "and (actor name) as (character name)" or "starring" or…you get the idea. After the actors come the "creative technical credits" such as director of photography, production designer, costume designer, etc. After those come the producers, the writer or writers, and finally the director. A typical main title credit sequence might look like the following:

Super Star Actor(s)
Picture Title
Actor 1
Actor 2
Actor 3 & Actor 4
Casting Director
Costume Designer
Production Designer
Director of Photography
Editor
Composer
Executive Producer
Producer(s)
Writer
Director

This order is subject to change, and positions can be added or taken away depending on the fame, notoriety, and agent power of each of the players. But the end of the list, producer—writer—director, is pretty firmly entrenched, especially if you have signed with the DGA and the WGA. If the main titles are to be placed at the end of the picture, the order is reversed.

The end titles or credit roll lists everyone else, including the producer's third cousin on his mother's side. There are only two rules pertaining to the order or content of the end titles, and those rules apply only if you are signed with the DGA and/or SAG. The DGA rule is that the DGA staff (unit production manager, first assistant director, and second assistant director) must be the first card or cards of the technical credits. The SAG rule is that you must list all the cast members up to 50. If you have more than 50 cast members, you can eliminate some in order to keep the list to 50 if you wish. The cast can be listed before the technical credits or after them. A typical end credit roll would look like the following:

Cast List
Stunt Players
DGA Credits
Shooting Crew Credits
Post production Credits
Visual Effects House Credits
Music Credits
"Thanks To" List
Contractual Vendor and Union Credits and Logos
No-Resemblance-to-Any-Person Disclaimer
Statement of Authorship and Copyright Notice

859-01 Main & End Titles

In budgeting for this account, it is vital to know what type of main and end titles you want in your movie. If you are doing a James Bond type of main credit designed by a professional title designer and involving live-action filming, animation, and visual effects, the costs can run into the millions. If you are doing simple white lettering on black, you can probably do it on your computer, incurring only the film-out costs. A nice compromise is white letters with a drop-shadow over picture. The end titles can start over the end of the picture and change to white letters over black, or the entire end title credit roll can be white over black. In *Anarchist*, we had our main titles over picture with some animation that the editor did on his computer. Our end titles were white letters over a black field. We put $10,000 into the budget in this account and spent $3248. This included the quotations that appear at the beginning of the film and the dictionary definitions that appear in the body of the film.

859-02 Title Designer

If you go the James Bond route or want something a little fancier than white letters over picture, you might employ a title designer who will conceive of the titles, choose the fonts, and oversee the artwork and the shooting of the titles. The designer's salary depends on how much time it will take to generate your titles and the designer's experience. In other words, it is completely negotiable.

859-03 Optical Effects

These are editorial opticals such as fades, dissolves, and wipes. Often these can be generated on an editing system without need to do an actual optical on an optical printer.

859-04 Inserts

In the opening of *The Lord of the Rings: The Fellowship of the Ring,* we see Gollum's hand reach into some water and scoop up a half buried golden ring out of the sandy bottom. That is an insert. The shot is tight enough that it could have been done in an aquarium. When a character rips open a letter and we cut to a close up of it, that is an insert. If Sherlock Holmes suddenly bends down to look at a torn piece of cloth on a protruding nail and we cut to a close up of it, that is an insert.

At one time, it was standard practice to save all inserts for the end of the schedule so that they could be shot with a minimum crew in one or two days. It was felt that this made better sense than shooting some small item while you have eighty people plus cast standing around. Nevertheless, I find that it is often more efficient to shoot the inserts with the rest of the scene, especially on a low-budget film where you are shooting with a minimum crew anyway. Sometimes it is only a matter of tilting the camera down and shooting what the actor was looking at in the previous shot. If you do save the inserts for the end of the schedule, you need to make sure you can gather the items that appear behind the object being shot such as sections of floor, rugs, tables, car seats, or anything else that would appear in the shot.

There are companies such as Howard Anderson who specialize in insert shooting (**http://www.haopticals.com/**). They are expert at matching the lighting in a clip or an eight by ten still, and they normally charge by the hour. Typically they will use a crew of about four people and are very efficient. *The Anarchist Cookbook* did use Howard Anderson's services for one insert shot. As originally shot, when Puck opens the suitcase of pills in the attic, the trade name of the drug is clearly evident. The manufacturer of the drug in question did not want us to use the trade name, so the shot had to be redone with the bottle labels changed to carry the generic chemical name of the drug. The shot was made perfectly by Howard Anderson and at a low cost. The total cost was a small fraction of what it would have been if I had had to pull together a crew for a minimum day to shoot it.

859-05 Trademark, Logos, & Rating

This is the cost to add trademarks, logos, and the film rating to the negative. This would involve some printing costs once the logos had been appropriated. This cost was handled within our title budget.

859-06 Other Titles / Sub-Titles

The quotations at the beginning of *Anarchist* could be covered here, as would subtitles that were needed because of a character speaking in a foreign language. Again, this was covered in our title budget.

859-08 Optical Development

This is where to put the cost for photographically developing the editorial opticals in account 859-03.

21

Other Expense

This section of the budget is often called General Expense. These items generally apply to the film as a whole and do not fit into any particular category level of the budget.

861-00 Insurance

Making a motion picture is a risky business—both physically and financially. It makes sense to minimize the risk to the project and its financiers whenever possible. One way of doing this is through a producer's insurance package. The only insurance that you are legally compelled to carry is worker's compensation insurance. In addition, if you are signed with any unions, certain unions will require flight insurance on their members who are required to travel by air or who need to go up in aircraft for filming purposes. Nevertheless, it makes good sense to protect the project from as many unforeseeable risks as possible. A good producer's insurance package is designed to do just that and should be bound early in your preproducton phase.

In dealing with insurance companies, brokers, and adjusters, it is vitally important that you understand your obligations and responsibilities. As the producer or production manager of a film, you must do whatever you can to minimize the damage in case of a possible claim. If an actor is hurt or falls ill and cannot continue, then you must try to reschedule other scenes that do not include that actor in order to continue filming. In *The*

Blues Brothers, John Belushi hurt his back while we were filming the scene inside the federal courthouse building where he and Dan Aykroyd were barricading the doors by pushing heavy objects in front of them. Belushi was unable to continue for a day or two, but we were able to reschedule and shoot other scenes that did not include him. We lost no time and therefore we had no insurance claim other than Belushi's medical bills. If you do not make every attempt to minimize any damage you may incur, your claim could be denied by the insurance company. Notify your broker immediately upon any event that could generate a claim, and keep the broker informed as to how you are proceeding. Be honest, communicative, and document everything. Motion picture claims can be very complex and the more documentation you have, the better your chances are to have your claim honored in full. It is important to realize that any insurance claim payout will be less the deductible as stated in your policy.

The cost of your insurance package is best estimated by your broker. The broker will ask for a copy of your script, schedule, and budget. You also need to point out any unusual events that may occur in the course of your filming, stunts, and your use of any watercraft or aircraft. The *Anarchist* package estimate was $27,500. Our final bill was for $29,613. The following sections describe each of the areas of coverage.

Cast Insurance

On Monday, June 14, 1999, the assistant director on the set of *Hollow Man* called the lunch break. Elisabeth Shue, playing the leading lady role of Linda, decided to go to a nearby gym during the lunch break for a quick workout on a trampoline. She is an expert gymnast and keeps herself very fit. She finished her workout and sat down on the edge of the trampoline. As she stepped off onto the floor, the Achilles tendon in her right leg ruptured, detaching from the heel bone, and she collapsed to the floor in considerable pain. She was unable to walk and was rushed to a hospital immediately.

While the consequences to Ms Shue were severe, the consequences to the film were devastating. Ms Shue was in almost every scene that there was to be shot. In addition, the prognosis was that the earliest she could be walking would be at least eight weeks into the future. She made a remarkable recovery, and she was working again on Sunday, August 15, 1999, nine weeks after her injury. In those nine weeks, the production company incurred many expenses due to the delay that were not in the original budget, such as holding on to key crewmembers, the continuing rental of our stages, equipment costs, etc. These costs, which were several million dollars, were all covered in full by our insurance company. That is what cast insurance can do for you.

Cast insurance will cover any extra expense necessary to complete principal photography of an insured production due to the death, injury, or sickness of any insured performer or director. Insured performers (or directors) must take a physical examination prior to being covered by this insurance. Coverage usually begins two weeks prior to the beginning of principal photography.

Negative Insurance

This coverage protects against all risks of direct physical loss, damage, or destruction of raw film or tape stock, exposed film (developed or undeveloped), recorded videotape, soundtracks and tapes, up to the amount of the insured production costs. This does not cover a loss caused by fogging, faulty camera or sound equipment, faulty developing, editing, processing, or manipulation by the cameraman, exposure to light, dampness or temperature changes, error in judgment in exposure, lighting or sound recording, or from the use of an incorrect type of raw film stock or tape.

Faulty Stock, Camera, & Processing

This covers the loss, damage, or destruction of raw film or tape stock, exposed film (developed or undeveloped), recorded videotape, soundtracks and tapes, caused by or resulting from fogging or the use of faulty materials (including cameras and videotape recorders), faulty sound equipment, faulty developing, faulty editing or faulty processing, and accidental erasure of videotape recordings. Coverage does not include loss caused by errors of judgment in exposure, lighting, or sound recording from the use of incorrect type of raw stock, or faulty manipulation by the camera operator.

On *Anarchist*, our only insurance claim was under this provision. The emulsion of the exposed film from one full morning's shoot was scratched by the camera magazine, causing us to go back and reshoot the scene. Our insurance covered the extra expense of reshooting the scene, but not the expense of the added work that we did that day.

Props, Sets, and Wardrobe

This provides coverage on the actual costs of props, sets, scenery, costumes, wardrobe, and similar theatrical property against all risks of direct physical loss, damage, or destruction during the production. In reality, the deductible is often more than the claim unless you have had a devastating loss such as a set burning down. On *Starship Troopers*, we had a flash flood wipe out a set in Wyoming that was fully covered (less the deductible, of course).

Extra Expense

This coverage reimburses the production company for any extra expense necessary to complete principal photography of an insured production due to the damage or destruction of property or facilities (props, sets, or equipment) used in connection with the production. Coverage includes losses due to faulty generator operation.

Miscellaneous Equipment

This covers all risk of direct physical loss, damage or destruction to cameras, camera equipment, sound, lighting, (including breakage of globes) and grip equipment, owned by or rented to the production company. Coverage can be extended to cover mobile equipment vans, studio location units, or similar units upon payment of an additional premium.

Third Party Property Damage Liability

This coverage is vital for the renting of locations. It pays for damage or destruction of property belonging to others (including loss of use of the property) while the property is in the care, custody, or control of the production company. The coverage does not apply to liability for destruction of property caused by operation of any motor vehicle, aircraft, or watercraft, including damage to the foregoing, or liability for damage to any property rented or leased that may be covered under Props, Sets or Wardrobe, or Miscellaneous Equipment Insurance (except the loss of the use of any such equipment is covered). This coverage is not included under a Comprehensive Liability Policy. Property Damage coverage written as part of a Comprehensive Liability Policy excludes damage to any property in the production company's care, custody, or control.

Errors & Omissions Insurance (E&O)

This covers legal liability and defense for the production company against lawsuits alleging unauthorized use of titles, format, ideas, characters plots, plagiarism, and unfair competition. This also protects for alleged libel, slander, defamation of character, or invasion of privacy. This coverage will usually be required by a distributor prior to release of any theatrical or television production.

Once a filmmaker has applied for E&O coverage, the underwriter will require that the script be examined by a clearance company. The clearance company will go over each line of the script looking for items that may need any sort of rights clearance such as personal names, artwork (including murals on buildings), music (see the discussion under 853-01 Clearances), film clips, copyrighted written material, photographs, references to living persons, publications, logos (these are protected vigorously by sports teams), trademarks, and products. After this process is complete, you will receive a list of recommendations from them as to how to proceed. For example, with personal names, they will check the phone book of the city in which your story is set for names that may match. If they find one, they will suggest that you change it and may even give you a list of permissable names. With most other items, they will suggest that permission for their use be obtained from the appropriate source.

It is important that these instructions be fully complied with in order to keep the E&O policy in effect. When revised script pages are issued, they must be similarly cleared.

Watercraft & Aircraft

If you use any type of boat or aircraft, either on-camera or off, it is important to notify your insurance company. Normally an extra premium will be required for this coverage. Hull insurance protects you against damage to the craft itself. You should try to have the aircraft or watercraft owner carry the hull insurance because the vehicle will be under the control of the owner or the owner's agent in most instances, and the owner no doubt has an insurance policy in effect on the craft already. If you can do this, it will lower your costs considerably.

Worker's Compensation

This coverage is required by state law and applies to all temporary or permanent cast or production crewmembers. Coverage provides medical, disability, or death benefit to any cast or crewmember who become injured in the course of his/her employment. Coverage operates on a 24-hour per day basis whenever employees are on location away from their homes. Individuals who call themselves "Independent Contractors" will usually be held to be employees as far as worker's compensation is concerned, and failure to carry this insurance can result in having to pay any benefits required under the law plus penalty awards. Normally, this coverage is carried by your payroll service, which means that it does not need to be part of your insurance package. Individuals who are paid by their loanout corporations should be paid through the payroll service so that they also are covered under the payroll service's policy. If you have interns or other unpaid volunteers on your set, you need to investigate how to cover them while they are working for you.

Comprehensive Liability

This coverage protects the production company against claims for bodily injury or property damage liability arising out of filming the picture. The coverage includes the use of all non-owned vehicles (both on and off camera), including physical damage to such vehicles. This coverage will be required prior to filming on any city or state roadways, or any location sites requiring filming permits. The coverage does not apply to use of any aircraft or watercraft, which must be separately insured before any coverage will apply (see above).

Guild or Union Flight Accident

This coverage satisfies motion picture and television guild or union (IATSE, NABET, SAG, or DGA) contract requirements for aircraft and accidental death insurance to all production company cast or crewmembers. Coverage is inclusive and the limits of liability will meet all signatory requirements.

862-00 Publicity

This account is not the money to publicize or market your film. (That is a distribution expense.) This account is for the expenses in generating the raw materials for your marketing campaign such as the EPK (electronic press kit), production stills, and third party interviews.

862-01 Unit Publicist

The unit publicist is responsible for creating and managing the opportunities to generate those raw materials. If you have a well-known star in your film, the publicist will arrange for interviews of the star with various magazines, newspapers, and TV shows such as *Entertainment Tonight.* In addition, the publicist will write stories on the production, biographies of the key people involved, and generally work to prepare materials for the marketing campaign. The publicist will also check the production stills and have them approved by the actors if contractually required. (Each major actor is usually allowed a certain number of *kills* of stills in which he or she appears. This allows the actor to mark certain pictures so that they will not be used.) If you have a really well-known star who will generate a lot of paparazzi activity, a unit publicist can help run interference for them.

Experienced union publicists make a minimum of $1,537.14 per week. Most make over scale. On small pictures, you may not need a full-time publicist and can arrange for someone on a part-time basis. We did not have a unit publicist on *Anarchist.*

862-08 Film and Processing

This covers the expense of the raw film and the processing for all the production stills that the still photographer will be taking. We budgeted $500 and spent $1044. Do not underestimate the importance of production stills.

862-60 Miscellaneous Expense

One cost that might go here is the cost of the electronic presskit (EPK) crew and equipment. If you are having someone shoot the-making-of type footage, it can be invaluable to your marketing campaign. If you contract with an outfit to do this for you, it will run into several thousand dollars. Pick the days in your schedule that will give them the most to shoot.

865-00 General Expenses

The is the catch-all account for those expenses that are not broad enough to require their own major account.

865-01 MPAA Seal

The Motion Picture Association of America is the organization that rates your picture. If you are going for any type of wide theatrical distribution, you should have your film rated. If you are concerned that your picture may be a borderline R when you want a GP, or if you are afraid that you may get an NC-17 when you would prefer an R, you can try to find out the criteria for each of the ratings in advance. I know of no list that enumerates how many curse words or how many minutes of nudity are acceptable for each of the ratings. It is how the film strikes the ratings board as a whole rather than how many *f---'s* you may have in the dialogue. They will rate it based on theme, use of violence, language, nudity, sensuality, drug abuse, and "other elements." Once you have had your film rated, if you are dissatisfied with the rating, you can ask them for suggestions on how to change it, or you can appeal the rating. The ratings (G, GP, GP-13, R, and NC-17) are all registered trademarks and cannot be use without the MPAA's permission. The X rating was never trademarked and can be used by anyone for whatever purpose desired.

At the time *Anarchist* was made, the fee to rate a feature film under $2,000,000 was $4000. Check with the MPAA (**http://www.mpaa.org**) for their current fees. *The Anarchist Cookbook* was never rated for theatrical release, but it was rated for its DVD release. It received a rating of R for "language, sexuality, and drug content." I feel it was an appropriate rating.

865-11 Legal Fees

Legal fees on a feature film can be as much as $25,000 to $50,000. On a really big picture, they can run much higher. Most of what your picture attorney will be doing for you is writing and reviewing contracts. There are several way that you can help lower these expenses.

1) Do as much of the copying of documents as you can so that you do not have a highly paid legal aid standing at the copy machine for hours.

2) Try to use standard contracts, such as the SAG daily or weekly contracts, as much as possible instead of special "long-form" contracts.

3) Learn to read and evaluate simple contracts yourself. For instance, most equipment-rental contracts follow a standard pattern. The exceptions here are to beware of clauses promising credit to the vendor, and clauses making the individual signing the contract personally responsible for any costs.

Freedonia Productions, the company that produced *The Anarchist Cookbook*, used legal services purchased by its parent company, Anarchy Movie Partners, LLC.

865-12 Bank / Exchange Costs

Since Anarchy Movie Partners (based in Los Angeles) was financing the film, it needed to be able to transfer money to the production's bank account in Dallas, Texas, where the film was being shot. This was done by wire transfer and for that reason we budgeted $500 in this account. Our actual costs were $686.

865-32 Preview Expense

This account covers the expense of conducting previews and surveys for solicited audiences. Typically, a solicited preview conducted by a market research company will cost about $25,000 per preview. This is in addition to the time and money expended getting the film ready for the preview. Low-budget filmmakers should have informal screenings for friends and family if they must, but trust their own instincts.

865-51 Office Purchases

This covers normal office supplies: paper, staples, three-ring binders, envelopes, etc. We vastly underestimated this account at $2000. We actually spent $8478.

865-55 Computers and Software

This account covers the computers and software that you will use for your accounting. On *Anarchist*, we used the Vista Accounting® package supplied by Entertainment Partners, the payroll service company we were using. Although we budgeted $2250, our actual costs were $1985.

865-58 OSHA Safety

Movie sets are inherently dangerous places to work. On any given movie set, you can be exposed to explosives, dangerous stunts, people working in high places, temporary constructions, low flying aircraft, cables and equipment littering the floor or ground, power tools, heavy equipment, people working in the dark, and innumerable, never-before-attempted, first-time-ever operations. With all the chances for injury, it is amazing that anyone survives unscathed while working on a movie set.

Yet in 2002, according to the U.S. Department of Labor Bureau of Labor Statistics, the rate of injury for workers in motion picture production was 1.8 per 100 full-time workers (**http://data.bls.gov/servlet/**). It was more dangerous to work in a movie theater than on a movie set in full production. The rate of injury for workers in motion picture theaters in 2002 was 3.9 per 100 full-time workers! The credit for motion picture production having an injury rate of less than half that of the injury rate for exhibiters can be given to the aggressive and comprehensive safety program which has been instituted by the motion picture industry.

Every studio has a Department of Safety charged with making sure that all OSHA (Occupational Safety and Health Administration) guidelines and requirements are met. In addition, there have been extensive training programs established to insure that the crew members are aware of the latest techniques to reduce the possibility of injury, and that they are fully schooled in the safe use of their equipment. For example, crew working up high in areas that do not have guard rails are required to make use of a positive fall-restraint system usually consisting of a harness and tether.

Failure to use available safety equipment can be cause for dismissal.

Every safety complaint by a crew member is taken seriously and acted upon. On *Starship Troopers,* the company had just moved onto the stage where the bug tunnels had been built. The tunnels were sculpted out of large blocks of Styrofoam which had been "pointed up" by the plasterers and painted to look like rock. The floor of each tunnel was covered in clean playground sand—the sand that parents buy to fill their children's sand boxes.

As the crew began to set up for the first shot, one crew member came to me with an empty, discarded bag that had contained fifty pounds of the playground sand. He pointed out to me a warning label on the bag written in large red letters. It said "DANGER! Breathing dust may cause silicosis!" I immediately had the propmaster buy enough particle masks to supply everyone in the crew who wanted one. In addition, the studio safety department had a testing facility sample the air in the bug caves to determine how much dust was actually in the air. It turned out that very little dust was being stirred up and the environment of the stage was deemed to be safe. Nevertheless, some of the crew continued to wear the dust masks for their own piece of mind.

Although *Starship Troopers* was a large studio picture with huge resources, even small independent projects should emulate the aggressive attitude for safety taken by the prodution. In addition to preventing injuries, you will gain the trust and respect of your crew when they know that their well-being is important to you.

A resource open to all filmmakers and free for the taking is the collection of safety bulletins distributed by the AMTPT Industry-Wide Labor-Management Safety Committee of the Contract Services Administration Trust Fund (**http://www.csatf.org/bulletintro.shtml**). A list of these bulletins can be found in the appendix.

You may encounter expenses in your pursuit of safety ranging from environmental testing, to purchases such as dust masks or safety harnesses, to copying and distributing your company's safety program. An allotment of $1,500 to $2,500 should be sufficient. As can be seen in the budget, *Anarchist* did not have money specifically set aside for this account. Nevertheless, money was available in the contingency had we needed it.

22

Tracking the Film's Progress

Are We Ahead or Behind?

Imagine that you are in the midst of a lengthy 52-day production. On day 3, you fall a little behind your schedule but you can shoot the missing scene almost anywhere, so you figure you will make it up at some point. On day 7, you are rained out mid-day, but you have cover sets you can go to, so you move to the stage and finish out the day there, shooting scenes that were originally spread through days 27 and 28. On day 8, an actor gets food poisoning and cannot finish the day so you grab a scene from day 42 and finish the day using that, but you do not entirely finish the scene. On day 9, you are beginning to get a little confused and decide to reschedule the rest of the picture. Are you ahead? Are you behind? If you keep the schedule to 52 days, is it realistic? Will you be able to finish on time? Originally you had Scene 33A scheduled for half a day, but now you have it boarded as three quarters of a day. Does that matter? Does that mean some other scene is shortchanged? What does that dull ache in the pit of your stomach mean?

When I started in this business, the standard practice was to listen to that dull ache in your stomach. Most production managers had a bottle of Mylanta in their desk drawers. If the Mylanta could not make the ache go away, then you were probably in trouble and should talk to the director about making some adjustments. Films routinely went over schedule and over budget. If you turned in a budget of twelve million, the studio would give you ten million figuring that if they actually gave you the twelve million, you would spend fourteen. By giving you ten million, they counted on you going over and coming in on your original estimate of twelve. There was so much second-guessing going on that I do not think anyone ever really knew where the picture was in relation to the budget and schedule until the picture was over. Of course, by that time it was too late.

I realized early on that this was a game that could not be won. Most directors would take advantage of the confusion to steal more time, and the length of a picture's shooting schedule depended on how long it took to shoot the picture. Apparently no one had figured out an objective way to quantify a film's progress. Before I bought my own bottle of Mylanta, I met Lindsley Parsons, Jr. At the time, Lindsley was Vice President of Production at MGM Studios and I was starting to work there on Mel Brooks's *Spaceballs: The Movie*. Lindsley introduced me to a way that he had developed to quantify the progress a film made, no matter how you scrambled the schedule. In addition, the method always related any new schedule to the original schedule that the budget was based on.

How Many Widgets?

If you were the production manager of a widget factory, it would be easy to know if you were ahead or behind schedule. If your target was 2700 widgets per day and you made 2600, you would know that you were behind schedule. Likewise, if you made 2800 widgets you would be celebrating that you had pulled ahead of schedule. Now imagine that some widgets take longer or shorter amounts of time to produce than other widgets. Things become a little more complicated. Maybe the day you only made 2600 widgets, you were making widgets that take longer to produce.

This is similar to film production, only in film you are not producing widgets but are shooting pages of the script instead. That is your product. Now some pages take longer to shoot than other pages. Remember our eighth of a page "Atlanta burns to the ground"? That will take awhile to shoot. So the problem becomes one of quantifying how long it will take to shoot each shooting sequence, and getting everyone to sign off on the estimate. Well, guess what? Once you have an approved budget and schedule, that has already happened. Presumably, your director has gone through the schedule in minute detail with the assistant director and has decided that the film can be shot with that plan. The director has committed to how many widgets he or she can produce on each and every day of the schedule.

Lindsley's Method

Lindsley had me go through the shooting schedule that the final budget was based on, and assign to each shooting sequence a percentage of the day that each would take to shoot. For the most part, you can use the page count of the sequences to do this, tempering your assignments with common sense and good judgment. Figure 22.1 shows the first page of the original one-line shooting schedule from *The Anarchist Cookbook* with a

The Anarchist
ONELINE SCHEDULE

Page 1
May 21, 2001

Shoot Day # 1 Wednesday, May 23, 2001

Scs.						
Scs.	155	INT	**Computer Company** Puck's boss compliments him. **Cast Members: 1.Puck, 27.Boss sc. 155**	Day	2/8 pgs.	.1
Scs.	160	INT	**Computer Company** Puck gets an email from Jody. **Cast Members: 1.Puck**	Day	1 pgs.	.3
Scs.	163	INT	**Computer Company** Puck continues to slave away. **Cast Members: 1.Puck**	Day	1/8 pgs.	.1
Scs.	169	INT	**Computer Company** Puck call Johnny B names in an email to Jody. **Cast Members: 1.Puck**	Day	2/8 pgs.	.1
Scs.	161	INT	**Computer Company - Boss's Office** Puck tells his boss the reason for the party. **Cast Members: 1.Puck, 27.Boss sc. 155**	Day	1 pgs.	.3
Scs.	162	INT	**Computer Company** Puck works late into the night. **Cast Members: 1.Puck**	Night	1/8 pgs.	.1
Scs.	164	INT	**Computer Company** Puck is asleep. Carolyn tells him to go home. **Cast Members: 1.Puck, 28.Carolyn sc. 164**	Night	1/8 pgs.	.1
Scs.	170, 171	INT	**Computer Company** Puck turns down an invitation from Carolyn to wait for an email from Jody. **Cast Members: 1.Puck, 28.Carolyn sc. 164**	Night	3/8 pgs.	.1

End Day # 1 Wednesday, May 23, 2001 -- Total Pages: 3 2/8

Shoot Day # 2 Thursday, May 24, 2001

Scs.						
Scs.	52, 53	EXT	**Neiman Marcus - Service Entrance** Johnny B. hits the guard. Puck checks to see if he is okay. **Cast Members: 1.Puck, 3.Johnny Black, 22.Guard sc. 52**	Day	1 1/8 pgs.	.3
Scs.	55	EXT	**Neiman Marcus - Service Entrance** Cops examine the crime scene. **Cast Members: 22.Guard sc. 52**	Day	1/8 pgs.	.1
Scs.	44	EXT	**Restaurant** Puck and Double D pose as valets and steal an SUV. **Cast Members: 1.Puck, 2.Double D, 40.Man #1**	Day	2/8 pgs.	.1
Scs.	44A	EXT	**City Street** Puck and Double D pose as valets and steal an SUV. **Cast Members: 1.Puck, 2.Double D**	Day	1/8 pgs.	.1
Scs.	138	EXT	**Sidewalk** Cops questions the computer laden lads. **Cast Members: 1.Puck, 2.Double D, 15.Officer Roger**	Day	1 2/8 pgs.	.3
Scs.	223	EXT	**FBI Building** Establish FBI.	Day	1/8 pgs.	.1
Scs.	220	EXT	**FBI Building** Puck walks away from the FBI past the parking meters and Neiman Marcus.	Day	3/8 pgs.	.1

Fig. 22.1. A page from ***The Anarchist Cookbook*** one-line schedule.

percentage of the day assigned to each shooting sequence along the right-hand margin. The percentages are shown in tenths of a day. Notice that both day one and day two each add up to more than one day. This will be addressed shortly.

The percentages in figure 22.1 are based strictly on each sequence's page count compared with the total page count for the day, with the one rule that no sequence can be less than one tenth of a day. For example, Scene 155 is $\frac{2}{8}$ of a page. The total page count for the day is $3\frac{2}{8}$ pages. Scene 155 is actually 0.077 of the day's page count (2/8 divided by $2\frac{6}{8}$). This is not very useful since 0.077 times a 12-hour day is 55.44 minutes. Can you complete the sequence in 55 minutes? It seems reasonable, but it is also overly complex. This is not an exact science, it is an estimate. Besides, no one will be standing there with a stopwatch. If you restrict yourself initially to assigning no less than full tenths of a day to any given shooting sequence, you do not need to go into complex computations that are promising accuracy that is not real.

So by assigning nothing less than a tenth of a day, we end up with 1.2 days' work for the first day. Nevertheless, we must take on face value the declaration of the director that the work can be shot in a day. We therefore need to reexamine the time we have assigned to each sequence. We should examine the sequences which are $\frac{1}{8}$ page in length first. The first sequence

The Anarchist
ONELINE SCHEDULE

Page 1
May 21, 2001

Shoot Day # 1 Wednesday, May 23, 2001

Scs.						
Scs.	155	INT	**Computer Company** Puck's boss compliments him. **Cast Members: 1.Puck, 27.Boss sc. 155**	Day	2/8 pgs.	.1
Scs.	160	INT	**Computer Company** Puck gets an email from Jody. **Cast Members: 1.Puck**	Day	1 pgs.	.3
Scs.	163	INT	**Computer Company** Puck continues to slave away. **Cast Members: 1.Puck**	Day	1/8 pgs.	.1
Scs.	169	INT	**Computer Company** Puck call Johnny B names in an email to Jody. **Cast Members: 1.Puck**	Day	2/8 pgs.	.1
Scs.	161	INT	**Computer Company - Boss's Office** Puck tells his boss the reason for the party. **Cast Members: 1.Puck, 27.Boss sc. 155**	Day	1 pgs.	.2
Scs.	162	INT	**Computer Company** Puck works late into the night. **Cast Members: 1.Puck**	Night	1/8 pgs.	.05
Scs.	164	INT	**Computer Company** Puck is asleep. Carolyn tells him to go home. **Cast Members: 1.Puck, 28.Carolyn sc. 164**	Night	1/8 pgs.	.05
Scs.	170, 171	INT	**Computer Company** Puck turns down an invitation from Carolyn to wait for an email from Jody. **Cast Members: 1.Puck, 28.Carolyn sc. 164**	Night	3/8 pgs.	.1

Fig. 22.2 One-line schedule with corrected shooting time assignment.

that is ⅛ page is Scene 163. After speaking with the director, I know that he plans a visual effects shot for that sequence and it will take the hour and twelve minutes assigned to it. The next two ⅛-page sequences are scenes 162 and 164. Can they be done in about an hour together? Yes, since they each are only one shot, they could be done in an hour so I can reasonably assign 0.05 of a day to each (see fig. 22.2).

We are now at 1.1 days' work. Examining each of the other sequences, I know that the director intends to do Scene 161 in two shots. It is slated for 0.3 days, which is about three and a half hours (12 hours x 0.3 = 3.6 hours). Could we shoot that sequence in 0.2 days (12 hours x 0.2 = 2.4 hours)? Yes, easily. So I will change Scene 161 to 0.2. (See figure 22.2.) That makes day one equal to one day's work.

By going through each day in the schedule in this manner, you will end up with a portion of a day or days assigned to each shooting sequence. When you must rearrange the shooting schedule, those assignments should go with each shooting sequence. If Scene 161 can be shot in two hours and twenty-four minutes in the original schedule, it should be possible to shoot it in that approximate amount of time in any schedule you make.

With this as our premise, we can now know exactly where we are in relation to our schedule at any given time by tracking how much work we accomplish on each day. We can do this best by creating a chart. Figure 22.3 shows the chart created for *A Lot Like Love.*

It is assumed that every day of the schedule, a full day's work has been planned, so on every day, *Days Scheduled* is equal to one. The column labeled *Days Shot* shows the actual work accomplished that day as measured by adding up the portion of a day assigned to each shooting sequence completed. The *Variance* column simply shows the difference between what was shot that day and a full day's worth of work. In other words, if the variance is zero, then a full day's worth of work was accomplished. If the variance is above zero, then less than a full day's worth of work was completed and the company fell behind that day. A negative variance means that more than a day's worth of work was accomplished and the company is ahead of schedule. The *Cumulative Variance* column is a running total of the *Variance* column. If the cumulative variance is at zero, then the picture is on schedule. If it is more than zero, then the picture is falling behind schedule. If it is less than zero, the picture is ahead of schedule.

The *Scenes Credited* column simply records the scenes shot each day. The *Location* column is a reference as to where the company was shooting on each day. *Days Over Shown* is a record of how many days over or under schedule was shown on the production report for that particular day. If the projected-days-over box is changing back and forth on the production

Film Progress
2/18/2005

	Day	Date	Days Sched	Days Shot	Var.	Cum. Var.	Scenes Credited	Location	Days Over Shown	Comments
M	**1**	4/12/2004	1	1.00	0.00	0.00	25, 26A, 27. Version of 28 dropped (credit .4)	NY	0	
T	**2**	4/13/2004	1	1.00	0.00	0.00	17, 18, 22A ('B' unit 19pt not shot)	NY	0	
W	**3**	4/14/2004	1	0.50	0.50	0.50	20, 20A (B: 19pt, 22Bpt)	NY	0	
T	**4**	4/15/2004	1	1.30	-0.30	0.20	19, 22B, 26, 35, 28pt. 28Apt	NY	0	
F	**5**	4/16/2004	1	1.20	-0.20	0.00	21, 28, 28A, 30A	NY	0	
M	**6**	4/19/2004	1	1.00	0.00	0.00	32	Restaurant Bar	0	
T	**7**	4/20/2004	1	1.00	0.00	0.00	4, 5	LAX terminal 2	0	
W	**8**	4/21/2004	1	1.00	0.00	0.00	5A, 8, 13	LAX terminal 4	0	
T	**9**	4/22/2004	1	1.00	0.00	0.00	22, 33	Tattoo Parlor, Pizza P	0	
F	**10**	4/23/2004	1	0.40	0.60	0.60	9, 10, 11pt (3/8 of 5/8)	Air Hollywood	0	
S	**11**	4/26/2004	1	1.60	-0.60	0.00	7, 11, 12, 115, 125, 130 (6 omitted)	Air Hollywood	0	Shot Sat. because of actor avail.
T	**12**	4/27/2004	1	1.00	0.00	0.00	42, 135	El Matador Beach	0	
W	**13**	4/28/2004	1	1.00	0.00	0.00	116, 117, 118, 119	Venture Capital	0	
T	**14**	4/29/2004	1	0.70	0.30	0.30	111, 104, 110pt (2/8 of 4/8), 103 (3/8 of 5/8)	Lancaster	0	
F	**15**	4/30/2004	1	1.00	0.00	0.30	110, 102, 103, 103A, 112, 101pt.	Lancaster	0	
M	**16**	5/3/2004	1	0.90	0.10	0.40	92, 48pt (2 of 2 5/8)	Villa Elaine	0	
T	**17**	5/4/2004	1	1.20	-0.20	0.20	148, 152 (171 omitted)	Villa Elaine	0	
W	**18**	5/5/2004	1	0.90	0.10	0.30	114, 128A, (113 omitted)	Villa Elaine	0	
T	**19**	5/6/2004	1	0.90	0.10	0.40	108, (141pt time lapse still shot)	Desert Stage	0	
F	**20**	5/7/2004	1	0.30	0.70	1.10	105, 106, 109	Desert Stage	0	Casting office not shot
M	**21**	5/10/2004	1	1.00	0.00	1.10	139, 149, 151	Echo Park	0	
T	**22**	5/11/2004	1	2.10	-1.10	0.00	2, 168, 178, 179, 181, 186pt. (1/8 of 7/8) Omit 180, 170, 172, 173, 174, 175, 176,	Ext. Martin House	0	
W	**23**	5/12/2004	1	0.30	0.70	0.70	186, 186A, 186Bpt (2/8 of 1 6/8)	Int. Martin House	0	
T	**24**	5/13/2004	1	0.40	0.60	1.30	187alt, 187pt (7/8 of 1 7/8)	Ext. Martin House	1	Alternate ending being shot.
F	**25**	5/14/2004	1	1.00	0.00	1.30	131, 47A, 187, 186B (Omit 183, 184, 185)	I/E Martin House	1	Actual day over.
M	**26**	5/17/2004	1	1.10	-0.10	1.20	132, 133, 138, 159A, 166B, 166D, 47pt. (Omit 136, 137)	Int. Martin House	1	
T	**27**	5/18/2004	1	1.00	0.00	1.20	132A, 154, 155A, 155C, 47pt, 60Apt. (Omit 1)	Int. Martin House	1	
W	**28**	5/19/2004	1	1.00	0.00	1.20	79, 89, 91, 129 (omit 78A)	I/E BabyRush.Com	1	
T	**29**	5/20/2004	1	1.00	0.00	1.20	55, 50pt (1 of 2), 53pt (1 of 1 5/8)	Sunset Junction	1	
F	**30**	5/21/2004	1	0.90	0.10	1.30	50, 51A, 52, 53	Sunset Junction	1	
M	**31**	5/24/2004	1	0.90	0.10	1.40	140, 141, 142, 143, 88, 145pt. (146A, 144 omittied)	Sunset Junction	1	
T	**32**	5/25/2004	1	0.90	0.10	1.50	71, 72, 73, 75, 76, 74pt. (1/8 of 2/8)	Oliver's LA Apt.	1	
W	**33**	5/26/2004	1	0.80	0.20	1.70	57, 60pt (4/8 of 6/8), 60Bpt (5/8 of 7/8)	Natural History Museum	1	
T	**34**	5/27/2004	1	0.60	0.40	2.10	60, 60B, 60D, 69pt (0/8 of 1/8), 70pt (4/8 of 6/8).	Natural History Museum	1	
F	**35**	5/28/2004	1	1.40	-0.40	1.70	58, 60A, 60C, 62, 62A, 69, 70	Natural History Museum	1	
T	**36**	6/1/2004	1	1.00	0.00	1.70	100, 159F	IHOP & Brooks Bros.	1	
W	**37**	6/2/2004	1	1.00	0.00	1.70	82A, 83, 84, 128 (138 credited but not shot)	Carroll Avenue	1	
T	**38**	6/3/2004	1	0.70	0.30	2.00	37, 38, 38A, 35B, 38C	Barwick Stages	1	
F	**39**	6/4/2004	1	1.30	-0.30	1.70	47, 48, 49, 41, 43	Barwick Stages	1	
M	**40**	6/7/2004	1	1.20	-0.20	1.50	93, 97, 99, 95pt (3/8 of 5/8). 96A omitted.	Barwick Stages	1	
T	**41**	6/8/2004	1	0.90	0.10	1.60	145, 98, 122, 125A, 125C, 123pt (6/8 of 1 5/8)	Barwick Stages	1	
W	**42**	6/9/2004	1	1.50	-0.50	1.10	147, 166, 166C	Barwick Stages	1	
T	**43**	6/10/2004	1	0.50	0.50	1.60	159C, 101, 159D, 74, 72pt, 38Bpt (last 2 previously credited.	Barwick Stages	1	
F	**44**	6/11/2004	1	1.10	-0.10	1.50	39, 40, 54, 62B, 124B, 125B	Barwick Stages	1	
M	**45**	6/14/2004	1	1.30	-0.30	1.20	23, 51, 120, 121, 123, 124 (omit 153 & 169)	Chinese Rest, Cemetary	1	
T	**46**	6/15/2004	1	1.00	0.00	1.20	90, 94, 96, 159E	Michelle's House	1	
W	**47**	6/16/2004	1	1.00	0.00	1.20	155, 155B, 155BA, 155D, 155E, 159B, 159G	Ben's House	1	

Fig. 22.3. The progress chart from ***A Lot Like Love***.

report, the studio or financier may begin to wonder if you really have a handle on the progress of the picture. You should show a day over when you know it is real and when you know you cannot make it up. The *Comments* column is there for notes explaining the progress or lack thereof.

Looking at a few days in detail will make this clearer. On Day 1, we completed the day's work and took credit for one full day. This is not as wonderful as it sounds. There were two versions of Scene 28 scheduled to be shot that day and only one was completed. The second version (scheduled for 0.4 of a day) was dropped. We credited the second version as having been shot since it was never going to be shot and would no longer need to take up space on the schedule.

Day 2 was largely successful except for a B-unit shot that was not done. Nevertheless, a full day's credit was taken since the main unit did complete its work. However, on Day 3, we only completed half the day's work and so we only took credit for 0.5 of a day. That put us a half day behind. On Days 4 and 5, we made up the work we had dropped, and then we were back on schedule for the move back to Los Angeles.

Things went fairly well for a while until Day 14 when we started to fall behind again. This continued until Day 22 when the company made a super human effort and with much cleverness on the part of the director, we shot work on that one day that had originally been scheduled over two days. That put us back on schedule. It was short-lived though, because the production company decided they wanted us to shoot an alternate ending. That along with some additional slow progress put us a day over on Day 24. At that point, since we really had no way of making up the extra day, and with the concurrence of the studio, I began showing our status on the production report as one day over schedule. And so it went until the end of the picture. It should be noted that the production report never reflected more than one day over even though on days 34 and 38 the company was actually a full two days behind schedule. This was because we knew we would be able to make up the time during the stage sequences.

Looking at a chart full of numbers is not the best way to evaluate the trends. Making a graph from the *Cumulative Variance* column shows the trend immediately. Figure 22.4 shows the graph from the chart of *A Lot Like Love* just discussed. As can be seen in the graph, we never did make up that first day over, but we did keep it to no more than one day over. The show was originally scheduled for forty-six days and we finished it in forty-seven. These charts and graphs are useful tools in that they can show a trend.

I do not recommend running to the director every day waving one of these graphs in his or her face. You are likely to get a poor reception, and rightly so. The value in this system is that it can show the line producer or production manager what trends are developing, and it can illuminate the problems early enough so that something constructive can be done to fix them.

On *Robin Hood: Men In Tights*, I explained to Mel Brooks in the first two weeks of filming that if he continued at his then current pace, we would be two weeks over by the end of the picture. He said, "Oh yeah?

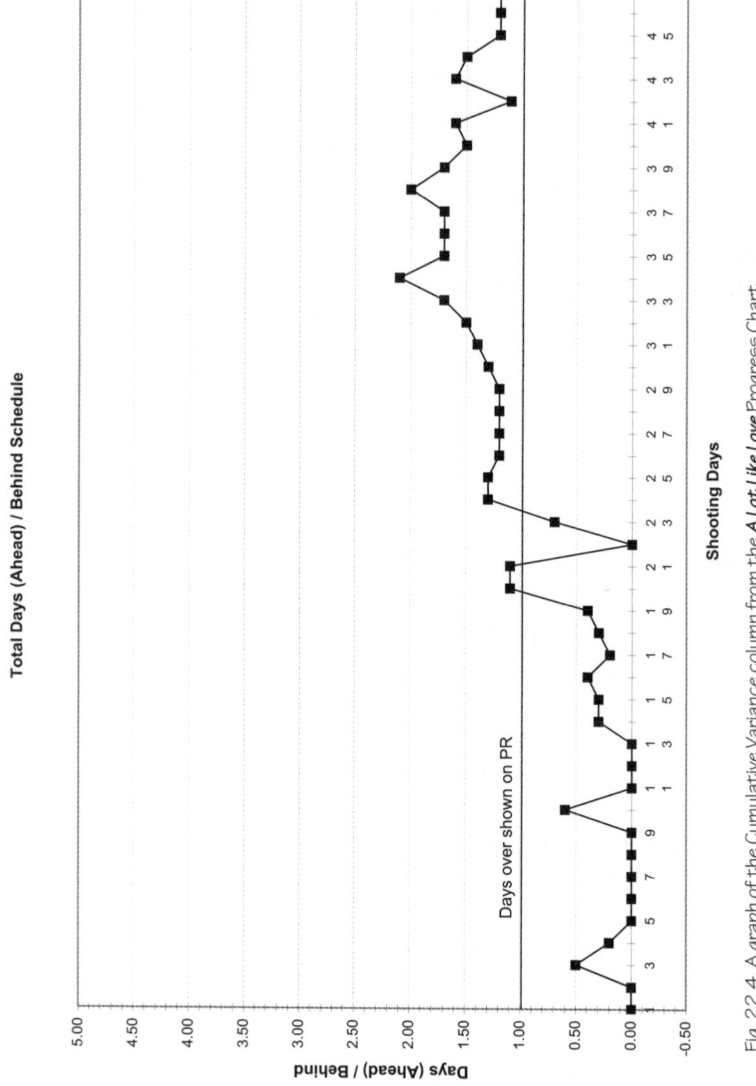

Fig. 22.4. A graph of the *Cumulative Variance* column from the ***A Lot Like Love*** Progress Chart.

Watch this." He ripped out several pages of script and we were back on schedule. (One of the advantages of working with Mel Brooks is that he is both producer and director. When Producer Mel is presented with a problem, Director Mel is able to come up with a creative and effective solution.*) It should be noted that we were falling behind through no fault of Mel; it was just an unfortunate set of circumstances.

* Another instance of this was on *Spaceballs: The Movie.* See the next chapter.

Sometimes a picture can be all over the map. Figure 22.5 shows the graph from *S.W.A.T.* A graph like this tells me that we did not do a very good job of estimating what could be accomplished each day.

Most of the time though, the trend is apparent early and it stays consistent. Figure 22.6 shows the graph on *Starship Troopers*. In this case, we had used the director's pace on a previous dramatic film to determine how much work should be put into each day. Our mistake was that we did not take into consideration that a picture with many visual effects shots takes longer to shoot because of the extra passes required by the effects. So although the director's pace did not change, the work that could be accomplished did change. With this chart, the trend was detectable within the first two weeks of shooting.

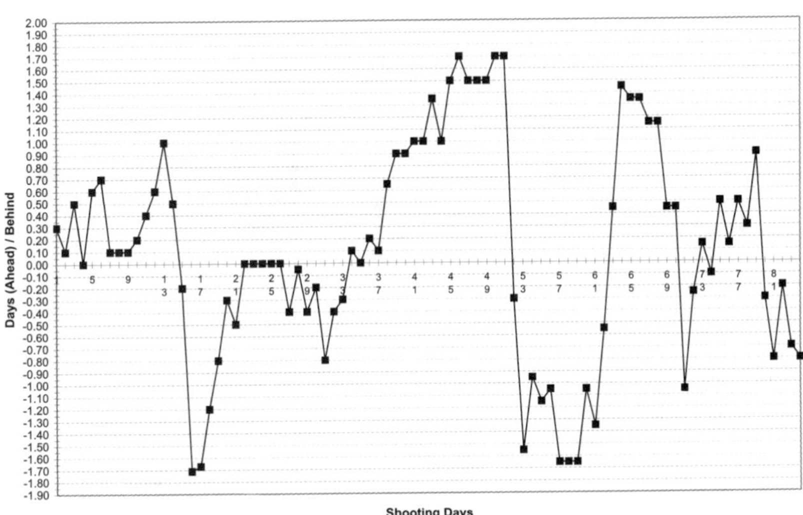

Fig. 22.5. Progress graph from ***S.W.A.T.***

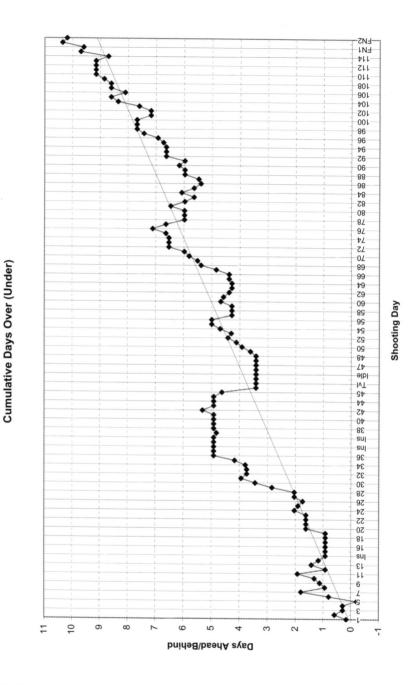

Fig. 22.6. The progress graph from ***Starship Troopers***. Note how consistant the progress trend was from the very beginning of the schedule all the way through to the end. Often the first two weeks of a schedule will predict how the rest of the schedule will go.

The Cost Report

The cost report is another vital tool that will help you know where you are. Each week, the line producer and/or the production manager should meet with the production accountant to go over each account in the budget. They do this with a report known as the *Estimate to Complete* or *Estimated Final Cost* (EFC). Figure 22.7 shows a part of the EFC from *The Anarchist Cookbook* at a point two weeks into the shooting of the picture.

THE ANARCHIST COOKBOOK
PRODUCTION COST REPORT
Period Ending 06/02/2001 — Page 0002

Acct. Num.	Account Description	Actual This Period	Actual To Date	PO Commits To Date	Total Cost Plus Commits	Estimate To Complete	Current EFC Amount	Current Budget Amt	Variance
819 01	Chief Lighting Tech	1,500	2,500	0	2,500	5,000	7,500	7,500	0
819 02	Asst. Chief Lighting Tech	1,200	1,400	0	1,400	4,960	6,360	6,360	0
819 03	Light Technicians	2,000	2,000	0	2,000	9,664	11,664	11,644	(20)
819 11	Loss & Damage	0	0	0	0	2,500	2,500	2,500	0
819 51	Purchases	1,375	1,375	53	1,428	1,572	3,000	3,000	0
819 56	Rentals	3,973	6,635	9,257	15,892	796	16,688	15,200	(1,488)
819 58	Box Rental	134	134	666	800	0	800	800	0
819	**ELECTRICAL**	**10,182**	**14,044**	**9,976**	**24,020**	**24,492**	**48,512**	**47,004**	**(1,508)**
821 01	Set Decorator	1,500	3,000	0	3,000	6,250	9,250	10,500	1,250
821 02	Leadman/Buyer	1,200	1,200	0	1,200	2,400	3,600	0	(3,600)
821 03	Swing Gang	2,250	4,750	0	4,750	5,700	10,450	8,746	(1,704)
821 11	Loss, Damage & Cleaning	11	11	0	11	0	11	2,000	1,989
821 51	Set Dressing Purchases	6,342	17,889	8,205	26,094	7,000	33,094	33,825	731
821	**SET DRESSING**	**11,303**	**26,850**	**8,205**	**35,055**	**21,350**	**56,405**	**55,071**	**(1,334)**

Fig. 22.7. Part of the EFC report for ***The Anarchist Cookbook***.

The two main accounts shown here are Electrical (Set Lighting) and Set Dressing. Of course in a complete report, all the accounts of the budget would be represented. The columns that make up the report deserve a little explication in order to be fully understood.

Account Number. This is the subaccount number from the budget for the particular expense being reported. Each subaccount is examined on its own. The report can be printed in even more detail, giving the actual individual transactions that are summed up in the total of the subaccount. This particular chart of accounts uses hyphenated numbers, others don't.

Account Description. This is the account name describing what expenses the account covers.

Actual This Period. The amount shown is what was paid in the most recent reporting period, usually the week preceding the date of the report. As noted in the heading, since this report is for the week ending June 2, 2001, amounts in this column will be for all monies paid out from May 27, through June 2. The exceptions to this are labor accounts. Labor is usually a week behind because of the payroll cycle. This is explained further below.

Actual To Date. This is the total of all monies actually paid out up through the period-ending date, including the amounts shown in the *Actual This Period* column.

PO Commitments To Date. All purchase orders issued to vendors, including purchase orders issued to employees for box rentals or other predictable payments (not including labor), are summed up in each account in this column. This represents money that the company owes or anticipates paying, but for which no check has been written. An example might be a PO for the camera truck issued to a truck rental company. If you knew that you were going to rent the truck for a total of 5 weeks and pay $500 each week in rental, then you would issue a PO to the rental company for a total of $2500. Each week when a $500 payment was made for the truck, the payment would be deducted from the PO and added to the *Actual To Date* column.

Total Cost Plus Commitments. This is merely the total of *Actual To Date* and *PO Commitments To Date* columns. In other words, this is the total of all monies actually spent or committed.

Estimate To Complete. This column needs to be evaluated carefully. This represents how much money is needed in each subaccount to finish the picture, based on what is currently known. If you know that you will need 6 more work days in lamp operators, this is where the money should be added. If you do not know of anything more than the information that you used to budget the subaccount in the first place, then this account is merely the difference between what was budgeted for the subaccount and what has been spent and committed to date.

Current EFC Amount. This is the estimated final cost of the subaccount to the picture, or in other words, the sum of the *Total Cost Plus Commitments* column and the *Estimate to Complete* column.

Current Budget Amount. This is the figure from your budget for each account. This figure is never changed once the budget is locked. Adjustments to the account are made in the *Estimate To Complete* column instead.

Variance. This is the *Current Budget Amount* column minus the *Current EFC Amount*. Depending on which cost reporting program you are using, overages can be either positive or negative numbers. In the report shown in figure 22.7, if the variance is positive, we are under budget. If it is a negative number, we are over budget. If it is zero, then we are on budget. The *Variance* column is the only one of the last four columns that can show a negative number.

Using the Cost Report

Going through a few lines of the report segment shown in detail will help explain the purpose and use of this report. At first glance, things do not look well. Both the Set Lighting account (819) and the Set Dressing account (821) are over budget. We will concentrate on Set Lighting for the moment. It is showing an overage of $1,508. When an account is over, look at the individual subaccounts that make up the main account to see which of those are causing the problem. In Set Lighting, we have a large overage in Rentals (819-56) and a small overage in the Light Technicians (819-03).

In general, when a subaccount is over, we first want to try to remedy the problem within the subaccount. When that is not sufficient, we then look to the rest of the subaccounts within the main account. When the account overage cannot be covered by the monies allocated to the account, then the only choice is to range further in the budget to see if there are other main accounts that might have a surplus of money.

Prior to your cost report meeting, the production accountant will go through each line in the account and determine how much money is needed to finish the picture. In other words, the accountant is refiguring the estimate to complete to make sure it still holds true. If the estimate to complete has changed, the accountant will pencil in the figures to be added or subtracted from the estimate to complete. When these figures are presented, the production manager should consider them carefully. There may be information of which the accountant is unaware. Let's go through this process for the electrical account.

The first line shown (account 819-01) is for the Chief Lighting Technician or gaffer. In the column headed *Actual This Period*, the amount shown is what was paid in the most recent reporting period. As stated above, this will be a week behind the accounts payable costs in the non-labor subaccounts. In this case, that would be the week ending May 26, 2001. This is because of the way the payroll cycle works. Crewmembers are usually paid on the Thursday following the close of the work period. That means that the payroll for the current week (week ending June 2) has not yet been calculated and therefore has not been entered into the cost report. Accounts that are paid directly by check in response to an invoice (accounts payable) are entered into the costs automatically as soon as the check is written.

Our gaffer was paid $1500 in the most current payroll period (May 20 through May 26), and has been paid $2500 for his entire time on the picture (May 16 through May 26). We do not issue purchase orders for labor, so the *PO Commitments To Date* column is zero. Because of that, the *Total Costs* column is equal to the *Actual To Date* column. To estimate how much is needed to finish the picture, we calculate how much the gaffer will make through the rest of his anticipated time on the picture. We expect him to work from May 29 (May 28 was Memorial Day) through the final day of photography, June 20. That equals 20 days since we were shooting six-day weeks. His rate was $250 per day, so 20 days x $250 equals $5000. In this subaccount, our ESTIMATE TO COMPLETE plus the TOTAL COST PLUS COMMITMENTS equals our budgeted figure so our variance is zero and we are on budget.

Account 819-02, ASSISTANT CHIEF LIGHTING TECH (best boy), is showing a total cost to date of $1400. We expect the best boy to work another 22 days: May 29 through the end of the picture on June 20 plus two days of wrap. His rate is $200 per day, or 22 x $200 = $4400. We need $4400 to finish the picture with him. The estimate to complete column is showing $4960. That means that we can subtract $560 from the estimate to complete ($4960 - $4400). We make a notation to that effect next to the $4960 figure (see fig. 22.8).

THE ANARCHIST COOKBOOK
PRODUCTION COST REPORT
Period Ending 06/02/2001 Page 0002

Acct. Num.	Account Description	Actual This Period	Actual To Date	PO Commits To Date	Total Cost Plus Commits	Estimate To Complete	Current EFC Amount	Current Budget Amt	Variance
819 01	Chief Lighting Tech	1,500	2,500	0	2,500	5,000	7,500	7,500	0
819 02	Asst. Chief Lighting Tech	1,200	1,400	0	1,400	4,960 -560	6,360	6,360	0
819 03	Light Technicians	2,000	2,000	0	2,000	9,664 +23	11,664	11,644	(20)
819 11	Loss & Damage	0	0	0	0	2,500	2,500	2,500	0
819 51	Purchases	1,375	1,375	53	1,428	1,572 -971	3,000	3,000	0
819 56	Rentals	3,973	6,635	9,257	15,892	796	16,688	15,200	(1,488)
819 58	Box Rental	134	134	666	800	0	800	800	0
819	**ELECTRICAL**	**10,182**	**14,044**	**9,976**	**24,020**	**24,492**	**48,512**	**47,004**	**(1,508)**
821 01	Set Decorator	1,500	3,000	0	3,000	6,250	9,250	10,500	1,250
821 02	Leadman/Buyer	1,200	1,200	0	1,200	2,400	3,600	0	(3,600)
821 03	Swing Gang	2,250	4,750	0	4,750	5,700	10,450	8,746	(1,704)
821 11	Loss, Damage & Cleaning	11	11	0	11	0	11	2,000	1,989
821 51	Set Dressing Purchases	6,342	17,889	8,205	26,094	7,000	33,094	33,825	731
821	**SET DRESSING**	**11,303**	**26,850**	**8,205**	**35,055**	**21,350**	**56,405**	**55,071**	**(1,334)**

Fig. 22.8. The Set Lighting account with changes to be made in the EFC noted.

In the film business, it is always wise to look a gift horse in the mouth. Why do we have this savings? Is it a mistake? If we look at the budget (see the appendix), we see that the best boy was slated to have a week of prep. That would have started him on May 16. Actually, he did not start until May 19, saving three days' salary on him. So why isn't our savings $600 (3 days x $200)? Because the budget is in error. Look at the best boy's wrap; it is listed as 0.3 weeks. That is supposed to stand for 2 days, which is one third of a six-day week. Instead of being entered as 0.34 weeks, it was rounded off to 0.3 weeks. This inserted a $40 error in the wrap figure and explains why the best boy's wrap days are listed as costing $360 instead of $400. So the savings is real, but not what it would have been if the budget had not been in error.

The next account, 819-03 LIGHTING TECHNICIANS, is already showing an overage of $20. We have spent, to date, $2000 in this account. We have been carrying two lamp operators every day of the picture at a rate of $166.67 per day ($1000/week). They each had two days of prep, so they each should have been paid for six days, or a total in the account of twelve work days which is 12 days x $166.67 = $2000.04. The cost reports rounds off the four cents and is showing $2000. That checks out. What about the rest of the picture? We expect the two lamp operators to work the entire picture plus two days of wrap. That's a total of 44 work days (2 x 22 days). At their rate of $166.67 per day, that amounts to $7333.48 needed to finish the picture. Our estimate to complete in 819-03 is showing $9664! Our hearts soar! We are saved! Not so fast. Be suspicious. Why is that extra money there? Look at the budget. There are fourteen extra work days in the account to pay for extra help on heavy days and night work. The extra days total $2324 and this must be added to our figures: $2324 plus $7333 totals $9657. We now see that our estimate to complete is high by only $7.

The fact that the account was showing such a weird number as an overage ($20) bears investigating. It could be that there is a bad charge in the account, or that someone was overpaid. Or more simply, we may have another budget error. Notice that the lamp operators' prep periods were figured at 0.33 weeks, intended to represent two days. Actually, they should have been figured at 0.34 weeks. The difference, 0.01, times $1000/week times 2 lamp operators equals $20. That is where the discrepancy comes from. Note also that the same error was made in the wrap period, and that will be reflected in another $20 at that time.

Another source of error is apparent in this account. Although the lamp operators are making $166.67 per day, the extra workdays were figured at $166. Fourteen work days times $0.67 equals $9.38. In making your budgets, round up, not down. In light of all this, we probably want to add $23 to our estimate to complete ($20 + $10 [round up, not down] - $7). We make a note to that effect next to the $9664 (see fig. 22.8).

Now we come to the 819-11 LOSS & DAMAGE account. We look longingly at that $2500 sitting there. Can we take it? It would easily cover our overages. Stop and think for a minute. The bills for loss and damage do not appear until after the shoot is over and you have returned all your equipment. There is no way you can anticipate what may happen here unless you are psychic, and my understanding is that psychics are terrible when it comes to numbers. You cannot tap LOSS & DAMAGE at this early date. That is why the estimate to complete for LOSS & DAMAGE must remain at the full $2500.

Account 819-51 for PURCHASES is showing on budget but we need to examine it more closely. Of the $3000 originally budgeted, we have spent almost half of the money. That seems appropriate since we are about halfway through our shooting. But is it? Most of the spending in set lighting purchases occurs during the prep period before shooting starts. This is when the crew is getting their truck outfitted and they are gathering the things that will be need for the shoot. Perhaps there is some money here. We can discuss with the gaffer and best boy what they think their future needs may be. When we do, they tell us that they pretty much have bought all the stuff that they will need except another roll of gel that they have just realized will be necessary. A roll of gel will be about $200. It's best to be conservative here. Something may come up that will require more purchases. So far, our ups and downs in the electrical account as a whole are netting out to a $971 overage. That results from adding our savings in 819-02 (+$560) and our overage in 819-03 (-$23) to the previous overall overage in the electrical account (-$1508). If we took out just what we needed to cover the balance of the overage from account 819-51, we would still have $601 left in the account. That would buy a roll of gel and then some. We note next to the $1572 estimate to complete in 819-51 to subtract $971 (see fig. 22.8).

We will leave 819-56 RENTALS with its balance of $796 to spend. Reducing this account would be foolhardy based on our experience with it so far. We have spent 95% of the budgeted amount already, although over half of that is in PO commitments on the rental package, and we should leave some room for added equipment. The 819-58 BOX RENTALS account is dead on and it should not change.

Figure 22.8 shows the cost report with the handwritten adjustments made. Figure 22.9 shows the cost report after we have made our adjustments to the SET LIGHTING account using the cost reporting software.

We have now brought the SET LIGHTING account under control. Nevertheless, constant vigilance will be needed to make sure the figures in the *Estimate to Complete* column hold.

The rental account is especially one that needs watching. This is because of the pricing structure that the equipment houses use. Equipment houses currently are renting the lamps based on a fraction of a day per week. In other words, the vendor may charge only 0.3 times the published daily rate for each week's use. If you use a lamp for one day, you pay three tenths of the published daily rate for it. If you use a lamp for a week, you still pay 0.3 times the daily rent for the entire week. Great deal? Actually, no. In essence, the going weekly rate is really 3⁄10 of the published daily rate and they charge you a minimum of a week's rent for each week or fraction thereof. Go one day beyond the rental week and you owe for another full week. They do not prorate for partial weeks. The daily rate is a fiction that the equipment houses use so that they can base all their rentals on weekly minimums. What proves that the daily rate is fictional is that no filmmaker in his or her right mind would rent a piece of equipment for five times the daily rate for a week's use. The cost would be prohibitive. The equipment vendors just do not want to be bothered with daily rentals.

This same procedure outlined above must be done on SET DRESSING and on each of the other accounts in the budget. Doing this each week will keep you fully abreast of where you are in your costs.

THE ANARCHIST COOKBOOK
PRODUCTION COST REPORT
Period Ending 06/02/2001 Page 0002

Acct. Num.	Account Description	Actual This Period	Actual To Date	PO Commits To Date	Total Cost Plus Commits	Estimate To Complete	Current EFC Amount	Current Budget Amt	Variance
819 01	Chief Lighting Tech	1,500	2,500	0	2,500	5,000	7,500	7,500	0
819 02	Asst. Chief Lighting Tech	1,200	1,400	0	1,400	4,400	5,800	6,360	560
819 03	Light Technicians	2,000	2,000	0	2,000	9,687	11,687	11,644	(43)
819 11	Loss & Damage	0	0	0	0	2,500	2,500	2,500	0
819 51	Purchases	1,375	1,375	53	1,428	601	2,029	3,000	971
819 56	Rentals	3,973	6,635	9,257	15,892	796	16,688	15,200	(1,488)
819 58	Box Rental	134	134	666	800	0	800	800	0
819 ELECTRICAL		**10,182**	**14,044**	**9,976**	**24,020**	**22,984**	**47,004**	**47,004**	**0**
821 01	Set Decorator	1,500	3,000	0	3,000	6,250	9,250	10,500	1,250
821 02	Leadman/Buyer	1,200	1,200	0	1,200	2,400	3,600	0	(3,600)
821 03	Swing Gang	2,250	4,750	0	4,750	5,700	10,450	8,746	(1,704)
821 11	Loss, Damage & Cleaning	11	11	0	11	0	11	2,000	1,989
821 51	Set Dressing Purchases	6,342	17,889	8,205	26,094	7,000	33,094	33,825	731
821 SET DRESSING		**11,303**	**26,850**	**8,205**	**35,055**	**21,350**	**56,405**	**55,071**	(1,334)

Fig. 22.9. The Set Lighting account with the changes implemented. Note that the account is now showing on budget with a zero variance.

23

THAT'S A WRAP

The Director's Big Ideas

Your director will get ideas. Dangerous ideas. Expensive ideas. They lay awake nights trying to dream up ever more outrageous stunts. They spend their weekends, when normal people are relaxing, creating subversive thoughts to throw at you on Monday morning before you have had your coffee: "I want a scene where our hero walks on water...supported by the backs of 5000 porpoises...on his hands...across the Irish Sea...to the bad guys' aircraft carrier." Obviously, none of this was budgeted.

What do you do? First, you must realize that this is what the director was hired for: his or her vision. Sure, it would be nice if you could have put the 5000 porpoises in the original budget but that is not how the creative process works. Sometimes the ideas come late. When that happens, you must try to help the director find a way to make it happen within the given resources of the picture. Sometimes an adjustment here and a compromise there can accomplish it, at least in part. It is important to give the director as many options as possible. ("Could you do it with whales instead of porpoises? We wouldn't need as many.") When that is impossible, then the director needs to explain to the studio or the financiers why the scene is essential and justify the extra expense. This is not to say that the studio or financiers will agree. Sometimes the great ideas just do not happen.

On *Clean and Sober*, the director, Glenn Gordon Caron, was called to task by the studio because we were slipping behind in our schedule and inching up in our costs. In his frustration, he declared to the studio that they had hired him for his vision but would not let him realize it. Actually, the studio had every right to expect the picture to stay on budget and on schedule. What was lacking was that the producer and I had not fully done our jobs. We had not given him alternatives to help him stay within the parameters of the picture. Perhaps he would not have been satisfied with the alternatives, but at least he would have had a choice. If a compromise will not work, and there is no more money, then the director needs to try to do it in another way, or give the idea up.

On *Spaceballs*, Mel Brooks had a great idea similar to a scene in Charlie Chaplin's *Modern Times*. Mel wanted Dark Helmet to be fed his dinner by an "eating machine" and become tangled up in it. When I came back to him and told him that to build and shoot the gag, it would cost $50,000, he paused a moment to consider it and shook his head saying, "If you had said $25,000, okay. But for $50,000, it's not that funny." Not all directors are so accommodating. Another director with whom I worked once asked me if this was a "money question" when I tried to approach him about our slow progress. When I told him that indeed it was, he said, "That's not my problem, that's a production problem."

Nevertheless, it *is* the director's problem when budget overages or schedule overruns threaten to affect the rest of the filming. The best approach is one of collaboration. Production should make every effort possible to realize the director's vision, and the director should be willing to exercise his or her creative powers to do it with the resources available.

When Things Go Wrong

I began this book writing about the complexity of filmmaking. In any endeavor this complex, things will go wrong. On *Hollow Man*, we had an underwater swimming pool sequence to shoot. We erected an above-ground swimming pool on stage at Sony Studios. Upon inspecting it soon after the pool was filled, I noticed that the water was cloudy. I mentioned this to the pool people and they said that I should not worry because that was what pool water did when a pool was newly filled, and that it would clear up in a day.

The next morning the pool was still cloudy. I again talked to my pool experts and they said they were adding more filters to the system that day. I was not to worry.

The next day, the pool was cloudier than ever. We had to shoot it in two days and I was worried. I was told that they were installing even *more* filter pumps. They said that the next day I would see sparkling, clear water.

On the fourth day, the water was almost opaque. It had also developed a strange greenish tint. My experts told me that they were sure it would soon be perfect. I had my doubts. I told them that the director would be there that afternoon to inspect the pool.

When Paul Verhoeven arrived to look at the pool that afternoon, the visibility underwater was no more than one foot. The color of the water had gotten even stranger: it was now a milky blue. It looked like we had filled the pool with blue custard. Paul turned to me and said, "This is unshootable." He was right. Paul left the stage realizing that he had nothing to shoot the next day. I stood there realizing that I had completely let him down.

I finally did what I should have done that first day: I got down on my hands and knees and looked closely at the water. With the aid of a stage lamp and the gaffer, I saw that that the cloudiness was caused by billions of very tiny air bubbles. I went to where the filter pumps were and saw that my pool experts had fifteen separate pumps running in a panicked effort to clear the water. I told them to shut off the pumps. They protested saying they knew that they could have the water clear within a few hours. I told them to shut off the pumps…*now!* So they did.

In an hour, the water was already much clearer. Evidently the pumps were generating the bubbles, and each added filter pump created even more bubbles and the water only got murkier. So we had solved the visibility problem. There was still the strange color. The pool experts told me that they had put blue dye in the water in order to correct the greenish cast that the water seemed to have. The greenish cast came from the cloudiness of the water and the yellow work lights on stage. I told them to drain the pool immediately, and to refill it with fresh water and to keep all the filter pumps off except one, and that one would be turned off two hours before we filmed. The next morning we had shootable water.

How you react when things go horribly wrong may mean the difference between successfully completing your picture or failing dismally. The natural reaction is to seek the head of whomever is responsible and to beat him or her unmercifully. This is not productive. It did not work for Ivan the Terrible*, and it does not work now. Your energy needs to be directed toward finding a solution to the problem. What is done is done, and now it needs to be fixed. The person responsible probably thought he or she was doing the right thing. Holding an inquisition or a witch-hunt does not solve the problem. All it does is make the inquisitor feel as though something is being done.

---

*Ivan was know for beating his subjects unmercifully when they did not comply with his instructions.

After the problem is solved is the time to take the responsible person aside (and it may be you who is responsible), and in private, calmly explain what happened and what can be done to avoid it in the future. The perpetrator will be grateful for the enlightened way you have handled the situation, and will be more anxious than ever to perform well.

So...?

Line producing or production managing a film is a tremendous responsibility. You are dealing with other peoples' money, hopes, and dreams. Careers in this business can rise or fall on the outcome of the weekend box office. You can be a hero one day and be discarded the next without even knowing why.

When talking about acting, George C. Scott said that it was a ridiculous way for a grown man to make a living. The same could probably be said for filmmaking as a whole. The business is filled with craziness. Look at a sampling of book titles about the business: *Bring on the Empty Horses* by David Niven, *You'll Never Eat Lunch In This Town Again* by Julia Phillips, *Which Lie Did I Tell?* by William Goldman. These titles belie a humor and often a cynicism which is unique to Hollywood. John Milius once complained that the studios take his scripts in which he has bared his soul, rip the heart out of his characters, and trivialize his meaning—and for all that they pay him a great deal of money. Larry Peerce, the talented director who began his feature career with *Goodbye, Columbus*, took aside the writer-director of *The Anarchist Cookbook*, Jordan Susman, and said, "My boy, any business that gives such great rewards for doing so little will attract the very worst sort of person." That is true. I have met those people.

But I have met many, many more who are their opposite. This business is not brain surgery. It is not rocket science. It won't feed the poor, or heal the sick. What it *does* do is capture and reflect the human spirit, both in its every day interactions, and the stories that it tells. And that is what makes filmmaking a worthy pursuit, the stories—stories that can touch someone sitting alone, in a crowd, in a darkened room.

APPENDIX

The Anarchist Cookbook Budget

On the following pages, I have reproduced the shooting budget of *The Anarchist Cookbook*. Where names were originally inserted, I have changed or eliminated them when necessary to protect the privacy of the individuals concerned. Although this budget was based on the Universal Studios chart of accounts, not every account or subaccount was used in the *Anarchist* budget. Please refer to the text in Chapters 18 through 21 for a more complete listing of accounts and subaccounts.

The Anarchist Cookbook
Freedonia Productions, LLC

Writer/Director: Jordan Susman
Producers: Brown, Susman, Greenspun
Script Dated: April 5, 2001
Budget Dated: 05/21/01
Revision #14

Start Principal Photography: 05/23/01
Complete Prin. Photography: 06/20/01
Dallas Local Location: 24 Days
Dallas Stage: 0 Days
Post Production: 16 Weeks

Acct No	Category Description	Page	Total
803-00	WRITING	1	20,000
805-00	PRODUCER & STAFF	1	72,277
807-00	DIRECTOR & STAFF	1	20,000
809-00	TALENT	1	295,855
810-00	**Total Fringes**		**42,904**
	Total Above-The-Line		**451,036**
811-00	PRODUCTION STAFF	3	95,440
813-00	CAMERA	4	75,543
814-00	ART DEPARTMENT	5	23,908
816-00	SPECIAL EFFECTS	5	1,800
817-00	SET OPERATIONS	5	66,032
819-00	ELECTRICAL	6	47,004
821-00	SET DRESSING	7	55,070
823-00	ACTION PROPS	7	24,228
825-00	PICT. VEH. & ANIMALS	8	6,100
829-00	EXTRA TALENT	8	40,820
831-00	COSTUME	8	39,395
833-00	MAKEUP & HAIR	9	18,500
835-00	SOUND	9	25,926
837-00	LOCATION	9	160,394
839-00	TRANSPORTATION	10	128,577
841-00	FILM & LAB	12	88,062
843-00	TESTS	12	1,100
847-00	SECOND UNIT	12	1,250
849-00	**Total Fringes**		**79,775**
	Total Production		**978,924**
851-00	EDITING & PROJECTION	13	78,500
853-00	MUSIC	13	75,000
855-00	SOUND (POST PRODUCTION)	13	105,000
857-00	POST PRODUCTION FILM & LAB	13	51,194
859-00	TITLES & OPTICALS	13	10,000
860-00	**Total Fringes**		**7,534**
	Total Post Production		**327,228**
861-00	INSURANCE	14	27,500
862-00	PUBLICITY	14	500
865-00	GENERAL EXPENSES	14	9,000
870-00	CONTINGENCY	14	200,000
	Total Other		**237,000**
	Total Above-The-Line		**451,036**
	Total Below-The-Line		**1,543,152**
	Total Above and Below-The-Line		**1,994,188**
	Grand Total		**1,994,188**

[*Note*: Actors work long and hard to increase their *quote* (the rate at which they will work). Sometimes a script that the actor really likes will come along and the actor will agree to work for a much lower than normal rate in order to accommodate an independent film's lesser resources. When actors make deals like this, they usually ask that it be a *no-quote* deal. This means that the producer pledges not to disclose the rate at which they worked so that this temporary lowering of their rate will not affect their future negotiations. In order to honor that commitment, I have blocked out the rates at which our principal cast worked in accounts 809-01 and 809-02. For similar reasons, I have done the same with the producers' rates in account 805-02.]

The Anarchist Cookbook
Freedonia Productions, LLC

Writer/Director: Jordan Susman
Producers: Brown, Susman, Greenspun
Script Dated: April 5, 2001
Budget Dated: 05/21/01
Revision #14

Start Principal Photography: 05/23/01
Complete Prin. Photography: 06/20/01
Dallas Local Location: 24 Days
Dallas Stage: 0 Days
Post Production: 16 Weeks

Acct No	Description	Amount	Units	X	Rate	Subtotal	Total
803-00 WRITING							
803-01	Writer's Salaries						
	Jordan Susman	1	Fee	1	20,000	20,000	
	Total						20,000
Account Total for 803-00							**20,000**
805-00 PRODUCER & STAFF							
805-02	Producers						
					See note on facing page.		
	Jordan Susman	1	Flat	1			
	Robert Brown	1	Flat	1			
	Amy Greenspun	1	Flat	1			
	Total						67,500
805-30	Travel and Living Expense						
	Per diem						
	Robert Brown	56	Days	1	30.0	1,680	
	Amy Greenspun	34	Days	1	30.0	1,020	
	Air Fare						
	Robert Brown	1		1	338	338	
	Jordan Susman	1		1	533	533	
		1		1	397	397	
		1		1	276	276	
	Amy Greenspun	1		1	533	533	
	Total						4,777
Account Total for 805-00							**72,277**
807-00 DIRECTOR & STAFF							
807-01	Director						
	Jordan Susman	1	Allow	1	20,000	20,000	
	Total						20,000
Account Total for 807-00							**20,000**
809-00 TALENT							
809-01	Principal Cast						
	Puck	4	Weeks	1	*See note on facing page.*		
	Double D	4	Weeks	1			
	Johnny Black	3.17	Weeks	1			
	No. of checks	13	Weeks	1	0.0	0	
	Total						91,001
809-02	Supporting Cast						
	Karla	3	Weeks	1	*See note on facing page.*		
	Johnny Red	2	Weeks	1			
	Sweeney	3.17	Weeks	1			
	Gin	2	Weeks	1			
	Jody	4	Days	1			
	Overtime	20	%	1	90,000	18,000	
	No. of checks	12	Weeks	1	0.0	0	
	Total						108,000
809-03	Day Players						
	Milo	4	Days	1	512.6	2,050	
	Dale	2	Days	1	512.6	1,025	
	Rich	2	Days	1	512.6	1,025	
	Lawyer (drop/pickup)	4	Days	1	513	2,052	
	Mr. Gold	2	Days	1	513	1,026	
	Tour Leader	1	Day	1	513	513	
	Mrs. Gold	1	Day	1	513	513	
	FBI Agent sc. 224	1	Day	1	513	513	
	Security Guard	1	Day	1	513	513	
	Teen	2	Days	1	513	1,026	
	Clean-cut Kid	1	Day	1	513	513	

The Anarchist Cookbook - May 21, 2001 Page 2

Continuation of Account 809-03

Acct No	Description	Amount	Units	X	Rate	Subtotal	Total
	Guard sc. 52	1	Day	1	513	513	
	Manager sc. 76	1	Day	1	513	513	
	Japanese Girl	1	Day	1	513	513	
	Sweet Thing	2	Days	1	513	1,026	
	Waitress sc. 127	1	Day	1	513	513	
	Officer Roger	5	Days	1	513	2,565	
	Boss sc. 155	1	Day	1	513	513	
	Carolyn sc. 164	1	Day	1	513	513	
	Susie	1	Day	1	513	513	
	Truck Driver sc. 231	1	Day	1	513	513	
	Burger Dude	1	Day	1	513	513	
	Newsman	1	Day	1	513	513	
	Old Codger	1	Day	1	513	513	
	Punk sc. 35	1	Day	1	513	513	
	Bike Messenger	1	Day	1	513	513	
	Businessman #1	1	Day	1	513	513	
	Businesswoman #1	1	Day	1	513	513	
	Black Man sc. 67	1	Day	1	513	513	
	Businessman #2	1	Day	1	513	513	
	Davie Crockett	1	Day	1	513	513	
	Latina sc. 67	1	Day	1	513	513	
	Santa Ana	1	Day	1	513	513	
	Astrud	1	Day	1	513	513	
	Bam-Bam	1	Day	1	513	513	
	Straightlaced Teen	1	Day	1	513	513	
	Woman sc. 100	1	Day	1	513	513	
	Sorority Girll sc. 121	1	Day	1	513	513	
	Sergeant At Arms sc. 142	1	Day	1	513	513	
	Child sc. 152	1	Day	1	513	513	
	Mother sc. 152	1	Day	1	513	513	
	Sales Guy sc. 185	1	Day	1	513	513	
	Overtime	20	%	1	29,238	5,847	
	No. of checks	45	Weeks	1	0.0	0	
	Total						35,085
809-10	Looping & Expenses						
	Looping Allowance	1	Allow	1	10,000	10,000	
	Total						10,000
809-15	Casting Directors						
	Liz Keigley	1	Allow	1	15,000	15,000	
	Total						15,000
809-16	Casting Asst. & Expenses						
	Sari Kiegley	1	Allow	1	5,000	5,000	
	Total						5,000
809-30	Travel & Living Expenses						
	Per diem						
	Puck	31	Days	1	60.0	1,860	
	Double D	27	Days	1	60.0	1,620	
	Johnny Black	28	Days	1	60.0	1,680	
	Johnny Red	18	Days	1	60.0	1,080	
	Karla	22	Days	1	60.0	1,320	
	Jody	8	Days	1	60.0	480	
	Sweeney	30	Days	1	60.0	1,800	
	Gin	16	Days	1	60.0	960	
	Mrs. Gold	3	Days	1	60.0	180	
	Casting	25	Days	1	30.0	750	
						11,730	
	Hotel						
	Puck	30	Days	1	60.0	1,800	
	Double D	30	Days	1	60.0	1,800	
	Johnny Black	30	Days	1	60.0	1,800	
	Johnny Red	17	Days	1	60.0	1,020	
	Karla	21	Days	1	60.0	1,260	
	Jody	7	Days	1	60.0	420	
	Sweeney	30	Days	1	60.0	1,800	
	Gin	15	Days	1	60.0	900	
	Mrs. Gold	2	Days	1	60.0	120	
						10,920	

The Anarchist Cookbook - May 21, 2001 Page 3

Continuation of Account 809-30

Acct No	Description	Amount	Units	X	Rate	Subtotal	Total
	Air Fares						
	Puck	1	FCRT	1	25.0	25	
	Double D	1	FCRT	1	1,620	1,620	
	Johnny Black	1	FCRT	1	25.0	25	
	Johnny Red	1	FCRT	1	620	620	
	Karla	1	FCRT	1	1,120	1,120	
	Jody	1	FCRT	1	455	455	
	Sweeney	1	FCRT	1	620	620	
	Gin	1	FCRT	1	350	350	
	Mrs. Gold	1	FCRT	1	120	120	
	Moonchild	1	FCRT	1	620	620	
	Susie	1	FCRT	1	290	290	
						5,865	
	Airport Pickups	11	rt	1	114	1,254	
	Total						29,769
809-49	Insurance Exams						
		1	Allow	1	2,000	2,000	
	Total						2,000
Account Total for 809-00							**295,855**
810-00	**Total Fringes**						
	FICA	6.2%			06,085.03	6,577	
	FUI	0.8%			70,085.4	561	
	SAG	11%			44,086.18	26,849	
	Medicare	1.45%			06,085.03	1,538	
	CA SUI	5.4%			28,000	1,512	
	ATL check fee	8	Weeks		525	525	
	TX WC	2.87%			53,085.4	1,524	
	TX SUI	6.27%			44,085.4	2,764	
	CA WC	2.45%			42,999.63	1,053	
							42,904
	Total Above-The-Line						**451,036**
811-00 PRODUCTION STAFF							
811-01	Production Manager						
	Prep	4.33	Weeks	1	1,500	6,495	
	Shoot	4.17	Weeks	1	1,800	7,506	
	Wrap	1.5	Weeks	1	1,500	2,250	
	Total						16,251
811-02	1st Assistant Director						
	Prep	2	Weeks	1	1,200	2,400	
	Shoot	4	Weeks	1	1,500	6,000	
	Total						8,400
811-03	2nd A.D.'s & Trainee						
	2nd Assistant Director						
	Prep	1	Week	1	1,000	1,000	
	Shoot	4	Weeks	1	1,000	4,000	
	Wrap	0.33	Weeks	1	1,000	330	
	Total						5,330
811-04	Script Supervisor						
	13 hrs/day shoot						
	Prep	1	Week	1	1,500	1,500	
	Shoot	4	Weeks	1	1,500	6,000	
	Total						7,500
811-05	Location Manager						
	Prep	1.67	Weeks	1	1,500	2,505	
	Shoot	4	Weeks	1	1,500	6,000	
	Wrap	1	Week	1	1,500	1,500	
						10,005	
	Additional						
	Assistant Loc Mgr #1	6	Days	1	250	1,500	
	Assistant Loc Mgr #2	14.5	Days	1	250	3,625	
	Assistant Loc Mgr #3	30	Days	1	100.0	3,000	
	Location PA	2	Days	1	100.0	200	
	Assistant Loc Mgr #4	5	Weeks	1	500	2,500	
	Additional Labor	15	Allow	1	100.0	1,500	
	Total						22,330
811-07	Production Coordinators						
	Production Coordinator						

Continuation of Account 811-07

Acct No	Description	Amount	Units	X	Rate	Subtotal	Total
	Prep	3.33	Weeks	1	720	2,397	
	Shoot	4	Weeks	1	720	2,880	
	Wrap	1.5	Weeks	1	720	1,080	
						6,358	
	Production Secretary						
	Prep	4.33	Weeks	1	500	2,165	
	Shoot	4	Weeks	1	500	2,000	
	Wrap	1.5	Weeks	1	500	750	
						4,915	
	Additional help	2	Weeks	1	600	1,200	
						1,200	
	Total						12,473
811-08	Prod. Accts. & Assists.						
	Production Accountant						
	Prep	1.83	Weeks	1	1,200	2,196	
	Shoot	4	Weeks	1	1,200	4,800	
	Wrap	1.5	Weeks	1	1,200	1,800	
						8,796	
	Payroll Clerk						
	Prep	0.33	Weeks	1	800	264	
	Shoot	4	Weeks	1	800	3,200	
	Wrap	1.5	Weeks	1	800	1,200	
						4,664	
	Total						13,460
811-09	Production Assistants						
	Production Assit #1	4.33	Weeks	1	600	2,598	
	Production Asst #2	4.33	Weeks	1	600	2,598	
	Additional M/Days	8	Days	1	100.0	800	
	Total						5,996
811-12	Pre-Prod. Breakdown						
	Preliminary Board and Budget	1	Allow	1	1,500	1,500	
	Total						1,500
811-51	Purchases						
		1	Allow	1	500	500	
	Total						500
811-58	Car & Box Rentals						
	Computer Rentals						
	UPM	10	Weeks	1	50.0	500	
	Production Coordinator	10	Weeks	1	50.0	500	
	Assistant Director	6	Weeks	1	50.0	300	
	Accountant	8	Weeks	1	50.0	400	
	Total						1,700
Account Total for 811-00							**95,440**
813-00 CAMERA							
813-01	Director Of Photography						
	Prep	1.83	Weeks	1	2,500	4,575	
	Shoot	4	Weeks	1	2,500	10,000	
	Total						14,575
813-02	Camera Operator						
	Steadicam Operator	4	Days	1	500	2,000	
	Total						2,000
813-03	First Assist Camera						
	13 hrs/day						
	Prep	0.3	Weeks	1	1,500	450	
	Shoot	4	Weeks	1	1,500	6,000	
	Wrap	0.17	Weeks	1	1,500	255	
	Total						6,705
813-04	Second Assist Camera						
	2nd Camera Assistant						
	Prep	0.16	Weeks	1	900	144	
	Shoot	4	Weeks	1	900	3,600	
	Wrap	0.16	Weeks	1	900	144	
	Total						3,888
813-08	Loader						
		4	Weeks	1	600	2,400	
	Total						2,400

Acct No	Description	Amount	Units	X	Rate	Subtotal	Total
813-11	Loss and Damage						
		1	Allow	1	1,500	1,500	
	Total						1,500
813-51	Purchases						
		1	Allow	1	500	500	
	Total						500
813-56	Rentals						
	Camera Package						
	Shoot	4.3	Weeks	1	6,800	29,240	
	DV Allowance	5	Weeks	1	300	1,500	
	Steadicam Camera	1	Allow	1	1,000	1,000	
	16 mm Camera	4	Weeks	1	1,600	6,400	
	Video Sync	1	Allow	1	1,000	1,000	
	Additional Equipment	1	Allow	1	4,585	4,585	
	Total						43,725
813-58	Box Rental						
	1st Camera Assistant	5	Weeks	1	50.0	250	
	Total						250
Account Total for 813-00							**75,543**
814-00 ART DEPARTMENT							
814-02	Art Director & Assistant						
	Prep	4	Weeks	1	2,000	8,000	
	Shoot	4.17	Weeks	1	2,000	8,340	
	Wrap	0	Weeks	1	2,000	0	
	Total						16,340
814-04	Illustrators						
	Graphic Artist	2	Weeks	1	500	1,000	
	Total						1,000
814-06	Production Assistants						
		8.33	Weeks	1	600	4,998	
	Total						4,998
814-11	Blueprinting						
		1	Allow	1	1,000	1,000	
	Total						1,000
814-51	Purchases/Research						
		1	Allow	1	250	250	
	Total						250
814-58	Car and Box Rentals						
	Computer	6.4	Weeks	1	50.0	320	
	Total						320
Account Total for 814-00							**23,908**
816-00 SPECIAL EFFECTS							
816-01	Effects Coordinator						
	Key Effects						
	12 hrs/day						
	Prep	1	Day	1	400	400	
	Shoot	3	Days	1	400	1,200	
	Total						1,600
816-51	Purchases						
		1	Allow	1	100.0	100	
	Total						100
816-56	Rentals						
		1	Allow	1	100.0	100	
	Total						100
Account Total for 816-00							**1,800**
817-00 SET OPERATIONS							
817-01	First Company Grip						
	Key Grip						
	Also pushes dolly						
	12 hrs/day, 250/day						
	Prep	1	Week	1	1,500	1,500	
	Shoot	4	Weeks	1	1,500	6,000	
	Total						7,500
817-02	Second Company Grip						
	Best Boy						
	200/Day						
	Prep	1	Week	1	1,200	1,200	

Continuation of Account 817-02

Acct No	Description	Amount	Units	X	Rate	Subtotal	Total
	Shoot	4	Weeks	1	1,200	4,800	
	Wrap	0.3	Weeks	1	1,200	360	
	Total						6,360
817-04	Company Grip						
	Grip #1						
	12 hrs/day						
	Prep	0.33	Weeks	1	1,000	330	
	Shoot	4	Weeks	1	1,000	4,000	
	Wrap	0.33	Weeks	1	1,000	330	
						4,660	
	Grip #2						
	12 hrs/day						
	Prep	0.33	Weeks	1	1,000	330	
	Shoot	4	Weeks	1	1,000	4,000	
	Wrap	0.33	Weeks	1	1,000	330	
						4,660	
	Additional Labor	15	Days	1	166	2,490	
	Total						11,810
817-07	Craft Service Labor						
	Craft Service						
	13 hrs/day shoot						
	Prep	0.5	Weeks	1	720	360	
	Shoot	4	Weeks	1	720	2,880	
	Wrap	0.17	Weeks	1	720	122	
	Total						3,362
817-11	Loss & Damage						
		1	Allow	1	500	500	
	Total						500
817-16	First Aid & Expenses						
	1st Aid - shoot	4	Weeks	1	1,200	4,800	
	Expendables	1	Allow	1	500	500	
	Total						5,300
817-51	Purchases						
		1	Allow	1	3,000	3,000	
	Total						3,000
817-52	Craft Service Purchases						
	Incl. occasional 2nd meal	24	Days	1	500	12,000	
	Total						12,000
817-56	Grip Rental						
	Main Package	4	Weeks	1	1,400	5,600	
	Crane	3	Days	1	1,000	3,000	
	Dolly	4	Weeks	1	900	3,600	
	Total						12,200
817-58	Box Rentals						
	Key Grip	4	Weeks	1	200	800	
	Craft Service	4	Weeks	1	500	2,000	
	1st Aid Kit	24	Days	1	50.0	1,200	
	Total						4,000
Account Total for 817-00							**66,032**
819-00 ELECTRICAL							
819-01	Chief Lighting Technician						
	Gaffer						
	12 hrs/day, 225/day						
	Prep	1	Week	1	1,500	1,500	
	Shoot	4	Weeks	1	1,500	6,000	
	Total						7,500
819-02	Asst Chief Lighting Tech						
	Best Boy						
	Prep	1	Week	1	1,200	1,200	
	Shoot	4	Weeks	1	1,200	4,800	
	Wrap	0.3	Weeks	1	1,200	360	
	Total						6,360
819-03	Light Technicians						
	Lamp Operator #1						
	12 hrs/day						
	Prep	0.33	Weeks	1	1,000	330	
	Shoot	4	Weeks	1	1,000	4,000	
	Wrap	0.33	Weeks	1	1,000	330	

The Anarchist Cookbook - May 21, 2001 Page 7

Continuation of Account 819-03

Acct No	Description	Amount	Units	X	Rate	Subtotal	Total
						4,660	
	Lamp Operator #2						
	12 hrs/day						
	Prep	0.33	Weeks	1	1,000	330	
	Shoot	4	Weeks	1	1,000	4,000	
	Wrap	0.33	Weeks	1	1,000	330	
						4,660	
	Additional Labor	14	M/Days	1	166	2,324	
						2,324	
	Total						11,644
819-11	Loss and Damage						
		1	Allow	1	2,500	2,500	
	Total						2,500
819-51	Purchases						
		1	Allow	1	3,000	3,000	
	Total						3,000
819-56	Rentals						
	Electrical Package	4	Weeks	1	3,800	15,200	
	Total						15,200
819-58	Box Rental						
	Gaffer	4	Weeks	1	200	800	
	Total						800
Account Total for 819-00							**47,004**
821-00 SET DRESSING							
821-01	Set Decorator						
	Set Decorator						
	Prep	2	Weeks	1	1,500	3,000	
	Shoot	4	Weeks	1	1,500	6,000	
	Wrap	1	Week	1	1,500	1,500	
	Total						10,500
821-03	Swing Gang						
	Swing #1						
	Prep	1.33	Weeks	1	750	997	
	Shoot	4	Weeks	1	750	3,000	
	Wrap	0.5	Weeks	1	750	375	
						4,373	
	Swing #2						
	Prep	1.33	Weeks	1	750	997	
	Shoot	4	Weeks	1	750	3,000	
	Wrap	0.5	Weeks	1	750	375	
						4,373	
	Total						8,745
821-11	Loss, Damage & Clean						
		1	Allow	1	2,000	2,000	
	Total						2,000
821-51	Set Dressing Purchases & Rentals						
	Purchase and Rentals	1	Allow	1	33,825	33,825	
	Total						33,825
Account Total for 821-00							**55,070**
823-00 ACTION PROPS							
823-01	Propmaster						
	Propmaster						
	Prep	1	Week	1	1,500	1,500	
	Shoot	4	Weeks	1	1,500	6,000	
	Wrap	1	Week	1	1,500	1,500	
	Total						9,000
823-02	Assistant Propmaster						
	Prop Assistant						
	Prep	1.33	Weeks	1	750	997	
	Shoot	4	Weeks	1	750	3,000	
	Wrap	1	Week	1	750	750	
	Total						4,748
823-51	Purchases						
		1	Allow	1	10,000	10,000	
	Total						10,000
823-58	Car & Box Rental						

The Anarchist Cookbook - May 21, 2001 Page 8

Continuation of Account 823-58

Acct No	Description	Amount	Units	X	Rate	Subtotal	Total
	Propmaster Box	4	Weeks	1	120	480	
	Total						480
Account Total for 823-00							**24,228**
825-00 PICT. VEH. & ANIMALS							
825-01	Picture Vehicles						
	8 cop cars	1	Day	8	200	1,600	
	Bus	2	Days	1	200	400	
	cop car	5	Days	1	200	1,000	
	Total						3,000
825-10	Animals						
	20 cows	1	Allow	1	500	500	
	5 Minks	2		5	100.0	1,000	
	Total						1,500
825-12	Wranglers & Handlers						
	Trainer #1	3	Days	1	400	1,200	
	Trainer #2	1	Day	1	400	400	
	Total						1,600
Account Total for 825-00							**6,100**
829-00 EXTRA TALENT							
829-01	Standins						
	Standin #1	4	Weeks	1	600	2,400	
	Standin #2	4	Weeks	1	600	2,400	
	Total						4,800
829-02	Extras						
	Non-union 60/10hrs						
	Day 1	2	M/Days	1	60.0	120	
	Day 2	12	M/Days	1	60.0	720	
	Day 3	7	M/Days	1	60.0	420	
	Day 4	20	M/Days	1	60.0	1,200	
	Day 5	12	M/Days	1	60.0	720	
	Day 6	22	M/Days	1	60.0	1,320	
	Day 7	22	M/Days	1	60.0	1,320	
	Day 8	13	M/Days	1	60.0	780	
	Day 9	56	M/Days	1	60.0	3,360	
	Day 10	53	M/Days	1	60.0	3,180	
	Day 11	30	M/Days	1	60.0	1,800	
	Day 12	50	M/Days	1	60.0	3,000	
	Day 13	7	M/Days	1	60.0	420	
	Day 14	30	M/Days	1	60.0	1,800	
	Day 15	26	M/Days	1	60.0	1,560	
	Day 16	16	M/Days	1	60.0	960	
	Day 17	30	M/Days	1	60.0	1,800	
	Day 18	31	M/Days	1	60.0	1,860	
	Day 19	12	M/Days	1	60.0	720	
	Day 20	20	M/Days	1	60.0	1,200	
	Day 21	12	M/Days	1	60.0	720	
	Day 22	0	M/Days	1	60.0	0	
	Day 23	13	M/Days	1	60.0	780	
	Day 24	11	M/Days	1	60.0	660	
	Total						30,420
829-39	Extras Casting Ser. Fee						
	Extras Casting Director						
	Prep	1	Week	1	1,000	1,000	
	Shoot	4	Weeks	1	1,000	4,000	
						5,000	
	Casting Assistant	4	Days	1	150	600	
	Total						5,600
Account Total for 829-00							**40,820**
831-00 COSTUME							
831-01	Designer/Supervisor						
	Prep	1.33	Weeks	1	1,500	1,995	
	Shoot	4	Weeks	1	1,500	6,000	
	Wrap	1	Week	1	1,500	1,500	
	Total						9,495
831-06	Costume Labor						

Continuation of Account 831-06

Acct No	Description	Amount	Units	X	Rate	Subtotal	Total
	Costumer						
	Prep	1.33	Weeks	1	1,000	1,330	
	Shoot	4	Weeks	1	1,000	4,000	
	Wrap	0.67	Weeks	1	1,000	670	
						6,000	
	PA	6	Weeks	1	600	3,600	
	Total						9,600
831-10	Cleaning & Dyeing						
	Cleaning	1	Allow	1	3,000	3,000	
	Total						3,000
831-51	Purchases						
	Purchases and Rentals	1	Allow	1	17,000	17,000	
	Total						17,000
831-58	Car and Box Rentals						
	Costume Designer/Supervisor	6	Weeks	1	50.0	300	
	Total						300
Account Total for 831-00							**39,395**
833-00 MAKEUP & HAIR							
833-01	Makeup Artists						
	Makeup Artist	4	Weeks	1	1,500	6,000	
	Second Makeup	1.5	Weeks	1	1,000	1,500	
	Total						7,500
833-05	Hairstylists						
	Hairstylist	4	Weeks	1	1,500	6,000	
	Second Hair	1.5	Weeks	1	1,000	1,500	
	Total						7,500
833-10	Makeup Supplies						
		1	Allow	1	925	925	
	Total						925
833-12	Hairdressing Supplies						
		1	Allow	1	925	925	
	Total						925
833-58	Box Rental						
	Makeup	24	Days	1	25.0	600	
	Second Makeup	9	Days	1	25.0	225	
	Hairstylist	24	Days	1	25.0	600	
	Second Hair	9	Days	1	25.0	225	
	Total						1,650
Account Total for 833-00							**18,500**
835-00 SOUND							
835-01	Mixer						
	Mixer						
	Prep	0.17	Weeks	1	1,800	306	
	Shoot	4	Weeks	1	1,800	7,200	
	Total						7,506
835-02	Boom Operator						
		4	Weeks	1	1,500	6,000	
	Total						6,000
835-04	Playback Operator						
		2	Days	1	1,000	2,000	
	Total						2,000
835-51	Purchases						
		1	Allow	1	700	700	
	Total						700
835-56	Rentals						
	Sound Package	4	Weeks	1	1,200	4,800	
	Walkie Talkies	24	Days	30	6.0	4,320	
	Video Playback	2	Days	1	300	600	
	Total						9,720
Account Total for 835-00							**25,926**
837-00 LOCATION							
837-01	Site Fees & Rentals						
	Fees and Rentals	24	Days	1	2,000	48,000	
	Modifications & Restoration	1	Allow	1	40,000	40,000	
	Clean out attic	1	Allow	1	1,000	1,000	
	Set Chairs	1	Allow	1	1,866	1,866	

The Anarchist Cookbook - May 21, 2001 Page 10

Continuation of Account 837-01

Acct No	Description	Amount	Units	X	Rate	Subtotal	Total
	Total						90,866
837-02	Police/Firemen/Watchmen						
	Police	10	Days	2	400	8,000	
	Set Watchman						
	$15/hr 24/7	4.17	Weeks	1	2,520	10,508	
	Total						18,508
837-03	Scouting						
	Scouting Photos	1	Allow	1	500	500	
	Total						500
837-05	Travel Fares						
	Gas & Motel						
	Editor	1	Allow	1	500	500	
	Asst. Editor	1	Allow	1	500	500	
	Total						1,000
837-08	Living Expenses/Per Diems						
	Production Designer	58	Days	1	30.0	1,740	
	Editor	33	Days	1	30.0	990	
	Asst. Editor	33	Days	1	30.0	990	
	Total						3,720
837-09	Meals/Catering						
	Catered Meals	24	Days	80	12.5	24,000	
	Ice, Water & Propane	1	Allow	1	1,000	1,000	
	Total						25,000
837-15	Film Shipping						
		24	Days	1	200	4,800	
	Total						4,800
837-16	Baggage & Equipment Ship						
		1	Allow	1	500	500	
	Total						500
837-18	Mileage & Parking						
		1	Allow	1	2,500	2,500	
	Total						2,500
837-30	Location Restoration						
		1	Allow	1	1,000	1,000	
	Total						1,000
837-51	Purchases						
		1		1	3,000	3,000	
	Total						3,000
837-52	Office Rentals						
	Offices Cleanup	1	Allow	1	1,000	1,000	
	Total						1,000
837-54	Phone & Postage						
	Phone	1	Allow	1	5,000	5,000	
	Postage/FedEx	1	Allow	1	1,000	1,000	
	Total						6,000
837-56	Office Equipment Rental						
		1	Allow	1	2,000	2,000	
	Total						2,000
Account Total for 837-00							**160,394**
839-00 TRANSPORTATION							
839-02	Transportation Captains						
	Drives a Stake Bed Truck	5	Weeks	113	23.62	13,345	
	Total						13,345
839-03	Studio Drivers						
	Camera						
	Prep	0.2	Weeks	88	18.96	333	
	Shoot	4	Weeks	106	18.96	8,039	
	Wrap	0.2	Weeks	88	18.96	333	
	Holiday	1	Day	8	18.96	151	
						8,858	
	Grip/Elec						
	Prep	0.4	Weeks	88	23.32	820	
	Shoot	4	Weeks	106	23.32	9,887	
	Wrap	0.4	Weeks	88	23.32	820	
	Holiday	1	Day	8	23.32	186	
						11,716	
	Props/Special FX						

Continuation of Account 839-03

Acct No	Description	Amount	Units	X	Rate	Subtotal	Total
	Prep	0.2	Weeks	88	18.96	333	
	Shoot	4	Weeks	106	18.96	8,039	
	Wrap	0.2	Weeks	88	18.96	333	
	Holiday	1	Day	8	18.96	151	
						8,858	
	Honey Wagon #1						
	Shoot	4	Weeks	106	21.54	9,132	
	Holiday	1	Day	8	21.54	172	
						9,305	
	Honey Wagon #2						
	Shoot	3	Days	17	21.54	1,098	
						1,099	
	Set Dressing 24'						
	Prep	1	Week	88	18.96	1,668	
	Shoot	4	Weeks	106	18.96	8,039	
	Wrap	1	Week	88	18.96	1,668	
	Holiday	1	Day	8	18.96	151	
						11,528	
	Maxivan						
	Driven by PA						
	Stakebed						
	Driven by Captain						
						0	
	Cook Driver						
	Prep	2	Days	1	400	800	
	Shoot	24	Days	1	300	7,200	
						8,000	
	Cook Helper	24	Days	1	150	3,600	
	Addition Help	10	Days	1	125	1,250	
						4,850	
	Total						64,214
839-12	Repairs/Maintenance						
		1	Allow	1	2,500	2,500	
	Total						2,500
839-23	Gas & Oil						
		1	Allow	1	10,000	10,000	
	Total						10,000
839-24	Tolls & Permit						
		1	Allow	1	1,000	1,000	
	Total						1,000
839-51	Purchases						
		1	Allow	1	500	500	
	Total						500
839-54	Location Self Drives						
	Producer	6	Weeks	1	150	900	
	Producer	5	Weeks	1	150	750	
	Production Designer	6	Weeks	1	150	900	
	Total						2,550
839-56	Studio Vehicles						
	Camera	5	Weeks	1	425	2,125	
	15' Cube van						
	Grip/Elec	5	Weeks	1	1,594	7,970	
	Wardrobe trlr	4.5	Weeks	1	480	2,160	
	Pulled by stakebed						
	Props/Special FX	5	Weeks	1	375	1,875	
	Ryder truck						
	Honey Wagon #1	5	Weeks	1	1,275	6,375	
	Honeywagon #2	1	Week	1	1,275	1,275	
	Set Dressing 5 ton	5.5	Weeks	1	375	2,062	
	24' Ryder						
	Stake Bed	5	Weeks	1	375	1,875	

Continuation of Account 839-56

Acct No	Description	Amount	Units	X	Rate	Subtotal	Total
	Maxivan	5	Weeks	1	250	1,250	
	Total						26,968
839-58	Cranes & Insert Cars						
		1	Allow	1	7,500	7,500	
	Total						7,500
Account Total for 839-00							**128,577**
841-00 FILM & LAB							
841-01	Raw Stock						
	35mm Kodak						
	5,000 feet/day						
	Raw Stock						
	Total: 95, 000 ft	19	Days	5,000	0.51977	49,378	
	16mm						
	Raw Stock	6	Days	1,700	0.3	3,060	
						52,438	
	Total						52,438
841-02	Negative Develop						
	Processing at Fotokem						
	35mm						
	Develop 90%	19	Days	4,500	0.115	9,832	
	16mm						
	Develop 90%	9,000	FT	1	0.115	1,035	
	Total						10,868
841-04	1/4" Sound Stock						
	DAT	24	Days	1	15.0	360	
	Total						360
841-05	Sound Transfer						
	Sound Transfers						
	(70% of 4500' + 15%	24	Days	3,623	0.085	7,390	
	Total						7,391
841-06	Video Cassettes						
	Telecine for editing						
	100,000 Feet	78	Hours	1	160	12,480	
	Key number prep	100	reels	1	10.0	1,000	
	Video stock - DVCAM	20	cassettes	1	42.5	850	
	Tape Stock	1	Allow	1	700	700	
	Telecine 16mm	3	Days	1	325	975	
	Total						16,005
841-51	Polaroid Film						
	For all departments	1	Allow	1	1,000	1,000	
	Total						1,000
Account Total for 841-00							**88,062**
843-00 TESTS							
843-51	Purchases						
		1	Allow	1	500	500	
	Total						500
843-56	Rentals						
		1	Allow	1	600	600	
	Total						600
Account Total for 843-00							**1,100**
847-00 SECOND UNIT							
847-13	Camera						
	Camera Assistant	5	Days	1	250	1,250	
	Total						1,250
Account Total for 847-00							**1,250**
849-00	**Total Fringes**						
	FICA	6.2%			426,912.9	26,469	
	FUI	0.8%			57,426.04	2,859	
	Medicare	1.45%			426,912.9	6,190	
	Dallas Teamster weekly	210	Weeks		6,342	6,342	
	Payroll Fee	0.25%			424,912.9	1,062	

Acct No	Description	Amount	Units	X	Rate	Subtotal	Total
	TX WC	2.87%			426,912.9	12,252	
	TX SUI	6.27%			92,344.28	24,600	
							79,775
	Total Production						**978,924**
851-00 EDITING & PROJECTION							
851-01	Film Editors						
	Editor	20	Weeks	1	2,500	50,000	
	Total						50,000
851-02	Asst. Film Editors						
	Assistant	20	Weeks	1	800	16,000	
	Total						16,000
851-12	Negative Cutting						
	10 Reels	10	reels	1	1,150	11,500	
	Total						11,500
851-15	Post Ship/Messenger						
		1	Allow	1	500	500	
	Total						500
851-51	Purchases						
		1	Allow	1	500	500	
	Total						500
Account Total for 851-00							**78,500**
853-00 MUSIC							
853-01	Clearances						
	All Costs	1	Allow	1	75,000	75,000	
	Total						75,000
Account Total for 853-00							**75,000**
855-00 SOUND (POST PRODUCTION)							
855-06	Sound FX Package						
	All costs	1	Allow	1	105,000	105,000	
	Total						105,000
Account Total for 855-00							**105,000**
857-00 POST PRODUCTION FILM & LAB							
857-03	Stock Shots-Purchase						
		1	Allow	1	25,000	25,000	
	Total						25,000
857-06	Tape to Tape Transfers						
		1	Allow	1	2,500	2,500	
	Total						2,500
857-07	Lab Special Handling						
	Film out from DVCam	1	Allow	1	6,000	6,000	
	Total						6,000
857-08	Video Cassettes/Tape						
		1	Allow	1	250	250	
	Total						250
857-17	Optical Sound Track						
	Develope & Print Opt Neg	10,000	feet	1	0.458	4,580	
	Total						4,580
857-40	Answer Print						
	Composite Answer Print	10,000	Feet	1	1.2864	12,864	
	Total						12,864
Account Total for 857-00							**51,194**
859-00 TITLES & OPTICALS							
859-01	Main & End Titles						
		1	Allow	1	10,000	10,000	
	Total						10,000
Account Total for 859-00							**10,000**
860-00	**Total Fringes**						
	FICA	6.2%			66,000	4,092	
	FUI	0.8%			14,000	112	
	Medicare	1.45%			66,000	957	
	CA SUI	5.4%			14,000	756	
	CA WC	2.45%			66,000	1,617	
							7,534

Acct No	Description	Amount	Units	X	Rate	Subtotal	Total
	Total Post Production						**327,228**
861-00 INSURANCE							
861-03	Negative Insurance						
	Producer's Package						
	Estimate	1	Allow	1	27,500	27,500	
	Total						27,500
Account Total for 861-00							**27,500**
862-00 PUBLICITY							
862-08	Film & Processing						
		1	Allow	1	500	500	
	Total						500
Account Total for 862-00							**500**
865-00 GENERAL EXPENSES							
865-01	MPAA Seal						
		1	Allow	1	4,000	4,000	
	Total						4,000
865-11	Legal Fees						
	Legal Services	1	Allow	1	250	250	
	Total						250
865-12	Bank/Exchange Costs						
		1		1	500	500	
	Total						500
865-51	Office Purchases						
	Allowance	1	Allow	1	2,000	2,000	
	Total						2,000
865-55	Computers and Software						
	Accounting System	1	Allow	1	2,250	2,250	
	Total						2,250
Account Total for 865-00							**9,000**
870-00 CONTINGENCY							
870-01	Contingency						
		1	Allow	1	200,000	200,000	
	Total						200,000
Account Total for 870-00							**200,000**
	Total Other						**237,000**
	Total Above-The-Line						**451,036**
	Total Below-The-Line						**1,543,152**
	Total Above and Below-The-Line						**1,994,188**
	Grand Total						**1,994,188**

Shooting the Locket Sequence in *Robin Hood: Men in Tights*

To film the sequence discussed in Chapter 3, we were unable to use computer generated effects or any other visual effects method. In order to keep the expense down, it was necessary to shoot all of the shots in real time and make them work as scripted. This took a fair amount of ingenuity on the part of the production designer, special effects crew, and the director of photography.

An archway which appeared to be made of stone was actually made of wood and plaster, and was erected at an angle so that when the locket was swung on a wire, it would strike the archway in the center of its vault. When the locket hit the arch, a small explosive charge in the locket was detonated, causing it to shatter and release large pieces of gold glitter as well as a key that had been planted in it. This was filmed several times in slow motion with several prepared lockets until we were sure that we had the key emerging correctly from the explosion.

The key was then filmed several times more in slow motion, tumbling by in front of the lens of the camera. This gave us several shots showing the key descending through the air, and falling end over end. Finally, the key was inserted into the lock on the chastity belt with an air hose inserted into the lock from the far side so that the hose would not be visible. The camera was inverted, and once again in slow motion, the key was filmed as it was blown out of the lock with a puff of air. Once that piece of film was developed, printed, and reversed end for end, it appeared as though the key was miraculously flying into the lock.

Sources of Supply and Information

Budgeting and Scheduling Software

Movie Magic (EP) Budgeting
Movie Magic (EP) Scheduling
Entertainment Partners
http://www.entertainmentpartners.com

Production Pro Budgeting
Set Management, Inc.
http://www.setmanagement.com

Showbiz Budgeting
Media Services, Inc.
http://www.media-services.com

SunFrog Film Scheduling
Sunfrog Technologies LLC
http://sunfrog-tech.com/default.htm

Completion Bond Services

cineFinance llc
Los Angeles
Fred Milstein
1875 Century Park East, Suite 1345
Los Angeles, CA 90067
Phone: (310) 226-6800
Fax: (310) 226-6810
fmilstein@cinefinance.net
New York
Jim Berger
36 West 44th Street, Suite 600
NY, NY 10036
Phone: (212) 266-0202
Fax: (212) 266-0211
jberger@hccsu.com
http://www.cinefinance.net
(cineFinance prefers projects with budgets over $2 million.)

Film Finances, Inc.
9000 Sunset Boulevard, Suite 1400
Los Angeles, California 90069
Phone: (310) 275-7323
Fax: (310) 275-1706
http://www.ffi.com

International Film Guarantors (IFG)
10940 Wilshire Blvd.
Suite 2010
Los Angeles, CA 90024
Phone: (310) 208-4500
Fax: (310) 443-8998
http://www.ifgbonds.com

Film Commissions (Domestic)

Alabama Film Office
(334) 242-4195
http://www.alabamafilm.org
film@ado.state.al.us

Alaska Film Program
(907) 269-8190
http://www.commerce.state.ak.us/oed/film
alaskafilm@commerce.state.ak.us

Arizona Film Commission
(602) 771-1193
(800) 523-6695
http://www.azcommerce.com/film

Arkansas Film Office
(501) 682-7676
http://www.1800arkansas.com/film
jglass@1800arkansas.com

California Film Commission
(323) 860-2960
800-858-4749
http://www.film.ca.gov
filmca@film.ca.gov

Los Angeles Entertainment Industry Development Corp
(323) 957-1000
http://www.eidc.com
info@eidc.com

Malibu City Film Commission
(805) 495-7521
http://www.ci.malibu.ca.us
kim@sws-inc.com

Orange County Film Commission
(714) 278-7569
http://www.ocfilm.org
jarrington@fullerton.edu

Pasadena Film Office
(626) 744-3964
http://www.filmpasadena.com
apenn@cityofpasadena.net

San Diego Film Commission
(619) 234-3456
http://www.sdfilm.com
info@sdfilm.com

San Francisco Film Commission
(415) 554-6241
http://www.ci.sf.ca.us/film

San Jose Film & Video Commission
(408) 792-4111
http://www.sanjose.org/filmvideo
kmanley@sanjose.org

Santa Barbara CVB & Film Commission
(805) 966-9222
http://www.filmsantabarbara.com
martine@filmsantabarbara.com

Santa Clarita Valley Film Office
(661) 284-1425
http://www.santa-clarita.com/film/office/asp
film@santaclarita.com

Santa Monica Public Works, Construction & Film Permits
(310) 458-8737
http://www.santa-monica.org
vee.gomez@smgov.net
kathy.ruff@smgov.net

Santa Monica Mountains NRA
(805) 370-2308
http://www.nps.gov/samo
alice_allen@nps.gov

West Hollywood Film Office
(323) 848-6561
http://www.weho.org
wehofilm@weho.org

Colorado Film Commission
(303) 620-4500
http://www.coloradofilm.org
coloradofilm@state.co.us

Connecticut Commission on Culture & Tourism
(860) 571-7130
http://www.ctfilm.com
info@ctfilm.com

Delaware Film Office
(302) 672-6857
http://www.state.de.us/dedo/default.shtml
christine.serio@state.de.us

District of Columbia
Office of Motion
(202) 727-6608
Picture & TV Development
http://film.dc.gov/film/site/default.asp

Florida Film Commission
(850) 410-4765
http://www.filminflorida.com
susan.albershardt@myflorida.com

Georgia Film, Video, & Music Office
(404) 962-4052
http://www.georgia.org/film
film@georgia.org

Hawaii Film Office
(808) 326-2663 (Kona)
(808) 961-8366 (Hilo)
http://www.filmbigisland.com
film@bigisland.com

Idaho Film Bureau
(208) 334-2470
http://www.filmidaho.org
peg.owens@tourism.idaho.gov

Illinois Film Office
(312) 814-7160
http://www.illinoisbiz.biz/film/index.html
bhudgins@commerce.state.il.us

Chicago Film Office
(312) 744-6415
http://www.cityofchicago.org/filmoffice

Indiana Film Commission
(317) 232-8853
http://www.in.gov/film
film@commerce.state.in.us

Iowa Film Office
(515) 242-4726
http://www.iowalifechanging.com/filmiowa
filmiowa@iowalifechanging.com

Kansas Film Commission
(785) 296-2178
http://kdoch.state.ks.us/kdfilm/index.jsp
pjasso@kansascommerce.com

Kentucky Film Office
(502) 564-3456
http://www.kyfilmoffice.com
todd.cassidy@ky.gov

Louisiana Governors Office of Film & TV
(504) 736-7280
http://www.lafilm.org
schott@la.gov

Maine Film Office
(207) 624-7631
http://www.state.me.us/decd/film
lea.girardin@maine.gov

Maryland Film Office
(800) 333-6632
http://www.marylandfilm.org
filminfo@marylandfilm.org

Massachusetts Film Bureau
(617) 523-8388
http://www.massfilmbureau.com
massfilmbureau@aol.com

Michigan Film Office
(800) 477-3456
http://www.michigan.gov/hal
jlockwood@michigan.gov

Minnesota Film and TV Board
(651) 645-3600
http://www.mnfilmandtv.com
info@mnfilm.org

Mississippi Film Office
(601) 359-3297
http://www.visitmississippi.org/film
wernling@mississippi.org

Missouri Film Commission
(573) 751-9050
http://www.missouribusiness.net/film/index.asp
mofilm@ded.mo.us

Montana Film Office
(800) 553-4563
http://www.montanafilm.com
montanafilm@visitmt.com

Nebraska Film Office
(800) 228-4307
http://www.filmnebraska.org
info@filmnebraska.org

Nevada Film Office
(877) 638-3456 (Las Vegas)
(775) 687-1814 (Reno/Tahoe/Carson City)
http://www.nevadafilm.com
lvnfo@bizopp.state.nv.us
ccnfo@bizopp.state.nv.us

New Hampshire Film & TV Office
(603) 271-2665
http://www.filmnh.com
filmnh@dred.state.nh.us

New Jersey Motion Picture/ TV Commission
(973) 648-6279
http://www.njfilm.org
NJFILM@njfilm.org

New Mexico Film Office
(800) 545-9871
http://www.nmfilm.com/
film@nmfilm.com

New York Governor's Office for Motion Picture & Television Development
(212) 803-2330
http://www.nylovesfilm.com

New York City Mayor's Office of Film, Theater, & Broadcasting
(212) 489-6710
http://www.nyc.gov/film

North Carolina Film Office
(919) 733-9900
http://www.ncfilm.com
barnold@ncfilm.com

North Dakota Film Commission
(701) 328-2525
http://www.ndtourism.com

Ohio Film Commission
(614) 466-8844
http://www.ohiofilm.com

Oklahoma Film & Music Office
(800) 766-3456
http://www.oklahomafilm.org
filminfo@oklahomafilm.org

Oregon Film & Video Office
(503) 229-5832
http://www.oregonfilm.org
shoot@oregonfilm.org

Pennsylvania Film Office
(717) 783-3456
http://www.filminpa.com
jshecter@state.pa.us

Rhode Island Film and TV Office
(401) 222-3456
http://www.rifilm.com
steven@arts.ri.gov

South Carolina Film Commission
(803) 737-0490
http://www.scfilmoffice.com
filmsc@sccommerce.com

South Dakota Film Office
(605) 773-3301
http://www.filmsd.com
ann.garry@state.sd.us

Tennessee Film, Entertainment, & Music Commission
(615) 741-3456
http://www.state.tn.us/film/main.htm
tn.film@state.tn.us

Texas Film Commission
(512) 463-9200
http://www.governor.state.tx.us/film
film@governor.state.tx.us

Utah Film Commission
(800) 453-8824
http://www.film.utah.org
lvondere@utah.gov

Vermont Film Commission
(802) 828-3618
http://www.vermontfilm.com
vermontfilm@vermontfilm.com

Virginia Film Office
(800) 854-6233
http://www.film.virginia.org
vafilm@virginia.org

Washington State Film Office
(206) 256-6151
http://www.oted.wa.gov/ed/filmoffice
wafilm@cted.wa.gov

West Virginia Film Office
(304) 558-2200 ext. 382
http://www.wvfilm.com
phaynes@callwva.com

Wisconsin Department of Tourism: Communication Bureau
(608) 261-8195
http://www.filmwisconsin.org

Wyoming Film Office
(307) 777-3400
http://www.wyomingfilm.org
info@wyomingfilm.org

Film Commissions (Foreign)

Australia

New South Wales Film and Video Office
+61-2-9264-6400
Fax +61-2-9264-4388
GPO Box 1744
Sydney, NSW 2001, Australia
http://www.fto.nsw.gov.au/about.asp
fto@fto.nsw.gov.au

Queensland
Pacific Film & Television Commission
+61-7-3224-4114
Fax +61-7-3224-6717
GPO Box 94
Brisbane QLD 4002, Australia
http://www.pftc.com.au

Melbourne Film Office
+61-3-9660-3200
Fax +61-3-9660-3201
GPO Box 4361
Melbourne, Victoria 3001, Australia
http://www.film.vic.gov.au
mfo@film.vic.gov.au

Canada
Telefilm Canada
514-283-6363
Fax 514-283-8212
360 St. Jacques Street, Suite 700
Montreal, Quebec, H2Y 4A9
http://www.telefilm.gc.ca/accueil.asp
info@telefilm.qc.ca

Alberta Film Commission
780-422-8584
Fax 780-422-8582
10155 102 Street, 5th Floor
Edmonton, Alberta T5J 4L6 Canada
http://www.albertafilm.ca
dan.chugg@gov.ab.ca

British Columbia Film Commission
604-660-2732
Fax 604-660-4790
865 Hornby Street., Suite 201
Vancouver, BC V6Z 2G3
http://www.bcfilmcommission.com
shootbc@bcfilm.gov.bc.ca

Manitoba Film & Sound
204-947-2040
Fax 204-956-5261
410-93 Lombard Ave
Winnipeg, Manitoba R3B 3B1
http://www.mbfilmsound.mb.ca
explore@mbfilmsound.mb.ca

New Brunswick Film
506-869-6868
Fax 506-869-6840
P.O. Box 5001
Moncton, New Brunswick, E1C 8R3 Canada
http://www.nbfilm.com
nbfilm@gnb.ca

Newfoundland & Labrador Film
709-738-3456
Fax 709-739-1680
12 Kings Bridge Road
St. John's, Newfoundland, A1C 3K3 Canada
http://www.newfilm.nf.net
info@nlfdc.ca

Northwest Territories
NWT Film Commissioner
Industry, Tourism & Investment
867-920-6130
Fax 867-873-0101
P.O. Box 1320
Yellowknife, Northwest Territories, X1A 2L9 Canada
http://www.iti.gov.nt.ca/nwtfilm/index.htm
garry_singer@gov.nt.ca

Nova Scotia Film Development Corporation
902-424-7177 Fax 902-424-0617
1724 Granville Street.
Halifax, NS B3J 1X5 Canada
http://www.film.ns.ca
novascotia.film@ns.sympatico.ca

Ontario Media Development Corporation
416-314-6858
Fax 416-314-6876
175 Bloor Street East, Suite 501, South Tower
http://www.omdc.on.ca
Toronto, ON M4W 3R8 Canada
mail@omdc.on.ca

Prince Edward Island Film Office
902-569-7770
Fax 902-368-6255
94 Euston Street, 2nd Fl
P.O. Box 340
Charlottetown, PEI C1A 7K7 Canada
http://www.techpei.com
techpei@gov.pe.ca

Montreal Film & Television Commission
514-872-2883
Fax 514-872-3409
303 Notre-Dame Street East, 6th Fl
Montreal, QUE H2Y 3Y8 Canada
http://www.montrealfilm.com
film_tv@ville.montreal.qc.ca

Quebec City Area Film & Television Commission
418-641-6766
275 de l'Eglise St., 4th Floor
Quebec (Quebec) G1K 6G7
cctq@ville.quebec.qc.ca

Saskatchewan - Sask Film
306-798-3456
Fax 306-798-7768
1831 College Avenue
Regina, SKSK S4P 3V7
Canada
http://www.saskfilm.com
val@saskfilm.com

Yukon Film Commission
867-667-5400
Fax 867-393-7040
P.O. Box 2703
Whitehorse, Yukon Y1A 2C6 Canada
http://www.reelyukon.com
reel.yukon@gov.yk.ca

England

British Film Commission
+44-20-7861-7860 Fax 44-20-7861-7864
10 Little Portland Street
London, England W1W 7JG
UK
http://www.britfilmcom.co.uk
internationalinfo@ukfilmcouncil.org.uk

Mexico

National Film Commission-Mexico A.C.
(5255) 56-88-78-13 Fax (5255) 56-88-70-27
Av. Division Del Norte #2462 5th Floor, Col. Portales
Mexico City, 03300 Mexico
http://www.conafilm.org.mx
conafilm@prodigy.net.mx

Guilds and Unions

Directors Guild of America (DGA)
Los Angeles Headquarters
7920 Sunset Boulevard
Los Angeles, California 90046
Phone: (310) 289-2000
http://www.dga.org

International Alliance of Theatrical and Stage Employees (IATSE)
1430 Broadway
20th Floor
New York, NY 10018
Phone: (212) 730-1770
http://www.iatse-intl.org

IATSE West Coast Office
10045 Riverside Drive
Toluca Lake, CA 91602
Phone: (818) 980-3499
Fax: (818) 980-3496

Producers Guild of America (PGA)
8530 Wilshire Blvd., Suite 450
Beverly Hills, CA 90211
Phone: (310) 358-9020
Fax: (310) 358-9520
http://www.producersguild.org

Screen Actors Guild of America (SAG)
Hollywood
5757 Wilshire Blvd.
Los Angeles, CA 90036-3600
Phone: (323) 954-1600
New York
360 Madison Avenue 12th Floor
New York, New York 10017
(212) 944-1030
http://www.sag.org

Teamsters Local 399 (Hollywood)
(818) 985-7374
http://www.hollywoodteamsters.org

Writers Guild of America, west (WGAw)
7000 West Third Street
Los Angeles, CA 90048
Phone: (323) 951-4000
Outside CA: (800) 548-4532
Fax: (323) 782-4800
http://www.wga.org

Organizations

Independent Feature Project (IFP)
1964 Westwood Boulevard, Suite 205
Los Angeles, CA 90025-4651
http://www.ifp.org

Payroll Companies

Axium Payroll Services and Technology
300 East Magnolia Boulevard, 6th Floor
Burbank, CA 91502
Phone: (818) 557-2999
Fax: (818) 557-2990
http://www.axiument.com/offices.html

Cast & Crew Entertainment Services, Inc.
100 E. Tujunga Ave., 2nd Floor
Burbank, CA 91502
Phone: (818)848-6022
Fax: (818)848-9484
http://castandcrew.com/www/main.htm

Entertainment Partners
2835 N. Naomi Street, Suite 200
Burbank, CA 91504-2024
Phone: (818) 955-6000
Fax: (818) 845-6507
http://www.ep-services.com

Media Services, Inc. Los Angeles
500 S. Sepulveda Blvd., 4th Floor
Los Angeles, CA 90049
Toll Free: (800) 333-7518
Phone: (310) 440.9600
Fax: (310) 472.9979

Media Services, Inc. New York
30 West 22nd St., 5th Floor
New York, NY 10010
Telephone: 212.366.9390
Toll Free: 866.414.9615
Fax: 212.366.9398
http://www.media-services.com/

Production Boards and Strips

Chalk Hill Books
PO Box 606
Woodland Hills, CA 91365-0606
http://www.chalkhillbooks.com

Hollywood Production Boards
PO Box 461943
Hollywood, CA 90046
Fax: (323) 650-7349

The Writer's Store
2040 Westwood Blvd.
Los Angeles, CA 90025
http://www.writersstore.com

Safety Bulletins

These safety bulletins are published by :

Industry Wide Labor/Management Safety Committee
for the Motion Picture and Television Industry
Contract Services
15503 Ventura Blvd., Encino, CA 91436
Phone: (818) 995-0900

They can be read in their entirety on the Contract Services web site: **http://www.csatf.org/bulletintro.shtml**.

No.	Description
GCSP	General Code of Safe Practices for Production (7/01/02)
1	Recommendations For Safety With Firearms (April 16, 2003)
2	Live Ammunition (April 16, 2003)
3	Guidelines Regarding the Use of Helicopters in Motion Picture Productions (8/15/01)
3A	Addendum "A" to Guidelines for External Loads - Helicopters (8/15/01)
4	Stunts (5/28/97)
5	Safety Awareness (6/19/02)
6	Animal Handling Rules for the Motion Picture Industry (1/21/98)
7	SCUBA Equipment Recommendations for the Motion Picture Industry (10/3/95)
8	Guidelines for Insert Camera Cars (11/12/96)
8A	Addendum "A" Process Trailers/Towed Vehicles (11/12/96)
8B	Addendum "B" Camera Boom Vehicles (11/12/96)
8C	Addendum "C" Power Line Distance Requirements (6/19/02)
9	Safety Guidelines for Multiple Dressing Room Units (10/3/95)
10	Guidelines Regarding the Use of Artificially Created Smokes, Fogs and Lighting Effects (10/20/99)
11	Guidelines Regarding the Use of Fixed-Wing Aircraft in Motion Picture Productions (8/15/01)
11A	Addendum "A" to Guidelines for External Loads - Fixed Wing Aircraft (8/15/01)
12	Guidelines for the Use of Exotic Venomous Reptiles (9/19/95)
13	Gasoline Operated Equipment (10/4/95)
14	Code of Safe Practices - Parachuting and Skydiving (10/4/95)
15	Guidelines for Boating Safety for Film Crews (11/30/94)

No.	Description
16	Recommended Guidelines for Safety with Pyrotechnic Special Effects (11/30/94)
17	Water Hazards (1/21/98)
18	Guidelines for Safe Use of Air Bags (11/30/94)
19	Guidelines for the Use of Open Flames on Motion Picture Sets (11/30/95)
20	Guidelines For Use Of Motorcycles (2/23/96)
21	Guidelines for Appropriate Clothing and Personal Protective Equipment (9/18/96)
22	Guidelines for the Use of Elevating Work Platforms (Scissor Lifts) and Aerial Extensible Boom Platforms (6/25/93) (Updated 07/09/02)
22a	Addendum "A" Power Line Distance Requirements (6/19/02)
23	Guidelines for Working with Lighting Systems and Other Electrical Equipment (10/18/00)
23a	Addendum "A" Power Line Distance Requirements (7/09/02)
24	Recommended Safety Guidelines for Handling of Blood and Other Potentially Infectious Materials (5/23/00)
25	Camera Cranes (12/16/98)
25a	Addendum "A" Power Line Distance Requirements (6/19/02)
26	Preparing Urban Exterior Locations for Filming (9/20/00)
27	Nasty Plants (2/21/01)
28	Guidelines for Safety around Railroads and Railroad Equipment (11/30/94)
29	Guidelines for Safe Use of Hot Air Balloons (8/15/01)
29a	Addendum "A" Guidelines for External Loads - Hot Air Balloons (8/15/01)
30	Recommendations for Safety with Edged and Piercing Props (6/21/95)
31	Safety Awareness When Working Around Indigenous Critters (11/06/01)
32	Food Handling Guidelines for Production (6/19/02)
32a	Addendum "A" to Guidelines, Los Angeles County Health Advisory (06/19/02)
33	Special Safety Considerations when Employing Infant Actors (15 days to Six Months Old) (1/22/97)
34	Working in Extreme Cold Temperature Conditions & Wind Chill Chart (3/21/01)
34	Wind Chill Chart (3/21/01)
35	Working in Extreme Hot Temperature Conditions (3/21/01)
36	Remote Controlled Camera Helicopters (4/18/01)
37	Vehicle Restraint Systems (Seat Belts & Harnesses) (12/09/02)
	Informational Fact Sheet: Photographic Dust Effects (11/20/01)

GLOSSARY

2nd unit. *n.* See **second unit.**

accounts payable. *n.* The costs for equipment or services; monies owed by a production for everything but labor.

action. *n.* 1. The paragraphs in a script that describe what is physically happening or what the audience should see. *v.* 2. The command given by a director to tell the actors to begin the scene.

ADR. *n. Automatic Dialogue Replacement.* The computer-controlled process of having an actor record lines of dialogue in synchronization with previously shot takes (see **looping**).

AMPTP. *n. Association of Motion Picture and Television Producers.* The management bargaining unit that represents the motion picture studios in labor negotiations with the various guilds and unions.

angle. *n. Camera angle.* Camera postion from which a shot is taken. Synonym for *shot.*

answer print. *n.* The print that a lab makes from the original cut negative to show the filmmakers the result of the **color timing**.

APOC. *n. Assistant Production Office Coordinator.* (See **POC.**)

atmosphere. *n.* Nonspeaking players (see **extras**).

backing. *n.* A canvas or a translucent, plastic sheet used on a stage set outside a window or door to simulate scenery or sky. Canvas backings are generally hand painted while the plastic backings, also known as *translights*, usually are photographically produced.

backlot. *n.* Studio property on which building facades are erected to simulate city streets, residential neighborhoods, western towns, or other outdoor sets.

banner. *n.* On a **production board**, a strip denoting a **company move**, holiday, weekend, or other necessary information.

base camp. *n.* The place where the equipment trucks, dressing room trailers, and caterer of a company shooting on a location are set up.

best boy. *n.* Specifically, the assistant chief lighting technician; generally, any second-in-command on a department's crew.

blue screen. *n.* A method of photographing a subject in front of a specifically colored screen (usually blue or green) so that the background can be replaced with a separately photographed image.

boom. *n.* microphone boom (see **fish pole**).

breakaway. *n.* A prop, window, door, set wall, or other item designed and built to break apart when struck against or by an actor (e.g. breakaway chair, breakaway bottle, breakaway window).

breakdown. *v.* 1. The process of identifying and marking the essential elements needed when shooting the **shooting sequences** in a script. *n.* 2. The result of identifying the essential elements of a shooting sequence.

breakdown sheet or **page.** *n.* A preprinted form on which the essential elements of a **shooting sequence** can be listed.

camera angle. *n.* the position of a camera from which it views a scene.

CCD. *n. Charge coupled device.* The light sensitive chips in a DV camera. DVD quality requires a camera with at least three CCDs.

click track. *n.* An audio track played on set during a shot in lieu of music to allow actors and extras to maintain a rhythm such as during a scene in which dancing occurs.

coding. *v.* The printing of numbers on the edge of motion picture film at one-foot intervals in order to indentify specific frames.

color timer. *n.* The film lab technician who chooses the various printing lights for each cut in a film.

color timing. *v.* The process by which a color timer adjusts the printing lights used in the printing of successive shots which have been edited together to make the colors of each of the shots seem uniform or to achieve an effect such as moonlight.

company move. *n.* The act of moving the **base camp** of a shooting company from one location to another.

completion bond. *n.* A type of insurance that guarantees that a film will be completed for a given budget and schedule; used by banks that make film-production loans to guarantee that there will be a film produced to serve as collateral for the loan.

cover set. *n.* A set scheduled to be shot near the end of principal photography, which may be used as a place to continue working if a scheduled location cannot be shot due to weather.

coverage. *n.* the execution of a variety of camera angles of a scene to help tell the story and to give the editor choices. Typically, a **master** is shot of the scene and then the coverage consists of closer shots of individuals or objects important to the scene.

cut. *n.* 1. A synonym for **shot** or **angle** used by editors and directors in post production settings: *Let me see that cut again.* 2.The edited form of a film: *We went to see the director's* *cut. v.* 3. The command given by the director to let the crew know that the scene is over and the cameras can be turned off, and to let the actors know they can stop acting. 4. To edit a film: *It took ten months for them to cut that film.*

dailies. *n.* Positive prints of those **takes** that were marked to be printed, usually viewed the day after they were shot.

DAT. *n. Digital audio tape.*

day-and-date release. *n.* A type of release in which a film opens worldwide on the same calendar day.

decision list. *n.* A complete list of cuts based on key and frame number, created by a digital editing system from a cut picture, and which is used by the **negative cutter** as a guide to cutting and splicing together the original negative of a film in preparation for printing the **interpositive**.

DGA. *n. Directors Guild of America.* A collective bargaining unit that represents most professional motion picture directors, production managers, and assistant directors.

dialogue continuity script. *n.* A transcript of all dialogue and text from the final cut version of a film; used in the preparation of foreign language **dubs**.

dialogue track. *n.* One of three separate soundtracks mixed together to achieve the final soundtrack of the film. The track which contains the actors' voices as opposed to the music and sound effects tracks.

digital video. *n.* Video images shot with either a DV or 24P camera.

director's cut. *n.* The director's version of what the final edited form of a film should be.

double. *n.* 1. A photo double; a person who visually resembles an actor in a film and replaces that actor in a non-stunt shot. 2. A stunt double; a stunt player who replaces an actor in a stunt or action shot. *v.* 3. To replace an actor in a shot as either a photo double or stunt double.

DV. see **Digital Video**.

dub. *n.* 1. A mixing session. 2. The result of a mixing session. *v.* 3. to record or replace a sound on a soundtrack.

dubbing session. *n.* A mixing session. The process in which several soundtracks are mixed together into one.

edge numbers. *n.* The numbers printed on the edge of negative film stock at regular intervals that allow the identification of any frame.

EFC. *Estimated final cost* (see **estimate to complete**).

effects track. *n.* One of three separate soundtracks mixed together to achieve the final soundtrack of the film. The track with sounds that are not dialogue and not music.

EPK. *n. Electronic press kit.* Pretaped interviews, documentaries, and "behind-the-scenes" footage to be used in the marketing of a film.

estimate to complete. *n.* A report detailing how much has been spent and is expected to be spent in each account of a picture's budget.

estimated final cost. See **estimate to complete**.

extras. *n.* People who appear on-camera but who do not have a speaking role, usually used in the background and/or in crowd scenes. They are also referred to as background players or **atmosphere**.

favored nations clause. *n.* A clause in actors' contracts which states that all members of the cast will be treated equally, and that if any member of the cast is given something extra then all members of the cast will receive it.

film guarantee. See **completion bond**.

film guarantee company. *n.* An insurance company offering completion bonds.

final cut. *n.* The final edited form of a motion picture.

fish pole. *n.* A light-weight, telescoping pole with a microphone attached to one end and held by the boom operator to position the microphone over the actors' heads.

focus puller. *n.* The British term for the first camera assistant, the member of the camera crew who controls the focus of the camera lens during a take and who is generally in charge of the maintenance and care of the camera equipment.

foley. *n.* A process invented by Jack Donovan Foley, in which **foley artists** or **walkers** create and record sound effects in synchronization with a projected film scene.

foley artist. *n.* The person who creates the sounds on a foley stage.

foley walker. See **foley artis**t.

FX. *n.* An abreviation for *effects*, usually referring to *special effects*.

gaff. *v.* To boss or direct a crew: *He gaffed the pre-light on stage 30*.

gaffer. *n.* Specifically, the head of the set lighting crew. Generally, anyone who bosses a crew.

gofer. *n.* A runner, derived from the fact that they *go for* stuff.

green light. *n.* 1. The official approval to start spending money on a production. *v.* 2. To give approval to begin spending on a production.

greens. *n.* 1. A category of set dressing covering plants (both live and artificial), grass mats, and dirt. 2. The crew that handles greens.

grip. *n.* A member of the shooting crew primarily responsible for handling set walls, building camera platforms, and handling camera dollies and cranes.

header board. *n.* On a **production board**, a card listing the cast and other elements that are tracked on the board and which serves as an index for the board.

high-budget. *adj.* A relative term designating a class of fims costing approximately $5 million or more. There are many specific definitions depending on who is defining the term. (See **low-budget** and the text.)

hold-day. *n.* A day in which an actor is on payroll but not needed on set.

honeywagon. *n.* A two-axel truck and trailer combination containing dressing rooms and restrooms.

hot splice. *n.* A method of joining two pieces of film together that uses pressure, low heat, and cement—usually used with negative film.

IATSE. *International Alliance of Theatrical and Stage Employees*. An alliance of union locals that represents most of the crew positions on a film; also known as the IA.

insert. *n.* A shot narrowly focused on an object and usually cut into a sequence after a character is seen examining it, such as a close-up of a letter a character is reading. Inserts are sometimes saved to be shot at the end of principal photography with a smaller crew.

internegative. *n.* A negative made from an **interpositive** and from which **release prints** are struck.

interpositive. *n.* A low contrast **print** made from original edited camera negative as a step toward making an **internegative**.

loop. *v.* To replace lines of dialogue in a scene by re-recording the actor speaking the lines in synchronization with the projected filmed image.

looping. *n.* The process of having an actor re-record lines in synchronization with previously shot takes which have been formed into a loop for continuous play (see **ADR**).

low-budget. *adj.* A relative term designating a class of film projects in which the funds are extremely limited. There are many definitions but generally low-budget films are those costing $5 million or less. (See **high-budget** and the text.)

M&E. *n.* Music and sound effects tracks combined into a single unit for the use of foreign distributors so that they are able to replace the dialogue track with one in a different language.

magic hour. *n.* A period in the evening after the sun has set but while the sky is still somewhat light, which provides for an extremely flattering but subdued light. Magic hour usually lasts no more than about twenty minutes.

master license. *n.* Permission for the use of a specific recording of a piece of music.

master. *n.* master shot; a shot made with a wide camera lens that encompasses most of the action of a scene.

montage. *n.* In editing, the juxtaposition and joining of various shots in order to convey a story.

MOS. *adj.* Literally *mit out sound* meaning without sound. A designation put on the camera slate for a shot in which no sound was recorded. It is said to come from the German directors in early Hollywood who used the German word *mit* in place of the English *with*.

music track. *n.* One of three separate soundtracks mixed together to achieve the final soundtrack of the film. The track that contains the score of a film as opposed to the dialogue and sound effects.

ND. *adj. Nondescript.* Used to signify that there is nothing special about the item being described, as in *an ND vehicle*.

needle drop. *n.* Previously recorded music (usually from commercial albums) which has been purchased for inclusion into the soundtrack of a film.

negative cost. *n.* The cost of producing the original cut negative of a motion picture.

negative cutter. *n.* A person who cuts the original negative of a film and conforms it to the **workprint** or **decision list**.

one-light print. *n.* A positive print of negative film that is not color timed, usually used for printing **dailies**.

O.S. *adj. Off screen.* A designation placed in parentheses after a character's name in a script to signify that although the character's voice is heard and the character is present in the scene, the character is not seen (compare **V.O.**).

pay-hours. *n.* The number of hours for which an employee is paid after applying overtime premiums (e.g. an employee working for four hours at an overtime rate of time and a half will earn six times his or her hourly rate, or six pay-hours) (contrast **work-hours**).

per diem. *n.* Latin for *per day.* the term refers to monies given an individual on a distant location to pay for food, laundry, and other daily expenses.

perk. *n.* See **star perk**.

picture lock. *n.* The point at which no further changes will be made to the cut of a film.

post production. *n.* That period in the making of a film after the finish of **principal photography** during which the editing of both sound and picture is finished and the project is carried to completion.

POC. *n. Production Office Coordinator.* The person who runs the production office, oversees the flow of information (including script changes) to the cast and shooting crew, and is in charge of all travel arrangements.

POV. *n. Point of view.* A camera angle that purports to be what a character is seeing.

principal photography. *n.* The period in which the bulk of a script is shot, including all dialog scenes with actors.

print. *n.* 1. a positive copy of a film made from a negative. *v.* 2. to make a positive copy of a film from a negative.

production board. *n.* A device on which strips representing **shooting sequences** can be sorted and scheduled.

production dialogue track. *n.* The sound of the actors' voices recorded during the filming of a scene (see also **dialogue track**).

production number. *n.* 1. A number used by production companies to identify a particular project within their accounting system. 2. A large dance sequence involving music and extravagant costumes and sets.

prop. *n.* An object handled by an actor in a scene.

recce. *n.* In England and Europe, a scouting trip (see **scouting** and **tech scout**).

release print. *n.* The print of a film which is distributed to theaters.

run-by. *n.* A shot showing a vehicle or mounted person rush by camera. This type of shot is often used in chase sequences, or to show that a character is going from one place to another.

SAG. *n. Screen Actors Guild.* A collective bargaining unit to which most motion picture actors belong.

scene. *n.* A section of a script from a slug line to just before the next slug line, usually numbered in a shooting script.

scenic backing. See **backing**.

scoring session. *n.* The process in which live musicians are recorded in order to provide music for the soundtrack of a film.

scouting. *n.* The process of searching out and evaluating locations to be used on a film.

script timing. *n.* The process of predetermining how long the screen running time of a script will be.

second unit. *n.* A film unit shooting scenes other than those with actors speaking dialogue. Second units are usually not directed by the principal director and are often concerned with shooting action sequences.

shooting sequence. *n.* A portion of a script that maintains unity of time, place, action, and cast, of which any significant change in any of the foregoing elements signifies a new shooting sequence. A shooting sequence is a section of the script that can be shot in one place at one time with a defined group of actors performing a specific action. It may consist of part of a scene, an entire scene, or several scenes.

short end. *n.* The unexposed film left after a reel of raw stock has been partially used in a camera; typically short ends are under 200 feet.

shot. *n.* 1. An instance in which a camera records action by means of photographic motion picture film or electronically by means of a video process. *v.* 2. The act of recording action by means of either a video or motion picture camera (see also **take**).

show and tell. *n.* A session in which the propmaster shows the director the **props** that have been gathered so that they can be approved or rejected.

sides. *n.* Selected script pages.

slug line. *n.* In a script, the first line (printed in all caps) of a scene that gives the scene number, the set name and indicates whether the set is exterior or interior, and the time of day (e.g. 43 EXT. EWOK FOREST. DAY 43).

sound designer. n. A person who creates and records sounds which normally do not exist, such as the growl of a rancor pit monster.

sound stage. *n.* A soundproof space in which sets are built for the purpose of filming.

special effects. *n.* 1. The process of creating unusual elements while shooting a scene such as rain, wind, smoke, explosions, and unusual movement of objects and sets; sometimes referred to as *floor effects* or *mechanical effects.* 2. The crew that produces special effects.

spotting session. *n.* A viewing of the cut picture in which the director, composer, music supervisor, editor, and music editor discuss the placement and nature of the music in the film.

stage set. *n.* A set built on a **sound stage** or in a warehouse as opposed to a practical location.

star perk. *n.* Short for *perquisite.* A benefit demanded by an actor or the actor's agent over and above salary, such as extra airline tickets, special accommodations, or personnel hired only for the actor; often budgeted above-the-line in the cast account and considered part of the actor's cost to the picture.

stand-in. *n.* A member of the crew who stands in the place of an actor while the scene is being lit.

steadicam. *n.* A harness worn by a camera operator on which a motion picture camera can be mounted and which helps to smooth the motion of the camera as the operator walks.

still photographer. *n.* The member of the crew charged with taking photos of the actors in the various scenes, to be used later in the marketing campaign.

stock footage. *n.* Film that is bought from a **stock film library**, saving the production crew from having to shoot it.

stock film library. *n.* A collection of previously shot film of various locations or events, which may be licensed and made a part of another film.

storyboard. *n.* A series of sketches showing the action and camera angles to be used in filming a sequence.

stunt player. *n.* A person who specializes in doing dangerous stunts on-camera in place of an actor playing a particular role (see **utility stunt player**).

synch license. See **synchronization license.**

synchronization license. *n.* A license purchased from the copyright holder of a musical composition giving the purchaser the right to use the composition in the soundtrack of a motion picture or video production.

take. *n.* The filming of a scene or part of a scene from a specific camera angle; several takes are shot from each camera angle until the director is satisfied and says that the take is a print; the take and scene numbers are used to identify any given shot: *Scene 3B, take 4.* (see also **shot.**)

talent. *n.* Generally, a reference to the actors of a film.

teamster. *n.* A member of the International Brotherhood of Teamsters, whose job is to drive production vehicles.

tech scout. *n.* A trip or series of trips in which key crewmembers are shown the locations for the picture so that they can determine what equipment they will need.

telecine. *n.* The process of digitizing film footage so that it can be edited electronically.

timing. See **color timing.**

translight. *n.* A scenic backing made from a giant translucent photograph.

utility stunt player. *n.* A stunt player who is not doubling a particular role, such as the non-descript driver of a car who has a near-miss with the principal car.

visual effects. *n.* The manipulation of a camera image after the fact, usually with the use of computer generated effects.

V.O. *adj. Voice-over*, short for *voice over picture.* A designation placed in parentheses after a character's name in a script to signify that the character is not present in the scene and the following lines are to be considered narration (contrast **O.S.**).

VPB. *n. Video Playback.* The playing of a video tape or DVD through a monitor on set.

WGA. *n. Writers Guild of America.* A collective bargaining unit that represents motion picture screenwriters.

work-hours. *n.* The actual elapsed hours an employee works regardless of any overtime premiums: *I was paid fourteen times my hourly rate even though I only put in twelve work-hours.* (compare **pay-hours**).

workprint. *n.* The edited version of a film that the editor makes by cutting together printed footage of the **dailies.**

Works Cited

Detmers, Fred H. ed. *American Cinematographer Manual.* 6th ed. Hollywood, California: ASC Press, 1986.

Directors Guild of America. *2002 Basic Agreement.* Los Angeles: 2002.

Entertainment Partners. *The Paymaster: 2004 – 2005.* Los Angeles: DISC Intellectual Properties, 2004.

Producers Guild of America. "Producers Code of Credits." *Membership Roster*, 2004-2005. Los Angeles: PGA, 2004.

Pudovkin, V.I. *Film Technique and Film Acting.* Translated and edited by Ivor Montagu. New York: Grove Press, 1960.

Susman, Jordan. *The Anarchist Cookbook.* Unpublished motion picture script. Copyright 2001.

Index

Filmography

Robert Latham Brown has worked on over 40 films ranging in cost from $1.6 million to over $100 million. In addition, he teaches a class in Production Planning at USC's famed School of Cinema and Television. A partial list of his production experience is as follows:

Airport '79–The Concorde
Ali
All Night Long
Anarchist Cookbook, The
Babylon 5 (pilot show)
Best Defense
Blue City
Blues Brothers, The
Bustin' Loose
Car, The
Charlie's Angels 2
Child's Play
Child's Play 2
Child's Play 3
Clean and Sober
Dracula: Dead And Loving It
Elvira, Mistress of the Dark
Ghost Story
Goonies
Hindenburg, The
Hollow Man
Howard the Duck
Iceman
Indiana Jones and the Temple of Doom
Local Color
Lords of Dogtown
Lot Like Love, A
Maxwell Smart and the Nude Bomb
One Crazy Summer
Other Side of the Mountain, Part 2
Parent Trap, The
Pastime
Return of the Jedi
Robin Hood: Men In Tights
Showgirls
Spaceballs
Spiderman
Starship Troopers
S.W.A.T.
Thing, The
Vampires: Los Muertos
War of the Roses
Warning Sign

Quick Order Form

·or additional copies of this book:

Fax orders: 818-999-9478. Send this form or a copy.

Email orders: orders@chalkhillbooks.com

Online orders: http://www.chalkhillbooks.com

Postal orders: Chalk Hill Books, PO Box 606, Woodland Hills, CA 91365-0606

Name: ______________________________

Address: ______________________________

City: ______________ State: _____ Zip: _________

Telephone: ______________________________

Email Address: ______________________________

# of copies: __________ × $29.95 = $ __________

Sales Tax: Please add 8.25% for books shipped to California addresses.

Shipping and handling
U.S.: $6.00 for first book. $10.00 for 2-5 books. Larger orders please contact us.
International: Please contact us for shipping options.

Payment: ☐ Check ☐ Credit Card ☐ Money order

☐ Visa ☐ MasterCard ☐ Amex ☐ Discover

Card number: ______________________________

Name on card: ______________ Exp. date: __________

✶ Volume discounts are available for quantities of 10 or more books.

CHALK HILL BOOKS